HOW BOTHA AND SMUTS CONQUERED GERMAN SOUTH WEST

A Full Record of the Campaign from Official information by Reuter's Special War Correspondents who accompanied the Forces sent by the Government of the Union of South Africa.

WRITTEN BY

W. S. RAYNER *and*
W. W. O'SHAUGHNESSY,
CAPE TOWN.

With Special Illustrations and Maps.

Issued in Aid of the New Dominions Wing of the Union Jack Club, The Governor General's Fund of South Africa, and "The African World" Red Cross.

BY

LEO. WEINTHAL, F.R.G.S.,
Chief Editor of "The African World."

LONDON :
SIMPKIN, MARSHALL, HAMILTON, KENT & Co., Ltd.
STATIONERS' HALL COURT, E.C.

1916

Published by
The Naval & Military Press Ltd
Unit 10, Ridgewood Industrial Park,
Uckfield, East Sussex,
TN22 5QE England
Tel: +44 (0) 1825 749494
Fax: +44 (0) 1825 765701
www.naval-military-press.com
www.military-genealogy.com

© The Naval & Military Press Ltd 2010

The Naval & Military Press ...

...offer specialist books for the serious student of conflict. The range of titles stocked covers the whole spectrum of military history with titles on uniforms, battles, official histories, specialist works containing Medal Rolls and Casualties Lists, and numismatic titles for medal collectors and researchers.

The innovative approach they have to military bookselling and their commitment to publishing have made them Britain's leading independent military bookseller.

In reprinting in facsimile from the original, any imperfections are inevitably reproduced and the quality may fall short of modern type and cartographic standards.

HOW BOTHA AND SMUTS CONQUERED GERMAN SOUTH WEST

A Full Record of the Campaign from Official information by Reuter's Special War Correspondents who accompanied the Forces sent by the Government of the Union of South Africa.

WRITTEN BY

W. S. RAYNER *and*
W. W. O'SHAUGHNESSY,
CAPE TOWN.

With Special Illustrations and Maps.

ISSUED IN AID OF THE NEW DOMINIONS WING OF THE UNION JACK CLUB, THE GOVERNOR GENERAL'S FUND OF SOUTH AFRICA, AND "THE AFRICAN WORLD" RED CROSS.

BY

LEO. WEINTHAL, F.R.G.S.,
Chief Editor of "THE AFRICAN WORLD."

The Naval & Military Press Ltd

Reproduced by kind permission of the Central Library, Royal Military Academy, Sandhurst

Pro Patria.  Pro Rege.

[Photo by Russell & Sons.

HIS GRACIOUS MAJESTY KING GEORGE V.

After taking German South West.

Botha to Britain: "Carried out your wish and in accordance with our compact at Vereeniging."

Specially drawn for THE AFRICAN WORLD, *by* LOUIS RAEMAEKERS, 1915.

[Photo by Leon Levson, Johannesburg.

GENERAL THE RIGHT HON. LOUIS BOTHA, P.C.,
Commander-in-Chief of the Union and Rhodesian Forces in the
South West Campaign.

GENERAL THE HON. J. C. SMUTS, K.C.,
Minister of Defence for the Union of South Africa.

HOW BOTHA & SMUTS CONQUERED GERMAN SOUTH WEST.

SYNOPSIS OF CONTENTS.

PART I.
By W. S. RAYNER.

			PAGE
CHAPTER	I.	THE PLAN OF CAMPAIGN AND THE COUNTRY	7
,,	II.	ABOUT PEN AND SWORD	17
,,	III.	THE OCCUPATION OF LUDERITZBUCHT	26
,,	IV.	SANDFONTEIN	39
,,	V.	MARITZ THE REBEL	48
,,	VI.	ENTERING THE NAMIB DESERT	56
,,	VII.	AEROPLANES AND OTHER WARFARE	71
,,	VIII.	DISTINGUISHED VISITORS	89
,,	IX.	GARUB	94
,,	X.	AUS	108
,,	XI.	CONVERGING ON KEETMANSHOOP	119
,,	XII.	GIBEON. THE FINAL STAGE	135

PART II.
By W. W. O'SHAUGHNESSY.

CHAPTER	I.	OPERATIONS AROUND UPINGTON AND THE ADVANCE NORTH	151
,,	II.	AT WALVIS BAY	162
,,	III.	AT SWAKOPMUND	173
,,	IV.	GENERAL BOTHA TAKES COMMAND	183
,,	V.	THE BATTLE OF RIET	192
,,	VI.	THE TREKKOPJES FIGHT	199
,,	VII.	ADVANCE TO WINDHUK	203
,,	VIII.	OCCUPATION OF WINDHUK	212
,,	IX.	THE FINAL ADVANCE	221
,,	X.	SURRENDER	231

PART III.

SOME OBSERVATIONS AND REFLECTIONS	241
NAVAL TRANSPORT DEPARTMENT	243
AVIATION	248
"CAPTAINS ALL"	250
IN GERMAN HANDS	252
SOUTH AFRICAN HORSES	254
HOSPITAL AND MEDICAL	255
ABOUT THE CENSORSHIP	256
NATIVE AFFAIRS	260
POSSIBILITIES OF SOUTH WEST AFRICA	264
APPENDICES	267

The Nett Profits of this book are devoted as follows:—One half to the Fund for the new Dominions Memorial Wing of the Union Jack Club, and the balance to the Governor-General's Fund of South Africa and the "African World" Red Cross Work.

HOW BOTHA & SMUTS CONQUERED GERMAN SOUTH WEST.

PART I.

GENERAL OUTLINE.

WITH THE SOUTHERN ARMIES.

By
W. S. RAYNER.

PREFACE to PART I.

IT is fitting that the story of the triumph of General Botha and General Smuts in German South-west Africa should be utilised in some way for the general benefit of the South African wing of the British Army. Devoting the proceeds to and dividing them between the fund to build a Colonial wing to the great Union Jack Club in the Waterloo Road, London, whereto South African soldiers may resort when " in town," and know that they are not strangers; the Governor-General of South Africa's Fund for soldiers' dependents; and "The African World" Red Cross Fund, which has almost specialised, one might say, in the needs of Africa and Belgium, but works hard for the common weal, is a purpose that will not go un-noted by the great British public, nor, I am sure, will the appeal that it all suggests go unheeded. Those who have assisted me have, all in their own way, contributed something, a sensible something, and I would like to take this opportunity of acknowledging their kindness. In this connection, I would specially like to mention Lieut.-Col. Dawson Squibb, 1st Transvaal Scottish; Lieut.-Col. H. T. Gripper, 1st Eastern Rifles; Chaplain-Capt. H. F. de Lisle; Surgeon-Capts. R. L. Girdwood, W. J. May, T. Welsh, and M. B. Lawrie; and Capt. H. Frew (Post Office) for their photographs. But there are others.

I believe it is usual on such an occasion as this to attempt to forestall criticism by admitting shortcomings in the work that one has done. It appears to me that the admissions I could make would be in a sense belated. For in one journal that affects criticisms of the candid variety I have already read a demand that the next expedition shall be accompanied by a *War Correspondent* (I feel I must rope in my colleague to share this implied criticism with me, since it embraced the German South-west African Expedition as a whole); and a callow youth, in recording his impressions, has by supercilious inference permitted himself to castigate me for severity of style and lack of imagination—his imagination—in dealing with facts. Shortcomings depend very largely upon the standpoint from which the matter is viewed. So far as my effort is concerned, I would only say this—that throughout I have attempted to record the facts as they arose and to convey the fairest idea I have been able to of the atmosphere which surrounded those facts. The narrative is in no sense official, nor have I in any way received official help, but I claim that it is comprehensive and reliable.

I have one *enlargement* to make. It is this, that though the name of General Smuts is mentioned on only few occasions, and then only at the end, it must not be supposed for one moment that this even indicates the sum total of his contribution to the campaign. General Smuts' work as Minister of Defence, the director-general as it were of the whole Expedition, was greater, harder, more exacting, more responsible, and more effective than the work done by anybody else, the Prime Minister of the Union only excepted. But he was hardly ever in the limelight.

Capetown, November, 1915. W. S. RAYNER.

ACKNOWLEDGMENT.

OUR *grateful acknowledgments are due to numerous friends who went to a great deal of trouble to supply us with topical photographs to illustrate this work. Amongst them special acknowledgments are due to Mrs. Louis Botha, Pretoria; Lieut.-Col. Danie de Waal, who sent a valuable variety of photographs from Windhuk when Provost Marshal; Mr. W. Johnson, of Pretoria; Mr. R. C. Nissen, of Johannesburg; Messrs. Underwood & Underwood; The "Cape Times," Limited; and Mr. Leon Levson, of Johannesburg, whose photographs of General Botha and General Smuts will be particularly appreciated. Our special thanks are also due to Mr. Louis Raemaekers, for his telling and in every way admirable special cartoon, and to Mr. Alexander Gross, F.R.G.S., Managing Director of Geographia, L·mited, for the excellent maps contributed by his office for this publication; also to the Union Defence Department at Pretoria, for kindly placing official maps of several battles fought at the disposal of the authors and publishers.* L. W.

CHAPTER I.

THE PLAN OF CAMPAIGN AND THE COUNTRY.

On the 7th August, 1914, the Imperial Government, through the then Acting Governor-General (Lord de Villiers) invited the Union Government to "seize such part of German South-west Africa as will give them the command of Swakopmund, Lüderitzbucht, and the wireless stations there or in the interior." Three days later, General Botha announced that he and his colleagues "cordially agreed" to do so. Exactly a month later, the Union Parliament, which had adjourned on the 7th July until October 2nd, but which was called into special session on the 9th September, confirmed the Government's action by the overwhelming majority of 91 votes to 12.

In the meantime, the Union itself had been invaded by the common enemy. Very shortly after the outbreak of war in Europe, and certainly before the 14th of August, a strong patrol of the German Colonial Forces in German South-west Africa advanced over the border at Nakob and entrenched itself in Union territory. The official announcement was made on August 21st. There was another incident on August 22nd.

In view of the controversy that arose at the time over Nakob, the result of suspicions on the part of a small pro-German or, at any rate, an intensely non-British element, in the Union, it will be as well, perhaps, to explain here that police posts were maintained at this point of the German-Union border by both the German and Union authorities. That of the Germans was known as Nakob; the Union post was also spoken of as "Nakob," but it was really named Groendoorn. The two commanded the road running through from Upington to Warmbad. Both posts were small ones—that of the Union seldom being more than three men strong; but the Germans had a big military post at Ukamas, about 18 miles behind, and Ukamas was connected with railhead at Kalkfontein by a good military road. It has been stated that there was a regular garrison of at least 500 men at Ukamas, and that the place was a remount depôt. There was nothing of this kind on the Union side of the border. The headquarters of the frontier post was Upington, 70 miles away, along the most atrocious of roads, which took every minute of nineteen hours to cover; and there was a trek of 150 miles from Upington to railhead—Prieska—which was also frightful going. But Upington was not a military centre, nor even Prieska.

When the Germans "entrenched themselves at Nakob," the Nakob referred to was the Union post of Groendoorn. They effected their crossing some distance, of course, from the Union police quarters, but they were unmistakably in Union territory. Mr. F. C. Cornell, of Cape Town, who brought back details of the affair, describes how, desiring to get a photograph of the German post, the *personnel* of which had just been changed from police to military and increased to one officer and twenty-five men, with a machine gun, he went to a certain prominent hill in Union territory. But he had not climbed far up it when, to his surprise, he came across new spoors and a freshly built schanz neatly loop-holed. Proceeding with caution, he made out schanz after schanz, stretching along for 15 or 20 miles; and within very few yards of him was a camp oven, in which fire was still burning. There were bottles about, and the remains of food; drills, hammers, and freshly broken stones. And finally he saw enemy soldiers themselves moving about on top. Mr. Cornell tarried not, but he came away with valuable photographs, as well as other information.

So the Union had other and perhaps weightier reasons for considering and taking military measures against German South-west Africa.

Once the proposal to take such measures had been ratified, it was, of course, necessary that the blow should be struck quickly. It has since been admitted that the Union was not prepared for a war; but the tellers in Parliament had hardly announced the result of the voting than troops were on their way to German territory. The plan of campaign was to attack at four different points—at Nakob, at Raman's Drift, at the port of Lüderitzbucht, and at the port of Swakopmund. To get to three of these places involved oversea travelling (not necessarily in the case of Raman's Drift), and called for a considerable amount of shipping. Fortunately, the Union Government was able without delay to command sufficient bottoms for its purpose.

Four columns, known as "A," "B," "C," and "D" forces, were organised for the first phase of the campaign:—

"A" Force, composed of five regiments of South African Mounted Rifles, three batteries Transvaal Horse Artillery, and the Witwatersrand Rifles, under Brigadier-General H. T. Lukin, C.M.G., D.S.O., Inspector-General of the Union's Permanent Forces, was deputed for Raman's Drift, and left Cape Town on September 2nd, 1914, for Port Nolloth, whence it proceeded to Steinkopf, which was made the base.

"B" Force, under Lt.-Col. S. G. Maritz, a District Staff Officer of the Permanent Force, was to proceed to Schuit Drift after establishing a base at Upington. For reasons which are explained later, this column never materialised.

"C" Force, made up of the 1st Transvaal Scottish, Rand Light Infantry, D Squadron of the 1st Imperial Light Horse, the 7th Citizen

Battery (15 pounders), a section of the Cape Garrison Artillery with two 4.7 guns, and Engineers, with Col. P. S. Beves, of the Permanent Force, in command, went to Lüderitzbucht, sailing from Cape Town on September 15th.

"D" Force, under Brigadier-General Sir Duncan McKenzie, C.B., was destined for Walvis Bay and Swakopmund, but never got there. Before it could embark, the horizon had become clouded by the resignation of the Commandant-General of the Union Defence Force, General C. F. Beyers, and also by the shadow of rebellion, which certain other events, which may or may not have been read aright, intervened, notably fighting inland from Raman's Drift and also near Lüderitzbucht; and so the whole plan of campaign underwent revision.

"D" Force, instead of going to Walvis Bay and Swakopmund, was disembarked at Lüderitzbucht. It sailed from Cape Town on September 30th, and was composed of the 1st Natal Carbineers, the 1st Eastern Rifles, the Kaffrarian Rifles, the 1st Kimberley Regiment, and the Pretoria Regiment, with the 12th Citizen Battery (15-pounders) and such essential units as field hospitals, engineers, etc.

Such were the original forces that were chosen to open the campaign against German South-west Africa. What about the country against which they were proceeding? Let me briefly run through its history.

The first we hear of the territory was in 1485, when Bartholomew Diaz called there on the great journey that led to the discovery of the Cape of Good Hope. Diaz erected one of his famous crosses here, at a point some ten miles south of the present Lüderitzbucht, which is still known as Diaz Spitz or Point. It is said that the original cross is in the Museum at Berlin, having been placed there by order of the Kaiser. Anyhow, a steel cross, not a marble one, stands on Diaz Point now.

In 1761 the Dutch Government at the Cape sent an exploring expedition into the territory with, however, no very great results beyond the discovery of a hot spring. The present township of Warmbad is a sufficient indication of the place where they found it.

Missionaries entered in 1805, when the London Missionary Society established itself at Warmbad. German missionaries, representing the Rhenish Society, followed in 1841, and first settled at Bethany, opening a number of other stations later on, notably at Keetmanshoop, which they named after one of the presidents of the Society, Herr Keetman, and at Otjimbingue, which the German Government subsequently first made its capital. The Wesleyan Missionary Society was also represented at some time or other, though it does not seem to have maintained its activities for long, nor to have kept any very close record of the venture. But the Society's representative, whoever he was, must have been a very thorough and impressive worker. In very truth his work lived after him, as the remarkable incident I am about to relate will show.

One of the chaplains of the force that operated from Lüderitzbucht was Chaplain-Capt. Wilkinson Rider, of the Wesleyan Church. One day Capt. Rider got into touch with the native element at the port. To his unbounded surprise he found that some of them were Wesleyans already. He inquired into it, and his investigations disclosed a branch of the Wesleyan Church, with "ritual" all complete, right down to the offertory. It was no pretence at religion that they made, either. They had local preachers, class leaders, and properly constituted members. They maintained themselves and even put a bit by each week, or month, or whenever they made up their accounts, so that when the opportunity should arise they could be the means of passing on the glad tidings of the Gospel to other people, just as it had been passed on to them. Quite voluntarily they handed over their balance, in all the circumstances a goodly sum, to Capt. Rider for transmission to Wesleyan headquarters. Altogether a splendid advertisement for Christianity and Wesleyanism, and, incidentally, no small testimony to the ability and willingness of "native" communities themselves to defray the cost that their religious needs involve.

The first mining discovery, the location of copper in Namaqualand, was made in 1854. It gave rise to a boom to which people at the Cape lent themselves with truly astounding readiness. The end, unfortunately, was almost complete ruin for everyone who had had anything to do with it. Nevertheless, the discovery led to a great deal of mining activity, with consequent concessions from the natives. One of these concessions embraced the present Pomona diamond mine, and was obtained by the Cape Town firm of De Pass, Spence and Co. Another embraced the area of the present Otavi copper mines, and was granted to one Robert Lewis. Copper, of course, was the attraction in each case, though there was no material development until many years afterwards. It is interesting to note that all this activity was carried on chiefly if not wholly by British subjects.

In 1867 the British Government was urged to annex the territory. The prompting came from the Cape. At intervals during the next fifteen or sixteen years the Government was continually being approached with the same object. At one time it was the German missionaries who appealed, fearing that the natives, with whom they never seemed to get on, would carry out their oft-repeated threat to wipe them out; and their own Prussian Government forwarded the appeals and at first supported them, but that was in the days when Germany had no thought of colonial expansion. At another time it was the Herero natives who appealed, worn out, no doubt, with their constant warring with the Damaras, and desiring peace. The Hereros went so far as to offer two-thirds of their lands and all their copper mines if Great Britain would only annex the territory.

Most frequently, however, it was the Cape who appealed. There were substantial Cape interests at stake. The Cape held many land titles and mining concessions, and was continually sending adventurers and prospectors to explore and exploit them, incidentally finding much money to defray the cost of these expeditions. Cape merchants were supplying the territory with its limited requirements, and Cape traders were in constant communication with the interior. By 1875 a fair trade was being done in ivory and ostrich feathers.

But appeals and offers alike had little effect. The Home Government shrank from the responsibility that annexation would place upon them. They nibbled twice, as it were, but they stoutly refused to bite a third time.

They nibbled first in 1867, when they took over the Guano Islands, some twelve in number, that skirt the coast in the vicinity of Angra Pequena Bay. The islands, all very small ones, were formally annexed to the Cape in 1874. That is the reason why, when we sailed up the coast on the expedition to Lüderitzbucht, we had the curious and cheering spectacle of Union Jacks waving proudly and throwing their shadows almost on to the mainland itself.

The second nibble was in 1878, and resulted in the annexation of Walvis Bay, along with a 40 by 20 mile stretch of land. A resident was appointed, and there seemed reason to hope that some extension of British influence would be brought about in due course. It was so much delusion. In less than three years the Resident was withdrawn, and, strangest thing of all, the taxes that he had levied on the traders were refunded. At the same time, Germany, who was not asking for something definite in the way of a Declaration of Rights, was informed that British responsibility in the territory ended with Walvis Bay. In 1884 Walvis Bay was incorporated with the Cape.

In all these overtures the Germans undoubtedly acted with scrupulous regard for the diplomatic proprieties. All the same, events could not have shaped themselves better to their liking, for by this time the colonial expansion idea had taken root in Germany. An African Society was formed in Berlin in 1878. In the year following, people were fed with a very thoughtful but very insidious article by Ernst von Weber, which not merely set out the possibilities of South Africa for German colonisation, but insisted on the "Low German" origin of the Boers, and spoke openly of an inevitable Dutch rising—very interesting reading in view of the Maritz treachery thirty-five years later. Still, the right of way to

11

Damaraland and Namaqualand was not quite undisputed. Though the territory was not the coveted of nations, it is perhaps not surprising that Germany took advantage of the new position. British diplomatic circles professed to be astounded when she actually did make her move, nevertheless.

The German flag was hoisted over "Germany's first colony" on the 2nd May, 1883. It was a small affair then, a matter of ten miles of coast at Angra Pequena and twenty-four miles of hinterland. This was a concession that Herr Luderitz, a Bremen merchant, who had opened up business with the territory the previous year, had secured from a native chief the previous day. In August, 1884, however, Germany annexed the whole territory, and thus became the nominal overlord of 322,450 square miles, having a coastline of 930 miles. The new colony was about equal in size to the German Empire in Europe and the United Kingdom combined. In the meantime, German traders and concession-hunters had been very busy, and concessions covering almost every conceivable thing, even previous concessions, so it is asserted, were won from the natives.

Thus was the territory's national destiny settled.

The rest of its pre-war history is the one story of Germany's efforts to Germanise and develop it, according to her pre-conceived ideas. She set about her task with ruthless determination. Human considerations deterred her not, neither was she daunted by any physical shortcoming on the part of the territory itself. Money and energy, and even men, were lavishly expended.

There are two outstanding landmarks in this period.

In 1904 the Hereros and Hottentots, admittedly goaded to it by what the Germans themselves call "a lack of wisdom" in their native policy, broke out in rebellion. This rebellion took three years to subdue, cost 22 millions sterling, and necessitated the employment of nearly 20,000 regular troops from overseas; and there was a casualty record of 179 officers and 2,165 men killed, died of disease, and wounded. It is said that 50,000 natives were involved, and that fewer than 15,000 reported at the final surrender on the 23rd December, 1906, which is some, and yet only faint, indication of the utterly heartless severity which the Germans infused into their campaign. British eye-witnesses speak of Herero prisoners being huddled together on Shark Island, where the Lüderitzbucht hospital now stands, like penguins. Wounded and unwounded alike were dumped on this most inhospitable spot. Some were quite naked; none was given shelter: food was insufficient and often lacking altogether. We scarcely need to be told that they died off like flies—some from thirst, some from hunger, some from madness mostly through drinking sea water.

In short, to borrow a cynical and candid phrase from Professor Bonn, of Munich University, the Germans tried to assume to themselves the functions of Providence and to exterminate the native race. They succeeded in smashing tribal life.

In 1907 diamonds were discovered in the Lüderitzbucht area, and German South-west Africa got the industry of which it was so much in need.

So this was the position when war broke out:—
(1) There was a European population of 15,000, of whom about 2,250 were Protectorate troops and about 800 police; 4,300 were women. There was a British element close on 2,000 strong, mostly from the Union. The death-rate was about 11 per thousand, which we are given to understand are flattering figures, as the colonists took particular care to die out of the country if they could arrange it so! The native population, exclusive of the natives of Ovamboland and the Caprivi Zipfel, the stretch of territory that reaches, tongue-like, to within fifty miles of the Victoria Falls, totalled about 100,000. It is estimated that there are between 125,000 and 150,000 natives in Ovamboland and the Caprivi Zipfel.

It is interesting to turn aside here and see what kind of population this was, what its feelings and tendencies. According to Professor Bonn, the German colonist was "not of the class that Germany wanted for her colonies." Incidentally, the Professor shows that men were wanted who had capital and the capacity to manage native races; "more like the younger son that Britain has been sending overseas."

According to the *Lüderitzbucht Zeitung*, six months before war broke out some shrewd people in the colony were even then anticipating a political junction with the Union of South Africa. And, according to refugees and to prisoners, who were all unanimous on the point, though coming from various parts of the country and at different times, the farming element at any rate, had decided not to leave the country after the British had conquered it, being convinced that farmers would be better off under the Union Government than ever they had been under the German Government.

As for the natives, the corollary of the events leading up to and occurring during the three years' rebellion is sufficiently clear. But the Germans never did enjoy the native confidence. They were always in a state of nervous apprehension. Thus the Lüderitzbucht journal, on July 31st, 1914: "There are many elements of danger, both natives and bastards possessing arms in varying quantity. If you were to tell an

13

Ovambo despot of the far north that he was under German protection, he would laugh himself to death." Professor Bonn has to admit that "we rule the natives not always very wisely." There was more than one minor revolt between our arrival in the country and our return to the Union, notably a serious affray at Rehoboth in April, 1915. Perhaps nothing could be more eloquent of native feeling than the scene that greeted Sir Duncan McKenzie and his mounted column on their entry into Berseba, hot on the perspiring heels of the enemy. It was just a band of natives offering up heartfelt prayers to Heaven for this severance of their German bonds!

(2) There was a railway system which linked up most if not all townships of note and all the districts with the two ports of Swakopmund and Lüderitzbucht. Most critics have declared that these railways were far ahead of the colony's needs, that they were built primarily for military reasons. German publicists themselves agree; indeed, Herr Lattmann went so far in the Reichstag in one debate as specifically to explain that they were built "to facilitate considerably our attack on Cape Colony." A few years previously one of Bismarck's organs had bluntly declared that "the next piece of African territory to belong to the Fatherland will be the Transvaal."

There were 1,260 miles in use at the time of our occupation, and they ran as far north as Otavi, Tsumeb, and Grootfontein; as far east as Windhuk and Keetmanshoop; and as far south as Kalkfontein. During the campaign the Germans dynamited practically the whole of the railway more or less heavily, and it had, therefore, to be almost entirely rebuilt before the Union army could make use of it.

(3) There was a trade running into between five and six millions sterling in one year, imports turning the two million mark. Over 80 per cent. of the trade was with Germany, and the Union secured 12 per cent. of the balance. The exports were principally diamonds. Copper, tin, stock, wool, hides, and skin were other exports. It is an interesting fact, and one that is not a little peculiar in all the circumstances, that much of this trade, both mineral and agricultural, was due to the development schemes of British companies, notably the South-west Africa Company and the S.A. Territories, whose manager, Mr. Scotland, was, by the way, arrested at the very outbreak of hostilities and tried for his life on a ridiculous charge of "instigating a Berseba Hottentot to rise." At one time it was reported that Mr. Scotland had been shot. Both the rumour and the allegation were, happily, proved to be devoid of substance, Mr. Scotland eventually being released.

(4) There was a mining industry. It was chiefly confined to diamonds and copper, but not wholly so. Tin was worked

on a small scale, and there had been prospecting and, in some instances, more advanced operations in respect of lead, wolfram, iron, coal, asbestos, galena, and gold (in quartz), while everything was ready for the quarrying and exporting of ornamental marble. But money and native labour were both scarce and so activities were eventually concentrated on diamonds and copper. In 1913 the outputs of diamonds and copper were respectively of the value of £2,800,000 and £400,000. The German Government had latterly modified its exactions on the diamond industry to one of 66 per cent. less 70 per cent. of the working costs, which were arrived at by regulation. Revision of the taxation on diamonds was rather badly needed. It is on record that in 1911 one company paid a million marks in taxation and yet ended up the year with a deficit! The Kaiser owned a diamond mine at Pomona.

(5) There was an agricultural industry, in which probably 1,750 principals were engaged, mostly in pastoral pursuits. Quite 75 per cent. of the country comes under the head of "pastoral," and this area is capable of carrying three million head of cattle besides a few million sheep and goats. So says Dr. Rohrbach, a German colonial authority. The veld in south-west has a peculiar characteristic, in that it retains its nutritive qualities even in very prolonged droughts. About 1,400 farms had been taken up. The average size of the farms was 20,000 acres; and such a farm is calculated to carry some 500 head of cattle and numerous small stock. Roughly, there were in the country 225,000 head of cattle, 1,250,000 sheep and goats, 17,500 horses, 14,000 mules and donkeys, 750 camels, 1,250 ostriches, 7,000 pigs. Very close attention was paid to stock-raising. Pedigree animals were imported free.

One feature of farming operations in German South-west was the success attending efforts to breed pure and half-bred Karakul sheep from stock that was specially imported from the mountains of Araby and the Steppes of Russia. I have been assured that in South-west Africa the common Afrikander sheep after three or four crossings yields a fleece that is equally marketable with the pure Karakul of the Union. The German breeder was said to have been getting as much as £2 per crossbred Karakul lambskin. There were isolated irrigation schemes in operation. There are only two running rivers in the country, and they are border rivers—the Kunene and the Orange. Water, however, is found in almost all parts at no great depth. The rainfall is fair, though variable, being from 8 ins. to 12 ins. in the south and gradually increasing as you go north until a maximum of 20 ins. in the season is recorded. Fewer than 15,000 acres were under cultivation in 1914. Maize and tobacco were the principal crops, and did well, and good results had attended the planting of lucerne, onions, and such-like crops, while grapes and citrons and certain stone fruits grew easily. The price of land ranged from 6d. to 1s. 3d. per hectare (2.47 acres), and among private landowners was the Kaiser himself, who had two farms in the Gibeon district.

(6) There was a fairly well developed general administration. A Governor, the representative of the Kaiser, was the supreme head. A Landesrath, or Parliament, supported him, but in an advisory capacity only. A Commander-in-Chief controlled the military side, the expense of which was, until 1913, borne entirely by the German Government. Thereafter, a yearly call was to be made on the colony. For the year ended March, 1914, the colony's contribution was about £5,000. Notwithstanding this, the Budget in this year showed an equal revenue and expenditure at £1,640,274. The principal revenue items were:

Military subsidy from Berlin	£737,782
Taxation (including £330,000 from diamonds)	357,250
Customs	111,700
Mining	49,900
Fees, fines, etc.	82,200
Railways and harbours	183,145

The various votes were:—
Military .... £742,438 (£51,098 being non-recurring).
Civil .... 437,560 (£139,622 being non-recurring).
Police .... 195,411 (£4,880 being non-recurring).
Railways and harbours £99,300.
Interest on Public Debt, etc., £165,515.

Since 1910 revenue and expenditure have balanced, but every year previously had recorded deficits, amounting in the aggregate to 14 millions sterling, all of which was made good from Berlin. What with one thing and another, German South-west Africa cost the German Imperial Government from first to last 50 millions sterling.

District Councils looked after the districts, and the most important towns had all a form of municipal government; Windhuk (the capital), Lüderitzbucht, Swakopmund, Keetmanshoop, Karibib and Taumeb (which were the towns proper), and Omaruru, Okshandja, Usakos, and Warmbad (which were "centres of population"). All had telegraph and telephone services, and numerous out-stations, the destruction of which was the main object of the Union army's expedition. These wireless stations were situated at Lüderitzbucht, Swakopmund, Aus, and Windhuk, and that in the capital was one of the most powerful in the world. When weather conditions were favourable it communicated direct with the Nauen station near Berlin; on other occasions viâ Togoland. The public wireless service cost 9d. per word, with a minimum of 7s. 6d. per message.

H. E. VISCOUNT BUXTON, G.C.M.G

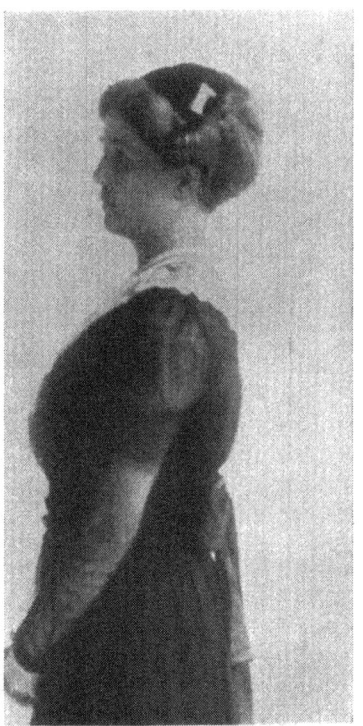

H.E. VISCOUNTESS BUXTON.

GENERAL SMUTS AND STAFF.

BRIGADIER-GENERAL LUKIN AND HIS STAFF.
Front row (left to right):—Col. Burn, General Staff Officer; Brigadier-General Lukin, C.M.G., D.S.O.; Col. Sir Abe Bailey.
Back row : Capt. Stewart, Staff Captain; Capt. Clarke Kennedy, A.D.C. to G.O.C.

General Sir DUNCAN McKENZIE, K.C.M.G.,
G.O.C. Central Force.

Brig.-Gen. H. T. LUKIN, D.S.O., C.M.G.

Brig.-Gen. COEN BRITS.

Brig.-Gen. M. W. MYBURGH,
Commanding 3rd Mounted Brigade.

RHODESIA

Within 21 days of the United Kingdom.

THE LAND OF SUNSHINE.

A long summer, a short and mild winter, a healthy, open-air life, with freedom from the trammels of over-civilisation; a new country where a man can build up and make for himself a settled position. RHODESIA is the Active Man's Land—a land of sunshine, enterprise and success.

New Settlers leaving for their Farm.

The British South Africa Company sells land very cheaply, and payment may be spread over a number of years. The Railway and Shipping Companies grant special facilities for settlers.

Illustrated pamphlets on request.

The British South Africa Company
(Incorporated by Royal Charter),
2, London Wall Buildings London,
E.C.

CHAPTER II.

ABOUT PEN AND SWORD.

I propose here to note the arrangements in vogue for recording the progress of the Expedition as unofficially as Press Censorship would allow, and to write of the conditions under which the Union forces went into the field. The Department of Defence was not in the least eager for newspaper correspondents to accompany the troops, and I believe that the first representations on the point from certain daily newspapers received a distinctly cold reception, if they were not actually turned down. Perhaps it was not to be expected that anything in the nature of what I may call competitive correspondence, with its consequent hustle and possible straining after "human" stories, would be allowed. On the other hand, it would have been a bad mistake to have gone to war, as it were, with no independent "eye-witness" at all, and I think the authorities were wise when in the end they permitted themselves to be influenced by the suggestion that the News Agency familiarly known as "Reuter's" should represent the South African Press as a whole. At the same time, even this scheme did not go far enough. There were several columns on which Reuter was not represented.

Unfortunately, the campaign was like no other campaign on earth, if I may borrow an expressive phrase from colloquial English. It was full of failings—but not of failures—from a correspondent's point of view. Comparatively, it produced only blood smears, singularly little maiming, hardly one of those scenes to which the piercing cry of anguish draws your attention, as in Flanders any hour this last twelve months and more. So, curiously enough, it was not a campaign of outstanding *human* interest! No one came within hailing distance not of a V.C. but of a D.C.M. even, unless it were of a District Court Martial, for unbecoming conduct in cursing the Fates that sent men to war and yet gave them only sparingly of war's excitements, of war's abiding sensations.

Still, the human interest was not entirely absent. Mention of courts-martial brings one little incident to mind that I may perhaps interpolate here, though it has nothing to do with conditions under which newspaper correspondents worked. I was walking in the streets of Lüderitzbucht one very hot day along with a regimental medico, when the two of us, turning a corner, all but fell over a non-commissioned officer of my friend's regiment, who had been breathing over, and had imbibed, apparently, a goodly quantity of very good liquor. I should mention that at this particular period McKenzie's force had struck what it emphatically called a "frightfully dry patch." The doctor mentioned the incident to the Colonel at mess that night. The delinquent was then in the guardroom.

"Yes," said the Colonel, "he's in for it; a double dose for him."

"Really?" I observed.

"Most certainly. He shall be made a sergeant for getting what the Colonel can't get, and then reduced to the ranks for abusing what the Colonel would have respected!"

All the same, there was precious little opportunity for fine writing. Whether the campaign justified the correspondent or the correspondent the campaign is something on which I have not yet made up my mind; and I have not dared to inquire as to whether or not the reading public was satisfied.

Originally four correspondents were selected for the four forces, but as "B" force did not materialise, only three of them got into the field—Mr. Vere Stent, with "A" Force, and the two authors of this narrative. After Sandfontein "A" Force was withdrawn with, of course, the correspondent, and the new columns that were organised for the southern and eastern attacks, after the suppression of the rebellion, got clear away without accredited correspondents at all. Mr. O'Shaughnessy and myself remained in the field throughout.

All four correspondents had first to meet with the approval of the Department of Defence. I interviewed the Secretary, Captain (afterwards Major) Bourne, on Friday, September 11, 1914, was given a document or licence which implied something about punishment for disobeying orders, was warned against having any truck with lies, sensationalism, and other unclean newspaper things, and was sped on my way with good wishes for my safety and success. Two days later I had embarked on H.M.'s transport "C" for Lüderitzbucht. Transport "C" in private life was the Union-Castle S.S. Co.'s intermediate liner "Galway Castle." At the start I joined the mess of the Transvaal Scottish Regiment; later on, for geographical reasons, I went over to the 1st Field Ambulance mess. In the first instance I have to thank Lieut.-Colonel Dawson Squibb for his kind invitation, and in the second, Major Pratt-Johnson and Captain R. L. Girdwood, both of the S.A.M.C., for theirs. My kit I bought on experience gained in the Boer War, and it conformed more or less to that of Union Defence Force officers, which officially weighed 35 lb.

Throughout the campaign I had the utmost freedom of movement. Mostly I enjoyed courteous treatment, and those in authority were considerate on the whole. The censorship restrictions, however, were most irksome; in a few instances they were distinctly stupid. On one occasion, I remember, I obtained some information from a German publication about the Kolmanskuppe diamond fields, which I used as a sort of vein of interest to liven the otherwise bald announcement that we held this rich but sickly spot. As far as I can make out, it never saw the light of day, so the Germans never learnt that we knew all that they knew themselves about Kolmanskuppe and its magnificence. Very possibly the elimination was justified, Germans do not necessarily read all books that emanate from German sources. No one, so far as I know, has yet hurled this accusation at them. I have also in mind the detailed description of the only bit of fighting that came Sir Duncan McKenzie's way. This story was mailed at Lüderitzbucht on May 6. It was released for publication on June 21. In the meantime censored letters from soldiers describing the same action were being published all over the place. On the other hand, one newspaper complained that I was getting too much through of what was happening in McKenzie's division.

Early in the campaign my messages were censored on the spot and despatched by Headquarters to the Union. The plan I followed was to try to get away brief telegrams of actual events and to follow up these messages with amplified accounts by mail. All means of communication were in the hands of the military. Very soon I was to find that the word "telegram" at the head of a message was merely a nominal indication of how I fancied I should like it sent. My very first telegram was sped to Cape Town by boat and was beaten on the tape at the finish by my mail letter describing the very same event, which was nothing more than the occupation of Lüderitzbucht, one of the four specific achievements that the Union Army set out to accomplish. For some time, as I shall explain later, we had only a limited use of our wireless service, and flush of official wires alone frequently caused a block. Against these, of course, Press messages paled in importance. Nothing that I wrote could, for example, hope to displace such a thrilling and urgent instruction that in all future messages staff officers must write " aaa " in place of the more popular " stop." The position eventually became impossible, and towards the end of October I was notified that in future my messages would be censored in Pretoria by the Intelligence Department, and that I was to send them there direct, telegrams and letters too. Under the address of " Significant, Pretoria," Press telegrams henceforth seemed to carry an official flavour, and they reached the Union, at any rate, without delay.

By the Intelligence Department Press matter was passed on to Reuter. The new arrangement was much preferable to the old, without itself being perfect.

The troops that were called upon to open the campaign against German South-west Africa belonged to the Permanent Force (South African Mounted Rifles) and the Active Citizen Force. The latter was in annual camp assembled when war broke out, and thus ready for instant disposition so soon as South Africa's particular plans were decided. The S.A.M.R. were experienced, well-drilled, disciplined troops, an extremely fine body of men. The A.C.F. embraced the youth of the country in process of training. It was thought at the time by some that the authorities would have been better advised to have requisitioned the Reserves, who were seasoned men, for the business in hand. No Active Citizen Force ranker, however, thought like this.

But certain changes in the personnel of the various regiments were necessarily brought about by the special medical examination that was instituted. Into the gaps caused by rejections were brought volunteer recruits, mostly the seasoned campaigner, who literally tumbled over each other in order to get enlisted. There was no difficulty about men. The difficulty was in refusing them. Men in good positions, as employers of labour and magistrates, clamoured to be taken on, if only in the ranks.

It was much like the scene described by General Botha. After his decision himself to go to German South-west Africa, the General called up thirty-five officers who had served under him in the Boer War, on the Boer side, of course. Telling them his plans, he said he wanted fifteen of them to go with him as officers. Then he left them for five minutes to decide among themselves. When he returned, their spokesman simply said : " Take the fifteen you want; the remaining twenty intend to go anyway as privates ! "

That was the spirit all through. I was walking down King George Street, Lüderitzbucht, one morning with a Colonel when an elderly man passed, saluting.

" No, not if I know it, old man," suddenly rasped out the Colonel. " You're not passing me without a word."

A few minutes later. Col. —— was explaining to me that the man just passed and himself were captains in the Boer War, and served in the same regiment. Not being in the Union Defence Force when this German war broke out, the ex-captain found that he could not take up a commission in a regular corps, so he joined as a trooper; "and by strict attention to duty," he said, with twinkling eyes on parting, "I hope to finish up with the stars again. You see, I'm getting on," pointing to the three stripes on his arm.

The medical test for the volunteer recruits was not severe, and there soon came a time when regrets that it had not been exacting and uniform could not possibly have been keener. There was very little disease, nevertheless; but every conceivable precaution to prevent disease was always being taken. Camps, particularly the infantry camps in McKenzie's division, were kept scrupulously clean; some were laid out with French drains, even. Woe betide the regiment that was careless with its refuse, or whose French drain became choked! Practically every man was inoculated against enteric fever, and to this proceeding is undoubtedly due in the main the fact that enteric fever cases were so rare. I have been unable to get complete figures, but in the first four months of hostilities only ten cases of enteric fever occurred on our side in German South-west Africa.

But the hospitals were seldom on light duty, for all that, though hospital arrangements were conceived on a big and, I think, adequate scale. Each force was equipped with hospitals and field ambulances—McKenzie's division at one time had three hospitals and two field ambulances—and there were large stationary hospitals at the Cape, notably at Wynberg. The medical service was particularly strong on the personal side, but at one time its supplies got disturbingly thin.

In the tending of the sick and wounded, the Defence Department was assisted by an Official Advisory Committee on Voluntary Aid, of which Sir Thomas Smartt, K.C.M.G., was the chairman. It will ever be difficult to estimate the real value of the services that this body was able to render. The Government chartered a steamer, the British and African Steam Navigation Co.'s (Elder Dempster Co.), "Ebani," a West African liner, as a hospital ship; the Committee equipped the boat for its special work. The Government wanted convalescent homes; the Committee arranged for three in various parts of the Cape Peninsula, and furnished and equipped them; while a "Women's Hospital Ship and Convalescent Homes Equipment Fund Committee," of which her Excellency Viscountess Buxton was the head, took in hand the work of collecting the necessary funds, and of providing hospital linen. The most notable donation to the "Ebani" fund was one of £30,000 from the Transvaal Chamber of Mines; and an interesting contribution was one of £500 from the late Sir George Farrar, given as he stepped on board a transport at Cape Town in September, 1914, on his way to the front, from which he was fated not to return alive.

As a Red Cross ship, the " Ebani " was almost ideal: she might have been constructed originally for the purpose. Completed, she gave eight wards holding 199 cots in all, besides operating theatre, dispensary, and other indispensable conveniences; and every room or cabin was rendered mosquito-proof. She was formally put into commission on December 1, 1914, and Lady Buxton travelled over a thousand miles for the express purpose of performing the opening ceremony.

The pay of the Union Army ranged from 3s. per day for men to 6s. per day for warrant officers; and from 10s. per day for junior officers to 20s. for lieut.-colonels as officers commanding regiments. There was, of course, special pay for special duties: in the ranks, cooks were given an extra shilling a day, and the sergeant-cook got still another shilling; machine gunners (machine guns in McKenzie's force were not brigaded, but attached to the various regiments, two going to each unit) got an extra shilling, and so did " pioneers," who may be called the tradesmen of a regiment; and signallers got 2s. a day extra. Regular monthly cash advances were made to the troops in the field ranging from 10s. in the case of privates to £5 in the case of senior officers. The balance of pay was handed over with the certificate of discharge. While in South-west Africa, the troops used a great deal of German money at $20\frac{1}{2}$ marks the pound sterling (official rate of exchange). Married men at first had their pay made up to 5s. a day, inclusive of allowances, but with the commencement of the New Year a distinct separation allowance of 2s. a day was given, provided the N.C.O. or man, by "stop order," gave half the pay of his rank to his wife. In the case of a widower with children, a shilling a day was allowed for the first child and 6d. for each succeeding child, provided the children were dependent on him.

Rations, valued at 1s. 6d. a day, and first kit with reasonable renewals were all free. This was the ration list: $1\frac{1}{4}$ lb. bread or 1 lb. biscuits or flour and baking powder; $1\frac{1}{4}$ lb. fresh meat or 1 lb. " bully," or (at the option of the officer commanding) 1 lb. fresh meat and 6 ozs. mealie meal, with 1 oz. sugar; 2 ozs. cheese (an optional ration); $\frac{1}{4}$ oz. tea; $\frac{3}{4}$ oz. coffee; 4 ozs. jam, or dried fruit, or syrup; 4ozs. sugar; salt; pepper; $\frac{1}{2}$ lb. potatoes, or any of the following—onions, rice, peas, beans, 2 ozs. compressed vegetables, 4 ozs. dried fruit; special issues—2 ozs. milk when obtainable and transport permitted: 4 ozs. fresh vegetables; lime juice (every day at the front and in blockhouses); dop (weekly); 4 ozs. tobacco (weekly); 1 box of matches (weekly). The list is almost identical with that in force in the British Army. In the latter 4 ozs. bacon appears as a ration, 3 ozs. of cheese is a fixed ration, cocoa is sometimes issued in place of tea or coffee, and whichever is the issue, the allowance is ⅝ oz., the sugar allowance is 3 ozs., double the quantity of fresh vegetables is allowed, and the weekly smoking ration is either 2 ozs. of tobacco or fifty cigarettes.

According to the technicians, the daily ration was fully equal to 5,000 calories, which is 500 calories more than are actually required for an able-bodied, fully worked soldier. There were other ways of measuring its sufficiency. One was the state of the swill tub, which was usually gorged after meals. The surplus (but unwasted) would have been even greater had the cooks had previous rudimentary instruction in the culinary art, while the health of the men, or, at any rate, the sense of satisfaction that usually follows a good meal would not have suffered. The cooking question often became a sore point of debate, though I, personally, had never once cause to become interested. A feature of the ration list on McKenzie's force was the number of times that bread and fresh meat were served. Until the rush for Gibeon, their alternatives, biscuits and bully—how trippingly the three words come from the tongue!—intruded only once a week. I suppose it was this unfamiliarity with "hard tack" that led to one man posting a biscuit as a curio for his friends. He posted it as he would a postcard, having first written a facetious message on one side and the address on the other. The postmaster must have thought the proceeding much too bare; he confiscated the potential curio.

For the fewness of the biscuit and bully issues and the plenitude of fresh bread and meat, McKenzie's men had undoubtedly to thank Sir George Farrar and his great gift of organisation, for without the smoothly working transport that he organised this result would not have been possible. Rations, as a rule, were of excellent quality, and when they weren't they were condemned without compunction or loss of time. A huge consignment of Australian "bully" was not of the tastiest, and a shipment of Union jam was a libel on South Africa's fruit-growing capacity, while the early issues of a local tobacco came in useful for "footer," being neatly tied up in bags. And yet on more mornings than I can remember I have breakfasted off mealie porridge and milk, curried bully with rice (the mess bought the curry), steak and onions, coffee, and the loveliest bread and jam. This was the common breakfast.

It was possible while in the field to supplement rations and, of course, meet personal requirements, at the S.A. Garrison Institute, which is the successor of the old Field Force Canteen. The "Sagi," as it was generally referred to, was in evidence with well-stocked cases wherever the troops moved, and was indeed a boon and a blessing. Heaven knows there was little enough occasion to supplement rations, but as man does not live by bread alone, taking a little cake occasionally, so does a warrior on service now and again hanker after the flesh-pots of ordinary life—a tin of fish paste, which, sometimes, I recall, we had to take willy nilly, in lieu of copper change; a jar of pickles; a packet of fancy biscuits. Within reason you could buy almost anything from "Sagi": fancy soap, choice cigarettes, writing paper, and so forth. The Garrison Institute is a semi-official institution, and in McKenzie's force was managed by a committee of officers, who regulated prices and dealt with complaints. When they did one they usually did the other. Early in its South-west career, "Sagi" had a mania for fluctuating prices. Cigarettes that were 3s. 9d. the hundred one day were 5s. the next day. This was the reason, as a matter of fact, why the local committee of management was appointed. Incidentally, I may mention that a welcome effect of this innovation was a reduction of 40 per cent. in the price of those cigarettes.

There were complaints about boots, and at one time the condition of the men in this respect gave rise to some anxiety. Otherwise clothing was plentiful and good, if varied in design and colour. Infantry, by the way, were allowed 20 lbs. of travelling kit, and at a pinch it could all be carried by the man himself. The pinch never came, thanks to the railway. The 20-lb. kit was composed of greatcoat, blanket, waterproof sheet, towel, soap, shaving tackle, handkerchief, laces, socks, Balaclava cap, hussif, and shoes. When tents were pitched ten men were told off to a tent.

The troops signed on for the duration of the war or for a less period, according to requirements. Through a curious blunder early recruits were enlisted for "six months or the war, whichever is the lesser period," and when six months had passed and the campaign had hardly begun, the authorities found themselves in a predicament, for these men demanded their release, and it was not convenient to comply. To their credit, the authorities fulfilled their part of the contract to the letter. I shall return to this subject in a subsequent chapter.

The troops had special postal arrangements. Wherever they went they were followed by a branch of the Army Post Office. The Army Post Office was manned almost exclusively by men of the Union General Post Office, and so far as McKenzie's division was concerned, achieved uncommonly good results. The percentage of lost letters and parcels was no more than in civil life, and mails were distributed with both certainty and despatch. No postage was charged on letters from the troops to places in the Union; elsewhere the ordinary rates prevailed. All postal matter going to the troops was paid for in the usual way. Letters from the troops were censored. As much of this censoring as possible was done by the field postmasters; the balance was done in Cape Town.

At the outset the censorship was a very sore point with the troops. Raising the question in the Union Parliament, a protesting Labour member declared that 94 texts from the Bible had been censored as unfit for mental consumption. But it wasn't chagrin at hearing later on that his favourite Bible text had been expunged from his letter home that led "Tommy" to complain. It was annoyance at finding that his continual attempts to tell his people where he was had as continually ended in ghastly failure and thick black dashes, and that his people were becoming terribly anxious in consequence. This censorship of private letters was nevertheless not nearly so strict as in Flanders and France, and yet it was often inexplicable. For instance, I should never have deflected a certain postcard on which the sender had in a phrase given a whole history of Kolmanskuppe, the place to which I have already made reference.

"Kolmanskuppe," wrote this soldier-historian, "is a terrible place—miles on miles, on miles, on miles, on miles, on miles of dam-all!"

The actual wording is certainly toned down a little here, the original having been conceived in unhampered vigour, but after all, strong language nowadays is only a question of degree.

In course of time the troops developed a greater philosophy, and censorship restrictions ceased to worry them greatly.

CHAPTER III.

THE OCCUPATION OF LÜDERITZBUCHT.

About the middle of September there were several happenings of importance. The enemy began to invade the Union in real earnest. No less earnestly Union forces began to return the compliment, and led off with the occupation of Lüderitzbucht. A few days later, unfortunately, another Union column met with reverse at Sandfontein, in the south; but even from the German point of view nothing was so vital at the moment as the fall of Lüderitzbucht.

When " C " force put out from Cape Town it was in very truth taking a plunge into the unknown. It was not a very formidable force either, so far as numbers went, being not more than 2,000 strong, though it made a brave display with its fleet of five ships. One of these boats was H.M.S. "Astrea," sent in the first place to keep watch and ward over us, lest a roaming German cruiser should swoop down and swallow us up; and in the second to shell Lüderitzbucht if needs be, when the troops would land under cover of its guns. The other four were transports—the "Galway Castle" and the "Gaika," which carried the troops, and the "Monarch" and "Clan Macmillan," which carried munitions. The "Monarch" was a remarkable boat in her way, and rendered us most valuable service. Of 12,500 tons, she was the biggest cargo boat that had traded with South Africa. She was to remain with us as a supply ship and a medium of communication with the Cape, for which purpose she was specially fitted with wireless, taken, by the way, from a captured prize ship, the "Berkenfels." The "Monarch's" cargo consisted principally of horses and mules, nearly 4,000 of them, 500 tons of meat in cold storage, and over 750,000 gallons of fresh water drawn from the reservoirs on Table Mountain; and while at Lüderitzbucht she condensed sea water, and by this means added some sixty tons of potable water, or over 13,000 gallons, to her tanks daily.

This ocean transport service was organised and controlled by a Naval Transport Staff, under the direction first of Commander Lambert and then of Commander Lockhart, and the activities of September, 1914, were the very beginning of it. It wasn't a perfect service by any means, and I have heard of some weird loading orders that—well, delayed operations and added to their expense; but it did the work that was required of it, and that, anyhow, is a big something. In course of time the fleet of transports, exclusive of tugs and lighters, of course, rose to twenty ships. Three of these vessels were captured from the German East African mercantile fleet—the "Professor Woermann," the "Erna Woermann," and the "Rufidji." Another transport was the "City of Athens," which in the early days acted the part of a sort of semi-hospital ship.

Colonel Beves had Major F. A. Jones, D.S.O., an ex-Imperial officer like himself, as his Chief of Staff, and his Intelligence section was under the control of Captain C. K. de Meillon. About de Meillon, a special service man, there was quite an air of romance. A Dutchman, he fought in the Boer War, in which he earned a reputation for colossal daring. Twice he was captured; the first time he showed in a very material way that stone walls do not a prison make, nor iron bars a cage, by completely regaining his freedom after once failing in the attempt, and regaining it in spite of the special precautions that were taken to prevent his escape. After his second capture he was sent to Ceylon, but when he left the island of "soft, spicy breezes " he flatly refused to live under British rule. He preferred German South-west Africa.

His ideas of justice and freedom, however, never coincided with those of the Germans, and he was never in love with his new surroundings, personal or impersonal. When the local courts had deprived him of what he considered were his rights in a certain mining venture, he "gave the country best" and returned to the Union. This was three months before war. He thus came to meet General Smuts again, and as a result of conversations with the Minister, who told him exactly what had happened since the Boer War, as between the English and the Dutch, his resentment against the English vanished entirely. When the new war broke out he took up the British cause whole-heartedly, and was one of the first to offer his services to the Union. A valuable offer like this, which brought with it a fund of recent information about German South-west Africa, was, of course, gratefully accepted.

De Meillon's knowledge of Lüderitzbucht and the great hinterland enabled him to advance a pretty shrewd theory as to the conditions that we should find ourselves up against on arriving there. Twenty-four hours after leaving Cape Town a general order was issued stating that there was reason to believe the port was held by 250 men, mixed Regulars and Town Guard, and protected by entrenchments. Engines with steam up, however, were no doubt standing in the station, to enable the garrison to wait until the very last moment, so to speak, before retiring inland. As and when they retired the Germans would, naturally, dynamite the line after them. It was presumed that the plant for condensing water from the sea (which constituted the Lüderitzbucht water supply), the wireless station, and the lighthouse were already prepared for demolition. We had no information about their guns. There was also reason to believe that a force was entrenched at Kolmanskuppe for the purpose of holding the diamond fields and, possibly, to work in conjunction with German naval forces that were almost hourly expected from over-sea. In this last-named event I am afraid the Union force would have been in a pretty pickle indeed.

After-events showed that this outline was extraordinarily well-drawn.

By means of a flank attack, Col. Beves sought to make a bid for both the Lüderitzbucht and Kolmanskuppe garrisons and their supply trains, and then prevent the destruction, if possible, of the condensing plant and wireless station which, though they were not essential to our purpose, were uncommonly important factors. The scheme was to land a mixed party about 300 strong at North Long Island Bay, some thirteen miles south of Lüderitzbucht, soon after dark on the night of Thursday, September 17, and to support it with another mixed party of similar strength, which would move out a few hours later. The railway was to be cut at kilo. 21 and also at kilo. 5. The remainder of the force was to make a frontal landing at Lüderitzbucht.

The scheme, unfortunately, had not—could not take the weather into account, and the weather came to be the dominant factor. Almost while the men were rearranging their equipment and drawing rations, heavy seas developed, and by the time darkness set in conditions were such that a landing was quite out of the question. The scheme was regretfully dropped when there seemed no prospect of an early improvement.

No, not entirely dropped. Early on Friday morning the G.O.C. came out with a much modified plan. He detailed Capt. de Meillon and a small party of engineers off to land at the same bay and endeavour to cut the railway just behind Lüderitzbucht. In harmony with this, the force would steam boldly into Lüderitzbucht harbour and doubtless thereby bring about the instant retreat of the garrison—with disastrous results, it was hoped.

De Meillon's party were taken off the "Galway Castle" by the "Magnet," a whaler skippered by a hardy, hefty Australian salt, if ever there was one; Wearen was his name. From the "Magnet" they were to be landed, in batches of three, by means of the only rowing boat that the whaler possessed. The first batch, which included Capt. de Meillon, was landed safely enough, but in returning, Wearen lost his boat through a capsize in the surf, and the only way he could get back to the "Magnet," which was anchored fully half-a-mile out, was by swimming to it, which he did. No other rowing boat being available, no more men could be landed. That was doubly unfortunate, because no tools or explosives had been taken ashore.

In the meantime, de Meillon and his supports had been espied and engaged by an enemy mounted patrol, and there were sharp exchanges of rifle shots. One German was unseated, but all of them managed to get away to tell their presumably breathless story of a British landing.

So this second scheme went agley also, and the garrison at Lüderitzbucht made a complete and uninterrupted evacuation on to its inland supports. De Meillon and his men witnessed the final stages of this movement. After the encounter with the patrol they struck out for Lüderitzbucht, which they reached in the early hours of Saturday morning in rather an exhausted state. They had had a wretched tramp over some fifteen miles of sand, and, being without goggles or veils, they were half-choked and half-blinded at the finish. Arrived in the town, they saw a brilliantly lighted house standing invitingly open. They entered it. It was deserted, but there was hot coffee on the dining-room table, and in an adjoining room was a bed still warm from recent occupancy. Evidently the Germans had stood not on the order of their going.

De Meillon afterwards asserted that coffee never did a greater service to man than those lashings he so providentially encountered in that house; and as for the bed, he admitted being indebted to it for four hours' delicious sleep, full of danger though his surroundings were.

"You had a nerve," someone said to him.

"It's not that," he answered quietly; "I know the Germans!"

The Germans also know de Meillon, but that is the story of how the force lost its chief scout, and must be told later on. When we set foot on the jetty next morning the first man we saw was Captain de Meillon. Behind him was arrayed half the population of the town, whom he had rounded up just to "welcome the victorious British troops"! Amongst the residents of Lüderitzbucht was a fair sprinkling of naturalised British subjects, mostly Russians and Rumanians, who had at various times migrated from the Cape, and so our welcome was not entirely a sullen and stony stare.

After the "Magnet" mishap there seemed nothing for it but to steam straight into Lüderitzbucht. We did that, and shortly before dusk on the evening of Friday, September 18, 1914, boats anchored very near the spot where, over four centuries before, had halted the first fleet that ever visited those parts, and before what in the gathering shadows of twilight appeared to be a pretty township nestling on a hillside slope.

There was no communication with shore until early morning, when a party, consisting of Lieut.-Colonel E. Müller, British Consul in German South-west Africa, who had only recently left the country on holiday, Major Jones, and Captain Esselen, A.D.C., with a couple of signallers, went in to demand the surrender of Lüderitzbucht. Almost simultaneously the white flag was hoisted above the Town Hall.

The party returned with the Burgermeister, who was Herr Kreplin; Dr. Dommer, an attorney; Herr Otsen, the editor of the local *Zeitung;* and a Customs collector named Schmolke. Through Colonel Beves, these gentlemen formally surrendered the port to the British Empire.

The last act in the drama was witnessed at noon, when the white flag at the Town Hall was replaced by the Union Jack, and we had completely taken possession. A special detachment of the Transvaal Scottish Regiment was the flag-hoisting party, and the G.O.C. and Lieut.-Colonel Dawson Squibb (officer commanding the Transvaal Scottish) were the principal officers present. If severe quiet and masterly method go for impressiveness, then this ceremony was the most impressive I have ever attended. I remember, nevertheless, heartily wishing that someone would desecrate the whole scene by starting the strains of the National Anthem and raising lusty cheers for his Majesty the King. It was all so different from what one expected. It was very different, for instance, from the manner in which the Transvaal Scottish installed their headquarters at Kapps' Hotel an hour later. The Scottish flag was hoisted in anything but silence. The bagpipes played, and there was great and unrestrained rejoicing all round.

From first to last nothing untoward happened during the landing of men and munitions. It was feared we should find that the harbour was mined, and when the first tug, which was laden with men, just missed a sunken barge by the proverbial hair's-breadth, as it approached the jetty, worst fears began to creep uppermost. It was stated from German sources that the harbour had been mined, but that the mines had since been removed. (All the buoys, however, had been displaced.) This seems to square with information that we were able to extract from the Burgermeister, a very polite but very stolid gentleman, who said it was touch and go as to whether or not Lüderitzbucht should be defended, and, when the psychological moment for retreat came, then destroyed. The military authorities were all for the policy of blood and iron, the civil for the *status quo* and such peace as they could get. The Governor had virtually promised that full compensation would be forthcoming for all damage and loss sustained in the course of military operations, and the civil authorities would appear to have made a trump card of the sum that would have to be disgorged for Lüderitzbucht alone. Herr Kreplin played a prominent part in these negotiations, for, either out of his own wealth as the first diamond magnate in the country, or through his various companies, he practically controlled the place. In the result, the civil section won. That is why the military retreated after doing no more damage than destroying the wireless installation, which was the only piece of State property in the neighbourhood, and why there were no mines in the harbour, or in the streets, for that matter.

The Germans who were left behind—about a hundred men and their families, representing an essential business organisation—affected a pugnacity and arrogance that I rather fancy they did not honestly feel. Only just previous to our arrival these and some others, about 200 in all, had, in solemn conclave, agreed to appeal to the Governor and urge him to hand the country over to the Union on demand. Whether this appeal reached his Excellency, and, if it did, what happened to the appellants, I never heard. There was no prevarication amongst the natives. Those from the Union, at any rate, got tremendously excited over the British occupation. Saturday, the 19th September, 1914, they regarded as a sort of Day of Liberation, and they celebrated it right royally, according to their lights. They started off with a sort of holy war on any and every German native in the place on whom they could lay hands. That was to compensate and satisfy themselves for all the rough treatment that had been meted out to them when the German native was relatively top dog. They then got most efficiently drunk, no doubt to satisfy us that there was nothing half-hearted about their loyalty to the British!

It transpired that the Germans began preparing very early for eventualities. When we landed we were nonchalantly informed that " we really expected you three weeks ago "! They could have added another three weeks on, and more. They began removing foodstuffs inland from the coast towns—that is to say, nearer the Union border—before even war was declared: on the 29th July, in fact. This date is very significant, for the menace to Colonial Germany, if such a thing ever existed, was not Russia, nor France; and war with Great Britain did not break out until the evening of the 4th of August. One may well ask why this extraordinary activity. On August 1 operations ceased at the whaling station,

near Lüderitzbucht, and at Kolmanskuppe diamond fields.
The native labourers, who were all Cape " boys," were paid
off with paper money; and, assuring them that they would be
able to cash this paper at Cape Town, the Germans packed
1,800 of them on to the Italian barque "Mincio," bound for
the Cape, where, of course, they were stranded, for, outside
German territory, their paper money was so much dead weight.

On August 2 the Germans started to dismantle the
wireless stations and harbour works both at Lüderitzbucht
and Swakopmund, but the wireless station at the former port
was re-erected later on and brought into use again. About
the time war was declared the s.s. "Freda Woermann"
called in at Walvis Bay and delivered mails, but did not
trouble to land a consignment of foodstuffs that the small
local community there was expecting also, and waiting for;
she put away to sea again hurriedly. And about the same
time the German gunboat " Eber " abandoned her moorings
at Lüderitzbucht and sped away for a port unknown.

By August 19 the Germans were experiencing a monetary
stringency which even the quarter of a million marks saved
from the natives, who had so considerately been given paper
instead of cash for their wages, could not avert. So the
Governor, Dr. Seitz, issued five million marks of Treasury
notes. These notes were no doubt useful, but they sorely
displeased a Swakopmund lady, who complained that the
paper was " of miserable quality, looks awful, and will not
wear long "! Synchronising with this issue arose a complaint that Lüderitzbucht traders had increased their prices
by no less than 120 per cent., and Government was constrained to step in and curb their rapacity. It is interesting
to note that this trade ring embraced all tradesmen but one.
The exception was an Austrian, but a naturalised and, on
the face of things, a very conscientious British subject, whose
prices are said never to have gone above normal by more
than 20 per cent. !

Before the end of August the Germans were in active
conflict with the natives. There was an émeute of the
Bethany Hottentots. The members of this tribe were loyal
to the Germans during the Herero campaign, and they were
allowed to retain their rifles as a reward for their loyalty.
They were now called to a meeting by the local missionary,
but that man of peace declined to address them until they
had piled their arms. They did pile their arms, and the
meeting took place some little distance away. During the
proceedings a German patrol came along and quietly gathered
the rifles in. When the Hottentots found out the trick that
had been played upon them, insurrection followed. All that
transpired afterwards is not known, but it is known that the

Lieut.-Col. ROYSTON, C.M.G., D.S.O.,
Commanding 9th Mtd. Brigade.

Col. Sir ABE BAILEY, K.C.M.G.

Senator Col. the Hon. J. J. BYRON, C.M.G.,
Comdg. 2nd Infantry Brigade, Central Force.

Col. C. A. L. BERRANGE, C.M.G.,
Commanding Eastern Force.

Col. P. S. BEVES, Commanding "C" Force and afterwards Military Governor of South West Africa.

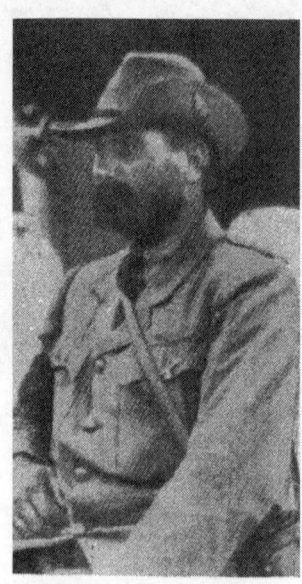

Brig.-Gen. VAN DEVENTER.

Major H. B. M. BOURNE, Union Secretary for Defence.

Col. Sir WILLIAM W. HOY, Commanding S.A. Union Contingent.

General Botha at Breakfast in South West.

Union Forces Landing an Engine at Luderitzbucht.

The Church, Luderitzbucht, after service on Sunday afternoon.

General Sir Duncan McKenzie returning from a Harbour Inspection at Luberitzbucht.

natives killed three German farmers. Subsequently the German Colonial Government announced that the insurrection "was speedily suppressed," an announcement that was brief enough, anyhow.

Some time during September a British auxiliary cruiser shelled Swakopmund. No official announcement was made on the subject from our side until the end of the year, and after the Germans in Europe had declared that Scarborough, the well-known watering-place on the east coast of Yorkshire, was bombarded because Swakopmund, an open town, had been bombarded. Then came a British Admiralty explanation that the cranes on the (south) pier at Swakopmund were shelled by the auxiliary cruiser "Kinfauns Castle" on September 24, as a reprisal for the dynamiting by German soldiers of the pier and a steamboat that same day, at Walvis Bay, also an open township.

According to an official announcement issued from Windhuk, and published in the *Lüderitzbucht Zeitung* of September 18th (the day before our arrival), a converted Union-Castle liner shelled the wireless station at Swakopmund on the 14th of that month, and then returned to the open sea. The communiqué spoke of a few houses having been demolished.

Apparently there was more than one naval visit to Swakopmund. But by the end of September two of the German South-west African wireless stations were out of action. I don't suppose this added greatly to the Germans' inconvenience. They still had the powerful stations at Aus and Windhuk, though by this time there were few sympathetic stations with which they could speak. For instance, in November they were making desperate efforts to get into direct touch with "our East Asia fleet," and Major Franke was offering a hundred marks to any operator who effected it. There was never any necessity for Major Franke to make his offer good. But all that was not from any incompleteness in their own wireless equipment.

But while these stations may not have had a great positive value, they were undoubtedly of value in a negative sense. No wireless message circulated within reasonable distance of Windhuk or Aus could escape being tapped, and when it suited their book the Germans could, and did, prevent certain of our stations from sending out messages at all. This exactly was our plight at Lüderitzbucht, as I recall with no little feeling on the matter. So soon as our operators got going, the German operators would "chip" in with a jarring note, or, rather, a perfect medley of jarring notes, and the wave would be broken. In one particular twenty-four hours we got exactly six words over to the Cape. Occasionally we would get a spell of freedom—always in the wee sma' hours when, presumably, the German operators had played themselves to sleep—and to the most riotous use would it be put. All arrears would be wiped off, and sometimes a more or less insignificant press message would get carried along in the rush.

It is doubtful if the Germans ever gained any vital information by their tapping, for the simple reason that while their wireless stations remained intact, wireless service in the Windhuk radius was utilised as little as possible. They were thus more bamboozled than anything else. Cape shipping, for instance, used the wireless only under extreme pressure of circumstances. Thus, in eight months Windhuk picked up the messages of seventeen vessels that were making Cape Town; and, addressing the Landesrath in March, 1915, the German Governor pointed with pride to this apparently wonderful effect on our shipping of the so-called German naval blockade! As a matter of fact, Cape Town docks were never so busy as during those eight months of 1914-1915, and more than the average hundred vessels a month were dealt with.

A connection with the trunk cable was effected early in November, and our interest in German vagaries then ceased.

First impressions of Lüderitzbucht were not ratified by close inspection. It turned out to be distinctly an unpleasing place, bare of everything in the way of natural growth, as a residential spot without one single advantage unless it were a healthy climate. There was a land-locked and apparently well-sheltered harbour, but it was small, and ships anchored nearly a mile from the jetty, which the largest tug could not reach at low water. There were streets of deep, loose sand—even those that were cut from solid rock—and it were punishment itself to walk through them; and there was a conglomeration of most irregular buildings, a few of them imposing and even handsome, the most of them quite unpretentious, but practically all of them either of brick or stone. A notable building was the offices of the German Diamond Company, which the force made its headquarters on arrival. The upper storey consists of residential quarters, which were furnished with taste and elegance. They had been furnished in this way, so we were informed, specially to receive the Crown Prince, who had arranged to tour the colony some time during 1914, and who was to have occupied them while he remained at Lüderitzbucht.

But most of the houses, indeed, were well furnished. Their occupants obviously "did themselves well." As a whole, these people must have been a pretty Bohemian lot, to employ a euphemism. Few houses were without a collection of filthy pictures and literature, mostly pornographic; in some the evidences of moral depravity were incomprehensibly amazing.

There were several little bonfires about the time of these discoveries. With irony, the troops were wont to declare that the least depraved place in Lüderitzbucht seemed to be the licensed brothel—in our day the headquarters of the Transport Section—which produced nothing more dreadful than a painting of the nude that could only have been objected to on the score of bad workmanship!

Another notable building was the hospital on Shark "Island," a double-storeyed building having eight wards, with fifteen beds, and an operating theatre, all most completely equipped. There were wood and iron buildings near by which gave accommodation for native patients. We took the hospital over at once. The outbuildings we thoroughly renovated and fitted up as ordinary wards, thus providing for over 100 soldier patients. The main building was reserved for officers. Later on two other hospitals were opened up, both in the town itself. One was in the Drill Hall, which was ideal for the purpose; the other was in the transformed Europaischer Hof Hotel, low-lying and sand-swept, where men got well in spite of their situation. This costly policy of opening up separate hospitals in the same place seemed to be preferred to an extension of existing accommodation.

Lüderitzbucht was taken over as a going concern, as it were, and its various services went on without interruption. The responsibility of maintaining them was not heavy, for the normal population scarcely reached 750 whites. The electric light service would have been somewhat curtailed had we known at first what we afterwards learnt. The power station was a huge building housing very powerful machinery, which was designed to supply the diamond mines at Kolmanskuppe and elsewhere, as well as the town and port of Lüderitzbucht. It had only just been completed; indeed, the contractors' representative was still in possession when we arrived. He is reported to have introduced himself with a murmur about payment, mentioning many, many thousands of pounds; but as ours was not a financial commission, he was not encouraged in such talk. S.A. Engineers assumed control straight away. From the start they became aware of an apparent wastage of power without being able to account for it; no amount of overhauling had any appreciable effect. Some days later a native employee asked them if they had "switched Kolmanskuppe off." There was the secret. Before clearing out, the Germans had "switched Kolmanskuppe on," and as they were at this time at Kolmanskuppe, we were supplying them with light and power without knowing it! The sin of commission soon became one of omission.

The whole of the first week was spent in fashioning defences and in dealing with the German elements, who became rather obstreperous. Signalling between the Germans within and the Germans without undoubtedly went on every night, yet it was only with difficulty, spite of all vigilance, that individuals inside the town were tracked down. This trouble, however, became automatically eliminated, as it had been decided to shut down the Germans in Lüderitzbucht entirely and send them to the Union for internment. In all the circumstances, it was the best policy, but it made the Germans very wroth. Dr. Seitz, the Governor, called it a "flagrant violation of all principles of international law," in so far as it concerned the women and children. But the fact was, the women and children were not permitted to starve; it was insisted that they should continue to live, and the means to live in comparative comfort were extended to them. There is little credit for humanity in war! A few civilians remained throughout, being the proved British element.

The defences of Lüderitzbucht entailed an enormous amount of work. There was barbed wire to lay, blockhouses to build, big guns to impose on commanding points, and the surroundings of the town were the reverse of flat. One of the 4.7's alone took 400 men two days to disembark and take away and mount. Also, there were innumerable fatigues by day, and quite sufficient pickets by night to find. It was exacting duty on so small a force, and it was a real relief when reinforcements came along. But, throughout, the men worked with great goodwill. There were, perhaps, occasional signs of irritability, as when a new junior subaltern and a member of a quarterguard had a tempestuous outburst. The former espied a dirty rifle and gave the owner a fairly complete "choking-off." But the man was not long from an exhausting fatigue, and for the moment he was in a state known in the Army as "fedupedness." Turning suddenly on his officer, he bluntly told him to "go to hell"!

For the moment the officer was flabbergasted. Then he stalked to a telephone near by and acquainted the long-suffering Brigade Major with the happening, asking, "What shall I do?"

"Don't go, my dear fellow, don't go!" came back the unexpected and perhaps not too soothing reply. All the same, the man lived to regret his loquacity.

A week after the landing, some of the troops had their first smell of powder. It was known that after leaving Lüderitzbucht the Germans moved out to Kolmanskuppe, ten miles away, blowing up the railway after them. A few days later, they continued the retreat as far as Grasplatz, two miles further on; and still later they moved on Rothkuppe, another eight miles, but they left an advanced post at Grasplatz. It was decided to try to cut off this post, and a force of 100 Imperial Light Horse, under Lt.-Col. Donaldson, D.S.O., and 250 Rand Light Infantry, under Lt.-Col. Fairweather, D.S.O., was deputed to do it.

Marching by night among the treacherous sand-dunes, the Light Horse suddenly appeared at dawn in positions which barred the way from Grasplatz to Rothkuppe. Simultaneously the Infantry, facing eastwards, lined a ridge of hills between Kolmanskuppe and Grasplatz, which commanded the road to Pomona, along which the Germans were believed to have established numerous small supply depots. The mounted men then commenced to sweep the country lying between them and the Infantry. At Grasplatz station they broke in upon quite a busy scene. Four Germans were directing the operations of about fifty natives who were loading up stores. As the natives were unarmed, the Light Horse refrained from firing. The Germans took advantage of this by getting well in among the natives and opening fire. They slightly wounded two men, and managed to get away. A couple of hours later the infantry and mounted men between them put up a party of eight Germans, killing four (one an armed native) and capturing one, an officer, who was slightly wounded. The fighting was entirely done by the mounted men, who opened fire at a thousand yards and finished up at fifty. They lost four men killed and three wounded, one of the latter being Captain de Meillon. One of the killed, Trooper Gruman, had already been wounded that morning, but would insist on going into the second action. Two of the other killed were brothers named Winslow. There was something truly pathetic about the death of the second Winslow. He heard his brother cry out for water, and naturally rushing to comply, was himself shot down as he was holding his water bottle to his brother's lips—shot doubtless by the same German. Over their grave in Lüderitzbucht cemetery now stands this very impressive declaration :

" Tell England, ye that pass this monument,
That we who rest here died content."

Their death cast a gloom over camp, for they were the bearers of a well-known name in the South African sporting world.

The movement was repeated a few days later, when Transvaal Scottish, under Lieut.-Colonel Dawson Squibb, supplied the infantry support. On this occasion only the left flank of the infantry, which had moved round Charlottental, a police post lying to the north-west of Kolmanskuppe, came in touch with the enemy. Eight well-mounted Germans were surprised in a building at Charlottental. Firing was soon pretty furious, but not of long duration. When they saw three of their number down, including the officer in charge, the unwounded Germans bolted into the sand-dunes and got clear away. None of the Scottish was hit. One of the Germans was very seriously wounded.

A goodly number of the force had thus come under fire very early in the campaign. For the most part they were youngsters without war experience. They came very satisfactorily out of the ordeal. They showed themselves alert and fairly self-reliant.

The captured equipment disclosed the enemy to be armed with a bayonet one edge of which was a saw. A saw-bayonet seemed a strange weapon for a European to be armed with while fighting a European. Its teeth literally gaped with ferocity. The mere sight of it almost made one shudder; and the Scotties began to wonder whether they had not been too kind in taking prisoners men who were armed with such a shameful weapon. Very soon these thoughts were fashioned into words. Two of the prisoners could speak English. They seemed anxious to explain that the bayonet was a sort of dual purpose affair: as it was teethed they were able to saw up wood with it; and it still remained a bayonet. It was pointed out that it would make a jagged, sickening, ghastly wound—one that was not likely to heal. That was so, they admitted, " but," with a shrug of the shoulders, " we are not likely to use it as a bayonet."

A prophecy, did we but know it! True enough, the Germans never came near using it.

A very good story is told in connection with these bayonets. When German prisoners were taken they were invariably put under a guard with fixed bayonets. Their officers protested against this, contending that Union soldiers were not subjected to such an indignity as a bayonet guard. " Oh, well, you see," was the answer, " we are not ashamed of our bayonets ! "

Before any further operations could be ordered of it, " C " force ceased to be. On October 3rd, Sir Duncan McKenzie arrived unexpectedly with his " D " force. The two forces were amalgamated, and henceforth were known as the Central Force.

CHAPTER IV.

SANDFONTEIN.

From the point of view of casualties, the biggest engagement fought by any of the Union forces was Gibeon, towards the end of the campaign. From the point of view of sheer, severe fighting there was no engagement to compare with Sandfontein, which was the first of the campaign. Sandfontein was fought by "A" force under Brigadier-General Lukin. General Lukin's Chief of Staff was Major (now Lt.-Col.) Burne.

"A" force was the first to leave Cape Town, but that was for the purpose of concentrating at some other spot in the Union—at Steinkopf, which was to be its jumping-off place for German South-west Africa. It sailed from Cape Town on September 2nd, which was some days earlier than was arranged originally. But in the meantime reports indicating that the Germans were concentrating on the frontier with a view to an invasion of the Union were received, and its departure was expedited in consequence.

Port Nolloth, 280 miles from Cape Town, was the place of disembarkation. It offered very few facilities for the business. The nearest water, moreover, was five miles inland, and that was distinctly brackish, while a few steps beyond the boundary of the township commenced the great sandy, waterless waste that is the characteristic of a vast portion of this western coast belt.

Port Nolloth exists principally for the service of the rich copper deposits of O'okiep, 92 miles inland. The deposits are being worked by the Cape Copper Company, which ships the metal, in the form of regulus, direct to Europe. Port Nolloth and O'okiep are connected by a 2 ft. 6 in. railway, the property of the company, and one of the stations on the system is Steinkopf, 61 miles from the coast. The troops had the use of this railway, of course, and, in spite of the narrow gauge and the limited amount of rolling stock available, it did really wonderful work. The line traverses desert country all the way, which is usually devoid of vegetation save when the average three-yearly rains drench it. Happily enough, fair rains had just preceded the troops, who traversed not bare sand but a track most richly carpeted with flowers of gorgeous colouring, in all the circumstances an incongruous scene, amazing, but a scene that greatly delighted the eye and mightily pleased the nostril.

By September 14 the force had its base fairly well established. The situation permitted an early move forward, and so Lt.-Col. Dawson (an ex-Imperial officer, Northumberland Fusiliers) and Lt.-Col. Berrange, with the 4th and 5th Regiments, respectively, of the S.A.M.R., were ordered to take up positions which would give them command of Raman's Drift on the Orange River, by which the force was to advance into German territory. The drift was held at this time by an advance post of the enemy.

From Steinkopf Raman's Drift is a distance of 45 miles, and the route produces neither water nor grazing. Of grazing, indeed, it were ridiculous to speak, where there was not sustenance for the veriest weed. Yes, there was one thing it produced, and it produced it in profusion. It produced bones. Hardly any turn on the whole route is without bones. At one spot there are more bones than anywhere else in the 45 miles, as if on some great trek exhausted nature had sank down here and died *en masse*. Good Chaplain Aldridge, of the Anglican Church, declared when he first saw it that his thoughts flew irresistibly to the passage in Ezekiel where the great prophet speaks of being set down in the midst of a valley full of bones which were very dry; only had these bones received breath, and sinews, and flesh, they would have become an army of horses and mules, not the exceeding great army of Israel. Mr. Stent, who penned an intensely vivid account of the trek, also called it the Valley of Dry Bones.

While animals, whose requirements are greater, suffered worse than men, one can give only an inadequate idea of the sufferings of both, however one conjures with positives, and comparatives, and superlatives. Men had their water-bottles, but what was one bottle of liquid, even had it been wine nectared in Naxos by fair immortals, to a man whose mouth was being " stopt in dust " almost as precisely as Omar Khayyam sings of? From first to last, it was one long grind through interminable dust that choked, and blinded, and deafened, for men's ears also were filled, as from a funnel.

There was a water-hole eight miles off the road, but the nearest point to this eight-mile deviation was not reached until no fewer than 33 miles of the journey were done and finished with, and but 12 more remained to be covered. All the same, it was considered safer to outspan at mile 33 and let the disburdened animals trudge to their fill, though it meant an extra 16 miles, rather than attempt the remaining 12 miles unrefreshed and heavily burdened.

The trek was a great test of endurance for both man and beast. If any one march in this campaign of good marches can be said to stand out beyond its fellows, this one from Steinkopf to Raman's Drift will assuredly advance strong claim to the distinction.

Raman's Drift was commanded by a German blockhouse or police station. The Union troops reached here in sufficient time to attack at dawn. All the Germans save one, however, scuttled at the first rifle crack. The exception was an officer, apparently, who endeavoured, Horatius-like, to hold the position himself. He surrendered to superior numbers, but he managed to kill one of our men first.

A patrol of the 5th Regiment set out in pursuit of the Germans, and discovered them in position higher up the river. There was a sharp skirmish, in which we lost one man killed and another wounded. The wounded man, Nesbit, was very pluckily brought out of the firing line by Regt. Sgt.-Major Thomas, who ran the gauntlet of a heavy fire to do so. The patrol returned to the drift without further loss.

The Germans afterwards went inland. Scouts kept in touch with them until they finally landed at a camp some twenty-five miles north-east of the drift, where there was abundant grazing and evidently plenty of water. This was Sandfontein, which may be described as a sort of half-way house to Warmbad, and therefore a position of some value.

Sandfontein itself is actually a small kopje with spurs of huge boulders, giving a frontage altogether of a few hundred yards. Surrounding the kopje is a sandy plain, which, again, is almost surrounded by ridges of hills, the whole forming a basin in places about three miles across. In between the ridges are four or five defiles along which run roads to Warmbad in the north and Raman's and Hom's drifts on the Orange River in the south. There were about fifty Germans in the camp. The place, however, was completely evacuated by September 19, when the 4th and 5th Regiments of the S.A.M.R. reached it. All the pumps were destroyed and the water had been left seemingly unfit for further use, the wells each containing bodies of dead dogs. Fortunately, the Union troops came along hard on the heels of the enemy, and so sufficient time had not elapsed for the corpses to become decomposed and the water vitally contaminated. The wells were soon made fit for use again. But it was clear that the Germans in South-west Africa intended to conduct their campaign with no greater gentleness than was characterising their operations in Europe.

A squadron of the 4th Regiment was left in occupation of Sandfontein, after patrols had scoured the surrounding country and apparently cleared it of the enemy. One man was wounded in this work. So far, six Germans had been taken prisoners. The remainder of these advance troops was recalled to camp at Hom's Drift, fifteen miles east of Raman's Drift, and at Godoun's Drift, eight miles to the west, pending the advance of the main body to Raman's Drift, a movement which was completed by the 24th. The following evening a squadron of the 1st S.A.M.R. pushed forward to Sandfontein in order to relieve the garrisoning squadron there, which then rejoined its regiment at Hom's Drift. The following day patrols of the new garrison were attacked by the enemy, and reinforcements were sent for. These reinforcements consisted of a second squadron of the 1st Regiment and two guns, with about thirty men of the Transvaal Horse Artillery, and they reached camp shortly before eight o'clock on the morning of the 26th. Lt.-Col. R. C. Grant, D.S.O., officer commanding the 1st S.A.M.R., accompanied the reinforcements.

Before the day was out the battle of Sandfontein had been won and lost. The new arrivals had hardly outspanned than suspicious clouds of dust were observed north, east, and south. They betokened advancing German forces, and it was soon evident that Sandfontein was being surrounded. The body first sighted was in the north-east, and when it was about two miles off the Transvaal Horse Artillery opened fire with half-a-dozen shells, which fell short. Shortly afterwards the enemy's big guns began their reply. Their first shot fell 25 yards away; their fifth spread over our guns. It is thought the Germans occupied their time at Sandfontein marking out ranges, which is one more evidence of their thoroughness and farsightedness. They had prepared for an advance into the Union. They had also prepared for their own eventual retreat.

S.A.M.R. and Artillery, all told, the Union force numbered 257 officers and men, and they had but two field guns and two machine guns with them. The Germans, on the other hand, had anything from 1,500 to 2,000 men—the exact number never transpired. With them were ten field guns and six machine guns. Their main force was in the north-east; it was backed by six field guns, and evidently came from Ukamas. Another force came along from Warmbad and spread from north to west; it had two field guns. A third force crept up from the direction of Hom's Drift in the south and extended to the west; it, too, had two field guns, and was probably the force of 300 that was reported on the 22nd to be some twenty miles west of Schuit Drift, and marching in the direction of Pella Drift, where there is a small mission station. The machine guns were evenly distributed among each force.

The Germans spread along the ridges enclosing the Sandfontein basin, and were not long in reaching the last of the narrow defiles by which ingress to the basin is obtained. They made their dispositions very skilfully, and it was clear they were operating with well-trained and sternly disciplined troops.

Before any possible relief could come to the besieged, the besiegers were all in position; and when reinforcements did appear on the scene these found their further progress barred by entrenched troops with four machine guns, which were used to advantage. The reinforcements came from Hom's Drift, being two squadrons of the 4th S.A.M.R., under Captains King and Davidson. After several ineffectual attempts to break through these had no option but to fall back. They sustained several casualties, mostly from heavy machine gun fire.

So there could be only one ending to such an unequal contest. Yet it was a long time before there was any sign of weakening on the part of the British troops. The gunners —it was chiefly an artillery action—never lost their heads or their nerve. The Germans soon got the range. They soon lost it. Quietly and deliberately the Union gunners had moved nearer to the attack, going some 50 yards in. To this device is due the fact that for an hour or two no German shell fell within 30 yards of either piece; and at the new range the gunners temporarily silenced one of the guns in the north-east. Then a spring in " A " gun gave way, and men had to stand around for ten minutes, twenty minutes, thirty minutes, impotent, but unfortunately not invulnerable, while the defect was remedied. With what alacrity firing was resumed! With what enthusiasm the first of the new series of shells was launched! With what grim satisfaction a palpable hit was recorded! One of the German guns in the south ceased awhile.

The S.A.M.R. had entrenched themselves on the 100-yards-long kopje, and maintained a steady and deliberate rifle fire. They worked their maxims at full pressure. Time and again they brought daring enemy movements to a complete standstill; and during one period of three hours abandoned all attempts at closing in. It was a tremendous achievement this, for it must not be forgotten that the Riflemen were all the time exposed to a galling fire from the enemy's artillery. It was unshowy work, theirs, but it was effective. After it was all over the German Commander required some convincing that the Riflemen did number fewer than 1,500, which was alike a tribute to the skill with which they had constructed their schanzas and concealed themselves, and used their rifles, and no little indication of the imagination animating the German scheme of Intelligence.

The struggle was at its height between half-past ten and half-past eleven. It is calculated that in this period the Germans alone fired not fewer than 1,200 shrapnels.

"To me," wrote one survivor, "it seemed like hell let loose. I know it wasn't France, or Flanders, or Russia. If I were in one or the other of those places I should simply be unable to describe what goes on there at all adequately. I know that at Sandfontein there was an infernal din of shrieking, splitting, sickening shells, an interminable rat-a-tat of machine guns, a cracking of rifles that rose in waves but never died away entirely. All this noise was intensified beyond measure because it was caught up in the hollow of the basin and reverberated again and again until the echoes in their clash almost threatened to drown the original noise! I thought my head would burst, and if it had done so it would only have been in harmony with the song of the day."

As noon approached the T.H.A. gunners were found to be dwindling away, gradually but surely, mostly wounded. Ammunition, too, was getting thin. It was decided to remove the guns close in to the kopje, at a spot near which the garrison was now concentrating. About this time the rattle of musketry outside was faintly heard. It was the relief trying to get through. Later on the sounds had died off. The attempts had failed.

Within the next hour "B" gun ceased to fire and "A" gun had but two gunners left. "A" gun did not long survive. It was not itself damaged, but its unwounded survivors were unwounded no longer; a shell had burst close to them on the left. Lieut. Adler, the officer commanding the guns, was now the only unwounded survivor. He could do no more than render the guns useless, and all the breech blocks were accordingly removed. This action seemed to be suspected by the Germans, who sensibly increased the intensity of their fire without, however, interfering one iota with the operation, which was facilitated by reason of a heavy fire poured by the S.A.M.R. into the German lines.

The Germans then turned their attention to the animals, and in half-an-hour had practically wiped out the lot. Scarcely a dozen came through unscathed. Still later, the enemy closed in on the south and, concentrating on their machine guns, enfiladed the positions occupied by the S.A.M.R. Finally, they attempted a cavalry charge, also from the south, but this was repulsed—a slight negative success for the garrison. In no wise did it affect the position, however. The plight of the besieged was undoubtedly desperate. It was complicated by the fact that the officer commanding, Col. Grant, was himself wounded. All hope of receiving relief had been abandoned.

Surrender, therefore, seemed inevitable; and the inevitable happened at 4.30 in the afternoon, after the force had, metaphorically, held up its head for eight hours against overwhelming odds. " Cease fire " was ordered, and a white flag was improvised and hoisted. It took fifteen minutes for the flag to convey its message to the Germans, and meanwhile it attracted no little rifle fire to itself. Indeed, the officer supporting it was actually shot in the leg—a flesh wound only, but still a wound.

Throughout, the Britishers had shown nerve and grit as well as capable shooting, and their behaviour was undoubtedly worthy of the best traditions of the race. The German Commander, who was Col. von Heydebreck, the Commander-in-Chief of the German forces, himself complimented Col. Grant on the gallant stand that he and his men had made, and specially referred to the work of the artillery. He had, as it may be assumed, no little admiration for the work of his own men; and from an order that we found at Tschaukaib early in November, we learn that no fewer than seventeen of them received Iron Crosses in token of the victory. Still, Col. von Heydebreck's admiration of the behaviour of the Union forces seemed to be sincere. There was some confirmation of it in the fact that by his orders the British dead were buried first, and their captured comrades were allowed to attend the funeral, while, after full military honours had been accorded, he himself delivered a short oration extolling their heroism. All the same, it sounds very strange, when contrasted with the treatment that was meted out to the prisoners, for these had fought just as heroically as their unfortunate dead. Other Union soldiers who had the ill-luck to find themselves prisoners with the Germans have since remarked on this—that the Germans treated no prisoners so badly as those that were taken at Sandfontein. These men, notably at Franzfontein, were reduced to such straits that they were compelled to go about camp in sacks and raw hide sandals, having no other clothing. It is true that at this time there was another man at the head of the German forces: Col. von Heydebreck had passed to the great majority, and had been succeeded by Major Franke. That may be the explanation.

The British casualties totalled 12 killed and 40 wounded, and 205 officers and men captured. The German losses were officially returned at 14 killed (including a major and subaltern) and 25 wounded. Both German and British medical sections were on the scene, and the wounded received generally good treatment; but the Germans detained two British ambulances and two medicos " for the British wounded." During fight a small section of officers and men of the S.A. Medical Corps most heroically moved about rendering what service it could.

The enemy got very little booty. Apparently they wanted none, for they burnt most of what they did get. It was noted that they specially retained the horses' bits, "as they are better than ours," so they explained. The captured field guns were taken to Windhuk, and, as trophies, placed alongside the Herero Memorial there; but they were nowhere to be found when General Botha entered the capital.

To what may the disaster be ascribed? I have heard the scouting blamed. I have heard it contended that the Union forces allowed themselves to be foolishly trapped. But I do not think there can be much doubt about it that it was almost entirely a consequent of the rebellion. To say the force was trapped is to give undue credit to the Germans, who not only poisoned, or sought to poison, the water at Sandfontein, but destroyed the machinery by which it was raised. It is conceivable that if they had intended to trap the Union force by pretending to evacuate the place, they would have left some allurement in the form of a water supply that had not been interfered with. I think there is a tendency to overlook the fact that it was about this time that Maritz finally satisfied the Germans that he was their man. Thus and then the Union Defence Department's scheme to invade German South-west Africa by way of Nakob became stultified. In anticipation either of opposition to their own invasion of the Union or of this projected invasion of their own territory, the Germans had begun to mass fairly strong forces near the eastern border, notably at Ukamas. The defection of Maritz from the Union army, coupled with the signs and portents of a successful rising of the recalcitrant Dutch in the Union itself, had the direct effect of releasing these eastern forces for service elsewhere. The Germans were shrewd enough to see the advantage of this position, and had wit enough to utilise it. They knew that a Union force had moved into Sandfontein. Here was an objective almost to hand. So they withdrew practically every available man and gun from the eastern area and by forced marches got them to Sandfontein. They did the journey in three days, and in the last twenty-four hours it is said they covered nearly 70 miles.

In a situation such as this the odds would be on the Germans (or any similar force) every time. It may reasonably be contended, however, that the garrison deputed to occupy and hold Sandfontein was most unwisely meagre. It is doubtful if the whole of " A " force itself would have been adequate, in all the circumstances; and I think it is significant that the Germans, even after their victory, got away from the place with all dispatch. That was practically an admission that the position was too dangerous for them to hold, big as was their force. Nevertheless, Sandfontein, with its water, was essential to General Lukin's advance. Waterholes proved to be the keynote of the whole campaign.

After Sandfontein Raman's Drift was evacuated. "A" force concentrated at Godou's Drift, and for the most part remained quiescent there. The main German forces, on the other hand, moved back some 50 miles, leaving every water hole in their wake either destroyed or polluted, though a substantial patrol remained behind to operate in front of the British outposts. The men of this patrol drew their food and water from small bases known only to the Germans. In ten days, however. Union patrols had accounted practically for the whole of these men, mostly as prisoners. One or two surrendered, being in rather a distressful state. It seemed that the Germans had overdone their water-destruction policy, and left their own patrol short of supplies! This was not the only occasion on which the enemy were just a little too thorough unto foolishness.

A general retirement was ordered about the middle of October, and "A" force returned to Steinkopf. While in camp here the Witwatersrand Rifles, commanded by Lt.-Col. Smythe, received orders to join General McKenzie at Lüderitzbucht, and the S.A.M.R. and Transvaal Horse Artillery received orders to proceed overland to Bloemfontein, there to join the campaign for the suppression of the rebellion which had broken out in the Union. The force trekked through O'okiep and Van Rhynsdorp to Birdfield, the terminus of the Malmesbury line, where it entrained. The trek to railhead was 230 miles in all, and it occupied ten days, exactly the length of time it took to entrain at Birdfield and reach Bloemfontein.

Thus "A" force came to be disbanded after having been in existence a little less than two months.

CHAPTER V.

MARITZ.

The story of "B" force, which was to have been commanded by Maritz, then a Lieut.-Colonel in the Union Defence Force, is the story of Maritz's treachery.

Maritz had certain units in training at Upington when he was ordered to proceed with a strong force to Schuit Drift and act under the orders of, and in conjunction with, General Lukin. His force numbered 980 officers and men, fully equipped with rifles and carbines, and having four machine guns, together with 600,000 rounds of ammunition. Among his men he created an impression that they were too young and raw and ill-equipped to "invade German South-west Africa," before finally putting his traitorous scheme before them. There was no question of their being too raw to undertake a serious rebellion campaign in the Union, which, even he admitted, might end in disaster. "In the event of anything going wrong," he said, "and any of us escape to German territory, they will give us protection and recognise us as German subjects."

But this was by no means the beginning of things. Maritz became an irreconcilable during the Boer War, and he has since been regarded as an irreconcilable by everyone who knew him at all well. It is a curious concatenation that connects Maritz, the German Government official in Southwest Africa, with Maritz, the Union Defence Force officer. Bad-tempered, stubborn, and not at all brilliant, he declined to take the oath of allegiance at the conclusion of the Boer War. He became a veritable soldier of fortune, and any country was good enough for him so long as it was not the country of his birth, improved though its condition had become. First he threw in his lot with the mad Emperor of Sahara, and was in Madagascar with him. Later on, he took up transport riding, also in the French island. Then he migrated to German South-west Africa, where he became naturalised. At one time he filled the appointment of Head Conductor of Transport to the German Colonial Government. In 1906 we find him in Pretoria, but under notice to leave within twenty-four hours, yet he was back again immediately after the establishment of Union, and established in business at Braamfontein as a butcher.

First British Train out of Luderitzbucht. Signing the "Passengers' Book" on the Platform. Left to right: Major Wells (Intelligence); Lt.-Col. Muller; Col. Sir George Farrar, D.S.O.; Gen. Sir Duncan McKenzie, G.O.C.; Lt.-Col. W. Tanne· (Chief of Staff); Major Maynard, S.A.M.C.

Departure of British Train from Luderitzbucht.

[*From the "Cape Times."*]

The graves of Rex and Wilfred Winslow, who were the first to be recorded on the Roll of Honour in G S.W.A.

[*Photo: Kejn.*]

H.M. Auxiliary Cruiser "Armadale Castle" at Cape Town.

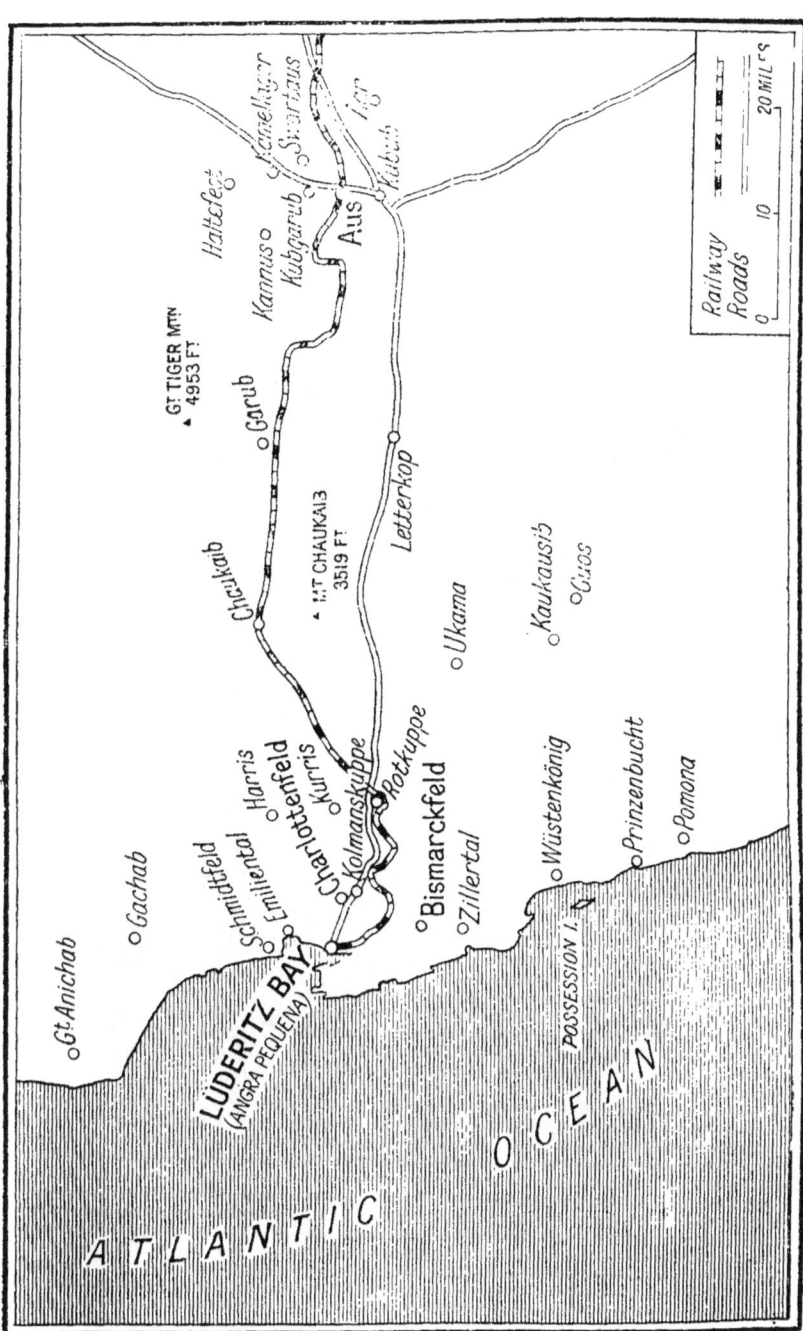

On Red Cross Service
From German South West.

African World.

The Hospital Ship "Ebani" at night, between Luderitz Bay and Capetown.

The "Ebani" is an Elder Dempster Liner and now engaged on Red Cross Work in the Mediterranean.

Very shortly afterwards he joined the South African Police and was made a Superintendent. In order that such an appointment could be made, the claims to promotion of established members having long experience and service had to be forgotten. It is not surprising to learn that the appointment was bitterly resented in the Service. In 1913, Maritz was put in charge of the enormous district bordering German territory on the north-west, of all districts in the Union!

He was plotting with the Germans in 1913. The overtures seem to have come out in May or June of that year, during the visit to his camp of an old irreconcilable crony in the person of Piet de Wet, a German subject. "We have a plan," he told de Wet one day, "should ever there be a war, to free our country. They have now placed me here to try to get into touch with the Germans." He did not say exactly who "they" were, but he mentioned that General Beyers, General de Wet, and others were in favour of the scheme. The most important result of this conversation, which was repeated in Windhuk on de Wet's return, as it was intended it should be, was an indirect message from the Kaiser himself declaring that he would "not only agree to your independence, but will guarantee it on condition that you start the rebellion immediately." There were also messages from the German Governor, who offered to "assist the Boers as far as possible with artillery and small arms." It is also said that Maritz was assisted financially as well, and the sum of £40,000 has been mentioned.

Prior to this, Maritz had attended a most important meeting in Pretoria of Staff-Officers and Commandants (August 14, 1914), when plans for the proposed German South-west African campaign were discussed. Maritz is then reported to have told Major Kemp, a District Staff Officer (who also went into rebellion). that he would resign rather than join the expedition). This form of virtuous protest does not appear to have developed at all. Maritz said nothing at the Conference, and he went back to his district ostensibly amenable to the discipline of his corps; while General Beyers, who was one of the triumvirate of the Republic *in posse*, addressed the first of the troops to be despatched to the front in seemingly the most loyal terms. Seated on his charger, the Commandant-General adjured them to "carry out your orders," and concluded by calling for "three cheers for his Majesty the King." General de la Rey, on a subsequent occasion, spoke similarly. The troops were to stand together in the cause of their country, and obey orders, for "this is not a question of nationality any more."

Such was the relationship between Maritz (and his like) and the Government.

With a view to facilitating measures both of defence and offence, the Defence Department arranged for the immediate extension of the railway from Prieska to Upington, a distance of 142½ miles. The survey was commenced on August 21, 1914, and the actual work of construction was begun on September 7. Incidentally, the new railway followed the course of the Orange River, and, advancing at the rate of 2¼ miles per day, was completed on November 20. Such rapid railway building was regarded at the time as a record for South Africa, but even better work was done before the campaign was over. The line was eventually pushed on to a junction with the German system at Kalkfontein, making 314½ miles of new railway in all. Though railhead was always well behind the military advance into German Southwest Africa, the line, so far as it was complete, was ever of inestimable value nevertheless; while, particularly in the Cape, the completed system will now serve a rich if somewhat limited farming area, which had been too long neglected in this respect.

I have referred in a previous chapter to the transgression of Union territorial rights at Nakob by the Germans. But Nakob was followed by a much more flagrant and serious incident. On August 22 a small force of Afrikander refugees from German South-west Africa, men and women, removed their stock and their belongings into the Union, crossing the border and the Orange River at a spot known as Beenbrink, some few miles south-west of Schuit Drift. They were observed here by a German patrol, the sergeant in charge of which ordered them to return, when no doubt their cattle would have been impounded as munitions of war. They refused to do so. They prepared to go into laager on an island in the river, which was unquestionably Union territory, and fight it out. The sergeant, who appears to have been a very officious and aggressive gentleman, first replied with the dramatic declaration that he was "no longer a policeman but a soldier"; then he solemnly warned them that "as you apparently mean to resist me, my shot shall be first." Simultaneously, he and his men opened fire.

The refugees returned the fire. The women helped their men-folk to entrench themselves, and a sharp engagement ensued. The result of it was that the sergeant was killed and one of his men wounded, while another was taken prisoner, though he escaped the next day. The wounded man succumbed. Two days later another German patrol, this time with an officer in charge, appeared at the drift and demanded that our police should hand the refugees over to them. It got no satisfaction. The Union Police merely pointed to the bodies of the dead Germans, which were actually lying in Union territory. The patrol buried their late comrades and then retired.

General Beyers called all this an "involuntary transgression of our frontier for which an apology was tendered," but this was after he had accepted the "corroboration of Lt.-Col. Maritz and his officers, who are on or near the frontier, that the report of the violation was unfounded." Parenthetically, I may here repeat the definite assertion of General Smuts that no apology for the involuntary transgression was ever tendered to the Union Government.

It is pretty patent, therefore, that so far as the officer in charge of the north-western district was concerned, the Union border there was unprotected, and the Germans had practically a licence to roam over it at will. "B" force being never anything more than a force in name, all the frontier ports were left unsupported, with the result that on the advance of the enemy our outposts had either to wage a conflict that they could never hope to win, or retire precipitately.

The first post to fall was Nakob or Groendoorn, which was on the principal trade route to German territory, and important, therefore, though small. There is abundant water at Nakob. Ordinarily it was a three-man garrison. At the time of the German attack there were eight men in camp; the nearest supporting post was Zwartmodder, where two men were stationed. Zwartmodder is 40 miles east of Nakob, and there is no water hole between the two places. Headquarters at Upington were 60 miles away.

It was on September 16 that the Germans appeared at Nakob, at daybreak. They were between 250 to 300 strong, and had three machine guns; they were operating from Ukamas as a base. They vainly called upon the garrison to surrender, and then attacked from two sides. The Britishers responded vigorously. Natives swear that they saw German horses "dropping everywhere." The garrison used up all its ammunition. Its personnel was then intact, having had the shelter of a building. The enemy, on the other hand, were more or less exposed. It is inconceivable that they came from under the fire of eight trained and entrenched men quite unscathed. After its ammunition was exhausted the garrison preferred to run the gauntlet of the enemy's fire, in an attempt to escape, rather than surrender. The odds were against the men getting through, but they took them. Three drew their winnings in the form of life and freedom; two got clear away, thanks to being well mounted, and the third got away after being captured. His captors became absorbed in a search for supposed buried ammunition, and while they were thus engaged he quietly walked off, fortunately finding a horse handy on the outskirts of their "outspan." The three of them were chased for miles, but without effect. Of the remaining five two were killed and three effectually made prisoners.

It transpired that the Germans were commanded by Andries de Wet, a Dutchman, but a naturalised German, a brother of the Piet de Wet already mentioned, and an irreconcilable like his brother, and like Maritz, of whom he was a great friend. Andries de Wet had raised this force himself with funds specially provided by the German Colonial Government. He and his men stayed at Nakob that day, clearing the adjacent farms of Aries and Gemsbok Hollow of cattle, and gathering in all the coloured and native residents, "as we are not going to have our movements reported at Upington." Later on, however, these people were released. While the Germans were in possession of Nakob, it is recorded that two Dutch farmers arrived on business, ignorant of the turn of events. They were made prisoners and ordered to be sent to Ukamas. One of them, who is described as old, unarmed, and, at the time, unmounted, on hearing of this, turned and ran. He was shot in his tracks.

Schuit Drift, on the Orange River, was captured two days later, possibly by the same force. The police in charge were taken prisoners.

On September 19 the enemy also occupied Rietfontein and Obobogrop. The Nakob force and this force most probably moved out of Ukamas at the same time, but while de Wet went eastwards, the other body went northwards, in the direction of Hasuur, a German police post and customs station, which practically faced Rietfontein. Ukamas and Hasuur are connected by a good road, one of those "military roads" of which we heard and saw so much in South-west Africa.

Obobogrop was ordinarily a six-man garrison, and the place is 50 miles north of Nakob. A German force of 50 men, 12 coloured men, and a Kaffir, with 10 camels and "lots of horses," doubtless a detachment from the larger body, rushed this post at daybreak. The police, however, had by then retired, having first destroyed the forage and stores.

Also at daybreak, a German force of 200 men appeared before Rietfontein, a further 45 miles to the north. Rietfontein is an important Union frontier post. It is the seat of a magistracy, and the garrison strength is usually an officer and nine men, all mounted on camels. The police here got away with their equipment before the arrival of the Germans, though they left certain stores behind. The stores, except a stock of dynamite which they destroyed, the Germans took away. They made the magistrate prisoner. It was at one time thought they were preparing for a march on Witdraii, a trek of twelve hours, in the direction of Kuruman, but their plans on this occasion did not materialise.

Meantime, Reuter had cabled out two messages from Amsterdam that make intensely interesting reading in the light of these events. The first message was apparently a Berlin communique which explained that the German Government never intended " permanently to occupy the South African Union." The second gave the gist of an apparently inspired statement which Dr. Solf, the German Minister of Colonies, had given to the German Press. In this Dr. Solf declared that Germany had been requested from the Boer side to explain its attitude towards the Union of first violating its own territory "in order to justify an unprovoked invasion of German South-west Africa, which the great majority of the Dutch inhabitants of the Union disapproved of."

The Press in general declared this statement to amount to an "impudent trap." I do not propose to go into the question as a whole. But I may fittingly point out here that in the very district where one might expect a great pro-German element to have arisen, and where, in fact, Maritz himself and the Germans themselves actually relied on finding one—I refer to Maritz's own district—the settlers were by no means unanimously sympathetic towards Germany. This is all the more surprising in view of the pretty well accepted fact that Government had rather neglected this area. In peace times some of the farmers had to rely on the Germans for medical attendance or else send a distance of about 400 miles, and, according to one commentator, English silver was rarely ever seen thereabouts—German silver was the currency. And yet one consequence of the fall of Nakob was the arrival at Upington of a batch of Dutch volunteers "anxious for a tussle with the Germans." Another body of burghers who had escaped from Maritz actually did have a tussle with a combined German and rebel force. One who took part in this affair says " we gave it them hot for three hours, and then we went into the veld and played the old de Wet game of hide-and-seek. Altogether, 300 of them chased us for 140 miles night and day. We lost one man."

Nothing of outstanding moment occurred in the district between September 20 and October 9. On the latter date a German force of 98 men, having a battery of four field guns and two machine guns, and commanded by Andries de Wet, crossed Nakob for the definite purpose of joining Maritz. They reached the region of Maritz's camp near Keimos the next day. Maritz had the greater part of his force here, dotted about in various small camps.

On October 10 the traitor broke the news of his treachery to the men of his command. He did it piecemeal fashion. It was told first to this batch, then to that. The first lot to be told were those on whose co-operation he most confidently relied, and so, by the time he came to the "doubtfuls," he had practically a complete rebel force around him; at any rate, it was quite numerous enough to subdue all the probable loyalists. Moreover, German forces were not far away.

Thus was a contretemps guarded against, but in order to make certain doubly sure, likely loyalists were got to the "indaba" by means of a trick, for which even Maritz himself shamefacedly apologised later. He called them to his quarters on the plea that he wanted to discuss the question of the insurance of their horses. Of course, they went along unarmed. As they reached headquarters, they saw a big gathering. A lane was made so that they could pass through to the centre. There they saw Maritz and his staff, but before the interview began the strange proceeding of searching them was gone through. Then and only then did the Traitorous Oracle speak.

In his speech Maritz outlined the scheme for the re-establishment of the South African Republic, and explained that he had entered into a compact with the Germans. In return for his assistance, not, however, to defend their own territory against invasion, but to help them capture other territory, Walvis Bay and the islands near it—the Germans would raise a volunteer corps to help him and his friends to fight the British and also take Delagoa Bay, "the natural port of the Union." It has been professed that an integral tenet in the rebel creed forbade the removal of "your neighbour's landmarks." Apparently it was to be held in abeyance what time "the Portuguese King." (Maritz's words) was being robbed.

Maritz gave his hearers five minutes to consider this new and startling position. Those that he wished to join him had to take two paces forward. Five officers and 58 men stood fast, including the whole of the machine-gun section. The gunnery officer, Lieut. Freer, told Maritz, moreover, what he thought of him, and declared that had he his four maxims he and his men would fight the whole band of rebels.

The offer was declined, "as in my opinion it would cause unnecessary bloodshed," but, as a sort of counterblast, and lest, perhaps, he be thought too squeamish, Maritz challenged any protestor to a duel. In the same breath, almost, he ordered the loyalists to be made prisoners and given to the Germans. This was done, as a wireless message to Windhuk, intercepted a few days later, proved. The hapless prisoners remained various periods in captivity; some escaped as opportunity offered, but none was in captivity less than eight months. Their treatment as prisoners always left something to be desired, but at times it was disgusting and scandalous.

One man, however, declared that the hardest thing for him to bear was the sight of rebels rifling his kit and leading his pet horse away. The last scene in this disgraceful episode was the announcement by one of his officers that Maritz himself was no longer an officer of the British but a General of an independent Dutch Republic. Later on in the campaign, however, Maritz was referred to as the representative of the Kaiser.

The Germans, now reinforced and numbering fully 300, actually joined their satellites the following day, and thereafter, for some time, German and Republican flags were always flying side by side in Maritz's camps. Maritz bragged that the Germans had agreed to place 6,000 men at his disposal, but that, one supposes, was in certain eventualities; eventualities that were never likely to occur once and so soon as the British Fleet had accounted for the German Atlantic Squadron. As the prisoners were crossing the border they noticed six German big guns on the way to the Cape.

Maritz formally declared the existence of a Republic on October 12, 1914. As was, perhaps, only to be expected, he was the President and Commander-in-Chief; his advisory statesmen were the two De Wets (who are no relation of General Christian de Wet), and Commandant de Villiers. According to original plans, General Beyers was to have been the prime mover in these events. It is on record that the German Governor waited in Keetmanshoop and Ukemas cooling his heels for many days, waiting for an arranged interview with Beyers, in order to conclude a treaty with him. Beyers never turned up. In the end Dr. Seitz left Herr von Zastrow to interview either Beyers or Maritz, and make all arrangements for combined action. (A copy of the treaty that was actually concluded with Maritz, with other documents, will be found as an appendix.)

Maritz then began his active rebellion. The Government was compelled to cease all vital operations in connection with the campaign in German South-west Africa for the time being, in order to deal with the new trouble, and a special force of 32,000 men was raised for the purpose. These new operations were in full blast two months. The rebellion was regarded officially as being "practically crushed" by December 10, 1914, and as being completely over by February 3, 1915, though the last rebels were not taken until March 23.

CHAPTER VI.

ENTERING THE NAMIB DESERT.

According to original plan, the early days of October should have seen Union troops closing in on the Germans from four different points. When October arrived there was only one force in enemy territory. That was the Central force, operating from Lüderitzbucht. No other force entered the country until the New Year. I am leaving the occupation of Schuckmannsburg out of reckoning. Schuckmannsburg is the chief town in the Caprivi Zipfel, and lies on the south bank of the Zambesi River, immediately facing Sesheke, a mission station in Northern Rhodesia. It fell unresistingly to a force of Rhodesian police, which crossed the river and occupied it on September 24. Its occupation by a British force was an essential in the campaign as a whole, but it involved no great or protracted military operation.

The new position was, of course, principally governed by the rebellion. But the authorities also took a serious view of Sandfontein and even of the fighting around Lüderitzbucht. The Union generally was inclined to be "nervy" at this time. Thus, when Sir Duncan McKenzie's force landed at Lüderitzbucht, both officers and men seemed surprised to find the Force of Occupation behaving quite as if the enemy were many miles away, and not very pressing in their attentions, which, as a matter of fact, was the case. They half expected to see haggard, grim-visaged men lying prone behind their rifles, every man Jack of them desperately keeping the foe at bay; and I am not so sure they weren't just a little disappointed that it wasn't so, for they were robbed of the thrill that relief parties should ordinarily experience! In such a way had the patrol affair at Grasplatz been interpreted.

The Beves column had really done very well, and the Minister of Defence was thoughtful and kind enough to wire and say so. The message went far to mollify officers and men, for "C" force was sorely disappointed at losing its identity and independence, being proudly confident in its ability. No member of it, I know, will ever be convinced that Aus, the first great objective after Lüderitzbucht, would not have fallen to them alone many months earlier than it actually did fall to them as an integral part of a much bigger force! "C" force, nevertheless, was too small for any great penetration inland.

Naturally, Sir Duncan McKenzie brought new ideas with him as well as new orders. His orders were, roughly, to sit tight, and, in any event, to do nothing that was outstandingly risky or dangerous, until the Defence Department saw its way, the grave situation in the Union being easier, to resume the aggressive on and in German South-west Africa generally. This release order did not come until about December 10, the time to which this chapter will extend. General McKenzie's Chief of Staff was Lt.-Col. W. Tanner, a District Staff Officer of the Union, and his A.D.C. Capt. Louis Botha, the Prime Minister's eldest son (who subsequently joined his father).

In all the circumstances, however, the most responsible appointment on the staff was that of the Deputy-Assistant Quartermaster-General, which was filled by Sir George Farrar, Bart., D.S.O. The Germans said that the 80-mile stretch of Namib desert separating Lüderitzbucht from the inland and comparatively fertile plateau which begins at Aus, would beat us. This desert, plus their own valuable assistance, would, they said, bring about our annihilation. It did neither. We beat the desert, and the forces that went to its aid, too. But victory came not through the rifle, but through those things that are the concern of the Quartermaster-General's department—transport and rations. The fact of Sir George Farrar, the head of the great Rand concern, the East Rand Proprietary Mines, with its vast organisation, being McKenzie's "D.A.Q.M.G." sensibly increased the authority attaching to the appointment. When German prisoners began to be brought in, the more enlightened of them generally asked where Sir George Farrar was. His whereabouts stood for them as the present measure of the invaders' success. The Union troops themselves saw the effect of his activities in the comparative comfort in which they went through the desert. That was the direct result of his own peculiar skill as an organiser. I recall as a typical instance of Sir George Farrar's way of doing things that from the day the railway started working—it began with ten miles of track—the supply train left at 6 o'clock every morning, prompt and regular. This supply train was also the *train-de-luxe* by which casual officers and men went or returned to the front, and any would-be passenger reaching the railway station five minutes after the hour found himself stranded for the day. A regular and punctual train service at the front is surely something of a novelty. It is not always an ordinary thing in civil life. Its real meaning here was that it helped to simplify the work of conducting the campaign as a whole.

At first there were about 6,600 men in the Central force, making two infantry brigades, and a section of mounted and general units, who were classed as divisional troops. The respective Brigadiers were Col. Beves and Col. Skinner, both now Brigadiers-General. Early in the campaign Col. Skinner was transferred to the Northern force, under General Botha, and the 2nd Infantry Brigade eventually came to be commanded by Colonel the Hon. J. J. Byron, C.M.G., to whom Captain Pepper acted as Brigade Major. They were *all* Union troops. The German colonial papers credited the Central force with 800 Portuguese soldiers, but this particular section of the world's Press was never quite regarded as an authority on the position. The bulk of the force was quartered in Lüderitzbucht until December 12, when a general advance inland was ordered.

There were two immediate problems to be solved. One was the provision of water, the other the getting of the water to the troops in the desert. It did not take long to find out that animal transport was practically out of the question. The iron horse was obviously the only possible motive power. So the railway had to be rebuilt. Meanwhile, an additional condensing plant was erected at Lüderitzbucht, and a reservoir holding 300,000 gallons constructed. The former was placed at the inmost point of Radford's Bay, out of sight from the open sea; and the reservoir was built on a ridge of lava kopjes that rise between Lüderitzbucht town and Lüderitz Harbour. The condenser supplies were supplemented by consignments of fresh water from the Cape, which were brought up by the various transports, and by this means the reservoir was generally kept at high level. There was thus no likelihood of disaster overtaking the force so far as its water service went, and that, of course, was its most vulnerable part.

The troops in Lüderitzbucht gradually settled down to the life of an ordinary garrison. No attempt was made to explain the situation to them, but there seemed an air of permanence about their stay, and so they proceeded to accommodate themselves to their surroundings. They laid French drains in their camps. They built incinerators. They erected substantial cookhouses. They even beautified their camps—the Transvaal Scottish particularly, who were camped around the local gaol. The Scotties laid out a drive from the tramway track to their headquarters, picking it out nicely in whitewashed stone; and in front of their headquarters soon rose a fearsome lion with pedestal and regimental crest complete. The builders had not a great choice of materials or tools, and for a model the sculptor was limited to a picture on a box of the weekly ration of matches. But a few bricks and a little plaster, a trowel and a penknife, and an empty matchbox sufficed, and the camp of the Transvaal Scottish became distinguished from all its fellows. The soldier-sculptor, a private under 21 years of age, was so pleased with his handiwork that he fashioned two more lions, but of smaller size, wherewith to guard the entrance to camp. These, however, being less able to take care of themselves, eventually succumbed to the wheels of a ration wagon under the guidance of a span of very truculent mules; but the bigger specimen, for aught I know, still casts its defiant gaze to the north front of Lüderitzbucht gaol.

Nor were the lighter forms of excitement overlooked. A Soldiers' Home soon opened its doors, and most camps had a gramophone or two. I should think that the percentage of gramophones to population in Lüderitzbucht was higher than in any other part of the world. The records were indicative of a good musical taste, and so the troops got both quantity and quality in their music. For the Soldiers' Home they were indebted to kindly Father Eustace Hill, C.R. Later on, the Anglican chaplain (1st Infantry Brigade) started other homes; indeed, he seemed to have the magician's art of producing, for wherever he turned, there, sure enough, sprang up a soldiers' home to dispense its mugs of tea or coffee and buns at a tickey (3d.) the two, and provide a common meeting-ground for men of the various regiments. The Home at Lüderitzbucht, which was established in the old Central Hotel, was, of course, the prince of the lot. It not only dispensed food and drink, but provided literature that was very comprehensive in subject-matter, and in date also, and offered all facilities for a "sing-song."

These "sing-songs," I recall, disclosed quite an array of talent, and set concerts became a frequent event as a result. Sometimes they would be given in the Home, sometimes in the camps (often round a big bonfire), occasionally in the quarters of the Engineers. The Engineers' concerts were held to be the "swankiest" of the lot, for they included bioscope items (the films were fairly frequently changed, thanks to the African Films Trust and the genial captain of the Clan McMillan transport), and an artist in evening dress! But no entertainment, I think, could quite compare with the St. Andrew's Nicht celebration in the camp of the Transvaal Scottish. The Nicht opened with a dinner party in one of the cells of the gaol, at which the General was the principal guest, and at which haggis, sent specially from the Rand, was solemnly played in, and solemnly served—and solemnly eaten. Then came a concert in the open, for which a covered-in stage, with a buck wagon as the foundation, had been erected. The stage was profusely beflagged, there were numerous (artificial) plants in pots; the lighting (all electric) followed the most approved stage design. There was a piano, and the bagpipes stood by ready to respond to any ebullition of Caledonian fervour. The pipes were frequently in evidence. And at a suitable moment a Presbyterian chaplain (Capt. McCulloch) began an oration that breathed a mighty patriotism and a mighty optimism. He sent everyone present into transports of joy, but it made the Germans, who were not present, but who read all about it a month or two later in the *Cape Times*, very, very wroth. It seems we had indulged in exultation before the victory was complete. In the vein known as "nasty," they commented on it in their *Windhuk Sudwest*. There was no occasion to apprehend any such chastening criticism at the time, however, and so I think it must be recorded that the celebration was a most enthusiastic affair. St. Andrew himself might have had reason to suspect the natal qualifications of some of his devotees, but if here and there the kilt did swing round the nether limbs of a sturdy young Jew, or hang on a hefty figure that mostly expressed itself in the Taal, that only added to the great uniqueness of the occasion.

In other ways had the troops reason to forget their isolation. Mails were fairly frequent, but they were irregular. There was a keen desire for the news of the day while it was yet fresh. "Reuter's" very thoughtfully met this desire by telegraphing a daily summary to all the forces. My colleague has shown me how the news was circulated on the Northern force. On the Central force a specially stern face was set against the luxury of a printed news sheet, my suggestion and offers notwithstanding. Here the wire was reproduced on a rotary-typed sheet, and as if to emphasise the penchant for the crude, it was reproduced in all its press-form nakedness, and printed without any lavish expenditure of care. Sometimes a genius would apply a weird system of punctuation, and the crude edifice was then complete. So our news was circulated in a way that left much to be desired, but such as it was, it was better than nothing at all, and the troops were very grateful for it.

Then "comforts" began to arrive very early—too early, as a matter of fact. Over 500 cases had arrived before the troops had been two months away from their homes, and well before they felt the need for anything of the kind. I am afraid it was ever thus in times of crisis: people allow their hearts to run away with their heads. Those 500 cases would have achieved the maximum of effect had they been sent two or three months later—say in January—when the kit of the men in the desert really was "thin." I am afraid, too, that the nature of the comforts left a lot to be desired. I say nothing about the most extraordinary shapes of cloth that were compelled to pass under the name of shirts; but why hefty, brawny specimens of humanity should be regarded as pining for glacé fruits, dainty chocolates, toothsome cakes, and the most expensive of cigarettes immediately they get on active service, though they are known religiously to refuse all truck with such things at ordinary times, passes all comprehension. I am afraid many large-hearted ladies (and men, too, for that matter) wasted both money and effort over these comforts. This was specially noticeable in the great heat of Tschaukaib and Garub, which quickly reduced all sweetmeats to a shapeless and unsavoury mess. What the men most desired were new and gossipy periodicals, cigarettes and tobacco of popular but economic, or substantial-but-good type, dried fruit (fresh fruit, where possible), socks, handkerchiefs, Balaclava caps, soap (also of the substantial-but-good type), plain postcards and indelible pencils, and footballs. I do not wish it to be understood that the men never got the right class of comforts, or, again, that when they most longed for comforts none were forthcoming. Far from it. I am merely pointing to certain incongruities which a little solid inquiry and clear thinking would have eliminated. One cannot but admit, and is glad to do so, that the good public of South Africa never forgot their men at the front. They will never be adequately thanked for what they did, because words will never fully convey the gratitude that the soldier himself felt for it all.

I have spoken of a garrison at Lüderitzbucht which made itself very comfortable. Coexistent with this garrison was a shifting camp of troops beyond Lüderitzbucht, who knew not comfort. The 2nd Infantry Brigade marched straight off into the desert from landing, and there they remained. Lüderitzbucht was always *terra incognita* to them. The matutinal dip at "Ostende," where the fashion of Lüderitzbucht was once wont to disport itself, and where, afterwards, the town troops took their compulsory tub (no fresh water could be spared them for washing purposes), was something they heard of but never experienced; at any rate, for many months afterwards.

By force of circumstances, this Brigade became the pioneers and the real advance party of the Central force during the time that the worst stretch of country was being negotiated. It is true that Sir Duncan McKenzie and the main body made a 45-mile breathless jump from Lüderitzbucht to Tschaukaib, but it was only the hard graft of those poor devils of the 2nd Infantry Brigade that rendered it possible; who the while lived and had their being in surroundings of undiluted misery. They will look back on those days as one prolonged wallow in the desiccated dregs of an abominable hell. (I divorce from the word "wallow" any association with filth and gross vice, which is one of the dictionary interpretations.) As often as not, sandstorms raged while they worked—sandstorms of inordinate length and unaccustomed violence, that enveloped them as completely as any London "pea-souper" could have done, when men see each other as through a glass darkly. Goggles and veils afforded them some protection from these fusillades of grit, but there were often moments when goggles and veils were the greater of two evils. I have seen toiling men rip the veils from off their faces because it was necessary for them to breathe freely and at once; and they have then taken in great, big, life-giving gulps of air, sand notwithstanding. I have seen them blindly snatch off their goggles, searching hopelessly about them the while for rag that was dry wherewith to wipe away the condensing moisture that clouded the glass and pained their eyes. And then they would return to camp to find that everything that they possessed had seemingly turned to sand. Their blankets were riddled with sand; their clothing was stiff with it; it lay on their food as scrambled eggs on toast. I do hope that when kudos is officially dispensed for the unwarlike work by which this German Southwest African war was won, officers and men of the Kaffrarian Rifles, the Kimberley Regiment, and the Pretorian Regiment, under the respective commands of Lieuts.-Colonel Smedley Williams, Harris, and Dales, will be permitted a liberal allowance. They deserve it.

The Germans blew up the line pretty artistically, as I have heard it put. What we actually saw, as a rule, was a clear-cut crevice in each line of rails (single track) about every 10 yards. It looked for all the world as if some giant assayer, very suspicious of the Krupp steel of which they were made, had passed along and scooped a "button" out of each rail or so, determined to put his suspicions to the thorough test.

The Germans commenced by laying their dynamite at the ends of each rail; thus, with one charge, they damaged two rails, together with the fishplate and its bolts. They used ordinary mining dynamite, which, I am told, has peculiar properties without being extraordinarily powerful; thus the resultant explosions (the charge did not always go off) did not do very extensive damage. Very rarely was the track itself disturbed. Sometimes the rails themselves were not broken through, only the upper flange blown away. An engine and trucks could have been driven over some of the wrecked stretches at a pinch; indeed, the first bit of rolling stock ever captured from the enemy—a water tank full of delicious well water, which was taken at Tschaukaib—was tugged by mules over ten miles of dynamited railway right to our railhead, which was then at Camel Camp. But it must be admitted that, for all practical purposes, this German policy of dynamiting the line was quite effective. I know that our engineers were confident they could have brought about more disastrous results, and yet where there had been explosions every inch of railway had to be relaid. Fortunately, the gauge was that of the Union—3 ft. 6 in. rolling stock had been brought along with us—and so it was possible to use the undynamited stretches without alteration. For some considerable distance the line was rebuilt with the old rails. The damaged portion was cut away, and the shortened lengths were brought into use again. It was not possible to treat every rail in this way, of course, but very few rails were irrevocably smashed up. The wastage was made good by rails imported from the Union. In course of time the Germans tumbled to what was being done, and then they began dynamiting the rails in the centre as well as at the ends. Thereafter few rails could be used again. But even this did not make us bankrupt in material, and when this fact was borne in upon them they resorted to the drastic and very laborious expedient of taking away the line altogether. We should have survived this appalling obstacle had it continued, but the Germans tired of the exertion after a few miles and returned to the easier work of dynamiting, and, more or less heavily, they dynamited to the end.

The Germans started their work of demolition at Kolmanskuppe, and continued without much interruption as far as Raalenberg, 32 miles out of Lüderitzbucht. Then, as the result of a sortie, they were pushed back at a bound almost as far as Garub, and a good 20 miles of railway were thereby saved. Subsequently the enemy were again able to destroy the line at will. The work of rebuilding went on very slowly at first. Now and again, for no reason that was apparent, the force as a whole would simply " mark time," and no work at all that was vital to the campaign was done; and irritating pauses these were. It was generally assumed that during October and November, at any rate, the waits had some connection with the more serious phases of the situation in the Union. Various suggestions were advanced to explain subsequent waits, but there were few that I would care to put into cold print.

Early work on the railway, anyhow, produced no record achievements. The first fifty-eight days saw only 45 miles in running order, and nearly two-fifths of that had required no repairing. The next 20 miles—the distance between two stations—occupied sixty-eight days, though quite a third, if not more, had not been destroyed. Thus far the line was guarded with blockhouses, which were placed a kilometre or so apart, and manned by men of the Eastern Rifles—crude, circular buildings of stone and sandbags and corrugated iron that accommodated a N.C.O. and six men, so long as none was more than 6 ft. high, or exceeded the average in rotundity.

These blockhouses must have had a great moral effect, as only once did the Germans spite them and cut the line. After Garub, however, they were dispensed with entirely, the enemy by this time having unmistakably left for other parts of the country.

It was sixty days later before the next station was reached, but the whole of the intervening $22\frac{1}{2}$ miles had been damaged, as well as three bridges, while a stretch of entirely new track $4\frac{1}{2}$ miles long was constructed. The railway was then open as far as Aus. At this time, following on a visit from Col. W. W. Hoy, general manager of Union Railways, it was decided to utilise the services of the numerous skilled railway workers in the Central force for the work of repairing and running the railway from Lüderitzbucht. A Railway Regiment was, therefore, formed, and officers and men were invited to transfer to it who in civil life were engaged on the Union Railways. Lieut.-Col. Fairweather, D.S.O., from the Rand Light Infantry, was placed in command, and the corps was soon at full strength. Thenceforward the wrecked line was put in order at a truly amazing pace. As much as five miles was repaired in the twenty-four hours. The men worked in shifts, of course, and after sunset the scene of their labours was brilliantly illuminated by means of searchlights and numerous electric lights. It was so bright hereabouts that one would not have been surprised had the very birds begun to sing, thinking it were not night! Within the next two months well over 200 miles of railway more or less seriously damaged, including over thirty bridges and culverts, also damaged, was brought once more into use, and so far as the Southern Army was concerned, railway construction was at an end.

But in all the circumstances the worst of the work was done in those first two months by the 2nd Infantry Brigade, which had such a long wait in the sand-dunes. Kolmanskuppe was not so bad as Grasplatz, perhaps, as a place of sojourn. It had advantages. There were diamonds to be kicked against and discovered, and one of the regiments, coming as it did from Kimberley, knew exactly how to kick. Once a diamond was seen, then that particular spot came to be searched with tooth-comb effectiveness, prohibition or no prohibition.

I heard of an amusing incident in this connection. A colonel of my acquaintance had noticed a knot of men—Irregulars. I may say, and it was in the early days—all kneeling on the ground staring very hard at something in the vicinity of their knees. His curiosity aroused, he walked over and looked on. His approach caused no diversion. The men were much too occupied to pay attention to any such insignificant happening as the approach of a field officer. They were searching for diamonds. But they were doing it so systematically. There was a sort of Master of Ceremonies, equipped with sacks of sand, evidently new ground. The men were all around him, each one with two heaps of sand in front, one heap constantly growing at the expense of the other, which the owner was most industriously sorting. Every now and again a man would get through the one heap of sand, and, Oliver Twist like, would ask for more, but he would get it. That M.C. was no Mr. Bumble. Eventually, and more or less aimlessly, the Colonel poked his stick into one of the growing mounds. Then the owner looked up. Somebody was claim jumping, surely—no, it was the wrong heap. He smiled in obvious relief. Then he spat out a mouthful of stones into his hand and spoke. "Sorry, sir," he said, "you won't find any there!"

I heard of many finds, without myself seeing more than two diamonds the whole time I was in the country. Once I did get on to my "tummy," and for fully ten minutes crawled and searched in the heart of diamond-land in quite the approved way. But the eternal wind blew so much sand into my eyes that I gave up the quest for glittering wealth in disgust then and there. Poverty, I thought, as I rubbed my now smarting eyes, is not entirely drawbacks! The average size of the Kolmanskuppe diamond is from 2 to 3 carats, if Herr Kreplin, the managing director of the Colmans Kop Diamond Company (a concern registered in the Cape; capital £125,000, four years' dividend since 1908: 152 per cent) be a reliable authority. The field covers 10,000 acres and there are 800,000 carats (estimated) "in sight," valued at something like twenty millions sterling. Nearly fifty white men and over 500 natives were employed on the field, and if the state of the residences there, the quality and style of the furniture, and the evidences of the table that was kept go for aught, then the Germans made a very good thing out of it. In this respect two of the houses that I looked over were superior to any I saw in any part of the country. The Colmans Kop Company was the principal owner of claims, and at the outbreak of war it was preparing to work on a larger scale than ever before. When Union troops reached the place the first thing they saw was a weird construction that looked as much like a giant see-saw as anything else. It was part of a huge washing plant that the company was installing in connection with its enlarged scheme of working. This new plant would, when completed, it was said, be the biggest individual diamond-washing plant in the world. There were only a number of independent workers at Kolmanskuppe. At one time our Captain de Meillon had claims there. As an interesting aside, I may perhaps mention that the first twenty diamonds discovered at this spot, which was in May, 1908, were presented to the German Emperor in the design of the Southern Cross.

It was while the troops were at Kolmanskuppe that the first British train steamed out of Lüderitzbucht station—October 19, 1914, exactly one month after the occupation. It consisted of an engine and seven trucks, all imported from the Union, and ran as far as Kolmanskuppe, the first station. The occasion was one for enthusiasm, and there was a lavish display of it, particularly as the train passed by the camps on Lüderitzbucht racecourse. The G.O.C. and staff and other prominent officers travelled as the first passengers, sharing such accommodation as there was with lengths of rail, piles of fish-plates, bolts, and tools, quarters of frozen beef, boxes of biscuits, jams, and so forth. But before entraining they signed a register which recorded the interesting and historic event, and which was afterwards presented to Lieut.-Colonel F. R. Collins, the officer commanding the Engineers Corps, and received a duly printed and dated ticket. In reality this was the antiquated German pasteboard rekindled into a sort of currency by the super-imposition of the date-stamp of the Engineers' Corps. The gathering then posed for the numerous cameras, which seemed the most prominent armament for the nonce.

Every effort was made, naturally, to keep the fact of this asset from the knowledge of the Germans. The driver was forbidden to blow the whistle while travelling to and fro, and the Reuter " wire " about it all was sent by mail and not allowed to see the light of print until November 24, thirty-five days later. Inasmuch as the Germans wirelessed their congratulations on our safely landing the body of the engine, it is possible that these exquisite precautions were just a little belated, even though the Engineers did get the engine into running order four days after landing it, which was undoubtedly very smart work.

The Germans had a veritable penchant for airing their great intelligence about our movements and operations. It was even extended to an intimation that the G.O.C. had addressed the troops at a church parade at Kolmanskuppe, which Sir Duncan McKenzie never attended at all! Once (before the end of October) they commented on the fact of a " footer " match having been played at Lüderitzbucht, and invited the force to a match with them on ground that was nearer their lines. Curiously enough, almost at the moment this wire was being transmitted a Union patrol was actually embarked on an operation that ended greatly in our favour. Next day the Germans were informed that their invitation had been accepted and the match played—and won by us. The scores given were the number of the casualties on either side, the killed counting as goals and the wounded as tries! These wireless interludes then ceased for a time.

From Kolmanskuppe the troops moved on to Grasplatz, where they were right in the heart of the famous sand-dune country. As a name Grasplatz is an awful fib. One would say it was a joke, only it comes from a source that is not usually associated with humour except of the very ponderous type. What justification there is for it is eloquently indicated by a notice that issued from their lines before the Union troops had been in residence many hours. Here it is:—

"GRASPLATZ.

"NOTICE.

"Protection of Meadows Act.

"Anyone found damaging a blade of grass in the vicinity of Grasplatz will be fined £5.
"By Order."

No breach of the act was ever reported.

There is no place in the country to compare with Grasplatz.

It is one mass of curious-shaped sand-dunes that are always on the move, wind or no wind. When there is no wind they can be seen "working," much as slaking lime works. When the wind blows, which is far more often the case than not, Grasplatz is simply one huge whirl of sand. The prevailing movement is from south to north, and a favourite tendency of the dunes is to stay awhile on the railway which cuts right through the area for a distance of nearly three miles. For this reason it is necessary to maintain a large staff of natives on the spot who keep the track clear of sand. These labourers are constantly at work. It has been no new thing for them to knock off at night with a line all clear, and to re-appear on the scene next morning to find that the line was under 6 ft. of sand.

There were no natives with the Central force to start with, and so this work of sand-clearing first devolved on the troops themselves. They thought it curious war work, and were not pleased; and certainly, at its worst, it was an appalling business. Accompanying the General once from Camel Camp to Lüderitzbucht by train, I passed through this area when things could not very well have been worse. No fewer than a thousand men were posted along the track, sweating, panting, struggling in an endeavour to keep it clear of sand, that the "General's train"—a few empty trucks and dry water wagons—could go through without interruption. As the present-day saying has it, What a hope! Mrs. Partington engaged on hardly a bigger task, though hers was a cleaner one and far less dry. Not a man, I'm sure, would have been loth to change his shovel for her mop on either account! Sometimes it was next to impossible to see anyone in the sand fog, and when the men could be seen, what a weird picture it all was! Everyone wore goggles; most had veils as well, and those who had not veils had their mouths and noses and ears swathed in handkerchiefs or rag of any kind. The best dressed of them had only slouch hat, shirt, shorts, and boots; they would have dispensed with shirt and shorts, which were ringing wet with sweat, had it been safe to do so, but this vicious, swirling sand would have swiped the less tender parts of their bodies almost as with cat-o'-nine tails. The train stopped awhile; the incessant sand had got the better of everybody, and the line was blocked. In thirty minutes it was reported clear again, and we prepared to hurry on. The train refused to budge. While everybody had been intent on the struggle ahead, the sand had executed a flank movement, as it were, and had almost completely buried the wheels of the train where they rested. So there had to be a new centre of attack. But this involved a weakening of the frontal attack, with the result that by the time the train was released the sand had once again got the upper hand ahead. Human effort and ingenuity told eventually, and we got through, but that 22-mile journey occupied exactly five hours and a-half.

After that, I believed all the weird stories I had heard about German South-west Africa and its rapacious, hellish sand-dunes. While I was in the country I received a letter from an old friend, a Rhodesian pioneer, who wrote: "I was through the country in which you are now roasting in quite the early days. Keep a sharp look-out, and you may find my wagons, which disappeared in a night, enveloped by the sand-dunes near the present Lüderitzbucht!" This seems to have been a pretty common experience before the advent of the railway. Only too often there was loss of life. The strangest story of all that was told me was of a police officer proceeding to Aus and other police posts with cash wherewith to pay the men. He left Lüderitzbucht all right, but he was never seen again. A fairly obvious conclusion was come to, and he was "posted." Fifteen months later a police patrol found a bag of money in the dunes—nothing else. It was the money that had been issued for police pay fifteen months before. Another conclusion is obvious—a dreadful one, too.

In German times this work of keeping a rail thoroughfare through Grasplatz involved an expenditure of £10,000 every year. It was not always successful work, as a mammoth dune lying across an abandoned stretch of railway track still demonstrates. Latterly the force employed about 250 natives on the work, but our engineers were always striving after a means to render the dunes innocuous. They were all agreed on this guiding principle: that the agency that brought the sand should carry it away. They made no practical headway with any new scheme, so far as I could gather, but they improved on a German expedient, and I believe the position is now very sensibly easier. The procedure followed is, roughly, to lay and pin sack-cloth over all the dunes that are dangerous to the railway. That prevents the sand being blown about. The cloth, however, stops short, say, a yard or so from the front of each dune. There is thus a strip of free sand left that is liable to be carried forward by the wind. In the course of time it is actually blown away, whereupon the foremost length of cloth is rolled up, leaving another stretch of sand free. This, too, is eventually blown away. And so the process goes on, and will go on, until all the dunes under treatment entirely disappear.

Eventually the troops moved on to Camel Camp, at kilo. 35, where, though they were still windswept and sandswept, they were beyond the dreaded and dangerous dunes. Camel Camp is German nomenclature. The Central force had no camels other than those it captured from the Germans, who used them rather extensively. The Germans had a corps of 500 camel-mounted men, but they do not appear to have made much use of it as an engine of warfare, though we expected to meet camel patrols on many occasions. The old " C " force captured three camels, all in the charge of natives. They had been sent into Lüderitzbucht with letters and other parcels from one of the outlying districts that was unaware of the change in régime that had taken place: the letters gave away a little information. The beasts themselves were handed over to the squadron of Imperial Light Horse, and Corporal Owen Letcher, F.R.G.S., was placed in charge of them. They were regarded as the nucleus of a camel corps that the force expected to develop on its own, but as the next captures were not made until Gibeon was reached at the end of the following April, after which the force took no further part in the campaign, the conception was more interesting than useful. The three beasts were well worked, however, and I suppose they earned their keep, but they were inclined to be a confounded nuisance, nevertheless. Camels and horses are seldom if ever boon companions. The mere whiff of a camel, as a matter of fact, sets a horse trembling with fright; a good smell of one positively sends it mad. Thus it behoved you when riding to be very careful lest camels should approach unawares, particularly when "warmed up," and, consequently, distinctly odorous; otherwise there was a buck and a bolt, and only a dismounted horseman was left to tell the tale. Riderless horses were not infrequently seen.

The 2nd Infantry Brigade, as an advance body, finally moved to Haalenberg, a kopje that stands in front of the plains of Tschaukaib and Garub. Thence they moved on with the forces as a whole.

CHAPTER VII.

AEROPLANES AND OTHER WARFARE.

THE TSCHAUKAIB CAMP.

McKenzie had little fighting, and little opportunity for fighting, during the time the railway was being built to Tschaukaib, which was the rebellion period. Then came a short but sharp skirmish at Garub. Thereafter, until the march on Gibeon, there was less fighting still, though the opportunities were perhaps greater. On the other hand, the Germans were fairly active with their aeroplanes and rarely visited our camps without result. From the point of view of casualties these results were comparatively poor, but as regards intelligence they could not well have been greater.

The first aggressive movement on the part of the re-organised Central Force was a drive over 120 square miles of country immediately to the south of Lüderitzbucht, and as far south as Elisabeth Bay. It spread over October 15 and 16, and the 1st Natal Carbineers, under Lieut.-Colonel Mackay, and the Transvaal Scottish, under Lieut.-Colonel Dawson Squibb, were the troops that mainly carried it out. The country they swept is one mass of lava kopjes, sharp and barren, which provided good mountaineering exercise, but nothing else. After a gorgeous sight of innumerable flamingoes, prettily cresting the waves in Lüderitz Harbour, not a living thing was seen. It was not surprising : a mountain goat would have met an early death from starvation there. But what did occasion great surprise was that the drive did not take in the Pomona diamond fields and their vicinities. Pomona is fifty miles south of Lüderitzbucht, and within an easy day's march of no fewer than five German police stations. There was never any reason, so far as I could make out, to apprehend a big German force using Pomona as a striking base, say, for an attack on Lüderitzbucht. There was always good reason, however, to fear that patrols working from here would threaten our communications ; and what between the police stations and the mining camps all the accommodation and supplies that they could possibly need were available.

Evidently, Pomona was not held of any account, and it was not visited until February 7, 1915, when two squadrons of the

1st Natal Carbineers went there on a week-end patrol; one of these squadrons also pushed on as far as Bogenfels, twenty miles further on. The General directed operations at Pomona and then returned to Lüderitzbucht to meet General Botha, the movement having coincided with the visit of the General Officer Commanding-in-Chief, who was on his way to Swakopmund to take up the command of the Northern Army.

The patrol did not actually encounter Germans either at Pomona or Bogenfels, but it received good evidence at both places that at any rate enemy soldiers were not far away. At Bogenfels the visitors found two buildings in flames—both stores that were full of foodstuffs. At Pomona one of their number, a sergeant, fell into German hands and was a prisoner for an hour, when he regained his liberty in the most providential of circumstances. The troops had off-saddled on the outskirts of Pomona. During the halt this non-commissioned officer walked away from his lines. He had not gone far—he was practically still within sight of his troops—when, to his utter consternation, he heard the order, "Hands up," and found himself the prisoner of a German officer and four men. They led him away first to a spot where their horses were picketed. Thence they rode, but they made their prisoner walk in front of them. Captors and captive had proceeded in this fashion for about two miles when the former trotted on ahead, after commanding their prisoner to follow as quickly as he could. The sequel, I think, is fairly obvious. The sergeant made a dash for freedom—what seemed so golden an opportunity could not be allowed to pass—but his captors made no attempt to follow him, except with bullets; they simply sat still on their horses and took pot shots at his retreating figure, and one supposes they got good sport out of it. Happily, the man reached his lines without being hit. His spoors were sufficiently clear throughout to confirm the story that he afterwards told Sir Duncan McKenzie.

The patrol resolved itself into a mere rounding up of stores. A tramway connects Pomona and Bogenfels with Kolmanskuppe. This was put into running order as far as Pomona, and a train load of supplies was brought away. The balance was destroyed. For some reason that I was never able to fathom, it was considered better to do this than to run the train backwards and forwards until all the supplies had been transferred to our own base. The patrol, of course, would have remained in occupation of Pomona meanwhile. Food and water were plentiful, and there was no urgent need just then of more troops either in Lüderitzbucht or Garub.

The troops bivouacked on the famous diamond fields, which are the richest in the country. The largest diamond that has ever yet been found in South-west Africa was picked up at Pomona. It weighed between 33 and 34 carats and had the appearance of being a piece of a larger stone. One of the mines is owned by the Kaiser, and real holy ground it looked in its ring of formidable fencing. Whether the visit of the patrol had any result in diamonds or not I cannot say definitely, but I think not. It would, however, have given a delicious touch of appropriateness to this particular expedition had any stones, or a stone even, fallen into the hands of one member of the patrol. But nothing of the kind happened, which shows how lacking this campaign was in a sense of the dramatic, for the individual I have in mind is a shareholder in one of the Pomona companies, and he is not likely to draw any more dividends for some considerable time yet. There would have been something quite Gilbertian about a shareholder escorted by an armed force, and himself armed, collecting his dividends in kind!

The Elisabeth Bay drive was followed by one in the vicinity of Rothkuppe station, twenty-three miles east of port, a week later. On this occasion no infantry were employed. The General was in command, and at dawn on October 23 the troops took up positions round a certain twelve miles perimeter, which there was reason to believe enclosed an advanced German post. The information was founded to the extent of nine n.c.o.'s and men. There was a short, sharp tussle, and the work of the patrol was ended for the time being. One German was killed, one wounded, and the remainder of the batch was taken unhurt. The wounded man had no fewer than five bullets in him, and there were two bullet marks on his mess-tin; his horse was shot in four places. But he showed himself to be very much alive, his wounds notwithstanding. He demanded a drink, and cold tea, the only liquid available, was handed to him. Of this he took a big gulp, but he spat it out with great vigour and greater disgust. He had laboured under the horrid delusion that every British soldier carried whisky in his water-bottle. He survived.

One of the prisoners was a German nobleman, Count Schwerin, I think his name was, a big, burly fellow, who was held up by the General. The next minute Sir Duncan thought he saw the opportunity of duplicating his performance, and dashed off after the prisoner *in posse*, whom, by the way, he didn't get, being forestalled. But he left the prisoner *in esse* in charge of the only other person near by at the time, who was his orderly. Now, the General's orderly was a very diminutive human, a mere bugler boy, in fact; and this was the incongruous spectacle that met the Chief of Staff when he turned up a few moments later: a slim, four-foot guard valiantly keeping a six-foot prisoner in complete subjection.

In some bewilderment, the Chief of Staff asked, "Who caught him?"

"Me and the General," was the proud and confident response. The guard, anyhow, had the situation well in hand. There were no Union casualties, and the skirmish, extraordinary to relate, occurred in a drenching rain.

There was an advance Union camp on the scene of this encounter when the next operation took place, which was a move on Tschaukaib, a railway halt twenty-two miles east of Rothkuppe, on November 8. Again the participating troops were all mounted—600 of them, with two field guns from the 12th Citizen Battery, and ambulances of the 1st Field Ambulance. A blank was drawn so far as regards *personnel*, but in other respects the movement had quite good results. Chiefly it had the effect of driving the enemy back on Garub, twenty miles further on, and of making him disgorge nearly twenty miles of line in good working order. It also caused him to leave a valuable overhead tank in its pristine state. This gain we consolidated by means of a continuous patrol, which worked first from Rothkuppe and later on from Haalenberg, and managed to confine the Germans to their new line. The Germans had probably maintained an officer and twenty-five men at Tschaukaib, judging by the amount of kit (from which the owners had parted obviously very hurriedly: several bottles of beer were found amongst it) that we lighted upon in the station buildings. The only official movable booty of note that was captured was a rail water-truck, with water all complete. As there was also water in the overhead tank there was a fair helping for all men and horses; altogether there would be about 3,000 gallons, and it was attacked with considerable relish—in the first place because everybody was right royally thirsty, in the second because it seemed delicious beyond compare after the unsparkling springs from the Lüderitzbucht condensers. The tank had been prepared for early demolition, and by all the principles of engineering logic it ought to have fallen about our ears. Before we could get to the water a broken pipe connection had to be restored, and a band of willing workers were hammering away at this for quite a long time and with tremendous energy. Then, and then only, it was found that the tank literally exuded dynamite charges.

There was some talk of continuing the march as far as Garub. Captain de Meillon keenly urged that this should be done, holding that the German post there (which, he said. was an officer and twenty-five men strong) would fall back in sheer surprise. There was a lot of worldly wisdom in what he said; and, strangely enough, the detachment was then better equipped for such an enterprise than it was when it eventually did go to Garub. The General, however, was unwilling to take the risk, being far from his base, which was very true, for the bulk of his forces and stores were still at Lüderitzbucht.

There was no other aggressive movement for exactly five weeks—until December 13, when the whole Central Force advanced. The Transvaal Scottish and Witwatersrand Rifles were detailed to occupy the important post of Haalenberg on the lines of communication. The rest of the force marched into Tschaukaib, arriving early in the morning of December 15. The infantry accomplished some really good marching. Three regiments did over twenty miles in the twenty-four hours, and of these three two started the trek after a day's blockhouse building, which, of course, had exhausted their best energies. But what mattered? They were advancing, and the possibility of a fight was in the offing. It was even whispered that they " might be taking Garub," and at that time Garub was a synonym for a sanguinary battle. And so on. A good many men, it must be admitted, cut up rather badly. It was not surprising. The going was extremely hard, much like an interminable stretch of the looser parts of sea-beach. At every step the feet slipped, and each man had just sufficient kit to make that slip an exhaust of energy that was distinctly felt.

No talking was allowed, nor smoking, nor singing; and so it was not possible even to pass any comment on a puffing, snorting, clanging engine that thundered by, throwing out the rich red glare of its glittering coals to heaven, as the fireman stoked up. The column was then still a mile or two short of its bivouac, and the men could have done with some stimulant, even of speech.

Late on the Tuesday (December 15) orders were issued for a march on Garub, mounted men only. After the movement the affair was called a reconnaissance, and certainly no wheels of any description were taken, neither guns nor ambulances. But there was a distinct impression at the time that we were going to Garub to stay, if the enemy were not too obstinate. Sir Duncan McKenzie was in command, and there would be about 700 of all ranks all told.

The march was uneventful enough. There was a two-hours off-saddle during the night. We were on the move again before dawn, and were behind an eminence overlooking the (to us) famous boreholes when the stars were being " put to flight." Other than ourselves, not a soul was to be seen; the boreholes machinery was in ruins and abandoned. The boreholes are on the north-west of the station, perhaps a mile or a mile and a-half away. The whole country round about is undulating, and yet a distinct plain stretching without interruption as far as the range, ten miles away, that so definitely divides the hinterland from the sandy coastal belt. On the north of the station, five miles off, rises Great Tiger Berg, or Dikke Wilhelm, as it was more generally called, commanding and gaunt. We felt sure Dikke Wilhelm was "held." On the south, two to three miles off, is a low, short range of hills, and small parties were detached for the purpose of taking up vantage points on these. Carbineers, under Major Park Gray, approached them from the east, and Imperial Light Horse, under Lieut.-Colonel Donaldson, D.S.O., went by way of their north front. The main body rode on for another couple of miles and then made its way back, having in the meantime crossed the railway. It halted a kilometre or so off Garub station, where there were three portable water-tanks at the line side; each tank was half-full of good water, which was plain indication that the place had not at any rate been finally abandoned. Indeed, before the column was five minutes halted someone unearthed a telephone wire that connected an outpost, as it turned out afterwards, with the trunk system; the connection was cut.

Men proceeded to water their thirsty animals. But before the operation was half completed a shot rang out in the distance. Then came a regular fusillade of rifle and machine gun fire. The time was about 7 a.m. Everyone stood to his horse and waited. In ten minutes or so an orderly arrived with the information that the Imperial Light Horse had been engaged by the enemy, and that the Germans were strongly entrenched in the hills. It seems that our men were crossing the second of two closely parallel dongas when they heard a single rifle shot, fired less than 700 yards away, possibly accidentally by a German who lived to rue it, as the Union troops instantly stopped their advance and made themselves "scarce." Another hundred yards and they would have found retreat out of the question. This was no doubt the position that the Germans played for, and would have got but for the untoward circumstance. As it was, the Britishers had barely time to "get down" before the full fury of the lead storm burst which had been prepared for them.

Two men fell from their horses at the first volley, as if hit. It transpired that one was killed on the spot; the other was thrown from his wounded horse and was later taken prisoner. Other men had very narrow escapes, as perforated hats and clothing eloquently told. One man, Moolman, of the Rand Intelligence Corps, had a particularly close shave. A Mauser bullet smashed up his cigarette case, which was in the left breast pocket of his shirt. As opportunity offered, officers and men withdrew to the larger donga that they had first crossed, and there awaited events.

Such was the position that was briefly reported to General McKenzie.

"Come on!"

There was a rattle of accoutrement, a rising cloud of dust, and five hundred horsemen went after the General hell-for-leather, in a short and glorious but furious ride that brought them to the great donga, whence, dismounted, they proceeded to certain positions.

The main idea seemed to be to work in very extended crescent formation, and get the Germans on their front and two sides. The Germans were more or less concentrated on the farther of two hills, and might number anything from a hundred to two hundred men, all sheltered behind entrenchments, mostly schanzes; they had three machine guns, including one that seemed to be firing a larger bullet than the ordinary Mauser, but no field guns. They maintained a terrific fire; they had the advantage of position. No real advance was possible in the absence of artillery, and we had only one machine gun. But we maintained a lively reply, and from first to last the enemy sustained a loss of one man killed and five wounded.

Shortly after nine o'clock huge clouds of dust were noticed issuing from Aus Nek, less than 10 miles away; clearly reinforcements for the Garub outpost. Clearly, too, that telephone wire had served its purpose before being cut. The number of the reinforcements was variously estimated, but the concensus of opinion favoured a thousand as the approximate figure, and the force was probably armed with light artillery. In face of this new position, Sir Duncan McKenzie decided to withdraw. As we were without artillery, it was the only thing to do.

Our casualties numbered five all told, being one killed, two slightly wounded, and two captured. One of the wounded men was a young signaller, who was hit in the hand. A doctor dressed the wound, and the youngster was off almost before the bandage was tied.

"Where are you going to?" this from the doctor, sharply.

"Off back again," was the blithe answer.

"Well, I think you had better stop; you can't do anything now."

"I can hold horses, sir."

And he was off before one could say "Jack Robinson!"

One of the captured men was Cpl. H. J. McElnea, 1st Imperial Light Horse. McElnea made his escape from the Germans five weeks later, in terrible circumstances that were subsequently related to my colleague of the Northern force. Before he rejoined his corps McElnea had gone through what was perhaps the most tragic and awful experience that befel any member of the Union's German South-west African expedition. Not only did he thirst and starve practically unto death, but he digged his own grave and then lay down to die. When discovered, life hung to him by the slenderest possible thread.

About ten o'clock the column was on its way back to Tschaukaib. The Germans made no move in this direction.

Garub at this time was evidently no more than an observation post, but a very important one, nevertheless. The station buildings were quite empty, but they had once been utilised by troops, the refreshment room as a stable! Two of the four overhead railway tanks were demolished, and attempts had been made to destroy the other two, while for nearly 10 miles in the direction of Tschaukaib the railway had either been dynamited or prepared for demolition, but actually was not badly damaged. From reports of explosions heard the next day we gathered that Garub was completely evacuated immediately after our visit. Scouts went all over the area, even round the hill fortifications (where there were thousands of cartridge cases), a week later and saw no one at all. There were two newly dug graves in the former German lines. When we occupied Garub practically ten weeks later we found all four overhead tanks demolished, the station house burnt out, and the refreshment room entirely gone; no further damage had been done to the railway west of the station, but to the east it had been systematically dynamited.

It was decided to build a camp at Tschaukaib and consolidate our position there before attempting any further advance. On the face of things it took just over nine weeks to do it, and Tschaukaib became an affliction—almost a moral disaster. The General remained three days, and then, with his Headquarters Staff, hurried back to Lüderitzbucht, and was not seen in the place again except on the day of General Botha's visit. Even those aristocrats of the Central force, the mounted men (at this time the 1st Natal Carbineers, a squadron of the 1st Imperial Light Horse, a squadron of mounted infantry drawn from the various infantry regiments, and a detachment of the Rand Intelligence Corps, left Tschaukaib, but that, it must be admitted, was because of the water question, which in two days became so desperate that they had to be packed off *instanter*. More infantry were brought up in their place; the Transvaal Scottish were advanced from Haalenberg, and as a stiff test of their powers of endurance, it may be, they were marched through in the full heat of a broiling day. Further comment is unnecessary.

About Tschaukaib camp, or "the front," there were two features and one pleasant memory. The first feature was its dust and heat; the second, the aerial activities of the enemy, which were almost wholly confined to the Central force and displayed here. The pleasant memory was the visit of General Botha with his stimulating presence and address.

Tschaukaib is an extensive, undulating, sandy plain, that during the greater part of the time that the Union troops occupied it developed a terrific dust-storm daily. There were few days when the visitation was not. The day that General Botha inspected the troops was one of them, both happily and unhappily, it was suggested. The storm would come at irregular times in the day, but it was almost invariably of eight hours' duration. Sometimes it worked overtime; and while it was with us it never worked less than industriously. Of itself, the sandstorm almost overcame us, which usually obliterated in an impenetrable fog anything beyond a five-yards radius, while itself penetrating everywhere. Reinforced by the torrid heat, which at times totted up to 127 in degrees in the tents, and we were "beat to a frazzle," as Mr. Roosevelt might say. So everything had to go by the board the while. Drills were impossible. Fatigues couldn't be thought of. It was every man for himself, to entrench himself as best he could against the storm and escape its enfilading fire; and, to the credit of the Garrison Commander, who was Col. Beves, be it said, there was little or no intrusion on the men in their affliction. The remedial measures did not make a very exhaustive array, but the first essential was to get inside your tent. Veils and goggles were of great assistance, but they had their limitations: goggles in time made the eyes sweat and thereafter smart, and veils would not exclude the finer dust which the eternally flapping tents sent into a vigorous and perpetual commotion. A tent became the worse for wear in a fortnight, and thence onward it was a distinct ally of the elements; as guide ropes went and rents appeared, the alliance attained completeness. Nor were towels a big success, in which men often wrapped their entire heads and fancied themselves asleep and oblivious of and impervious to the elements around. Towels defied the dust. coarse and fine, but they out-Turkished any Turkish bath that was ever improvised. Turkish baths are delightful body stimulants on occasions, but as a daily habit they certainly are not without their weak points, and that is why towels were not popular as a bulwark against sandstorm. As a matter of fact, the perfect remedy was never discovered. We achieved protection up to a point. Beyond that point we had to grin and bear whatever lengths the furies of sandstorm and heat thought fit to go. Thus, willy nilly, we breathed sand, we chewed it; we took it in our food—literally, there was sand with the sugar; we thought sand, we dreamt it.

After a month or six weeks the sand storm season undoubtedly began to wane. Instead of diurnal storms there would be one fine day a week, then two, and, if I remember aright, in our last week at Tschaukaib there were no more than four storms. The heat we had become accustomed to, after having adopted various devices. A popular one when the dust was not blowing was to go about in Nature's garb, plus a helmet; some who adopted this fashion wore veils as loin-cloths, but they were palpably over-dressed. In course of time sunshine began to tell, and I have seen one or two men so burnt that they were hardly distinguishable from Kaffirs. An ordinary coloured Cape boy would have considered himself white in comparison, I am sure. In any case, when these fashions were being promenaded, Tschaukaib was no place for ladies. Ladies—nurses from the hospitals who wanted to see what "the front" actually was like—once did run over on a rail motor-trolley. It was a surprise visit; and when their parasols first appeared over the last undulation, it seemed for all the world as if we were being routed by the Germans. Someone set up a cry of "Women!" The next minute naked and semi-naked forms shrieking the fateful word were careering all over the place in a mad scramble for cover. I'm sure those ladies must have thought Tschaukaib a very quiet camp, and its occupants very demure persons indeed, especially after all the stories that they had heard; *but honour was saved!*

But, apart from the atrocious sand and the atrocious heat, camp conditions were quite livable and even enjoyable. Rations were excellent and plentiful, except water, and water continually got less scarce, until in the end each man's ration was double the original allowance of three-quarters of a gallon. The water was never cold; it was never clear and sparkling; but, treated with chlorine as it was, it was always a safe drink. And eventually supplies of "brak" water began to come up from Kolmanskuppe for tubbing purposes; at various times and in sections the garrison would parade and disport itself in a huge tank that once did duty on the German railway as an overhead tank for serving passing trains. Camps were clean and sanitary and healthy, though they once threatened to become an intolerable nuisance and rout us out of the place altogether, there were not sufficient flies about after eight weeks to justify a census. That showed a watchful and efficient sanitary service, and, incidentally, proved the value of arsenite. It is true that vermin did make its appearance, but the cases were isolated, and the trouble was soon eliminated. Official orders for dealing with it were issued, and enlivening reading they made. The precise procedure to be adopted in order to obtain the articles mentioned, and the

Lord Buxton's Visit to Luderitzbucht. Boarding the "State Coach" outside the Jetty.

General Botha with Nurses at Luderitzbucht.

British Aviators with a Blackburn aeroplane.

S.A. Heavy Artillery with their "Long Toms" at Garub.

Convoy crossing the Desert.

A Running Fight in the Desert near Pomona.

Trench Fighting in the Desert.

Sand Dunes at Close Quarters, near Pomona Diamond Fields.

Camp at Tschaukaib being shelled by German Airman, who took the photo with a telescopic lens.

manner in which such trifles as flat-irons were to be carried about on trek were not indicated. As one never saw any flat-irons about or any steaming laundries at work, one supposes either that the remedy was regarded as rather worse than the disease or that other means of repelling the invaders were found.

Occasionally there were sports gatherings, notably at Christmas and New Year, when all sorts of contests were arranged. And there was a substantial inflow of "comforts." At Christmas, indeed, the inflow was a perfect deluge. Everyone got something from somebody, a plum pudding for sure. One regiment received over two hundred cases of comforts, which was equal on the average to a whole quarter of a case per man. Lest anybody should by chance be overlooked, an East London lady sent a cake to the Officer Commanding a certain regiment, with a note reading as follows:—

"If there should be two boys in your regiment who have no mother or sisters to care for them, please give them this token of my regard for them on the veld." The cake was inscribed "Good luck, boys." That woman was simply splendid. Her thoughtfulness and her action make an intensely human interlude which it will be hard to excel from all the interludes that the campaign produced.

And yet, in spite of all these brighter phases, there was dissatisfaction. This fact cannot be blinked. The men were getting no fighting—the infantry, that is, who were all practically at Tschaukaib. That which they went out into the wilderness to see they saw not, and as things were shaping themselves, they felt they were not going to see it at all. Only once had the Central force employed them on any fighting venture, and even then not so much as one German was seen! Now it was circumstantially rumoured that everybody was marking time pending the arrival of more mounted men, four thousand at least—five thousand horsemen to do the fighting, six thousand infantry to do fatigues! Of course, they did not like it. And those eternal sandstorms—they were "the limit." Thus did men argue.

The force lost men because of it. It lost some whom it never ought to have had—a few men who, in deference to their bubbling patriotism and transient enthusiasm, had been allowed to hurry by the doctor when being passed for active service; who found that their defective teeth, their varicose veins, and their phthisis (some, indeed, were *pensioners* of the Miners' Phthisis Board), which were going to be proof against any hardship that the Germans could bring about, were not proof against mere disappointment. Enthusiasm is a wasting asset at the front when it is not backed up by physical fitness. The doctors pointed this out at the time, but I understand they were overruled on the point.

The force also lost good men. About this time it was realised that a number of men, mostly in Rand regiments, had enlisted for six months' maximum service, and that their contracts would soon expire. Had rebellion not broken out, the contract would have been ample, but unfortunately the unexpected happened, and the question of these men was responsible for no little anxiety. The force wanted them. In the end many remained, but over 1,300 took their discharge, ostensibly because of agreements with their employers. Had there been less Tschaukaib, or occasional movements against the enemy, a continual nibbling into his domain, I somehow think that these agreements would have gone by the board (the employers tacitly concurring), and that there would have been 1,300 more re-enlistments on the spot. As it was, we heard a great deal of these men as potential recruits for the mounted regiments of the Central and other forces.

One could mark their spirit plainly enough on the occasion of the German aeroplane attacks. The airman was popularly called " Fritz "; and when " Fritz " came sick parades were hardly necessary, and six-months' men thought they would rather stay than go. This was war—something of the " real McKie," they said, and they were more satisfied. The worst of it from this point of view was that " Fritz " did not come often enough!

When war broke out there were three aeroplanes in German South-west Africa. It seems that at the beginning of 1913 the German Imperial Government conceived the idea of supplying their colonies with aircraft; it was a mere incident, of course, that the colonies were called upon to pay the cost involved. German South-west Africa contributed £5,000—a sum that was largely raised by private subscription. What the colony's apportionment of aeroplanes was to be I do not know, but in May, 1914, it received two machines. One was a Roland double-decker biplane, the " sister " of one that the previous February had achieved a reliability record and shortly afterwards made a 16-hour journey overland. This was stationed at Keetmanshoop, but it came to grief on August 23 of the same year while the pilot Fiedler (who was our " Fritz ") was alighting; Fiedler was not injured, but the aeroplane was irretrievably damaged. The second machine was an Aviatik, also a double-decker biplane, which the previous autumn gained a National Flying Union prize of £5,000 by putting up a world's record flight of 1,400 miles in twenty-four hours. This machine was stationed at Karibib, and Trueck was the pilot's name.

Lieut. von Scheele, a well-known German military aviator, was in command of the machines, and in addition to Fiedler and Trueck, he had under him four N.C.O.'s who were trained aviators. Both machines were of a modern military type; they were essentially military equipment; but they were also equipped for ordinary use, such as the carrying of mail matter and diamonds, and for effecting medical service in outlying districts. Both were fitted with 100-h.p. Mercedes motors, and were built almost exclusively of steel tubing, so that there should be no danger from warping or from white ants. They had, also, patent compasses, electric helios, telescopic cameras, and so forth, and their speed was from 65 to 70 miles an hour. Modernity and equipment notwithstanding, however, it was noticed that "Fritz" religiously refrained from flying after the cool of the early morning. We learnt afterwards that the machines were of a heavy pattern, and that their engines were not sufficiently powerful to maintain them in the air when the sun was well up. Whether this had anything to do with the disaster that befel the Roland or not did not transpire.

The third machine was a Hertzog, that was sent out specially for the Colonial exhibition that was held at Windhuk from May 29 to June 1, 1914, the occasion being the twenty-fifth anniversary of the foundation of the Colonial Corps. This machine did not compare with either the Roland or the Aviatik, and was not, in fact, of the military fleet, but one supposes it was not without its uses.

The Central force never had aeroplanes of its own, though it ever lived in hopes of being equipped with them. Aeroplanes would certainly have expedited matters substantially. Without them, of course, the force was waging a one-sided struggle. It is true that it had an anti-aircraft gun, and that at some time in his flight the airman came within range of field guns and four-inchers (manned by gunners from Antwerp), and 4.7's, but for fighting aircraft these cannot be compared with aircraft itself.

The anti-aircraft gun, or "Skinny Liz," as it was called for short, was a converted 15-pounder mounted on a special carriage that was made in the Army Ordnance workshops at Fort Knokke, Cape Town, and gave an elevation of more than 60°. "Skinny Liz," however, was by no means a quick-firer. She had to be set afresh after every shot, and so her utility was more apparent than real. In a second carriage which, I fancy, went to the Northern force, this fundamental defect was remedied and other improvements were made.

The ordinary 4-inch and 4.7 guns achieved the most success against the air raiders. They fired shrapnel, and on two occasions, at least, the spreading shot found its objective. "Our aviators," generously admitted the *Windhuk Südwest*, "have discovered that the British artillery can shoot very well." And then the paper speaks of two of their aeroplanes having been hit at an altitude of 6,000 ft.—one machine in 150 places.

Rifle fire was ever desultory. Once, an attempt was made to organise it. An engineer brought out a device for finding the range of the aeroplane, and a gunnery expert (a member of the Permanent Force, who, by the way, was made the issuer of loaves and jam and such-like munitions) got a school of marksmen together for the purpose of volley-firing according to the ranges that it registered. There was no proof that this scheme achieved even partial results. Perhaps the rangefinder was defective in some important particular. At any rate, it was never utilised again, nor was organised rifle firing either.

So no telling hit was ever registered. Still, with all their defects or shortcomings, anti-aircraft gun, big guns, and desultory rifle fire had a big moral effect. The airman was obviously afraid of them, and occasionally they kept him off camp altogether.

His effectiveness was, of course, assailed in other ways. He never surprised the troops, because a permanent look-out warned the camp by means of bugle blasts whenever he approached. The bugle wasn't always necessary. As often as not one heard the cry of "A-re-o-plane" being chanted along the lines before ever the warning "G" was given. Then, also, the camp was pretty thoroughly trenched. There were long, zig-zag trenches on the various fronts (a precaution primarily against attack by land), and in the lines were other trenches, and also numbers of individual six-foot-by-three trenches, serried rows of them, the mere sight of which set one's imagination at work in a sinister direction, suggesting, as they did, a huge and busy graveyard all ready to receive its myriad dead. Some units, like the field hospital (where they were very necessary), built bomb-proof shelters.

But neither trenches nor shelters realised their maximum of usefulness. A better precaution still was adopted. It was not found possible to get rid of the danger—i.e., the aeroplane—with which the troops were menaced, but it was possible to do the next best thing, which was to remove the troops. Thus it became the general rule for most units to leave camp soon after reveille every morning and not return until some time after 7 o'clock. It was reasonably certain that if the airman had not appeared by then he would not be coming that day at all. And on the occasions on which he did appear, he had only a thinly populated camp to bombard. The bulk of the men were in open country two or three miles away practising skirmishing tactics or going through other military evolutions. Parenthetically, I may observe that the training the men got at this time vastly improved their efficiency and kept them splendidly fit. The 2nd Infantry Brigade, under Col. Byron, did notably good work in this respect. Those who had, necessarily, to remain in camp utilised the trenches, of course, and it is worth noting here that not one man was hit while in a trench.

The first German flight over Union camps was made on November 14, 1914, by the German Flight Commander, von Scheele. It was for purely observation purposes. At times von Scheele flew very low, being no more than 1,000 ft. up, but mostly he maintained an altitude of 1,000 yards. He came as far as Kolmanskuppe, and after saying this and adding that a great deal of rifle fire was directed towards him without effect, there is really nothing more to be said from our point of view.

But the "Herr Lieutenant" has a picturesque turn of mind and a graphic pen, and he told the Germans all about it in a most interesting article in the *Keetmanshoop Zeitung*. He even went a little further, and told them of something that he didn't see at all. He talked about the sea that looked "like a blue wall," and spoke of six warships in the harbour at Lüderitzbucht. As a fact, on one occasion there were six warships lying off Lüderitzbucht, but it was not his occasion; it was on December 10, so one can say of Lieut. von Scheele what Mr. Balfour once said of another romancer—that he showed a lively appreciation of events before they occurred. The airman left Aus at half-past four in the morning, and was back again at seven; he thus flew about 150 miles in two hours and a-half. He says he manœuvred for an hour over Lüderitzbucht, but as that would have necessitated his flying out and home at a greater speed than his machine was capable of doing, we may safely assume that here he was writing for pure effect. Apparently it was anything but a comfortable ride, because the aeroplane, "which was one that had been sent over for trial purposes," was not adapted to local conditions; and as the thin, dry air became irregularly warmed, his machine leaned over first on one side, then on the other, ducked, was thrown upwards; then dropped in an air pocket.

The conclusion he came to was that to suit local conditions a machine needed to have bigger wings and a stronger motor than the one he was then flying. He drew quite a pretty picture of the desert mists below, from which the hills rose like islands from the sea. He asseverates that he saw everything while over our camps, even small flags and "the light colour of the Tommies' upturned faces." This is a very interesting admission, in view of the fact that when these German airmen commenced to shed their bombs they refrained from exempting the hospital lines from their theatre of opera-

tions. The hospital area was the recipient of several bombs—
once, three in a single morning, one of which fell in the
doorway of the operating tent—and overhead floated not small
flags but fairly big Red Cross flags.

However, on this first flight, he dropped no bombs. As
Reuter's representative, I remember making a special reference
to this fact, being, as it was, one of the points on which the
public would naturally look for definite information. The
Germans saw this message in a Union newspaper (it would
be interesting to know how they got those papers, which
seemed to reach them fairly regularly), and it was referred to at
the end of von Scheele's article in this piquant phrasing:
" Reuter's correspondent says we dropped no bombs. Well,
as soon as the coast mists allowed it, the flight was repeated,
and we obliged the English "—(always the " English ")—" by
dropping bombs "!

Altogether the Germans sent their aeroplanes thirteen times.
Explosives were dropped on nine occasions—once at Haalenberg, once at Rothkuppe, four times at Tschaukaib, and three
times at Garub ; the first time at Haalenberg on November 29,
1914, the last time at Garub on March 27, 1915. Through the
wireless " Fritz " intimated that he would be visiting us on
Christmas morn, and leaving a couple of cards, but he never
did. And we all got up so early so as to make sure of seeing
him—in time!

At first two (4.1-inch) shells were dropped per visit, then
four, and finally shells and dart bombs together—usually six
of the latter. There were no direct hits, except in the case of a
mule, which was struck by a dart bomb ; all the casualties were
from shell splinters, and all the men were above ground at the
time they were hit. As showing the security of the trench, I
may mention that on one occasion a 35-lb. shell fell and
exploded within 2 ft. of the edge of an occupied trench without
harming any of the occupants.

" I really thought," said one of these men to me later,
" that my last minute had come. I saw the shell falling,
then I heard it, so I just pulled my helmet over my face and
waited. But—we were first on the spot for splinters!" The
meaning of this last sentence will be apparent in a minute.
" Fritz's " total bag was three killed and nineteen wounded.
Ten of these casualties (including one killed) were sustained
by the 12th Citizen Battery, being a whole gun team that
was firing at the aeroplane ; six others (including one killed)
were of a fatigue party that was badly handled ; one (killed)
was a man who tried to change his trench between the dropping
of two shells.

Except in the case quoted, there were no casualties among
the animals, chiefly because few horses or mules were ever

in camp during the dangerous hours. They were always aware, however, of the presence of an aeroplane some time before it was seen. Often they could be seen looking apprehensively upwards, and it would be noticed that as a rule they were also trembling. This sensing of an aerial and an unseen danger was most noticeable in the case of a goat which the Pretoria Regiment affected as a mascot. When the alarm was given this animal could be seen sedately walking to the officers' mess tent. It would go in and take up a stand close to one of the sides; there it would remain motionless until the bombardment was over. The tent was frequently struck by shell splinters, but the goat always escaped, though once pieces perforated the tent just above and below where it was standing.

Equipment, of course, was frequently damaged, and sometimes the shell effects were weird, as in the case of a splinter that entered a water bottle, making a large and ugly hole, and yet it could not be extracted; a novel baby's rattle was the result. Once a rifle was cut into two so cleanly that it might have been a yard of Cambridge butter under the knife instead of a tube of hard steel facing a jagged splinter of a 35-lb. shell.

Not all the shells burst. Sometimes the limbo that was attached to them to act as a parachute became detached, and the shell would then fall harmlessly on its side. When no such providential happening occurred, those within a radius of two or three hundred yards of a dropping shell heard a fluttering of cloth as of a small but stout flag in a hurricane. Couple this with the noise of the shell itself, hurtling through space at I don't know how many miles an hour, and take into consideration the double illusion that the aeroplane is always exactly over you and that every shell is making straight for your very vitals, and you have a situation containing all those elements that fill the mind with horror and cause the heart to sink.

It all impressed men in different ways, of course. At first the airman was regarded as a terror: very shortly, and he was almost welcomed as an interlude. One young Afrikander was seen to jump from his trench trembling violently and full of rage. Shaking his fist at the retreating airman, he yelled: "You damned schelm; you aimed that at me!" But that was his first experience of aerial warfare. Later on, I saw the same young fellow showing quite another disposition. His eyes were just above the level of the trench. "Fritz" had arrived, and with no little humour he described the progress of the airman and of the shells after they left the airman's hands. He ducked simultaneously with each explosion, and re-appeared singing out "Any more for any more?" which is,

I believe, a familiar phrase to those who are addicted to such classic gambles as "Banker" and "Crown and Anchor." After the last explosion he assured everybody that there were "No more for no more!" Then he joined in the general stampede for the scenes of the explosions, to be in at the inevitable search for souvenirs, in the form of shell splinters, which was prosecuted with great energy and thoroughness. I should be inclined to say that if all the finds were pieced together they would make the whole of "Fritz's" thirty shells complete! Prof. Flinders Petrie never searched Egypt near so thoroughly as those Union soldiers searched the desert of Namib for pieces of nasty German shell.

It was not in bomb-throwing, however, but in intelligence work that the German airman really scored. The position of our camps and their approximate strength were always known to him, and, of course, to his superiors; he generally returned with telescopically taken photographs. Lantern slides were made from the films, and, as illustrated lectures, were subsequently shown and explained to gatherings of officers. All the same, the value of all this information was negative rather than positive, the views more interesting than useful, for the Germans never initiated any aggressive movement as a direct result of what these photographs told them.

A move on Garub was commenced on February 19, 1915.

CHAPTER VIII.

DISTINGUISHED VISITORS.

GENERAL BOTHA AND LORD BUXTON.

General the Right Hon. Louis Botha, P.C., Prime Minister of the Union and General Officer Commanding-in-Chief of the Union Expedition to German South-west Africa, visited the Central force at Lüderitzbucht and in its various camps along the railway line to Tschaukaib, on February 8, 1915. He saw all the troops, with the exception of two squadrons of the 1st Natal Carbineers, then out at Pomona. Lord Buxton, the Governor-General of the Union of South Africa, also visited the force on March 22.

General Botha at the time was on his way to Swakopmund to take up the active command of the Northern force. He was accompanied by his staff and travelled up from the Cape on the auxiliary cruiser "Armadale Castle" (an ex-Union-Castle mail-boat); he disembarked in the morning and re-embarked before dusk in the evening. He was, of course, ceremoniously welcomed at Lüderitzbucht, and troops were everywhere on parade to meet him. But there were certain features that stand out apart from these inevitable and proper courtesies. And of these features I would specially mention the sincere and frank pleasure of the troops at General Botha's visit, and, after all that he saw, the no less sincere and no less frank pleasure of General Botha himself at being able to pay that visit.

It should be understood that of the various columns then and subsequently at work, none was so strong in the "English" element as the Central force. It had no burgher units at all, though it had numbers of trained and disciplined young Dutchmen.

There were two main camps. There was the mounted camp at Lüderitzbucht and the garrison of infantry at Tschaukaib, "the front." Reviews were held at both places. In between were smaller camps. At Rothkuppe there were both mounted men and infantry, and No. 1 armoured train was in the siding parading its "Oom Louis" gun. In making Rothkuppe the armoured train had made great progress, but it was not persisted in long afterwards: conditions, as a matter of fact, were wholly against it. At Haalenberg the Witwatersrand

Rifles regiment (Lt.-Col. Smythe) was in occupation. The troops here were formally inspected. And along the railway, giving a 45-mile-long line of communication, was a series of blockhouses, each about 1,000 yards apart, and manned as a whole by Eastern Rifles under Lt.-Col. H. T. Gripper.

As General Botha travelled to Tschaukaib in an open railway truck he saw every blockhouse and every man in each blockhouse. Sensible of the monotony and thanklessness of the duty that these men were called upon to do, he took particular notice of them. Thereby he showed his greateartedness. He had a smile as well as a salute for everyone of the eighty-odd batches of them. At times his smile broadened perceptibly; that was when he caught sight of some of the appellations that were boldly lettered in front of most blockhouses—broadened in pleasure when he made passing acquaintance with " Fort Botha "; broadened in amusement when he saw strange and weird titles like " Fort Has Beans." And he laughed heartily as he passed a camp where boring operations were proceeding. The drill here was already down over 300 ft. and still in a dry formation. The engineers were sadly disappointed, and they called the place " Dryazell Halt." So was their humour in harmony with their surroundings—dry.

The two reviews were most impressive, because of the uniqueness of the surroundings. That at Tschaukaib was perhaps the more striking; I would say it was so for two reasons. It took place first, General Botha having proceeded straight to Tschaukaib from the jetty; and it had a spectacular advantage in that one of the units was a Scottish regiment that sported the tartan kilt and followed the bagpipes. I don't suppose that the Transvaal Scottish as a regiment differed very much from, say, the Rand Light Infantry or the Kimberley Regiment or any other of the infantry units in the Central force; indeed, I am sure it did not. They were all composed of sturdy fellows, deeply bronzed, in the pink of condition, and keen to impress on the revered General Officer Commanding-in-Chief that in them he had men on whom he could rely, men who were capable and fit and full of spunk. But the Scotties had just one extra film to their reel, as it were, and it must be confessed that they displayed it deliberately and self-consciously, sure of its effect. They marched brightly, even jauntily, past the saluting base in perfect and joyous sympathy with their pipers; they swayed their kilts with all the grace and harmony and ease of practised movement. General Botha admitted later on that as the troops marched past he felt more inclined to join in than watch, and I have no doubt he had the Scotties most in mind at the time. And yet every unit was soldierly to a degree, marched well and saluted smartly—infantry, artillery, all of them.

General Botha himself supplied a fitting climax when, so soon as the troops were back in position, he stepped forward and called for cheers for "His Majesty the King." Cheers! The desert literally trembled! Then Brigadier-General McKenzie called for cheers for General Botha. Cheers! The very hills rang with them. I have never seen such enthusiasm before, seen nothing quite so emotional at any time.

General Botha afterwards delivered a short speech to officers of the garrison, which was an unexpected pleasure, especially as it dealt with the position of officers and men at Tschaukaib (and elsewhere), and hinted at an early move forward. The speech was circulated in Orders the following day, and, coupled with the inspiring events of the day before, had an immense effect on the *morale* of the force as a whole, as no doubt was the design of it. The General spoke in Dutch, as follows, his private secretary, Major Bok, translating:—

It is a great pleasure to me to meet you and to see you all looking so fit. This morning as the men marched past I felt more inclined to step in and join them than to watch them. (Hear, hear.) Allow me to congratulate you most sincerely on the splendid exhibition you gave. Nothing impressed me more than the fine condition of both men and animals. I realise we have got to thank the officers for that. I have not come here to give you much advice, but to assist you if you want me. (Cheers.) To attain the object which has brought us all here we shall have to press forward with more energy from now on. (Cheers.) I know it is not your fault to-day you are still here. It is my fault. But in our country I had to deal with the rebellion, which gave me much pain and sorrow. I had to give much of my attention to that. Thank God! it is past. (Cheers.) I am here now, and I may tell you that 10,000 more mounted men are coming along to help us achieve our object. (Hear, hear.) It has been hard on you to have to be lying apparently idle here for so long a time, but, still, you have been doing very good work indeed. I know that the British Empire is grateful to you for the work you have done. We in South Africa have undertaken this task, and we are going to carry it through with all possible determination. (Cheers.) Your loyalty and your ability are going a long way towards achieving it. I am now going to discuss the whole situation with General McKenzie, and I hope you will soon get the order to go forward. (Cheers.) I wish you all possible success. God bless you! (Cheers.)

The troops had their own special, unceremonial, and unofficial say when General Botha returned to Lüderitzbucht. Garrison, small camps, blockhouse men all turned out in force to line the railway and cheer and wave as the distinguished soldier-statesman journeyed by. The cheering started at Tschaukaib; it died down 40 miles away. when the train was approaching the Lüderitzbucht parade ground. Helmets were doffed at the front, and a long, rolling wave set in motion; they were donned at the base, the wave just spent.

The mounted review was much of the nature of the one that had taken place earlier in the day. Horses were in excellent condition, all things considered. General Botha felt constrained to remark on this—and the men sat and rode them well. The General gave no address, but he received officers individually, and expressed warm admiration at what he had seen. He was to have passed on to the hospitals, but the day had been overcrowded, and the new military plans had yet to be discussed with General McKenzie. So the hospitals were regretfully cut out from the programme.

The day had been strangely and remarkably fine, really King's weather; a happy augury, surely, for the future under General Botha's personal command. There was only the merest suspicion of a sandstorm. Half-humorously the men were inclined to regret this. It threw doubts on, shall we say the *bond fides* of the Namib desert as a better desert than any other desert that the universe had produced! Their fears were unfounded. General Botha not only believed their stories and realised the terribleness of the times that they had gone through, but he had some taste of the dunes himself. Moreover, he benefited by their experience by resorting to the veil and the goggles that they had proved to be so useful! The day passed without hitch of anything. But perhaps I cannot do better than quote the very striking review of the whole visit that was penned by Mr. Roderick Jones, the general manager of Reuter's (who accompanied General Botha as far as his base), and reproduced in the South African Press.

At Lüderitzbucht (he wrote) we found a special train waiting to run us up to Tschaukaib, about forty-five miles inland from the coast, and the official " front." The first vehicle of the " special " was a long, open bogie truck, with about a dozen wicker chairs. Next came the engine, and behind the engine a commissariat and kitchen van, a water truck, and a long open truck containing an armed escort of about forty picked riflemen.

We occupied the leading truck, and so were " pushed " into the interior, instead of being dragged behind the engine in the orthodox way. This, and the fact of the truck being open, enabled us to get a most excellent view of the country ahead of us and on either side.

But what a country! North and south, sand to the very horizon, and beyond; east, sand also to the ridges that fringe the great interior plateau; a parched and, under the searching African sun, a blinding desolation as far as the eye can reach, with sand dunes and lava kopjes here and there to break the demoniacal monotony of the plains. The railway was destroyed by the Germans as they retired. It was rebuilt by the Union forces as they advanced. It is laid on a permanent way raised about a foot, sometimes more, above the surrounding waste, and along one section it has constantly to be watched by gangs of natives lest it disappear in a night. The dunes are eternally shifting, and we saw at one point several hundred yards of track which actually had been lost under a drift 20 or 30 ft. high, rendering necessary a deviation of the line.

The review at Tschaukaib was a most striking spectacle. "Only in the British Empire could this thing come to pass," said a Dutch officer (once a Cambridge "blue," by the way), when the ceremony was over. He had seen these British-trained troops, artillery, mounted infantry, and riflemen. English and Dutch, mingled in the commissioned and non-commissioned ranks, march past, all hard as nails, and darkly bronzed, after half a year's exacting service. He had seen General Botha's face light up with satisfaction as he marked the soldierly bearing of regiment after regiment passing the saluting point, and as, one by one, he congratulated the corps' commanders. He had listened while General Botha subsequently delivered his short impromptu address to the officers of all grades, thanking them for enduring these many months in this region of sand, wind, scorching heat, and waterless wastes, telling them to blame him only for keeping them back, and, finally, giving them the welcome hint that they might expect to advance against the enemy very shortly. All this from the man who, thirteen years ago, was Generalissimo of the Dutch Republics and now was Commander-in-Chief of a British expedition, impressed my Afrikander friend immensely, and was responsible for his ejaculation : " Only in the British Empire could this thing come to pass."

It was an event to be remembered, this review, in the heart of the desert, in sight of the enemy's outposts, under a blazing African sun and amid an apparently unfathomable expanse of sand, save on the east, where by now the ridges of the verdant interior rose high above the horizon. There was something unique in such a setting in the stirring skirl of the pipes as the Highlanders, men of magnificent physique, swung by, and in the drums and fifes and bugles playing the other units past this Dutch Commander-in-Chief, who, attended by a mixed Dutch and English staff, stood under a great Union Jack, the only splash of colour in this drab patchwork of sand and khaki, taking the salute, and, when all was over, doffing his helmet and lustily calling for " Three cheers for His Majesty the King!"

Lord Buxton's was a much less formal visit. His Excellency, who was accompanied by Major-General Thompson, C.B., commanding the Cape District, and other Imperial officers, also travelled up in the " Armadale Castle," and also remained ashore for the day. He was formally welcomed by Brigadier-General Sir Duncan McKenzie, and received by a Guard of Honour of Eastern Rifles. Immediately afterwards he entrained for " the front," which by this time had been advanced as far as Garub. There were no parades of troops, but the troops nevertheless turned out to do homage to the distinguished visitor.

While at Garub, Lord Buxton, under the guidance of Sir George Farrar, D.S.O., whom he was never to see again, inspected the operations that were being carried out with a view to the development of Garub as a huge water base—the sinking of boreholes, the raising of huge overhead tanks, the construction of a big underground reservoir. Altogether it was a very busy scene.

At Lüderitzbucht his Excellency toured the hospitals, where he spent some time. By dusk he had re-embarked, and was on his way to Swakopmund. On this occasion, too, the weather was remarkably fine.

CHAPTER IX.

GARUB.

Though there was an outpost affair, Garub itself was occupied by Union troops without opposition. This was on February 22, 1915. The force of occupation was the 1st Infantry Brigade, under Colonel Beves. It marched over from Tschaukaib in two stages.

On February 19 it reached and camped at Keishohe, a geographical spot in the desert eleven miles east of Tschaukaib. The railway had been put in order as far as Keishohe the day before; it did not require a great deal of attention as it was almost to Keishohe that the stretch of intact railway reached which was wrenched from the Germans the previous November. The remaining nine miles to Garub were fixed up in the three following days. From the perfunctory way in which this latter portion had been wrecked one would say that the Germans were very chary of restarting their work of demolition exactly where they did, scenting danger. By the time they reached Garub, however, they had regained their full confidence.

The Keishohe camp remained until the night of the 21st. There had been an enemy aeroplane reconnaissance that morning, and so there was no possibility of the Germans being surprised even had the idea of surprising them been entertained. The airman dropped no bombs on this occasion, but he covered the whole length of our line of communications. One assumes therefrom that they had become aware of our advance from Tschaukaib and feared a move of some proportions. "Fritz's" report evidently went to confirm their suspicions, for from the next day onwards they were observed working on fortifications in Aus nek at something akin to feverish pressure.

There was, however, no bar to our occupation of Garub, which Col. Beves' regiments effected in the early hours of the 22nd. The men marched notably well, for though the distance was not great, the way was very heavy of sand, which made the going not doubly but twice doubly hard. The Germans had their own reasons for relinquishing the place so unresistingly, and possibly those reasons were good reasons, but all the same the moment they did decide to go, that moment the Central force got them in the hollow of its hand. McKenzie's essential requirement was a water base forward.

By means of the boring drill one such had been searched for at Rothkuppe, at Haalenberg, at Tschaukaib, but always with unsatisfactory results. Either there was no water at all or the water was badly brackish. Garub was the solution to the problem, Garub, with its rich underground supplies of perfectly potable water. Thereafter, it was only a question of time when the hand would close and the Germans be squeezed to defeat. This process did not come about in the time or in the determined manner that was always possible, but that was not the result of any German influence.

Scouts under Captain de Meillon reconnoitred the Garub position the day before the advance, and were there when the troops arrived; indeed, in a way, they sort of handed over to the vanguard and then pushed on towards the German lines. Before dawn broke they were within sound of blasting, and soon after sun-up they saw a train approaching from Aus. The blasting probably came in the work of trench-making; the train was engaged on the work of railway demolition, which now took the form not of dynamiting but of wholesale removal. With the train was a fatigue of fifty men, who were soon busy pulling up the line and loading the material into the trucks. The Britishers crept towards this party and eventually fired on it from a distance of 1,500 yards. Work ceased instantly, for the time being wholly ceased; the train was hurried back to Aus. Scouts who returned assert that five men of this party were carried bodily to the trucks.

Almost simultaneously de Meillon and his men observed rising dust at the foot of a kopje some three miles to the north-west, that had hitherto been an outpost of the enemy. The Captain interpreted this as the sign of a complete retiral. "I knew those Germans would not fight," he said to Sergeant-Major Dreyer, his right-hand man; "I'm almost sure we can go straight into Aus." Without any hesitation, he led the way at a canter to this kopje. As they neared it they spread out: Captain de Meillon and Dreyer, with three Hottentots, took the centre, and Meintjes and Naude the wings.

They were within 200 yards of the kopje when a volley rang out almost at their feet, and Dreyer lost his horse. De Meillon dismounted and returned the fire, and it may be assumed that it was not without effect. Then a second volley spat out at them, and the Captain fell in his tracks, shot through the head and the chest; two of the Hottentots were also killed and the other severely wounded. Meintjes and Naude, unhurt, got away. It transpired that the marksmen were less than 30 yards away from their victims, in a skilfully concealed trench; they had fixed bayonets.

It was a complete ambush. There is no doubt, further, that de Meillon, who was well-known to the Germans, had been recognised. He was henceforth their mark. Thus it is difficult to avoid the conclusion that he was shot down in cold blood. Note that there was no call to surrender; note the range; note also the concentrated firing round him: no attention was paid to the flank men. Dreyer was blindfolded and taken away, after being relieved of his papers and money. I may observe, in passing, that Dreyer escaped from captivity four months later. In connection with his captivity, he speaks of two very interesting matters. One is that none of the prisoners, who included a number of burghers, would do any work for the Germans, such as railway construction, that was likely to militate against the success of the Union forces; the other that Union Rebel officers were treated with the utmost contempt by the Germans, who kept them on the same level as their N.C.O.'s. For a time he was in Windhuk gaol, and he mentions that while here he and others received many kindnesses from Mr. Scotland, a political prisoner, who was allowed a certain amount of freedom, and of whom I have made mention in a previous chapter.

Captain de Meillon the Germans buried where he had fallen, and on the mound they laid one of his spurs, while at the head they raised a cross of wood on which was inscribed his name and the date of his death; the cross-piece was fastened by means of an empty cartridge case—presumably the holder of the bullet that killed him. He was, however, buried so decently that the enemy can be forgiven this little bit of exultation. Later on, when Aus was in our hands and this part of the country was clear of Germans, the Transvaal Scottish remodelled the grave. They built it up to a height of 2 ft. in solid masonry, carrying a substantial cross of teakwood, duly inscribed, which was made by the Engineers. It was a striking piece of work in all the circumstances.

Memorial services were then held over the grave—a private one for the benefit of the widow, whom the authorities had allowed to come up from the Cape; a public one for the many members of the force who desired to pay a last formal tribute to his worth. For de Meillon had been a factor with the rank and file, and with the junior officers, at any rate, some even approached him with an appeal that he would form a Scouting Corps and take them on as the *personnel!* Higher up, and I am afraid he had a somewhat limited vogue. It was felt, I think I am right in saying, that he was too venturesome, too optimistic, that he wanted to rush matters; for his part, he literally chafed under the military inertia that seemed to have enveloped the force. He went five miles, ten miles ahead of the outposts, and the intelligence he gained led him to the conclusion that vital opportunities were being missed, and that by missing them the work of the future was being made all the harder. He was at one with Shakespeare in his warning that "delays have dangerous ends." I do know that he took the position very much to heart; and it was undoubtedly his keenness to make the very most of matters that led him into the trap in which he lost his life. Anyhow, the force in general was immensely attached to him: in the man they saw the gentleman, in the soldier the hero. At one time there was talk of raising a memorial fund to him, and I heard of promised donations of £1 from privates and £5 from N.C.O.'s, but the movement failed to get official sanction.

And so, though the service was purely voluntary, and the grave seven miles from the nearest camp there was a gathering of many hundreds of officers and men, all infantry, most of them members of the original " C " force. (The mounted men at this time were on the last stages of their march to Gibeon.) There was a firing party a hundred strong, with buglers. Chaplain-Captains Hill (Anglican) and McCulloch (Presbyterian), assisted by the Coadjutor-Bishop of Cape Town (Dr. Cameron), took the service, which was intensely impressive throughout, but perhaps never more so than when the crack of those hundred rifles and the surging notes of the bugles burst on the great stillness of the afternoon and echoed and re-echoed as they were caught up and thrown from hill to hill. The date of the event was April 25, 1915.

What became of the natives who fell with Captain de Meillon one can only surmise. The day after the scrap the Germans floated a wireless message to the effect that the three natives had been found to be German, and that consequently they had been hanged. "We *know* how to treat such natives," the message concluded. At the statement that they *did* treat such natives in the way they announced no one will cavil. It is conceivable that acquiescence will not go further. Two German-born natives were neatly buried near by de Meillon, and their graves inscribed. Possibly these were the two whom we believe to have been killed outright, but it is hardly probable; after their insolent message, the Germans are not likely to have shown so much sentiment and gone to so much trouble. It may be presumed, therefore, that these interred natives were the Germans' own casualties, especially as they admitted losing two "men." So far as regards de Meillon's Hottentots, the Germans may be taken at their word. When the force passed this way on the last day of March, the 2nd Imperial Light Horse, working through Kanus Poort, five miles to the north, came across the gruesome and shocking spectacle of three hanging natives, who had obviously been there some length of time; the bodies were cut down and given decent burial. Some of the troops have expressed the opinion that at least one was hanged alive and slowly strangled to death.

This way of treating natives who had incurred their displeasure was rather typical of German policy. The case I have quoted is by no means isolated. There is the case of the family of Cornelius van Wyk, Chief of the Bastards, as told by General Botha. The Bastards deserted from enforced service with the Germans rather than fight against Union forces. Among other reprisals that they resorted to, the Germans slaughtered the Chief's 70-year old mother and two of his children, aged respectively 14 (girl) and 4 (boy). Then they captured his wife and 21-year-old son, and when, on being cross-questioned, these two beat about the bush, the son was blindfolded and shot before his mother's eyes. There is also the case of a batch of natives who were buried alive. Their grave had all the appearance of a sunken mine, and that is how the Union soldiers came to investigate it, but they encountered not dynamite and bolts and bars; it was human bodies that they exposed, having faces that were hideously horrifying in their expression but plain in the story that they told. I could go on multiplying such instances. I mention these particular ones only with the idea of showing that, little as we know of the real fate of the natives who succumbed to the Germans in the region of Aus nek on February 22, 1915, the worst possible conception is quite justified.

The German version of the shooting was that "an English patrol, mainly comprised of Hottentots, was repulsed and driven back"; that Captain de Meillon, "formerly of Lüderitzbucht, and leader of the English espionage system there," was killed, and three others were captured; "we lost two men." From documents found at Aus, it would seem that the dead Captain's effects were distributed among the so-called victors; at any rate, a junior officer of guns received official sanction to take his Mauser pistol and field-glasses.

With modifications as to time, and with certain variations, the Garub camp was a replica of that at Tschaukaib. It endured for five weeks without change as "the front," and, so far as actual fighting went, the troops lay completely dormant. To them it was another camp of blighted hopes. Indeed, it was rather more disappointing than Tschaukaib. There, at any rate, except by way of the air, they saw no Germans, and, therefore, were not perpetually being reminded of the fact that Germans existed and were there to be subdued. At Garub, on the other hand, Germans were seen every day; certainly every day of the first three weeks. They showed themselves in and around Aus nek, and were obviously entrenching and fortifying. Day by day the garrison at Garub expected orders from headquarters at Lüderitzbucht at least to go out and harass the enemy; if possible to prevent his defensive works being completed; but none came. Not only so, but at one time all patrolling beyond two miles of the foremost trench was definitely forbidden. So, by order, the garrison restrained its overweening curiosity to know the nature and extent of the German defences, and simply looked on, which was a policy that had no terrors for the enemy. To the Union troops, however, it was the most galling experience that they had in all the campaign.

The force as a whole, nevertheless, was not in a position until some time afterwards to undertake a general offensive. It had to consolidate its own new position. The greatest problem, of course, was the water. Boreholes had to be reopened, and new ones sunk, and supplies of water had to be conserved. It was not expected that the daily yield would ever be equal to the capacity of the force, or, rather, that part of it, numbering quite 10,000 men and 6,000 animals, that would be concentrated for the attack on Aus. There was, too, always the danger of the pumping machinery becoming wrecked. The possibility of a German attack on Garub by land was never seriously contemplated, but "Fritz" was always a danger, though, try as he would, even he could never get near the boreholes, which were always his great objective. So water had to be conserved against the day when the daily consumption exceeded the daily yield, and also against the day when the pumping machinery might be damaged beyond repair. The latter, fortunately, never became more than a contingency, and the former position was fully coped with, thanks to the schemes and energy of Sir George Farrar. One of the chief measures adopted was the provision of a huge underground tank of cement; this and ordinary iron tanks stored probably a fortnight's restricted supply for the garrison at its full strength. Three days after occupying Garub the men were drinking borehole water and thanking God in that vague way that men have nowadays that at last they had finished and done with the chlorinated, rust-laden stuff that had for so long passed as their ration. Not very long afterwards—say within a fortnight—the boreholes were yielding 30,000 gallons a day, and the garrison was in some position at any rate to begin its offensive against the enemy; the daily yield finally reached 60,000 gallons.

Then an entirely new position arose. It was found desirable to build a railway deviation to the boreholes, in order, apparently, to facilitate the watering of engines and the filling of water trains. This involved further waiting. In German times the water was pumped from the boreholes to the railway station and there stored in four huge overhead tanks from which all supplies were drawn. The system gave quite satisfactory results. There seemed no reason, therefore, why it should not also serve the Union force; indeed, in the beginning, steps were taken to work on these lines.

The new scheme necessitated the building of a railway loop $4\frac{1}{2}$ miles long in all, at an estimated cost of £9,000, which is certainly not heavy expenditure as railway building costs go. It was to have been finished in ten days; it was not finished in twice ten days. It took practically a month, as a matter of fact, and while it was being constructed a force of about 12,000 men, with animals, was kept standing idly by. A Union soldier cost £1 per day, from first to last, i.e., dividing the total cost of operations by the number of men engaged. So that $4\frac{1}{2}$ miles of railway cost as near £350,000 as one can get, which is at the rate of £75,000 a mile. It must be about the most expensive bit of railway that the world has ever seen. Sir George Farrar, in conversation with me, condemned it, the engineers cursed it, the garrison reviled it; and when I travelled over it for the last time, on my return to the Cape, I was told authoritatively that it was to be pulled up!

Had it served any vital military purpose one could not have complained. But not only did it not do so; by the delay that its construction involved it positively hampered operations. When everything was ready for the great advance and Sir Duncan McKenzie came forward with his headquarters, the most terrifying danger that faced the troops was the danger of falling into unoccupied trenches and spraining their ankles or of running up against abandoned gun emplacements and barking their shins. For the enemy had flown; he, too, had tired of waiting.

Thus did the Central force come to have another long-standing camp. Happily, the conditions at Garub were a great improvement over those at Tschaukaib. Sandstorms were rather the exception than the rule, though when they did rage they beat as into a cocked hat anything that Tschaukaib could produce. Part of the garrison was camped on a sand-dune, and here, at any rate, tents fell like ninepins, and where personal goods and chattels previously stood appeared a glacis-like stretch of sand. But in heat Garub was far and away supreme. Where Tschaukaib registered only 127° in the tents, Garub came forward with 137°; where Tschaukaib merely toasted, Garub literally roasted, until our very skins almost were heard to sizzle and felt to crackle. Even natives were bowled over by it; one, indeed, succumbed to a heat stroke. During the greater part of the day one could only loll about and perspire, which was the common occupation. Once or twice I tried to do some writing. The first three lines I managed quite well. Then I seemed to be writing on blotting paper: perspiration from my arm and hand had turned the remainder of the sheet into pulp. After the third attempt I went to Lüderitzbucht, confident of encountering something like normal conditions there. But the port was in the throes of a heat wave, and my venture was like nothing so much as going out of the frying-pan into the fire. Lüderitzbucht, for the time being, was every whit as limp as Garub. Only then, I think, did I fully realise the thoughtfulness of the authorities in providing those ready-written postcards beginning, " I am quite well," and insinuating regrets, quite politely, that the letters—and the parcels !— had not yet begun to arrive. They must have been a real boon to the troops just then—sheer perspiration-saving devices.

Lüderitzbucht—going off at a tangent—was at this time very quiet, not a little respectable, and showing a distinct tendency towards a settled state. The mounted troops were encamped there, but some distance away from town ; on Sundays all store-yards and offices were closed, so regular were the demands from the front and so well organised was the supplies system ; and the "Base Depôt" men were sensibly careful about their dress, about their appearance generally. But the most striking change to me was the replacement of all German street names by names of British origin and Cultured application. The main thoroughfare was no longer Bismarck Strasse, but King George Street; there was, too, a Queen Mary Street. The road by the Town Hall, where Botha's troops first raised the Union Jack, had become Botha Road. Fittingly forming a junction with Botha Road was Smuts Street. There was, of course, a McKenzie Street. There was also a French Street and a Joffre Street, but no Kitchener Street, strangely enough ; there was, however, a Rhodes Street and a Roberts Street as well. As a tribute to the Navy, no doubt, another street carried the name of Mabel, the name of the wife of Admiral King-Hall, Commander of the Cape Station. The name of one street, however, was left unchanged —Diaz Street remained as a pretty compliment to the Portuguese and that celebrated navigator of theirs who effected the first known landing in the territory. One noticed, too, that the names of all offices were boldly inscribed on the walls, and the hours of business all marked in plain figures.

But to return to Garub and its heat, or, as one man who had obviously lived in a Bloomsbury "home from home" boarding-house called it, " Hell from Hell " ! No wonder (as we were told) the station-masters in peace times were given their £10 a month beer allowance. War times are not peace times, though our troops had, not without a certain mortification, seen empty lager beer bottles by the line side almost every inch of the way up, but there was no stint of water; and conditions were made more bearable still by the timely arrival of cases of luscious South African fruit, notably pears and grapes, which were in perfect condition. Apart from the heat, there is no doubt that Garub was not without its charm. The early mornings and the evenings were indeed most enjoyable; and the rising and setting sun, and the hills all around, and the sand beneath together produced some really exquisite pictures. Though the rich blues and the fiery reds were missing, one was frequently reminded of Egypt.

Then the authorities did a great deal to soften the harmful effects of the desert, both moral and physical, by the application of a holiday and leave scheme. The holiday part of it was really carried out at Tschaukaib, when each regiment in turn was given four days at Lüderitzbucht, to indulge in the luxury of an existence that was without parades or other official intervention, and mostly filled either with sea bathing or unrestricted visits to the Soldiers' Home and its master dish of eggs and bacon. The Soldiers' Home, now managed by the Garrison Institute, was at this time receiving large and regular consignments of eggs. The troops were not long in finding this out. At first there was just a demand for eggs and bacon; then there was a positive run on the dish, and so long as the Home could keep itself supplied, so long did the run continue. Business in other lines was quiet, as market reports do have it. During this holiday season, it was nothing unusual for the Home, spite of its limited accommodation and its small family-size cooking range, to dispose of a thousand cooked eggs of an evening! Eggs also began to filter through to the front, and the first consignment that got there gave rise to rather an amusing scene. They were a gift to a prominent but select mess, the president of which quietly handed them to the cook with the order, "Boiled eggs for breakfast." Next morning he sat by to notice the effect of such an immense and unlooked-for treat. The first arrival was the Second-in-Command, and this conversation ensued:—

"Orderly! Breakfast!"

Orderly: Sir. Porridge, boiled eggs, curried bully, and coffee this morning.

Second-in-Command: Coffee, boiled egg.

Boiled egg brought and consumed. Orderly requests the next order.

"Boiled egg."

Boiled egg brought and consumed. Orderly requests the next order.

"Boiled egg."

Boiled egg brought and consumed. Orderly requests the next order.

"Boiled egg."

Boiled egg brought and consumed. Orderly requests the next order.

Mr. President waited to hear no more. He fled. The monotony was too much for him! All the same, that egg boom, which was all too short-lived, was a feature of the fleshly side of the campaign.

The leave arrangements were announced as the troops were breaking camp at Tschaukaib for Garub. Under them, 7 per cent. of the force was allowed to be away at one time on a month's leave in the Union. Preference was given to men who had urgent matters of business to attend to. There was never any difficulty in making up the percentage. There were, indeed, many disappointments, but the concession was a generous one for all that, and probably left no officer or man out who was genuinely concerned about his business affairs, or his health either. It was no light undertaking for the authorities. In the first place it meant depriving the force of men at a time when it must have had need of them, and depriving it, moreover, of the very class of soldier (since the concession applied chiefly to infantry) who would in all probability have to bear the brunt of any fighting that the struggle for Aus brought about. Then officers and men had to be transported over a distance of more than 500 miles by rail and sea to Cape Town, but this was more easily done than was transporting them back again, when all boats and trains were mostly laden to their brims, as it were; in any case, accommodation was very limited. The troops received free railway passes to their homes, and these homes in most instances were from 600 to 1,200 miles away from Cape Town. Thus the holiday involved each man in some three thousand miles of travel, and so the concession was not without its material value.

Latterly there had been numerous rumours about the Germans gathering at Aus in strength. This strength was variously stated to be two, three, and four thousand men. Where the rumours originated Heaven alone knows, for no extensive scouting was being done; but subsequent events showed the statements to have had a pretty good substratum of truth. The Germans were in greatest strength at Aus during December, and they had a big array of guns. (An eye-witness speaks of having seen 180 big guns at Keetmanshoop just prior to the war). They may have expected an early assault on the place, or they may even have contemplated an offensive against the Central force. The more probable explanation is that they foregathered at Aus, after the failure of the Rebellion in the Union, to await events, as the only Union hostile troops in their country were in this area. Shortly afterwards, however, fresh dispositions were made to

meet the danger in the north, so that after Christmas Aus
was never held by more than perhaps a thousand men all
told. This body did not commence to dig itself in until the
Union troops were practically through the desert, which would
seem to show that right down to the last they never believed
they would have actively to defend the place. But the desert
and Von Spee's Naval Squadron failed them; the British
troops confounded them.

A part of these Garub rumours told of the death, through
the accidental bursting of a bomb, of the German Commander-
in-Chief, Col. von Heydebreck. This report was quite true,
but belated. Von Heydebreck died on November 12, 1914, at
Kalkfontein South, while experimenting with a dart-bomb, so
it is said, such as was used subsequently, in limited number,
by the airmen. His death was undoubtedly a severe blow
to the Germans, for he had been seventeen years in the
country, and in command of the colony's forces since 1910,
and, therefore, had an intimate and far-reaching knowledge
both of the requirements of the country and of the capacity
of the forces under him. Col. von Heydebreck was generally
credited with being a human soldier, though one who knew
him declares that "the soldiers dreaded him, the farmers
feared him, the natives only hated him, and nobody honoured
him." Be this as it may, he was essentially of the German
military caste, and had infused great energy into his plan
for the military development of German South-west Africa.
It was he who designed the military roads with which the
country is studded, who influenced the railway system, brought
about remarkable extensions of the telegraph and telephone,
and built up various water bases. He was succeeded by Major
Franke, with the rank of Lieutenant-Colonel. Col. Franke,
too, had a reputation among Union forces. His reputation
was that of a desperate and unscrupulous fighter. When we
reached the poisoned water of Aus we felt that his reputation
did him no great injustice.

There was one slight skirmish while the troops were facing
each other at Aus. It happened at a time when the German
railway destruction party had reached a stretch of the greatly
curving line that made them plainly visible to the Union
troops. No doubt knowing this, and fearing a sudden move
against them, they pushed their pickets nearer to our lines
than usual. These made a post on a couple of small hills,
close together, that stood alone in the sandy plain, themselves
sentinels of the desert. It was decided to rope these men in,
if possible, and a patrol of Rand Light Infantry and Natal
Carbineers was sent out on the night of March 10 for the
purpose. As luck would have it, the patrol rushed the hill
first that happened that night to be unoccupied. The Germans

were on the neighbouring height, and so they got away. By chance shooting they wounded a Corporal of Carbineers, but not badly. Next day the German fatigue was creating more dust than ever, and one supposed it had been reinforced, the quicker to be finished and done with work that was in front of their lines.

For the rest of their intelligence the Germans relied on their aerial service. "Fritz" paid several visits to Garub, though, as I have said, he bombarded the camp on three occasions only. On his last two visits he came armed with a new kind of ammunition, a sort of dart-bomb, in appearance very much resembling a doctor's ear syringe. The bomb and dart portion was about 8 ins. long and perhaps 2 ins. in diameter; emerging from it was a pencil-like shaft 12 ins. long, to which, again, wings of tin were attached to steady the whole in its flight. The airman dropped six dart-bombs each time, in addition to his customary 35-pounders. They were charged with high explosive, but human life was not affected by any one of them. As events turned out, the visit of March 27 was the last that "Fritz" paid to the Central force, and it had more the object, evidently, of keeping us occupied than anything else, for the Germans were then in full retreat.

A day or two previously—on the morning of the 25th—there had been an occurrence that was much similar in its design. The Germans were then on the eve of their retiral. With the object of distracting our attention, they sent a small patrol, probably of five men, to cut the railway in our rear. They may have hoped at the same time to delay our pursuit of them at this critical moment. The miserable, it is said, have no other medicine, but only hope. Without being a supreme test of skill and daring, the task these men had been set was not an easy one by any means, for, apart from the detour of something like 60 miles that it involved, they had to creep in among the blockhouses; but they accomplished it. They were, however, favoured by circumstances in the most extraordinary way. The night they selected for their enterprise turned out to be the very night on which a mounted regiment and a consignment of transport were moved up from the base. The column kept close to the railway throughout, and the transport followed more or less leisurely—and labouredly—in the wake of the troops. The wagons were, therefore, not closely guarded, and thus they offered a certain amount of cover to the Germans. Of this cover the Germans took every advantage, and reached the line side unobserved. The rest of their work was easy. They blew up the railway in half-a-dozen places—very foolishly, because the blockhouse guards were instantly on the *qui vive*—but, cutely enough, they left a number of charges to be exploded by the first train that came along from Lüderitzbucht, when, of course, their venture would most probably have had uncommonly fine results.

But events did not quite happen in that way, though even so, they were sufficiently horrifying, since they placed the life of one of the most valued members of the force in the greatest jeopardy. This was because a rail motor trolley, conveying Sir George Farrar back to Garub, came along in front of the trains that morning.

Dawn was just breaking as men of the two neighbouring blockhouses pulled up the trolley at the edge of the broken system, but the machine had already passed over the trap that the Germans had left. It was only when Sir George Farrar later on commenced to walk back over the track that it was discovered—half-a-dozen charges of dynamite packed underneath the flanges of the rails, with percussion caps on the rails, that must have wreaked terrible damage had they exploded. The trolley, it appears, had escaped through the narrowness of its wheels, which did not reach as far as the vital spots. It was not a particularly nerve-soothing experience, but Sir George Farrar made little comment. " I could have made a better job of it than that," is all he said.

The Germans got clear away, though efforts were made to track them. If they remained long in sight of the railway they must have doubted if their efforts had been worth while, as trains were passing through to Garub before nine o'clock that morning.

About this time matters developed rapidly. Lord Buxton had visited the force on the 22nd, and at the conclusion of his visit orders were issued to the mounted men to proceed inland. There were now three complete mounted brigades: The 7th Mounted Brigade, consisting of the 1st and 2nd Natal Carbineers (Sir Duncan McKenzie's old regiment), which was commanded by Lieut.-Col. D. W. Mackay, with Major Tanner as Brigade Major; the 8th Mounted Brigade, consisting of the Natal Mounted Rifles and the Umvoti Mounted Rifles, which was commanded by Lieut.-Col. Arnott, with Major Hurst as Brigade Major; and the 9th Mounted Brigade, consisting of the 2nd Imperial Light Horse and the Natal Light ("Royston's") Horse, which was commanded by Lieut.-Col. Royston, C.M.G., D.S.O., with Capt. Burgess as Brigade Major. During the week all these brigades were either on trek or preparing to trek.

On the 26th General Botha paid a sudden visit from Swakopmund, and conferred with Brigadier-General McKenzie, and thereafter the arrangements for the move were substantially expedited. On the 28th General McKenzie advanced his headquarters from Lüderitzbucht to Garub. There were, however, already signs that the spurt had come too late. It is now known that the Germans commenced their retirement on the 26th. We had more than a hint of it on the following day in a big series of loud explosions coming from the plateau, and at night, in the glare of numerous fires. All was quiet by the 28th.

The actual advance was ordered for the night of March 30.

CHAPTER X.

AUS.

Aus was a bloodless victory, and so far as the troops were concerned, anything but inspiriting.

By March 30 the bulk of the force was in camp at Garub, which was now in a perpetual pall of thick dust, visible for miles around. The country about the boreholes is a limestone formation, and the thousands of horses and mules quickly pounded the surface to the fineness of powder. Watering horses was an experience; native servants returned literally as white men.

The first part of the advance was entrusted chiefly to the two infantry brigades, which were ordered to get astride Aus nek, and take up commanding positions on the plateau. A regiment of mounted men—the Imperial Light Horse, under Lieut.-Col. W. Davies, M.D., D.S.O., proceeded along the northern flank to command Kanus Poort, which, by the way, they found in the undisputed possession of three stark, hanging natives. The second part of the scheme one never heard outlined. It was generally assumed to embody a sweeping, swinging movement, embracing Aus itself, by Carbineers and other mounted men under the General. But it never materialised. The infantry themselves went on as far as Aus and encountered no living thing.

It is well worth remembering, however, that up to this point the country itself was just as much an enemy of the Union troops as the Germans themselves, and that, though the Germans had evacuated their positions, the very work of reaching those positions was of itself no mean triumph. The troops, of course, would much have preferred something more tangible and glory-giving; the infantry, a little real bayonet work, as a leaven to the soulless prodding of stuffed sacks, in which they had been indulging in the desert, in readiness for the great day; and the mounted men, some hard hell-for-leather galloping after an enemy actually in flight, with running fighting all the way.

But these things cannot always be. Solid work was done nevertheless. The infantry scored here, coming triumphantly out of a distinctly trying time. They had first of all to cover a stretch of loose deep sand and broken ground that extended a distance of practically 10 miles. Conditions so far were, of course, conditions with which they were quite familiar, but they were none the less unpleasant and exhausting. By the time the foot of the mountain ridge was reached men felt as if they had marched not 10 miles but 20 miles. From their looks they might have just escaped premature burial in a Grasplatz dune, while they swore there was just as much sand inside them as out. Heartfelt inquiries for the watercarts, which were still somewhere behind, robbed this assertion of all fantastic colouring. But they had harder work yet in front of them. There were the ridges to scale " as they came," which were to give them their first real grip of the German positions beyond. There might, of course, be a hot reception awaiting them—one never knew. After so many months' sojourn in the desert, with its almost imperceptible gradients—in 75 miles the altitude rose only 750 ft.—this sudden jump up another 700 ft. meant exertion in a pronounced form. But officers and men alike were full of enthusiasm, and the heights were carried at dawn with something of a flourish. Finally came the scouring of the five miles of broken scrub-covered country, reaching almost to Aus, hard going, every inch of it, in which the Germans had built their fortifications. Food and water, naturally, were an irregular quantity until a new camp was reached, which was three days later; indeed, until then, officers and men were on very short commons.

The movement, as I say, did not develop along the lines expected by the General, whose plans, therefore, did not come wholly into operation. Very little news of what was actually happening, however, reached him, though Garub produced some apparently fantastic stories of how Aus was captured at the point of the bayonet. There never was anyone to bayonet; so much was admitted; but we were all given to understand that some kilted gentlemen, fixing their bayonets as a sort of precautionary measure, had rushed into and through the streets of Aus with a long shout and a great shout of triumph. We were also given to understand that this elation was not due so much to the fall of Aus (Aus had always been a name to conjure with, right from the time we had set foot in Lüderitzbucht) as that infantry had got there before the mounted men. Time went to prove these stories rather than disprove them.

The General, I am afraid, got very perturbed about it all. It was said that his plans did not provide for infantry making the initial entry into Aus; and, therefore, about six o'clock on Wednesday evening, the 31st, he made a hurried departure from Garub for the scene of the new movements, accompanied by a force of Carbineers. He found the infantry bivouaced at Klein Aus, three kilometres short of Aus, but Aus was already a British possession. Those present thought that Sir

Duncan showed some disappointment, but, of course, the programme had been irreparably displaced.

I think that both officers and men of the 1st and 2nd Infantry Brigades, when recalling Aus in days to come, will lay some stress on that march of theirs that they stole on the mounted men.

Aus yielded no booty. The Germans had evidently evacuated the place at their leisure. There are probably a score of residences all told, with a couple of hotels and half-a-dozen stores. About the most imposing building is the school, which had been utilised as a hospital by the Germans, and was continued in the good service by ourselves. But every place had been pretty well depleted of its main contents; there was desolation everywhere. No one, of course, expected to find such a thing as a water service in full swing (I shall return to this matter shortly), or a wireless station that was in working order, or even an aeroplane shed, so there was no disappointment in any of these respects. The wireless station and the flying ground were close together some two miles east of the township; the former had contained elaborate and powerful machinery, but that was before the Germans themselves sacked it.

In normal times Aus carried a population of 160; but its importance to the Central force was measured not by its size but by its situation, and its situation made it a place of enormous value. The great thing was that in it Sir Duncan McKenzie got a footing and a base on the inland plateau where (here and there) grew grass on which animals could feed, and where (here and there) were roads on which animal transport could travel. Nothing of the kind had been met with up to this point. The plateau, nevertheless, is not park land, but it is as different from the desert below as chalk is from cheese; neither is it flat, but there are not the heavy, relentless gradients beyond Aus that there are before it.

After March 27 few really expected to see fighting in front of Aus, but I hardly think that anyone was quite prepared for fortifications of the nature and extent that opened up before the Central force when it came to pass along to Aus. Prisoners captured subsequently declared that Aus was as a rod in pickle for the Union troops. But that depends, of course, whether the point of view is German or British. If German, yes; but, then, that view gives Union strategists credit for horse-sense only. Aus nek, the flanks to Aus nek, and the country immediately behind it were so obviously fortified that to attempt to take them by direct assault were patent foolishness. Other openings were available; and I know that other schemes were considered. There was one to work round from Garub, in a southerly direction, by way of the farm Tsirub, where there were known to be underground sources of water. Capt. de Meillon and his scouts were over Tsirub as far back as Christmas, and, incidentally, had royal feeds of growing peaches and tomatoes there. After they had returned to Tschaukaib and related their experience, and spoken of big, well-constructed dams, Tsirub as a *via media* to Aus became quite a popular idea. From Tsirub the troops would have moved on Kubub, and from Kubub they would have threatened Aus immediately in its rear. There was another—it would have been attended with some risk, but it was feasible, and, after all, the force was out to take risks— to send a mounted detachment from Garub, first to the police post at Neissib, 50 or 60 miles away in a north-easterly direction, and thence to Bethany, 35 miles south-east, where there was a water supply which the Germans could not wholly interfere with. From Bethany, the main line at Brackwasser, 15 miles south, and 69 miles west of Aus, could have been threatened, and in this event the Aus fortifications would by the same stroke have been rendered null and void. The advance of Union columns from the east and the south had the same effect and was, as a matter of fact, the actual cause of the Germans' precipitate retreat. The solving of the problem was thus taken out of the hands of the Central force, and it was possible in the end to enter Aus from the front.

The Germans had a fortified front of about five miles, extending from Aus nek to Kanus Poort, the thoroughfare which the Imperial Light Horse took up the command of, and where the German Camel Corps had been quartered. The horsemen gathered this last piece of information before they had been on the ground five seconds; and their horses took some quietening down. Then from Aus nek fortifications stretched back to Klein Aus, along the railway and the road, also a distance of five miles. On the hills the enemy had built schanzes which were mostly indistinguishable from their surroundings when looked at some little distance away; every bit of natural cover was fully taken advantage of. Often one would come across schanzes built round trees or bush. On the level they had dug trenches, straight ones, as a rule, except for kinks here and there to prevent them being enfiladed. In each series of trenches the one communicated with the other, and they were all noticeably well constructed. Most of them were protected by wire entanglements of the "trip" variety, and "trip" wires were encountered in all sorts of unexpected places. Here and there were cement emplacements for guns— in the two neks and on eminences in front of Aus. The guns on the latter possibly commanded Aus nek. All the various posts had been in telephonic communication one with the other, and one post, on the hill Dikke Willem, would be 20 if not 25 miles away from Aus. There were indications that something like 90 miles of wire had been paid out over those defences.

The railway, of course, was badly damaged, perhaps worse than along any other stretch out of Lüderitzbucht, but, even so, less seriously than it might have been. The country is a sandy plain no longer. It is, on the contrary, very rugged, with deep indentations, and the railway must needs be carried now and again on heavy banking and on bridges. In places embankment rises to a height of 10 ft. and more, and here and there it is pierced by culverts, usually mammoth piping, to allow of the passage of storm water, for these are parts that get heavy rains in due season. Not one of these culverts was destroyed, which was fortunate for the Central force, for had any of them been dynamited, the embankment would have been erased from the landscape as a consequence, and then the work of reconstruction would have been immensely harder and the rate of progress become correspondingly slower. But not one of the three bridges was left intact; two, each a 30-ft. single-span, had been dynamited, and the other the Germans had taken away almost bodily. As a piece of baggage for a scuttling army, a two 30-ft span iron railway bridge must have become rather cumbersome, and it was not surprising to find this one later on dumped on the veld and abandoned, but the Germans got as far as Kuibis, 40 miles away, before tiring of it. The line itself had for the most part been dynamited, but over a stretch of about three miles it had been pulled up and taken away holus-bolus. It was here where the Germans were at work when seen from the Union camp at Garub, and when it was suspected that they were taking up the line altogether.

The Germans, however, were not content with demolishing the railway and running away. They indulged in other measures for the purpose of "getting at" their enemy, measures that were neither legitimate nor nice. They laid sunken mines promiscuously, and they left poison in the water. Within limits, this policy was effective long after the authors of it had fled. True is it that the evil that men do lives after them.

The mines, so the Germans said afterwards, were designed to protect their defences. But when the Union troops came along the German fortifications had ceased to be active works. The men whom they were to shield had abandoned them. The ground on which they stood was no longer contested ground. Five of the mines, even, were in the township of Aus, and, therefore, behind those defences. Altogether, there were three series of five mines each—five in Aus nek, five in the cleared railway track, and the others in a stock kraal in Aus township. In construction they differed somewhat from the variety affected by the Germans in retreat from

Swakopmund. All the mines were hidden from sight, and, therefore, it was a matter of riotous speculation whether a man's next step was to be his last or not.

A mine consisted of two boxes. One box, however, was a trap—it held nothing but a friction tube for sparking the fuse; the pin was attached to the lid, and the lid was lightly poised on four frail pegs so that anyone stepping on it pressed it to the bottom instantly and heavily. This movement brought out the pin, created a spark, and ignited the fuse. The other box held the mine proper, which generally consisted of a layer or layers of dynamite, sometimes as many as 200 sticks, and as much old iron as could be got in the remaining space : horseshoes and nuts and bolts, which were most probably "burnt" beforehand, in order to ensure them breaking readily at the explosion, were the favourite material, but sometimes pom-pom shells were also included. There was no limit to the variety of the contents; a Jew's harp was taken from one mine, but I must say that this was the most harmonious thing that these mines ever produced. The fuse ran from the friction tube to the dynamite, and was of two seconds' duration only. The mine box was well sunk in the ground and earth solidly packed on and around it; the trap box was sunk just low enough for concealment, and the covering of earth on the lid was necessarily as light in weight as possible. The human toll of the whole fifteen mines was only two killed (the men who actually stepped on the trap box), and two wounded.

The mines in the nek looked suspiciously like a ring round Captain de Meillon's grave. As a matter of fact they flanked the road from Garub to Aus, but one has little doubt that the possibility of numbers of troops crossing the ground hereabouts for the purpose of taking a reverent glance at the last resting-place of a dead comrade had not been overlooked. It is significant enough that it was not deemed wise to hold the memorial service at de Meillon's grave-side until the ground in the immediate vicinity had been thoroughly searched, lest there should be any untoward happening during the service itself. Nevertheless, a batch of men was caught not 200 yards away a couple of days later : Private Webb, of the 1st Transvaal Scottish, was killed, and two men of the Rand Light Infantry were wounded. If there can be any satisfaction in it all, the knowledge that the men who laid this mine were, that very day, being basted at Gibeon, 200 miles away, by Sir Duncan McKenzie is, surely, fair cause for it.

The animals suffered the worse. Four mules were blown up by the first mine located; two never came down again except as a rain of flesh, and only the trunks of the other two were left. Curiously enough, these mules and their wagon had already that day crossed that particular piece of ground, in common with the mules and wagons and limbers of all the field artillery and transport that supported the force in its advance on Aus. The explosion had the effect of exposing, in the same track, another mine that was ringed literally with a myriad marks of passing traffic, yet quite untouched by any. Exploding mines usually exposed other mines.

There were also miraculous escapes at the Aus stock kraal. Colonel Byron enjoyed one. He was struck with some force by one of numerous pieces of iron that came hurtling through the air, but his helmet parried the blow and he suffered nothing worse than a scratch on the forehead. At the time, he was in the midst of a group of officers and men observing the despairing efforts of Engineers to extract potable water from a poisoned well, and it was the greatest wonder there were not a few serious casualties to report. As an integral part of the German scheme of defence this kraal seemed to be quite above suspicion. It had no apparent strategical value, and was therefore utilised without hesitation. Yet it was heavily mined; and one of the mines that was subsequently dismantled must alone have been capable of pitching Aus into ruins. The discovery that the kraal had been tampered with was made on Good Friday afternoon, when a valuable horse put its foot into a mine there and was shockingly mutilated. The kraal was eventually rendered innocuous by means of systematic digging from the entrance inwards, after the expedient of firing the manure had been tried.

The most ingenious scheme for discovering sunken mines, however, was put into operation at Joselshohe, where the Germans had turned the railway track into a mine field, after having bared it of rails for a distance of three miles. Two of the mines had gone off and killed a private (Wattmore) of the Kaffrarian Rifles, and a native. Some set scheme of exploration was therefore imperative before the work of rebuilding the railway could be continued. After discussion with Sir George Farrar, Captain Beith, of the Transvaal Scottish, devised and directed the working of a harrow by which the surface of the track was probed for hidden obstructions. Mules, walking well at the side, dragged the harrow along. Every obstruction did not tell a mine, of course, but each one, nevertheless, had to be handled with delicate care until its good faith was established, and so the whole business was pretty exciting while it lasted. The device was entirely successful; all the mines were speedily discovered.

But the German penchant for fighting by means of dynamite and detonator went further than this. An ordinary tablelamp, in the stationmaster's office at Aus, was found to be "mined," but found out in time.

So much for the mines. The poisoning of the water was a far more serious matter. No harm befel anyone from drinking poisoned water; on the contrary, it has been humorously suggested that the weak mixture of carbolic and water that most men had to take, willy nilly, had tonic effects, though it was most nauseating as a drink of taste; but in conjunction with the wrecked boreholes the policy seriously delayed the future operations of the Central Force, almost nullified them. All open water, wells included, the Germans poisoned, generally by means of sheep dip or crude lysol; sometimes they contaminated it by the introduction of the entrails and offal of animals, as at Kuibis. At Klein Aus, at Aus, at Kubub, the agent employed was wholly sheep dip. The first poisoned water encountered was an open well at Klein Aus, which bore a label, the work of someone unlettered in English, indicating that the water was not fit for drinking purposes. The information was needed only by those suffering from cold, for in vulgar parlance the poison could be smelt a mile off. From another point of view, also, the information was not greatly helpful, for this particular well gave no more than fifty gallons all told, and the mixture was not weak enough by the time the last drop was raised to justify anyone taking the risk of his thirst being too drastically ended.

One is rather inclined to smile as one recalls such incidents as these, secure in a great and busy city not from hardship only but from mere discomfort also. Yet there was not much smiling at the time. This incident, for example, occurred just after men (infantry) had completed fifteen miles of the heaviest marching imaginable and when they were suffering acutely from thirst. It was one incident in a whole series that makes the campaign stand out as a campaign of uncommon hardships.

The procedure adopted for dealing with the poisoned and contaminated water was to run off the mixture until it was weak enough to do no hurt. This was a matter not of hours, but of days; the Aus water tasted of carbolic a fortnight after the cleansing process started. Thousands of gallons of water thus came to be run to waste. According to a German doctor to whom I spoke on the subject, the German point of view on this poisoning outrage was that, as the water belonged not to the Union force but to them, they were perfectly at liberty to do with it as they would. He conceded this much, that had the Germans poisoned water that did not belong to them, then they would indeed have been guilty of a violation of international conventions.

The ingenuity of the argument was not denied, nor its audacity, either. It was even thought that the example it set might be followed. This enemy doctor had been taken prisoner in order to attend to wounded and sick Germans, and at the time this discussion arose he was on his way to the hospital at Lüderitzbucht. He wanted beef tea for the journey. Beef tea was obtained for him. But as it was handed over this bit of logic was impressed on him, that while the beef tea belonged to us we had the right to do what we liked with it; if he discovered that it was mixed with sheep dip he must not complain. He was nearly furious. I believe he called it barbarous. We said it was *Kultur*. After that we felt somewhat compensated for that rising gorge that for ten days had followed the drinking of tea and coffee in which the flavour of sheep dip predominated.

When I come to reflect, I really am surprised that some elfish sprite did not mix sheep dip with the liquid rations of the first batch of German prisoners to reach Aus. The garrison at Aus, I know, was at one time inclined to adopt a rather threatening attitude towards the prisoners. All sorts of kindly suggestions of retribution that should be visited on them were made. I think the kindest of the lot was to take them for an afternoon gallop in the kraal that they had so industriously mined (in which four mines still remained), and, if any survived, then to quench their thirst with lashings of carbolicised water made according to their own precious formula!

The borehole machinery was wrecked and the boreholes filled in, and night and day work at feverish pressure became necessary in order to permit of the main force being brought up from Garub, and a flying column got away without a moment's unnecessary delay. The Germans were now in full retreat, with Windhuk as the first stop. Of the few documents found in Aus, one was an order containing instructions about the retirement on the capital. The garrison left on March 26; the rearguard followed on the 29th. But, unfortunately, the water position dominated the situation entirely so far as the Central force was concerned, and it simply would not allow of any instant pursuit. For many days only very limited numbers of horses and men could be maintained in Aus. Attempts were made to force the position on April 6, but the result was not encouraging, a thousand men and horses having to be sent back to Garub with all speed. These were very anxious times.

But the position improved daily. The countryside was scoured for water. One day some pools were found in rocky lands to the north; they were the result of recent rains, and were therefore unreached by the German poison mania. They did the force a good though limited service. Then another mounted detachment was sent out to Kubub; here the water was poisoned, but hard and continuous work for a few days resulted in the poison being toned down sufficiently to permit of both man and beast drinking the water with safety. And all the time attention was being paid to the water position ahead.

So by April 14 it was possible to concentrate the mounted troops at Aus and the vicinity, and the work of the Central force then entered on an entirely new phase. Hitherto, the work of the advance had been essentially infantry work, though the dispositions that were made at one time and another probably did not emphasise this fact. Henceforth the mounted ranks were to come into their own. Mounted men and infantry thus parted company. The former—three brigades, two batteries of field artillery, and a mounted field ambulance section, with, of course, engineers—were made up into a flying column, led by General McKenzie, and moved out of Aus on April 15. The latter were left to garrison the stations and guard the lines of communication, with Colonel Beves as the General Officer Commanding. Lieut.-Colonel Dawson-Squibb was temporarily placed in charge of the 1st Infantry Brigade, which was sent back from Klein Aus (kilo. 138) on April 1 to a new camp at kilo. 116, where it remained. The 2nd Infantry Brigade, with headquarters at Aus, actually did the garrison work. The Kimberley Regiment, supplemented by the Pretoria Regiment later on, garrisoned Aus and carried out the fatigues necessary to keep the mounted men ahead in supplies; companies of Kimberleys were also pushed forward to garrison Kuibis and Bethany. The 1st Eastern Rifles were withdrawn from the blockhouses and marched to Aus. The lines of communication were then taken over by the Kaffrarian Rifles; but the blockhouse policy was now abandoned, and, instead, detachments of troops were maintained at Rothkuppe, Tschaukaib, and Garub, which were rail watering places.

In the meantime the railway was pushed ahead, and reached Aus on the night of April 22. The average rate at which railhead had advanced from Garub was one mile per day, but this included the building of three temporary bridges and the delay occasioned by the search for sunken mines.

Henceforward railway construction was carried on under the new scheme that I made mention of in Chapter VI. Col. Sir George Farrar, D.S.O., who had hitherto controlled the work, now had the great problem before him of supplying an army with its needs that was disposed along a 200 odd mile line and had a rapidly moving front. The problem became all the more difficult because of the shortness of road transport, and also because the railway, by reason of the climb from Garub to Aus, was not able to maintain the service that had been such a feature in the desert. From kilo. 129 to 133 (Garub 104, Aus 141) the gradient is 1 in 30 compensated, thereafter 1 in 40 uncompensated. Sir George Farrar solved his problem, but it required and took the whole of his attention.

CHAPTER XI.

CONVERGING ON KEETMANSHOOP.

It will be recalled that the original plan for conquering German South-west Africa provided for a convergence of Union troops on to the enemy's centre from all points of the compass. The Rebellion intervened, but though it quashed the plan it did not quash the idea. Thus the operations that led to the suppression of the Rebellion in the north-western districts of the Cape gradually developed into a definite offensive against the Germans from that quarter. Col. J. van Deventer was in charge of this movement, and his force, which was known as the Southern force, worked in three sections. Simultaneously a new column entirely, known as the Eastern force, was fitted out under Col. Berrangé, C.M.G., of the S.A. Mounted Rifles, and it assailed German territory from the east, crossing near Hasuur.

These forces did uncommonly good work. Mobility was their keynote. They got the Germans on the run, and on the run they kept them. They chivvied them from pillar to post, giving them not a moment's peace anywhere. To this policy is due the fact that these Union forces sustained so few casualties. There were places which the Germans had previously prepared with a view to making a stand in their retirement, but they had not the time to utilise them.

The common objective of both Col. van Deventer and Col. Berrangé was Keetmanshoop "or thereabouts." They achieved their objective with notable success. As with the Central force, part of their triumph was over the country itself, part was over the disgusting methods that the enemy adopted as warfare, and the remainder, goodly in share, was over the enemy *per se*.

Each column had to cross the desert belt, which, though varying in width, was always intense. Curiously enough, it was mostly Union territory. Where Col. Berrangé crossed it the width was probably 300 miles, and how he crossed it stands for as clever a bit of work as will be encountered in the whole campaign, for there were no regular or frequent sources of water from beginning to end, and he had no railway to assist him. They all got through very rapidly, and this is where the experience of the Southern and Eastern forces differs from that of the Central force; and yet those men, too, have their terrible pictures to draw, of tracks enveloped in powdery billows from which, gasping and choking, they seemed eternally striving to emerge and never likely to succeed. When they did emerge they shook the dust from off them in clouds, but it was days and days before the smarting sensation of corroding vitals that the desert had set up left them. It was not only *personnel* that was affected. There were occasions when it seemed as if the transport as a whole must break down. There was a particular stretch of seven miles on the Eastern route that I might specially refer to. It contained gradients of 1 in 3 1-3, and motor-cars were helpless. To get over the difficulty, donkeys were stationed along the route, and, when necessary, they pulled the cars along; but, even so, it took three hours to get seventeen cars over a patch of 150 yards.

On the other hand, there were occasional stretches as level and smooth as a billiard table. These were the dry beds of pans. One such was met with at Tukoos; it was 12 miles long and six miles wide, and some of the cars rattled over it at a measured speed of 64 miles an hour. Mostly, and happily, these pans contained great sheets of water, as at Windhoek (on the Bechuanaland side of the border), where a magnificent lake 23 miles long gave the tired and dusty troops "some" swim and made new men of them; or at a spot between Ukamas and Nabas, where there was a 7 by 1½ mile pan of water that was 20 ft. deep in the centre.

In parts, naturally, grazing was excellent, but more than one man speaks of this curious fact—that where there was water there was often no grass, and where there was grass there was frequently no water. There were only too many occasions, however, when both grazing and water were conspicuous by their absence, and as it was not possible to carry feed in any great quantity, the animals had a very trying time. Those on the Eastern force got only 8 lbs. of grain in seven weeks. And yet they "wore" admirably. The mounted men with Col. Celliers covered close on 1,000 miles in the saddle in seven weeks, and only 25 horses fell out; but these animals got small quantities of grain fairly frequently.

Some of the country was extremely mountainous. In this respect, nothing was quite so bad as the Karas ranges, "Great" and "Little," between Keetmanshoop and Kalkfontein, which rise to a height of 2,200 ft. These mountains had to be closely watched and scoured, which necessitated an elaboration of the plan of campaign and sensibly stiffened the work that the troops had to do. The Germans had police posts in both ranges, but they never attempted anything more than a make-believe defence, though there were prepared fortifications. What they could have done is indicated by Lieut.-Col. van der Westhuizen, who commanded the 17th Mounted Rifles (from the Worcester district, Cape), which had a straight run through, as football enthusiasts say, in Col. Bouwer's column, right from Raman's Drift to Keetmanshoop.

Col. Westhuizen says that Noachebeb, which is the pass between the two ranges, is a regular Gibraltar. The Germans had intended to put up a defence here, but did not, and yet, adds the Colonel, fifty men with machine guns entrenched on those slopes could have kept a thousand men at bay for a month at least. The Germans, however, probably getting news of the Union columns that were threatening them from the east and north-east under the respective commands of Col.-Commandant D. van Deventer and Col. Berrangé, retired with great haste.

Both forces had to contend with poisoned water and dynamite traps from the moment they entered German territory. Some of the wells contained iodoform and pungent oils, others the carcases of dogs and other animals, but in no case did mishap occur to the troops. The big open vleis, of course, the Germans could not tamper with. As dynamitards they seem to have resorted to tricks rather than to such measures as subterranean mining. At Kalkfontein, for instance, they placed bombs in the houses and connected them to the doorknobs by means of wire detachments. Whether or not it was the Guy Fawkesian flavour about it that exposed the frolic I don't know, but the trap was not successful. The houses, however, were not left alone; they were entered by the windows. At Gross Aub, again, finding that they could not take a laden wagon with them, they charged it with dynamite and placed detonators under each wheel. The guiding star of Providence was over the Eastern force that day, for that wagon was never moved.

The real fighting was, for the most part, an affair of patrols, but two encounters assumed very respectable proportions. One at Raman's Drift lasted eight hours, and it was sufficiently intense to justify the authorities (so an uncontradicted report states) in recommending an officer for a military distinction; the other, at Upington, resulted, so eye-witnesses state, in a loss to the enemy of 61 killed, but the estimate of the Union commander was only 18. The Union casualties were always very few. But whatever the extent of the fighting, with one exception (Nous) it went decidedly against the enemy.

Such is a rapid survey of the Southern and Eastern operations as a whole. I propose now to refer to each movement individually, four in all.

It has been declared officially that the Rebellion was over by December 10, 1914, though surrenders were recorded up to February 3, 1915, and the last rebels were not actually captured until March 23. So I propose to pick up the broken threads of the German South-west African campaign, in so far as it concerns the advance from the south and south-east, as I find them on or about December 10. But the rebels were very active even after this date. There was an action at Nous on December 22, which was largely conducted by rebels, though Maritz and Kemp, who directed it, were unquestionably assisted by Germans.

Nous is in the Cape Province, a "water hole," 17 miles directly south of Schuit Drift. It was held by 480 officers and men, with two maxims, who were commanded by Major Breedt, of the Britstown Commando. Other units besides the Britstown Commando were the Murraysburg, Cradock, Kakamas, and Kenhardt Commandos, the 20th Mounted Rifles (Graaff-Reinet Ruiters), the Midland Scouts, and the Prince Alfred's Guards Maxim Gun section. They were attacked at dawn by 800 rebels and Germans, having four field guns and four maxims. A Kenhardt Commando patrol saw the enemy first and careered back into and through camp at a headlong pace. Alarm and confusion ensued naturally, and units were too flabbergasted to take up the positions that had been assigned to them for such occasions as these. Before they knew where they were, therefore, shells—German shells— were dropping into camp amongst them; and the fact that the very first shell fell only two yards away from the maxim guns only adds to the general significance of the whole affair. Before calmness could be restored the enemy were in the camp, and the camp was in the throes of a general mêlée. The official account says that the Kenhardt Commando (as then constituted) was conspicuous in preparing for flight, and that only about nine members of it remained behind. To say the least, the garrison was highly unfortunate in some of its constituent parts.

Out of the chaos, however. Major Breedt got a force of 250 officers and men under discipline, and in the end put up a notably vigorous resistance. He summoned assistance from Zwartmodder, and was reinforced by Capt. Bronkhorst and 120 men. Then he retired on Kakamas. 44 miles eastwards. keeping up a running fight the whole time. and preventing Maritz and Kemp from achieving their object of surrounding him. In the end he lost one man killed. two men wounded, and 92 real prisoners. a disabled maxim, two wagons containing 80.000 rounds of ammunition, and a convoy of 26 empty wagons. which had outspanned in direct disobedience to orders, and the head conductor of which had already gone over to the enemy. Maritz and Kemp also took an ambulance and its equipment away.

There was next an encounter at Schuit Drift. on January 5, 1915. where Major Vermaas. with the Calvinia Commando. engaged the enemy and eventually pushed him back, though not before the pontoon and all the boats had been destroyed. Hostilities lasted for eight hours, and the Union troops sustained five casualties, all wounded. It was in attending to these wounded men that an ambulance officer, Lieut. Hartley, behaved with conspicuous valour. His improvised Red Cross wagons and flag were hit, suggesting that he was deliberately fired upon, and his clothing was pierced by bullets. He persisted, however, until his work was finished, and has now been recommended for some distinction as a reward for his heroism.

About this time Maritz and Kemp, and also Stadler, another rebel leader, were reported to be again advancing on the border, respectively from Jerusalem, Ukamas, and Blydeverwacht. On January 14 they ambushed and captured, after a fight, 36 men of the 8th Mounted Rifles, who were at Langklip. 25 miles east of Nakob. Three days later they had reached Cnydas, where they attacked the main body of the same regiment, which retired on Van Rooi's Vlei, having lost 8 men killed and 20 wounded. At Van Rooi's Vlei these troops got reinforcements, turned the tables on the Rebel-German forces, and made them disgorge all their prisoners.

Maritz, with his forces, then gradually but quietly worked their way round to Upington, and appeared before the township on Saturday, the 23rd. During the day he called on Upington to supply him with provisions and surrender within 24 hours. Both demands were refused. Maritz was nothing if not insolent. It didn't matter, he retorted, as he would be having Sunday breakfast in Upington, anyhow; Kemp was sure he would be holding a Church service there at 11 o'clock. They were both out of their reckoning. Col. J. van Deventer was in charge of the Upington garrison.

The Maritz-Kemp-Stadler forces numbered about 1,200, with four 18-pounder guns, two pom-poms, and maxims. They commenced to shell the town at daybreak on Sunday, and thereafter ensued an artillery duel lasting three hours. The garrison guns were those of the Cape Field Artillery, whose men did some capital shooting. They disabled a pom-pom straight away, and, later on, blew a wheel of one of the 18-pounder limbers clean off; twelve dead gunners were found beside this piece when it was eventually captured. The Union troops were victorious, and the Artillery really were responsible for the result. "So beautifully were they handled," said a Colonel Commanding, "that they might have been British Regular troops going into action." The enemy tried to creep into Upington under cover of the guns, and they engaged in a very hot and very determined rifle duel at close quarters. Once they forced the Union troops back. Reinforcements, however, were brought up, and the whole force then, working in extended and disciplined order, gradually got the upper hand. Finally the enemy forces crumbled up in rout and fled, being chased 15 miles.

The official estimate of the enemy casualties was 18 killed, 19 wounded, and 90 prisoners. Union officers have since declared, however, that the Germans lost 61 killed and 23 wounded. All the Rebel prisoners were dressed in German uniforms. Among the wounded was the Rebel Commandant Stadler, a daring leader, who is said to have been far superior to Maritz. Stadler died soon after the engagement finished, and was buried at Christiana.

The Union casualties were 3 killed, 32 wounded. Among the units engaged were the Gordonia, Prieska, Graaff-Reinet, Cradock, Colesberg, Conroy's, and Kimberley Central (Scott's Horse) Commandos, the 8th, 18th, and 20th Mounted Rifles, and Malan's Hanover Mounted Rifles, with the Cape Field Artillery.

Out of this action arose an instance of conspicuous bravery. During the fighting Lieut. Theron, of the Graaff-Reinet Commando, was wounded and lay exposed to a hot, short-range enemy fire. He was noticed by a 17-year-old despatch rider named Brian Melvill, trooper, and, despite a perfect hail of bullets, was by him carried to safety. Trooper Melvill's parents received the congratulations of the Minister of Defence upon the action of their son—another instance of the kindly thoughtfulness of General Smuts—and, later in the year, General Botha, on behalf of the public of Graaff-Reinet, handed young Melvill a gold watch and highly commended him on the high example he had set to South African youth.

About this Upington engagement it is interesting to note that Maritz let it be known that he was "off to German South-west Africa for bigger guns." Those he had failed with were bigger than those that succeeded against him, and had a longer range. But the following day he wrote Col. van Deventer, suing for peace.

As an outcome of this letter, Col. van Deventer met Maritz, Kemp, and another rebel leader named de Villiers, outside Upington, under a flag of truce, when the Rebels expressed a desire to capitulate. Col. van Deventer, however, refused to extend any terms. They intimated then that they would surrender.

Kemp, with Bezuidenhout and the famous prophet, van Rensburg, surrendered at Upington the following Wednesday, with 40 officers and 517 burghers; they also brought in 4 officers and 46 burghers of Maritz's Commando. Officers and men were alike dressed in German uniforms, and most possessed German arms. It was understood that Maritz's Commando, being more scattered than Kemp's, would surrender in batches at various places, and it was reported that

Maritz himself had gone back to German territory to round up the remnants.

Then there was a most extraordinary turn of events. A batch of Maritz's men, numbering 100 all told, actually surrendered that morning, February 3, at Kakamas, 50 miles west of Upington. But they had hardly reached the Commandant's office when the township was subjected to a fierce artillery and rifle fire bombardment. It transpired that a force of Germans, 300 strong, with field guns, pom-poms, and machine guns, under Major Ritter, had formed up outside, intent on the capture of the place, which was then held by the Murraysburg, Britstown, Kenhardt, and Kakamas Commandos under Major Bronkhurst.

The Germans first directed their attention to the township and De Witt's drift. Kakamas drift was ignored. This was fortunate for the garrison, as it enabled a detachment to cross to the northern bank of the Orange River (which was in flood at the time) and take up good positions near the school and electric power station of Schroeder, and thus frustrate a vital movement in the same direction on the part of the Germans. Altogether the Union forces maintained a front of three miles, and fought at first stubbornly and then with dash. The German fire was gradually worn down; then it ceased suddenly, and the enemy was seen to be in full retreat. By this time reinforcements were on their way from Upington. The Germans left some horses and a quantity of baggage behind.

According to their own reports, they lost 5 officers (3 Regulars) and 7 N.C.O.'s and men killed, 2 officers and 21 N.C.O.'s and men wounded, and 7 prisoners. Other reports give the killed as 13 and the prisoners as 15. One of the wounded officers, who had both legs broken, shot himself through the head with his revolver. The Union casualties totalled but three—1 officer killed and 2 men wounded. The dead officer was Lieut. J. Neethling, of the Transport section, who, with 14 men, put up a most gallant defence of the drifts. Almost the first one to see Lieut. Neethling's dead body was his father, Major Neethling, M.L.A., who had charge of the hospital at Kakamas. A happier incident than this is related about the Kakamas Commando, which, in the absence through illness, of the Lieut.-Commanding, was led by a member named du Preez. One of the men fighting under du Preez was his aged father.

The reason for this sudden German attack on Kakamas gave rise to considerable speculation. At first people were inclined to put it down to treachery on the part of Maritz, but I don't think that that assumption is now generally held. Most probably the reason is that the Germans got wind of the Rebels' intention to surrender, and endeavoured to prevent it being put into execution. They were, however, ten hours behind Kemp's force, and so evidently they pulled up at Kakamas, determined on hostilities somewhere. Every movement round Kakamas showed the attack to have been hurried and ill-conceived and developed. It is, anyhow, fairly well established that at this time the Germans and their Rebel friends by no means enjoyed each other's confidence or respect.

The Germans generally were in the state that is colloquially spoken of as "sick." One of them, an officer, observed to a Dutch officer that " it is strange you Boers should be helping the British who fought against you." " Yes," replied the burgher, "it is strange how things turn. I have a relative of German descent who had in his sitting-room a picture of your Field-Marshal Blucher shaking hands with the Duke of Wellington on the field of Waterloo. And now to think of the ' Lusitania ' ! " The German had nothing further to say.

There were clear evidences now that not only were all the Rebels practically accounted for, but that the back of the German invasion of the Union was broken. Three weeks later Colonel van Deventer had assumed the offensive against the Germans, and on February 26 he was in German territory.

In passing, I may mention that the Government casualties in the Rebellion totalled 131 killed and 272 wounded. Those of the Rebels are estimated at 1,000 killed and wounded, and 3,885 Rebels surrendered, while 5,792 were captured. Of those taken prisoner, 293 are described as leaders, and they stood their trial before the Treason Courts ; the rank and file were allowed to proceed to their homes.

The first German post that was attacked was that of Nakob, fittingly enough—the post from which the Germans had advanced into the Union six months before. The capture was effected on February 26 by patrols without loss, but the Germans managed to get away, though they lost four men killed and one wounded. Coloured eye-witnesses asserted that Maritz was with the retreating force.

Exactly a week later there was a movement on Schuit Drift. Despite the mountainous nature of the country and the difficulties of crossing the river within striking distance of the Germans, the fort was captured without loss on March 6. The Germans lost ten officers and men and six natives, all captured. Vellor Drift, which is midway between Schuit Drift and Raman's Drift, was taken about the same time. The units engaged were the Calvinia, Kenhardt, Murraysburg (with maxims), and Namaqualand commandos, the Karoo Schutters, Naude's Scouts, and Cape Field Artillery.

Raman's Drift was occupied on January 12, 1915, by Commandant Van Zyl with his commando, working under Colonel Bouwer, after a series of bouts with a German patrol, which lost one man killed, an officer and a man wounded, and an n.c.o. taken prisoner. The patrol got away in a northerly direction. There was also a skirmish at Godou's Drift, to the west of Raman's Drift, which was at this time the camp of 60 German infantry. Van Zyl's commando routed this party, too, inflicting a loss on it of one officer and two men killed.

On February 3 there was a stiff encounter between Colonel Bouwer's column and German advanced posts near Sandfontein, the scene of the terrible fight of the previous September, and three Germans were killed. The Union troops lost an n.c.o. killed—Sergt. Smit, of Van Zyl's commando, who was wounded in the first exchanges, but later on was shot dead as he was being carried out of action by Trooper Malan. On February 15 the German patrols had been pushed back right into Sandfontein.

So when Colonel van Deventer got Schuit Drift the whole of the Orange River line was in our hands.

From Schuit Drift van Deventer moved straight up on to Nabas, ten miles west of Ukamas, where a German force, 200 strong, was reported to have entrenched itself. Despite the disadvantage of position, the Union troops, who were personally led by Colonel van Deventer, carried the place by storm on March 7, after five hours' fighting, all with the rifle. The Germans, leaving one man killed, one wounded, and ten prisoners behind, as well as valuable stores, fled in the direction of Kalkfontein, whereto, by the way, runs a good military road. One man wounded was the only casualty sustained by the victors.

Jerusalem and Hairachabis had been taken on the way; and a few days later Ukamas was occupied, falling tamely to two companies of mounted men under Captain Cruse. Ukamas was an important military post under German rule. In its beautifully built barracks and other residences, its telegraph and telephone connections, and its good roads, there was every sign of permanency about the place and no small suggestion of menace to the Union, eighteen miles away to the east.

The German Press at Windhuk declared that our occupation of Ukamas was the most depressing news it had yet received, while it admitted that "a certain unrest exists here on account of masses of Union troops having advanced to Nabas." The Germans consoled themselves with the thought that the Union troops were composed of "dissipated farmers and fat-bellied sluggards," whom "it will be an easy matter to finish off." Getting into this frame of mind must have been an outstanding triumph of hope over experience.

A base was built up at Hudab, fifty miles in, which was the next place occupied.

About this time Colonel van Deventer detached a portion of the 4th Mounted Brigade, under his brother, Colonel-Commandant Dirk van Deventer, to proceed by way of Dawignab (a German police station), Plattbeen, and Geitsaub, round the eastern and northern flanks of the Great Karas range; he himself proceeded direct to Kalkfontein, and at the same time Colonel Bouwer pushed up from Raman's Drift.

Dawignab (occupied on March 22) offered no difficulties, but the Germans put up resistance at Plattbeen, where they had a camp. Their position was attacked by the 11th and 20th Mounted Rifles and carried after a short bombardment, in which four Germans fell killed and six wounded; the Union casualties totalled three—one killed, two wounded. The Germans retired on Geitsaub, leaving great quantities of supplies, clothing, and ammunition behind, as well as horses, mules, and sheep.

Geitsaub was taken, after opposition, on April 2, but without loss; the Germans, however, had seventeen casualties—two killed, one wounded, sixteen captured.

The Southern force reached Kalkfontein on Easter Monday, April 5, and the same day also occupied Kanus, 15 miles to the north, both without opposition. At the former place the British flag that was hoisted was one that had been specially made for and presented to the 4th Mounted Brigade, commanded by Colonel Celliers, by the ladies of Potchefstroom.

Colonel van Deventer made Kalkfontein his headquarters for some days, and in the meantime Colonel Bouwer's column —consisting of the 17th Mounted Rifles and Hartigan's Horse, making nearly 900 of all ranks—arrived from the south after having formally occupied Warmbad (April 7) on the way. Warmbad is one of the oldest places in the territory, and was being developed by the Germans as a tourist resort. It had a white population of about 850, and a number of charming residences; in fact, Warmbad is aptly described as a distinctly stylish place. Unfortunately the Germans saw their way to blow up the famous swimming-bath (which was fed from a sulphur spring having a temperature of 102° F.) before retiring. Warmbad was untouched otherwise, though it had been effectively ransacked of all food contents.

Kalkfontein marked an important advance in that it was the railhead of the German railway system in the south, though presently of little use in the absence of rolling stock and through connections with Lüderitzbucht or Swakopmund. Kanus had been a big military station under the Germans, but it was now completely deserted.

All this while Colonel Berrangé had been creeping up on the enemy's eastern front. The Eastern force consisted of the 5th S.A. Mounted Rifles (of which Colonel Berrangé was formerly the Officer Commanding), the Kalahari Horse, Cullinan's Horse, and the Bechuanaland Rifles; heavy artillery, maxim guns, motor section, and the usual details. Colonel Berrangé's Chief of Staff was Lieut.-Colonel E. F. Thackeray (Permanent Force), and Capt. Murray was the D.A.Q.M.-G. Two other important appointments were held by Major Sir Thomas Cullinan (not of Cullinan's Horse), who was on the Headquarters Staff and controlled the water arrangements, and Major Rose, who was responsible for the motor transport by which that water and other supplies were on occasions conveyed. Kuruman, at the edge of the Kalahari Desert, was the base; as different from the desert itself as any place well could be. There are beautiful fruit gardens at Kuruman and there is water clear as crystal, which gushes from the famous " Eye " there.

The Eastern troops commenced their great trek across the desert on March 6, 1915, after having marched over from Kimberley, 147 miles away. They were in heavy desert almost before camp was out of sight, and in desert they remained for the greater part of the 600 miles that they afterwards negotiated. Water holes were few and far between, and at most irregular distances. From Bushman Pits it is no fewer than 110 miles to the next water hole, and there are natives in between, so I have been assured, who have never seen water in the whole of their lives; for liquids these rely on the contents of tsama, a sort of desert melon.

The force surmounted the water problem by means of its motor-cars, the organising skill of Col. Berrangé and his Chief of Staff, and the splendid endurance of the *personnel*. Where the distances between water hole and water hole were greater than could be negotiated by forced march, as on this 110-mile stretch, artificial water bases were set up—a series of portable tanks which were filled and kept replenished by the cars journeying to and fro carrying drums of water from the last water hole.

Motor-cars also fed the column with supplies on occasions. The force had ox transport also—mule transport was impossible in that sand—but in the desert this had its severe limitations. In order to prevent animals from being overtaxed and to minimise the wear and tear on the wagons, convoys were worked in easy stages throughout. When the column, by pushing ahead or for other reasons, got out of touch with its wagons, supplies were brought up by motor. Thus the fighting men were never without rations; and though only half rations were issued on several occasions, game was very plentiful and kept the pot full. Thus was the mobility of the column assured, even though the natural conditions of the country were inimical to mobility.

I have heard it said that the suppression of the Rebellion was the triumph of the motor-car in South Africa, which was so largely used by the troops; in other words, the motor-car proved itself as a reliable vehicle of transport in parts that are more or less untamed. But roads are tolerably good in the Union, and the conveniences for repairing motors are never very far from hand. Far more emphatically did the motor-car prove its reliability and capacity in the German South-west African campaign, particularly along this eastern route. Perhaps it would be fairer to say "Motor Transport Service" rather than "motor-car." "I hesitate to think," said an officer, "what would have happened to us if the motor service had broken down." It never did break down, because of the energy and ingenuity of the men in charge of it. To overcome accidents Major Rose opened up workshops in the wilderness, and when a car broke down the section repaired it almost on the spot. Often they were hard put to it to keep up with these individual breaks-down, as it was next to impossible to get spares from either the United Kingdom or France. They won, somehow. There were occasions when the motor-car was beaten by the sand and the gradients combined, and when animals had to be brought to the rescue, as I have mentioned, but this was exceptional.

The force had no heavy fighting. The enemy set the ball rolling early in February by a raid on Reitfontein, whence they took the magistrate and others prisoners; and on other places round about (all in the Union), including Witdraai and Witkrantz, where they captured a camel patrol, under Captain Munro, which had been keeping observation at the border. Soon after the column got going the German airman was sighted on a scouting flight. This was at Monpeppi. At Schaapkolk the force encountered a German patrol, and the following day, the 19th, it beat it back over the border after inflicting a loss of four killed and twenty wounded; its own casualties were three wounded. The border was crossed on March 31, when Hasuur was occupied without opposition. Hasuur, a cold, bleak spot, is fifteen miles north-west of the Union post of Reitfontein, and was a German police post. Its barracks are most substantial buildings; and there were fortifications.

From Hasuur a force of Kalahari Horse was sent to Koes, sixty miles away to the north-west, where it had a brush with the enemy. Each side made a prisoner, and we sustained a wounded casualty; large quantities of stock were captured. The enemy made a most determined attempt to recapture this stock, about forty officers and men swooping down on the escort, which was only one officer and four men strong and was off-saddled at the time. They were stubbornly resisted, however, and eventually driven off. The fighting extended over two hours. Very pluckily a trooper of Kalahari Horse, named Jacobs, pursued the enemy on his own. He did not stop to saddle up, riding his horse barebacked. He succeeded in shooting a horse, thus bringing down the rider, whom he captured. It was stated at the time that Colonel Berrangé had recommended Trooper Jacobs for military distinction as a reward for his bravery.

The main body after deviating to the south then made due east. One night it camped at Schanzkolk, a very progressive German farm; on another, at Gross Aub, a fortified police post situated on a hill which commands miles of surrounding country.

Kiriis West, sixty miles east of Keetmanshoop in a direct line, was occupied, after opposition, on the night of the 14th. Previously a small Kalahari Horse patrol under Lieut. Wessels had tried to reach and cut the railway near Itzawisis, about seventy miles away, but was not successful. Returning, it encountered the enemy in some force at Kiriis West on April 13, and got into a nasty corner. It fought hard, however, and eventually succeeded in retiring with the loss of only six casualties—two wounded (one of whom died) and four captured; the German losses were one officer killed, one man wounded, and two prisoners. The enemy evacuated Kiriis West the same night, but they returned at dawn on the 16th with two guns. The attack, however, was opened not by them but by the Eastern force, and the Germans retired with distinct haste, first on Dörstamp and then on Guruchab, minus one officer and two men killed, and one officer and six n.c.o's and men captured. There were no Union casualties. This movement had the effect of startling a body of Germans about a hundred strong that was advancing from the south-west, and it, too, retired.

The captured officer, when ordered to put up his hands, attempted to draw his revolver, "as," so he explained afterwards, "no German ever puts up his hands while he has a revolver in his possession." The Britisher promptly hit him over the face with the butt-end of his rifle, which was at least a novel and merciful way of emphasising the fact that he had the drop on his man. The prisoner later on asked when he was to be shot, and seemed surprised and relieved to hear that he need not anticipate anything near so drastic as that.

A junction with Colonel-Commandant van Deventer's column was effected at Kiriis West. Here, for the time being, I leave the Eastern force.

For the Union forces operating in the southern half of the Protectorate matters now took a very important turn. Major-General the Hon. J. C. Smuts, Minister of Defence, arrived at Kalkfontein on April 11 from the Union, and at once commenced to co-ordinate the movements of the Central, Southern, and Eastern forces, manipulating them as the Southern Army having one central headquarters. By this time the three forces were fast extending to their common centre, and it was vitally necessary that they should move in perfect unison. There was, too, every indication that the enemy had definitely resolved to refuse battle other than by the miserable expedients of dynamite and poison. Immediately on his arrival, General Smuts held a meeting of principal officers, who discussed and settled a revised plan of operations. The keynote of that plan was unity and rapidity of movement, in order to prevent the enemy concentrating on any portion of our advance, and yet lead up to as decisive an action as circumstances would allow. Thus the new G.O.C. developed the advances of General McKenzie, of Colonel van Deventer, and of Colonel Berrangé into one big enveloping movement with the object of bottling the German Southern force estimated at about 800 of all ranks, in Keetmanshoop or thereabouts.

The Central force had now reached Aus, and, like all other portions of the Southern Army, was in country which could reasonably be relied on to supply all that was necessary in the way of food, grass, and water. Therefore, with his mounted men General McKenzie left the railway and cut across country, through Bethany and Berseba, to Gibeon, 106 miles north of Keetmanshoop. Colonel Berrangé, instead of going direct to Keetmanshoop, left Kiriis West in a north-westerly direction, making for Kabus and Itzawisis, twenty-five miles north of Keetmanshoop. Colonel-Commandant D. van Deventer, on Colonel van Deventer's right flank, moved up to Spitzkoppe and Daweb to work in conjunction with Colonel Berrangé. Colonel van Deventer, with Colonels Celliers and Bouwer, moved up from Kalkfontein, but at Kanus an independent column under Colonel Celliers branched out to occupy Seeheim, following the railway route, and Colonel Bouwer, with Hartigan's Horse, the Karoo Schuiters, the 17th Mounted Rifles, and Enslin's Horse, proceeded with Colonel van Deventer through the mountains direct on Keetmanshoop.

By the night of the 16th all these forces were on the move. The first to encounter the enemy was that under Colonel Celliers, whose scouts had a brush with a strong patrol to the south of Seeheim on the night of the 17th. The Germans lost nine killed, four wounded, and fourteen taken prisoner, but themselves inflicted no damage. About the same time a special patrol belonging to the Central force approached Seeheim from the west. Seeheim was then occupied by a force of 300 Germans, with two guns, who, however, seem to have taken fright at these patrols, mistaking them, perhaps, for the main body. Anyhow, they beat a precipitate retreat, leaving rolling stock, including an engine, behind. They would not even stay to blow up the big £30,000 railway bridge over the Great Fish River, though the holes for the dynamite were already drilled. This was the only bridge on the whole southern railway system that the enemy left intact. Colonel Celliers entered Seeheim in force on the 19th.

The Germans left on the 18th and made for Keetmanshoop, thirty miles eastwards, where there was a big German camp, which they warned. A general and instant retirement followed the next day. At the same moment Colonel van Deventer was making a rapid march in an endeavour to cut off the enemy's retreat. He reached the outskirts of the town at dawn on the 20th, too late, of course, to achieve his object. The escape of the Germans was a severe blow. There was, however, a chance that they would be intercepted by the Union forces north and east of Keetmanshoop.

Keetmanshoop was formally surrendered to the Union forces by the Burgermeister, Herr Bruno Müller. About a hundred inhabitants were left behind. According to the Windhuk Press, " the women-folk were treated with every possible respect and with great courtesy by the enemy, who have paid in cash for all foodstuffs requisitioned and whose personal bearing towards the farmers and their families has in every case been thoughtful and friendly "! This was written, however, not at the time that the burghers were "known" to be "dissipated" and all the rest of it, but when the fall of Windhuk was imminent and the editorial person in some danger of meeting with retribution for the pictures that his profound knowledge of Union soldiery had led him to draw and print. So, perhaps, the testimony is suspect, having been written with ulterior motive. But it is the case, nevertheless, that not only the women but the men also were treated with every show of decency, elsewhere as well as in Keetmanshoop.

Curiously enough, in normal times the population of Keetmanshoop was very largely made up of Dutch South Africans. Out of a total of 350 civilians only 110 were Germans; 197 were Dutch South Africans, and 38 were English. This is the more extraordinary when it is understood that Keetmanshoop was not only the seat of the Deputy-Governor for the Southern portion of the Protectorate, but that it was the greatest military centre in the country. From a commercial point of view it had no significance whatever. Before retiring, the German troops demolished the telegraph and telephone installations, but did no other damage.

Subsequently General Smuts issued an order in which he reviewed the recent arduous operations and expressed grateful appreciation of the services of both officers and men, observing that the then position marked the conclusion of an important stage in the operations of the Southern campaign. He specially commended the work of Colonel van Deventer, and announced that in recognition of his services that officer was promoted to the rank of Brigadier-General.

General van Deventer earned his distinction by hard work and real results. He acted as "fighting general" to General Smuts during the Boer War. He thus came into this campaign with a fund of experience, which he utilised to the best effect. He is a big man with a kindly heart, and is admitted to be a military tactician of no mean order. His name, by the way, comes from the quaint old town of Deventer, in Holland, the home of his forebears.

CHAPTER XII.

GIBEON.

THE FINAL STAGE.

The new stage in the Southern campaign of which General Smuts spoke in his order to the troops turned out to be the last stage. It was wound up at Gibeon, 106 miles north of Keetmanshoop, in an engagement that had the effect of removing the enemy from this sphere of operations, entirely and completely. The final movement was carried out by the mounted men of the Central force, under Sir Duncan McKenzie, after a series of forced and arduous marches that constitute, undoubtedly, one óf the most dashing feats of the whole German South-west Expedition.

When General McKenzie's column left Aus on April 15 his three brigades had to follow each other at intervals of a day, owing to water troubles. They were not able to work together as one whole force until Berseba was reached, 150 miles away, where there was open water in plenty. Thereafter they had no anxieties on this score. But until then the position, if not actually fraught with danger, certainly resulted in clogging their movements; and McKenzie, be it remembered, was now marching against time. There was a 44-mile trek for the first water out of Aus, which was at Kuibis, where, however, the position was literally none too sweet. The wells that the Germans had not poisoned they had contaminated with putrid flesh, and when the supplies had been pumped to the required degree of innocuousness the wells gave out, as if in resentment at this overworking of them. The Engineers, assisted by a company of the Kimberley Regiment that had been installed as a garrison, worked at these wells like Trojans in order that the general scheme of things should be facilitated. Yet it took exactly twelve hours to water the horses of the first brigade.

Kuibis is a pretty little village lying in a ravine some two miles from the railway siding of that name, which is 127 miles out of Lüderitzbucht. Kuibis village is a veritable oasis in the desert. The western desert belt is really past and done with at Aus, but sandy, barren patches are occasionally met with on the plateau. There is one at Schakkalskuppe, a geographical spot midway between Aus and Kuibis; and compared with Schakkalskuppe, Kuibis is very green and very pleasing, and very refreshing. About two miles from the village, and still in the ravine, is what was a Government experimental farm, but it was nothing at all when we passed it, save a proved experiment in ruin and desolation.

From Kuibis the column went due north-west, crossing the railway and leaving it on the left some seven miles east of the siding, making the old mission station of Bethany for the first halt. Once away from the railway and no more poisoned or contaminated water was met with, nor were dynamite traps encountered. Experience on the Southern and Eastern forces shows that the Germans did not necessarily confine their poison and dynamiting exploits to the vicinity of the railway, and one can only assume therefore that in deviating from the railway route McKenzie quite upset German calculations and expectations. The Germans had sought to lure the Union troops on to a mine-field at Schakkalskuppe, but the lure was rather too obvious to succeed. It consisted of a fence erected across the road. The most natural thing for anyone to do when one's path is obstructed is to go round the obstruction; but other things, too, must be natural, and that fence was not natural. Hence the Engineers inquired into the matter and discovered and fired a series of no fewer than fifteen mines. Had these mines gone off exactly as the Germans devised them to—had Union troops walked round the obstruction—there would have been little left of the Brigade that first passed that way; as it was, pieces of scrap-iron the size of oranges fell harmlessly over a 250-yard radius, and huge chunks of iron rails and sleepers dropped 100 yards away. But that was the last of dynamite warfare.

On the way to Bethany and along other stretches beyond, the column encountered a formation of country that was quite new to them. Instead of sand or bush, the underfoot was one mass of stones ranging from the size of tennis balls to that of footballs, and often as smooth. The wear and tear on the horses was heavy, and shoes were cast almost by the hundred. Instead of open rolling plain, it was hilly, and the hills were noticeable for the reason that so many of them had table tops. It was as if some giant with a mammoth sword had strutted over this very route toying with the hills as a boy with a cane toys with dandelions, by slicing off their heads. Could one imagine this really to have happened one would say that this giant had made devastating progress.

Bethany was deserted, but it yielded stock and plenty of water of a kind, to which the troops had unrestricted approach. The water here wells up out of the ground at the rate of 144,000 gallons a day, but it is heavily impregnated with lime and carries a normal temperature of 82 degrees, so it was more refreshing as a bath than as a drink. A company of the Kimberley Regiment arrived at Bethany before the mounted men had all passed through to take up garrison duty. They covered the seventy miles from Aus in three days, and had stood the ordeal remarkably well. Some time before, I know, when the question of the capacity of the infantry cropped up, Colonel Byron guaranteed that the men of his brigade would do 100 miles a week, keep it up, and fight on it. Here was the proof of their marching capacity.

Though little more than a third of the distance to Gibeon, Bethany became a sort of "half-way house" to the front, and the garrison set itself out to play the part of host to everybody that halted there on the great rush north-eastwards. Food was a problem with them, because owing to the lack of transport their own rations were reaching them only irregularly, and at times they went on quarter issues in order to eke out their supplies. But they dispensed comfort and kindliness in other ways. They offered you a hot bath, or a swim in the small bath there; they gave you a shake-down in their guest chamber, which happened to be a part of the local gaol, but not the dark cell with its ankle and body irons firmly riveted in the walls; and they showed you fragrant flower-beds, for in the meantime they had directed all surplus water on to the cultivated but latterly neglected plots and revivified them. Thus, in addition to flowers, they brought up lucerne, which the lucky horses revelled in; and I have no doubt if the Gibeon rout had been delayed and this garrison had been retained at Bethany, that they would have produced fruits in due season, for there are orchards and one or two date-palm groves and a few vineries about.

After leaving Bethany Sir Duncan McKenzie got his first scent of the enemy. His scouts surprised half-a-dozen Germans at a small place called Besondermaid, 44 miles further on, and shot one, a sergeant. The scouts, by the way, were now in charge of Captain L. B. Nicholson, of the 1st Imperial Light Horse, who had reached the force just before the occupation of Aus. Captain Nicholson was a most energetic Intelligence officer, and rendered invaluable service.

Besondermaid gave open water and facilities for bathing, but there was little opportunity to take advantage of them. So far, the column had covered 115 miles in four days. After a six hours' bivouac it was pushed on to Berseba on information that the enemy were moving in that direction in some number. Six miles from Berseba it halted until near dawn, and at dawn it closed on the town. German pickets, however, raised the alarm and the movement resolved itself into a straight chase of a troop of enemy horse through Berseba into the country beyond. The Germans were practically all rounded up—two officers and 28 men; one man had been killed. The column also captured 54 rifles and bayonets, and ammunition, 700 head of cattle, and 5,000 small stock. Patrols from General van Deventer's column at Keetmanshoop rounded up other booty in the Berseba district a few days later : 60 horses, 20 ox-wagons, a number of donkeys, lots of cattle and several light carts.

A most interesting episode in this Berseba charge came to light after it was all over. It appears that shortly after leaving Besondermaid the column was not only observed but joined by a German scout. It was then quite dark. He left at the halt before Berseba and reported to his officers that an English force of tired men and exhausted animals had camped some distance back, and were likely to reach the town by about 9 a.m., but certainly not before. If his judgment had been near as good as his bravery the troop would have got away.

The prisoners were sent straightaway to Lüderitzbucht for transportation to the Union. On the way two escaped, but were recaptured and, one presumes, suitably dealt with. After they were recaptured it is recorded that the senior German officer approached the officer in charge of the guard with a request that the two men be handed over to him for punishment. It seemed an extraordinary request, but there was no mistaking its terms. These men must be shot, he said.

He was informed—with regret—that it could not be. But he was asked why he should be so severe on his men for attempting what, it was to be presumed, he would do himself if he got the chance.

His reply was first a look of great pity and then these words : "I have decided to shoot them for deserting from the German Army"!

About this time, also, a number of refugees were rounded up who were trekking, by order, to Windhuk with all their belongings, including much stock. Their trek was deflected, and it ended at Aus. There were several women in this party ; one the wife of a German officer who was also captured and who is the brother of a once-prominent professional man on the Rand. Both this officer and his wife spoke English well, but I am afraid the lady was no lover of the Union, and she never lost an opportunity of letting the Union troops know that they could never have been German soldiers, as in the German Army they took only gentlemen. They treated her well, her delusions notwithstanding.

There was good though limited water at Berseba, where circumstances compelled the column to remain a day or two. Officers and men were at breakfast next morning when they were startled at finding themselves under fire. The shooting finished as suddenly as it started. It transpired that the marksmen were a party of 150 Germans who had approached from the south-east, evidently unaware of our occupation of the place. On discovering their mistake they dropped a few chance shots into camp and cleared. The 8th Mounted Brigade, under Lieut.-Colonel Arnott, immediately gave chase, and hung on to them for several hours; indeed, it did not get back to camp until well into the following day. There were several exchanges of rifle fire, and in these the Brigade lost one man wounded and several horses, while an n.c.o. fell into German hands. But Colonel Arnott returned with several prisoners.

This party was no doubt the left flank of the German army that had fallen back from Keetmanshoop before General van Deventer's advance. It had since then been attacked by Colonel Berrangé and Colonel-Commandant D. van Deventer, and was now in hasty retreat northwards.

Colonel Berrangé, when he left Kiriis West on April 16, occupied Stampried and then moved north and north-west to beyond Spitzkoppe and Daweb, working on the right of Colonel-Commandant van Deventer. The object was to cut the railway near Itzawisis and intercept the enemy's retirement north. On the 19th it was decided to move on Kabus, where there were signs of German activity. Kabus was formerly a military training school, having accommodation for 1,500 men in substantial buildings; it is five miles east of the railway and twenty miles to the north of Keetmanshoop. It transpired later that the enemy had concentrated at Kabus with about 600 men, two field-guns, and ten machine-guns.

Colonel-Commandant van Deventer reached Kabus first and was soon heavily engaged with the enemy, who used their machine-guns to great advantage. This was on the morning of the 20th. Colonel Berrangé got up with the Bechuanaland Rifles, under Lieut.-Colonel Cowan, in the afternoon, and succeeded in working round the enemy and eventually in rushing the place. The Germans crumbled up with surprising suddenness, but they managed to make good their escape. They left behind two killed, twenty-five wounded, three prisoners. At one time we held fourteen other German prisoners, but these managed to escape during the fighting. Four of the wounded were found in a deserted ambulance. It is believed that the German killed and wounded altogether totalled at least forty. The Union casualties were twenty-seven, made up of two killed, eight wounded, and eighteen prisoners. A vast amount of military stores was taken.

The Eastern force camped that night, the 20th, in Kabus. Subsequently, patrols moved up the line, one getting to within twenty-three miles of Gibeon, but the country by this time was quite clear of enemy. On the 28th Colonel Berrangé formed camp at Daberos, some forty miles to the north-east of Kabus. The pursuit of the Germans was now entirely in the hands of the Central force, moving in from the left.

General McKenzie, however, was too late to cut the retreating force off, though he had not spared himself in any particular. Men were on quarter rations and feeling the want of sound, undisturbed sleep, while the horses, now living entirely on the country, were being only scantily fed, and as they were doing double duty the whole time they too were fast becoming exhausted. But the column was obviously on the tail of the enemy, and McKenzie determined to push on at all hazards. He left Berseba on the night of April 24, and next morning was beyond Kokerboom Naute, nineteen miles away, with water and grazing around him in plenty. It was a great temptation to stay here for rest, but before the day was out scouts reported suspicious dust clouds at Aretitis, forty miles south of Gibeon. There was no hesitation. " Boot and saddle " was the order, and the six miles to Aretitis were got over at a spanking pace. The results were disappointing—only two prisoners, besides wagons and stock. Next day the track of the enemy was followed to Gründorn, and the following night a surprise march to kilo. 152 was done. The force was now only twelve miles south of the important station of Gibeon.

The enemy, however, was still " somewhere ahead," and officers and men were inclined to become dispirited. In an hour the whole situation had changed. It was noticed that the telegraph and telephone wires appeared to be intact. They were tapped, and suspicions were proved to be well founded. The thorough-going German militarist had been guilty of a flagrant lapse. The messages that were subsequently read off, which were passing from one German station to another, showed that he was not only careless but also extremely stupid.

German scouts and others, it seems, had been reporting the approach of the " English "; even that the " English " were close to Gibeon. The Germans in authority not only doubted, they disbelieved. A Lieut. Fincke, who had been engaged in dynamiting the line from Keetmanshoop northwards, announced that the railway had been occupied by " the enemy " as far as Tses. To this point he had been able to damage the line only slightly, "owing to shortness of time," but onward he had " secured better results." The " English," he further reported, were moving along the Fish River route and a strong party was in advance, but their horses were tired. Lieut. Fincke's was apparently the Eastern patrol, and he inquired about the Western patrol, intimating that if the two could get into touch they would attack.

But the Germans as a whole would have none of it. Most messages contained this phrase : " Don't believe it, they only saw dust." " Quite impossible," said Gibeon to Marienthal, but this message also contained the naïve admission, "Don't know what is happening!" Someone asked someone else, "Where are the Tommies?" The Tommies were exactly twelve miles away, laughing hugely at Teutonic incredulity, and the Germans were soon to know it.

These, however, are the lighter turns in the information that was being gathered in from the wires. The meat of it all was contained in the statement that the German force was leaving Gibeon that night for Marienthal, a station forty miles northwards, where they were to establish a new post.

Almost simultaneously, his scouts reported to Sir Duncan McKenzie that a party of 200 Germans was on the move near kilo. 162, six miles further on. The column instantly pushed on, and by nightfall was some five miles south of Gibeon station. The advance party had already reported great activity at the station, where a train with steam up could plainly be seen. At last was there something tangible for those eleven days and nights of ceaseless manœuvring. No time was lost in drawing up plans for an attack. It was a moonlight night.

Within an hour a party of Intelligence men under Captain Nicholson, and of Engineers under Captain L. H. Grier, about thirty with all, was working round the German positions. Their instructions were to blow up the railway line to the north of Gibeon. Shortly afterwards Lieut.-Colonel Royston with his 9th Mounted Brigade and the Umvoti Mounted Rifles from the 8th Mounted Brigade was despatched with instructions to take up a position in the rear of the Germans and so prevent their retirement. The general advance from the south was timed to take place at dawn.

At first calculations went sadly agley. The railway line was blown up, Royston got right behind the German positions—so secure evidently did the Germans consider themselves that they had dispensed with outposts—and yet something like disaster occurred. The railway was blasted at eleven o'clock, and the noise naturally led to a German investigation. This was made by four mounted scouts, who ran right into the advanced lines of the 9th Mounted Brigade. Colonel Royston had disposed three squadrons of Natal Light Horse and one of Imperial Light Horse along the railway embankment some four miles north of the station. The remainder stood by away to the east, along with the horses. The country was exceptionally flat; it offered no natural cover of any kind. The German scouts were called upon to surrender, and on refusing they were fired at; one got away.

This, of course, brought the enemy along in force, and by 2 a.m., when the moon was still high up, terrific firing was in progress. The Germans took up positions on the west side of the railway and also behind a short embankment running from the railway embankment on the east side like the down-stroke of a T, and this was the most damaging position of all. From the others the Britishers were to some extent screened by the railway embankment, but this one they were wholly exposed to. The Germans mounted a machine-gun here, and they had of necessity to use it at point blank range. It were commonplace to say that the Brit'sn lines were enfiladed; they were swept as with a jet of molten lead. They also came under the fire of two field-guns spitting forth shrapnel, and they were in no little danger, too, from the enemy on the western face of the embankment, though this, perhaps, was more apparent than real. But the two sets of combatants were so near to each other that when it was decided to retire on the main body the fatal word had to be whispered along from man to man lest the Germans should overhear it.

Owing to a break in the lines the retirement order did not reach the whole length, with the result that 70 officers and men of the Natal Light Horse were left behind, and when daylight appeared and they saw the utter hopelessness of their position they surrendered. They had little option in the matter.

It is amazing, indeed, that any of them saw the dawn of another day, a miracle that at any rate they came through unwounded. Some of their comrades, it transpired, were hit in as many as thirty different places. The casualty list read: 24 killed, 47 wounded, 70 prisoners.

The unfortunate happening was much discussed at the time. I know that many men had great difficulty in appreciating the need for so ostentatious a manner of wrecking the railway as blasting it, since this gave good warning to the Germans that they were in peril. But nothing quite so much matters, I think, as the position that the Union troops took up. It has been said that when daylight appeared it was found to be much nearer the station than was contemplated. Be this as it may; but the position could not possibly have been worse. It could have been better, and that it was not better would seem to point pretty clearly to over-hurried dispositions. The failure to take in that storm-water embankment is a big responsibility, especially as the night was moonlight, which rendered some survey possible of the area that was being occupied.

And yet, one supposes, all's well that ends well. In three hours the tables were completely turned. In six hours the German Southern army was a beaten and demoralised rabble, greatly reduced in number, and in precipitate flight.

The Germans persisted in being stupid to the end. After the engagement on the embankment side they returned to their camp almost drunk with elation. They seemed satisfied that the seventy unwounded officers and men whom they had captured and the seventy-one officers and men whom they had killed and wounded constituted the whole of the force that had assailed them. They shook hands all round, they danced, they sang, and they smashed captured rifles over their cartwheels the while. They remained supremely indifferent to the needs of the moment.

But all this time Sir Duncan McKenzie was busy with fresh dispositions, and instead of moving at daybreak he expedited matters by over two hours. His object now was to strike quickly and strike hard. There was to be no attempt at finesse. In order to narrow the sphere of operations he sent one regiment of Natal Carbineers to the east (the 2nd, under Lieut.-Colonel Woods) and three squadrons of the 1st regiment (under Lieut.-Colonel Montgomery) to the west, with instructions to contain the enemy on their flanks; the remaining squadrons of Carbineers acted as the advance screen. Two squadrons of Natal Mounted Rifles, with their Brigadier (Lieut.-Colonel Arnott), remained with the General, a third acted as escort to the guns, and the fourth accompanied the transport.

Dawn found the Britishers on three sides of the Gibeon camp, close in. The first object to be sighted was the engine, still with steam up. On this the guns of the 12th Citizen Battery were trained and two 15-pounder shells loosed on it. The effect was electrical. Not only were there great confusion and commotion, but the white flag rose as if by magic. That, however, was for the surrender not of the force but of the train, which we found shortly afterwards, was replete with everything for carrying on war by dynamite. It was made up of engine, tender, water-tank wagon, four open trucks, and two box trucks. One of the box trucks contained several varieties of explosives; elsewhere in the train were three cases of land-mines and two of lyddite. Had our 15-pounders registered a direct hit there would have been no living thing left within a radius of half-a-mile. It is fortunate that no such happening occurred, as the captured Union troops were quartered near the train, which was the centre of the camp; as it was they came under the fire of their own comrades, which was, perhaps, inevitable in the circumstances.

The Germans, who were under von Kleist, then began a hurried retirement, but by this time our guns and all our troops were in action. The advance was like a hurricane. In a very few minutes after hostilities opened the Germans had been deprived of their prisoners and were themselves forced to fight or submit to capture. Mostly they fought. At first they put up a good rearguard action, and they handled their machine-guns magnificently, but nothing that they could do could stem the dash and the vigour of McKenzie's offensive. The 12th Citizen Battery, which raced from position to position, speedily put the German guns out of action; one shell blotted out a mule span as it stood; another disabled the second span, and though this was reinforced, the pursuing troops rode the whole piece to a standstill, as they did the four machineguns. At first advancing under cover of the guns, our mounted men manœuvred with conspicuous precision; they maintained perfect extended order; they advanced, dismounted, fired, mounted, and advanced again with disciplined smartness. The Germans frankly admitted their surprise, their discomfiture, and finally their admiration.

In all, the Germans were chased from position to position for a distance of twenty miles, until, in fact, exhaustion became the arbiter and decreed an end to the chase. It was with regret that it had to be given up, for the bulk of the enemy's Southern army had got away. That, however, was due to circumstances over which Sir Duncan McKenzie had little control. The Germans showed wretched horsemanship, but they were unquestionably better mounted. That was a big advantage. Then the country was " wicked "—rocky and difficult; but the Germans, knowing their line of retreat, nursed a road along the Great Fish River route, and this was not available to troops executing an enveloping movement. So here, too, they had the advantage.

The action ended at 11.30 a.m. There was no doubt about the state of men and horses. They were simply dead tired. They had been on the go incessantly, night and day, since the 16th, and it was now the 27th; and in the intervening eleven days and nights they had covered 210 miles of country, mostly " wicked " trekking country, lived on ever-dwindling rations until rations ceased to be, and gone more and more without sleep until sleep and they seemed strangers. It has been quaintly put that men had a possible fifty-two hours sleep on this trek, but that they had to find " stables " and pickets out of it; and a witty officer declared that after the first five days he was either trying to keep awake or endeavouring to get to sleep; there was almost invariably something turning up to intrude on the moments when sleep was permissible. At any rate, after the action, most men lay down and slept where and just as they were. The tension was broken. They had been triumphing over nature; now nature was triumphing over them.

The known German casualties were eight killed, 30 wounded, 166 unwounded prisoners. The booty included the train, two field-guns with limbers and 80 shells all in good condition;

Grave of Capt. de Meillon (Intelligence Staff) in Aus Nek, as remodelled by the Transvaal Scottish. On the left Col. the Hon J. J. Byron, C.M.G.

At Kuibis. On Railway Fatigue

Begoggled Officers of the 1st Transvaal Scottish in the Desert.

Brig.-General Skinner and Staff.

"*A very gallant gentleman.*"

[*Photo: Duffus.*

COLONEL SIR GEORGE FARRAR, D.S.O., Bart.,
whose death by a railway accident caused mourning
throughout South Africa.

The Trolley after the accident resulting in Sir George Farrar's death.

Motor Car emerging from the bed of the Great Fish River.

four machine-guns, two of them in working order, with large quantities of ammunition, rifles and loose ammunition, twenty wagons, spans of mules and oxen, thirteen draught camels, 2,000 small stock, cattle, and donkeys.

Our final casualties were twenty-two killed in action, six died of wounds, sixty wounded; but there were only four killed and eight wounded in McKenzie's great charge, and five others were wounded while they were prisoners in the German camp.

Thus did Sir Duncan McKenzie turn the initial disaster at Gibeon into a brilliant rout of the enemy, which will live in the pages of the history of the campaign. It is a notable achievement in many ways. It is a notable achievement because, of course, it smashed up a big enemy force and demoralised it. It is a notable achievement because it so utterly upset the enemy's calculations. One prisoner was mystified as to how the column got its water. He thought it must have a very large number of water-carts, but of an entirely new make. He would readily have believed us if we had told him that Burroughs and Wellcome had invented tabloid water and that the men had carried their water rations in their trousers' pockets! Another thought it impossible for the Germans to be overtaken; and he was surprised not only that they were overtaken, but that the column that did overtake them had sufficient vitality left to do battle against them, a strong force well equipped with guns. He was also surprised and not a little disappointed that the troops who had shown such great discipline, such great dash, and such great bravery were Colonial troops, and not British Regulars. This second point of view is one that was pretty generally held by all the Germans. Then it is a notable achievement because of the stamina and the dash both of the men and their leader.

But it is also a notable achievement because of the dogged determination to win over adverse circumstances that Sir Duncan McKenzie showed from the day that he left Aus. For some reason or other, prior to Aus there had been little display of those characteristics that had won him fame and distinction as a dare-devil, dashing leader of mounted troops. Until the Central force moved out from Tschaukaib he was, we know, more or less the subject or the victim of the effects of the Rebellion in the Union. Yet at Garub his troops were camped within striking distance of the enemy, and they did not strike. Some blow ought to have been struck, if only for the sake of the morale of the force, which was being gradually sapped away by the actual daily spectacle of the enemy working away at fortifications and entrenchments without the slightest let or hindrance. The opinion has been expressed that the work that was accomplished at Gibeon should have been done at Aus, and the cost of all subsequent operations thus have been avoided. At any rate, in the immortal phrase of General Joffre, Sir Duncan should have nibbled at the enemy's positions.

When he did move forward from Aus he was more or less out of touch with his enemy; that this should ever happen is bad military tactics. Then he received a nasty set-back in the poisoned water at Aus and Kuibis, which badly hampered his movements, and made it extremely doubtful if he would ever overtake the Germans or intercept them. Finally, there was the initial disaster at Gibeon. These were influences enough to dishearten any commander. General McKenzie rose superior to them, and that is why I make special mention of his set tenacity of purpose. In the march to Gibeon and in the charge at Gibeon he displayed all the dash and daring with which his name is associated.

The result of Gibeon was to bring the Southern campaign to an abrupt termination. The following day General Smuts, who had moved from Keetmanshoop to Aus, issued a proclamation announcing that the Defence Forces of the Union of South Africa were in occupation of enemy territory to the latitude of Gibeon (actually the territory known as Great Namaqualand); and controlling the movement of civilian occupants and of movable stock. General Smuts left Aus on April 29 for Swakopmund on a visit to and to confer with General Botha.

Orders were also issued for the early return of the troops to the Union, and the first transport left Lüderitzbucht for the Cape on May 19, 1915. The troops at Gibeon did not get back until some weeks later. The 1st Infantry Brigade, however, consisting of the 1st Transvaal Scottish, the Rand Light Infantry, the Witwatersrand Rifles, and the Pretoria Regiment, was transferred to the Northern Army and took a prominent part in the campaign under General Botha. Colonel Beves, the Brigadier, was eventually promoted to Brigadier-General.

It was at first decided to garrison the Southern territory with the Cape Town Highlanders Regiment, which was actually installed in the various centres, but later on the Highlanders were transferred to General Botha's command in the north, and replaced by the South African Mounted Rifles (which is the permanent garrisoning force) under Colonel Berrangé.

There was a certain amount of railway building to be done after the withdrawal of the troops, but a month saw the work completed, while by the end of June the southern system had been linked up with that of the Union, *via* Kalkfontein, Nakob, and Upington.

Unfortunately, the elation that was felt over the success of the Southern campaign became heavily clouded by an occurrence of the saddest possible nature. I refer to an accident that led to the most untimely death of Colonel Sir George Farrar, Bart., D.S.O., Assistant Quartermaster-General, who only a month before had been promoted to full Colonel and received the congratulations of the Minister of Defence " on this well-earned promotion." On May 19 Sir George Farrar had motored out by rail trolley from his headquarters at Kuibis (kilo. 203) to Brackwasser (kilo. 250) on the business of a new supply base wherefrom to despatch convoys to Gibeon. He returned late that night, in a driving rainstorm, which made it difficult to see very far ahead. When at kilo. 208, where there is a big curve, which is carried on banking about 12 ft. high, the motor colliding with a construction train coming from Kuibis. Owing to the rain-mist the oncoming engine could neither be seen nor heard until a second before the impact. Sir George, who was seated in front, jumped for safety, but the train caught him and he was hurled down the embankment; he sustained internal injuries. The driver, Pte. Henwood, of the S.A. Engineer Corps, received fatal injuries. The only other occupant, Lieut. Bradley, V.C., Witwatersrand Rifles, was severely but not dangerously injured.

Medical attendance was quickly on the spot. A fatal termination was not expected to Sir George Farrar's injuries, but at three o'clock next morning complications set in. An hour later he was delirious, and an hour after that he had passed away. The news sent a shock throughout the whole of South Africa, but it was particularly felt by those who had been connected with the Central Force and had experienced the great benefits of the capacity for organisation which he possessed in so remarkable a degree. I was a frequent visitor at his "caboose," and I have had occasion already in these pages to refer to his work. He was a great man. He never had in view more than the object of advancing the interests of the Expedition in general and of the Central force in particular in every way that he knew or could devise. He had his own methods, and they did not please everybody. The results of those methods gave satisfaction to and were the admiration of all ranks. They made the Central force a standard in those conditions that apply to Quartermaster-General's departments. He was always thinking of his work; it is pathetically significant that in his delirium he talked about little else, of the new transport that was arriving, about feeding the soldiers up at the front. That was typical of him, his looking ahead. At times he affected a despondency at the slow progress that the force was making; but almost the last words he spoke showed that he was not unmindful of what had been done. "When we consider the conditions," he said, "we find that a great deal has been accomplished." And a great deal of that "great deal" was the work of his own self.

W. S. RAYNER.

PART II.

THE NORTHERN CAMPAIGN.

By

W. W. O'SHAUGHNESSY

Reuter's Special Correspondent with the Northern Army).

MOSENTHAL, SONS & CO.

72, Basinghall St., LONDON, E.C.

General Merchants.

ADOLPH MOSENTHAL & CO.,
Port Elizabeth.

MOSENTHAL & CO.,
East London.

MOSENTHAL BROS. & CO.,
Kimberley.

MOSENTHAL BROS., LTD.,
Johannesburg, Pretoria, and Delagoa Bay.

THE MOSENTHAL RHODESIA AGENCY,
Bulawayo and Salisbury.

BECHUANALAND TRADING ASSOCIATION, LTD.
[Adolph Mosenthal & Co., Agents],
Bechuanaland and Rhodesia.

CHAPTER I.

OPERATIONS AROUND UPINGTON.

I had previously been warned to accompany "D" Force (Col. Sir Duncan Mackenzie's) to an unknown destination, the name of which, however, was fully whispered about the club and in obscure corners, but, owing to the treachery of Maritz, who had considerately acquainted the enemy with our intentions, this expedition was suddenly cancelled, and on October 5 I boarded a train at Cape Town bound for Upington with new credentials and with little knowledge of the situation ahead beyond casual and mostly irresponsible gossip. At that time the railway was being built on from Prieska to traverse the long gap of country to Upington, through farms of such sterility that their dimensions average 80,000 acres and their price about half-a-crown an acre, as compared with farms in the Union Highveld of two to three thousand morgen, at an average cost of £3 to £4 per morgen.

My railway journey ended at Prieska, only construction trains running over the new section as far as it had been built, and I had recourse to a motor-car to convey me over the distance of 150 miles odd to Upington. The fare was £25 —a staggering figure outside South Africa—and this financial burden we distributed among three of us bound for the same destination.

That a motor-car should even attempt to traverse such a forbidding territory was in itself surprising, but still more prodigious feats were being accomplished elsewhere. Leaving Prieska at 11 a.m. one morning in a heavily laden car, our way lay over a firm track, through surroundings little different from those to be seen from the train throughout the Karoo. All this soon gave way to a type of country never observable from the main line—long stretches of sandy flats studded with a small and attenuated thorn bush lying between barren kopjes close-set with variously-shaped stones about the size of ordinary cobbles. Soon the whole earth appeared to be covered with little else, suggesting a desperate battle in the Stone Age, when the cobbles might have been used as missiles. Our way twisted on for miles through this stony area, and out once more into a sandy belt, where a different sort of scrubby little bush struggled to maintain an existence. Still not a sign of grass nor a vestige of anything edible for man or beast, and frequent remains were seen of sheep out of the few flocks kept back by the sorely-tried farmers, who had mostly contrived to remove their herds to far pastures pending the blessed advent of rain, of which it was stated that none of any account had fallen hereabouts for three years. The motor hums gaily on, never daunted at the dreary prospect or the softness of the path where it had been badly cut up by the recent passage of much heavy transport, and merely takes the loose sand as a liner takes the billows. We are not yet half way, and a further transformation in the scenery is effected. Gnarled and stunted bushes heave in view at intervals, and their shapes are mostly so grotesque that the imagination instinctively conjures up queer visions. One tree at a little distance looked like a skeleton, fleeing at the sight of several hideously contorted Bushmen armed with a variety of strange weapons. And so the illusion may be carried on indefinitely.

At half way we rested for the cool hours of night, and proceeded again at daybreak, being well on the way before the sun recommenced its fierce work. More changes now occurred; our gnarled friends had left us entirely, and the flora of our new locality had become reminiscent of a winter aspect of gorse and bracken, set among a carpet of small white quartzite chips, giving an appearance of a recent hailstorm on a rather abnormal scale. The smooth, low-lying kopjes, which carried on ceaselessly on all sides, also conveyed a new impression, and nothing more so than the idea that the sea had lately receded, leaving only glistening pebbles covering the slopes from base to top.

Eight miles out from Upington we came up with a sick, though evidently brave-hearted mule, slowly plodding its way on to the river and succour ahead. It had doubtless been superseded in a transport team, which had perforce to push on and leave it to its own resources. One of the comparatively small but pathetic incidents of war.

Towards afternoon we arrived at the edge of the Orange River, with the town of Upington straggling along the opposite bank a mile or so distant at this point. The river presented one glorious oasis of large, green, shady trees dotted about promiscuously along the banks and among the numerous "islands," the majority of which were, at this season, without the surrounding accompaniment of water, the river itself occupying only a narrow section of the broad river bed. Part of the road lay through the deep sand among the "islands," and four horses being inspanned to our car, with the assistance of the engine we made remarkably quick time, taking the pebbly-bedded river itself at a jolting run.

A few cracks from the whip and a snort or two from the motor and the top of the bank and the town itself were gained.

A sigh of relief terminated a notable journey through a remarkably dreary country under a pitiless sun.

I reported my arrival to Col. Coen Brits, then in command of the Forces at Upington, consisting of 1st Imperial Light Horse (Col. Ligertwood), Enslin's Horse, a few South African Mounted Riflemen (Captain Fisher), and 1st Durban Light Infantry (Col. Wylie).

Maritz, whose treachery was by this date fully manifest, was in camp at Van Rooyen's Vlei, about ten miles out, having performed an act which for sheer baseness has no parallel in the history of the world. Chiefly for this reason it is not my intention to dwell at length upon this infamous chapter in the annals of South Africa, but merely to lead up through a sequence of events to the actual operations in German territory; for it must not be overlooked that in the subsequent conflicts with Maritz it was Germans and German artillery from over the border that played the principal part in the encounters around Upington. Maritz himself, for some inscrutable reason, declined to carry out his oft-repeated threat to attack Upington, which for weeks remained in a state of comparative siege; the lines of communication with Prieska were constantly interrupted by the rebels and caused isolation, often for many days at a time, of the meagre forces at Upington. With the arrival of reinforcements of the Natal Light Horse, under Col. Royston, and a quick-firing battery of artillery (S.A.M.R.), under Major Roy, it was eventually decided to end the suspense and march out upon the arrogant traitor and his weak-kneed following. The first encounter took place at Keimoes, which had been occupied by an advance guard of the Union Forces, temporarily commanded by Capt. (afterwards Major) Leipoldt, Chief Intelligence Officer to Col. Brits. Maritz, supported by a strong German contingent, with artillery, at 5.30 on the morning of October 22 commenced the attack upon the town, which was at that hour garrisoned by a mere handful of Imperial Light Horse and Enslin's Horse, numbering 120 in all, who, in spite of the desperate character of the assault, gallantly contrived to hold out until reinforcements of both Imperial Light Horse, under Major Panchaud, and Natal Light Horse, under Major Watt, arrived upon the scene. Although it is stated that Maritz intended to press home the attack on Keimoes, it is a significant fact that approximately 350 only of our men managed to convert this desperate intention by 800 men and ten guns into a complete rout, the enemy turning tail and fleeing to Kakamas, in their line of retreat to the German border. Among the Germans captured at Keimoes was Count von Schwerin. It was at this fight that Maritz was shot in the knee-cap and incapacitated for some considerable time afterwards. The credit for this lucky shot was earned by the Imperial Light Horse.

From Upington to Keimoes is roughly thirty miles, and on to Kakamas another thirty, the road leading mostly through heart-breaking stretches of deep sand, creating a stupendous task for transport of any kind. Kakamas, upon which place the Germans and rebels retired, was our next objective, and leaving Keimoes at sundown on October 23, Col. Brits' force arrived at dawn on the outskirts of the Farm Settlement town. Maritz, it afterwards appeared, had left the day before in a motor-car drawn by four mules. A bed had been constructed for him in the car, and he was reported to be undergoing much pain from his wound. The Germans, with their guns, also deemed discretion the better part of valour, and early departed for their own territory. The resistance put up by the rebels at Kakamas was altogether weak, and in about an hour after the first shots were exchanged (the rebels being the first to fire) our men had gained the heights overlooking the town and were soon following hard upon the enemy's heels through the Settlement. More might have been accomplished had it not been for the fact that our horses were feeling the strain of the long night march from Keimoes, when over thirty miles were covered, even before the work of the day commenced. A smug proclamation in German which was freely distributed about Kakamas by the German contingent with Maritz read as follows, as translated into English:—

NOTICE.

To the Dutch Inhabitants of South Africa.

WHEREAS English troops have taken Ramansdrift, invaded German borders, and thereby transferred the War from Europe to South Africa, therefore I declare emphatically that the Germans are not making war against the Dutch inhabitants of South Africa; that on the contrary they are using all measures to ward off the attacks of the British troops at all points, and that they will carry on the war against the English, and against the English only, to the uttermost.

(Sgd.) SEITZ,
Imperial Governor of German South-west Africa.
Dated Windhuk,
September 16, 1914.

Added is a translation of the agreement between Maritz and the German authorities:—

AGREEMENT made and entered into by and between the Imperial Governor of German South-west Africa, as the representative of his Imperial Majesty the Emperor of Germany, and General S. G. Maritz, who is acting in the name and on behalf of a number of officers and men who are prepared to declare the independence of South Africa.

That is to say:—

(1) The said General S. G. Maritz has declared the independence of South Africa and commenced war against England.

(2) The Governor of German South-west Africa acknowledges all African forces which operate against England as belligerent forces, and they will, after further discussion, support the war against England.

(3) In the event of British South Africa being declared independent, either partially or as a whole, the Imperial Governor of German South-west Africa will take all possible measures to get that State or those States acknowledged as such by the German Empire as soon as possible, and bring them under the terms of the general conclusion of peace.

(4) In consideration of such assistance the newly formed State or States will have no objection to the German Government taking possession of Walfish Bay and the islands opposite German South-west Africa and the Cape Province.

(5) The German Empire will have no objection to the above-named States taking possession of Delagoa Bay.

(6) If the rebellion fails, the rebels who enter German territory will be recognised as German subjects, and will be treated as such.

Commenting on this treaty at the time, the *Bloemfontein Post* remarked, *inter alia*: "The last clause of this delicious treaty is perhaps the choicest morsel: 'If the rebellion fails, the rebels who enter German territory will be recognised as German subjects, and will be treated as such.' The only objection to this provision is that the rebellion will fail, and there will be no German territory in South Africa into which any rebels will be able to enter."

A truly prophetic utterance.

The people of Kakamas, who, it may be stated, were unmolested by the enemy, informed us that Maritz and his rebels and the German contingent always occupied separate camps, each flying distinct flags: the Germans their own national banner, and the rebels the Vierkleur, or old Republican flag. Apropos of this and the agreement already quoted, Mr. Merriman, addressing a public meeting at Beaufort West on October 28 of that year, ridiculed Maritz's agreement with the Germans, saying that nobody in his sober senses could imagine the Germans were going to spend money and give men to help to set up the old Vierkleur flag of the Transvaal Republic. What might happen was that the Vierkleur might be hoisted, but the German flag would be hoisted above it. He added that if this country was not a Republic, it was as good an imitation of a Republic as could be got, and this was the system of Great Britain. At this same gathering Mr. Merriman referred to an interesting meeting which had just recently taken place between General Botha and himself. Not forty-eight hours before, he said, he was shaking General Botha's hand as he was going out to head the forces in the field. He (Mr. Merriman) had then taken the liberty to remonstrate with him, saying his life was too valuable to the country to be risked. To this General Botha had replied, with deep emotion, that he did not ask his people to enter into armed conflict with their brethren unless he led them. That was a noble sentiment, which, said Mr. Merriman, ought to be laid to heart by every man in the country.

A junior commander took over the reduced situation from Col. Brits, who was required to quell bigger rebellious happenings in other parts of the Union. No sooner, however, had Col. Ben Bouwer assumed the reins at Kakamas than news came that Kemp, with a large following of rebels, was scuttling across country from the direction of Kuruman, with the intention of skirting Upington in an attempt to join hands with Maritz in German territory. Taking most of the available force with him, Col. Bouwer force-marched back through Keimoes and Upington, and formed a long line of interception from the Orange River across to the impenetrable sands of the Kalahari Desert. The river, except for the drifts, which were each strongly guarded, being in full flood, formed a natural barrier in itself. The position taken up by Col. Bouwer, besides being a natural line of earthworks, formed by sand-dunes, with at intervals dominating kopjes, was strongly held by the Imperial Light Horse, Natal Light Horse, and various district commandos, and any attack made by Kemp must always have been repulsed. At the extreme right of the line was the Orange River, extending full and indefinitely across the Union. To the extreme left lay the Kalahari, through which, it was stated, no force could penetrate without water. But the unexpected happened, and a phenomenal rainfall covered this arid area with pools of refreshing water in pans in the sand. Kemp seized this golden opportunity, and, due to our indifferent Intelligence, was away behind us making for the German border as hard as his spent animals would permit, hours before Col. Bouwer was acquainted with the occurrence.

Off our troops thundered in pursuit, the Field Artillery (S.A.M.R. Battery), with mule teams, keeping pace with the rapid movements of the horsemen. At Rooidam Farm the column came up with the rebels, and held them at bay for a whole day in the sand-dunes, with several losses to both sides.

By nightfall it appeared evident that Kemp had run his course. Distributed across his front in a half-moon was a strong force of Union troops; at his back was the illimitable Kalahari, which offered at this time nothing but sand and water. Between the Government commandos pickets were to be placed at the customary time of sundown. Kemp was well aware of such a custom, and resolved on a bold stroke. In the gathering darkness, while the ambulance wagons were trundling to and fro, and some careless confusion prevailed (the blame for which it is difficult to apportion accurately), Kemp, leading the way in a motor-car, passed through our lines, and was never caught up with again. In the rear of our force Kemp, in the darkness, came upon three men of the Imperial Light Horse, who had been in search of water. These he compelled to accompany him for many miles before releasing them to return on foot. To these men he remarked, with a laugh, " I thought I had better get through before the pickets were put out! " These instances but serve to impress one with Kemp's misdirected abilities.

In the meantime General Botha had arrived at Upington with considerable reinforcements, in readiness to oppose a strong body of Germans reported to be marching on that town.*

While the now hopeless pursuit of Kemp was being resumed by Col. Bouwer, General Botha and his staff motored over to Steenkampsputs, when, it is understood, some plain language was indulged in by the General on the subject of Kemp's second success in breaking through our lines. (It may be said, *en passant*, that it was Col. Bouwer's first command of such importance, while Kemp possessed an old reputation for military strategy and general prowess, and the local Intelligence reports submitted to Col. Bouwer can only be described as entirely misleading.)

Having seen the dust of the rebels disappear in the direction of the Swartmodder Mountains, after they had been met overnight at the Grondneus farm by Maritz's principal leaders, I took advantage of a motor-car proceeding to Upington to return to that town for a spell, after several days and nights of very hard riding. Arrived there, I found a telegram awaiting me with instructions to proceed to Cape Town immediately for duty elsewhere. There is just one incident more in con-

---

* This information proved to be entirely false, and was a further reflection upon the Intelligence as administered locally at that time.

nection with the rebellion in the Upington area, my account of which was at the time suppressed by the censor. This was the shooting of a spy at Kameelpoort during Col. Bouwer's first " hold-up " of Kemp. This spy, a cosmopolitan gentleman (he admitted having been born in Armenia, having resided in France, claimed to be a Frenchman, and spoke half-a dozen European languages, in addition to South African Dutch), was brought into the headquarter camp one fine morning by an escort of Imperial Light Horse, who stated that the prisoner had ridden up to their patrol bearing a white flag. In conversation with Col. Bouwer at his headquarters (a motor-car which did duty as an office as well as a conveyance), the newcomer stated that he had been made a prisoner by Kemp at Kuruman, that he had been compelled to accompany the rebel commando, and that he had only that morning been released by Kemp, who gave him a pony to ride and told him he was free to go wherever he chose. A swarthy individual of beady eye and insignificant stature, the prisoner's appearance was about as prepossessing as his explanation was convincing, and it occurred to Col. Bouwer to order him to be searched. A few men of the S.A.M.R., old police warriors, were accordingly " told off " for the purpose.

Denuded of every scrap of clothing, it was a pitiable figure that stood in the open camp protesting its innocence, until the suspicious appearance of the lining of one of his gaiters led to its being ripped open with a penknife, when out dropped a slip of paper upon which was written a message from Kemp to Maritz. The note, which was signed " Kemp " and countersigned by the prisoner, read as follows :—

" To Maritz,—The bearer of this note, Russell, was sent by me to you."

" To think that I just gave him my last cigarette to smoke," murmured the signalling sergeant in aggrieved tones.

A Field Court-Martial was then and there convened, the court consisting of Col. Ligertwood (I.L.H.), Major Panchaud (I.L.H.), Lieut. Munro (S.A.M.R.), Major Roy (S.A.M.R., Judge Advocate), and Lieut. N. Clarke (S.A.M.R., Prosecutor). The recommendation of this properly constituted Court was confirmed later in the day by Col. Bouwer, and the following morning at dawn the exposed spy and apparent world-adventurer was shot by a squad of the Imperial Light Horse. The prisoner, in spite of his timid appearance, remained perfectly calm to the end, even sarcastically adjuring his guard overnight " to be sure and see that the cord with which he was bound was properly tied."

In the grey chill light of early dawn, while the earth seemed to be undergoing a final shiver before the re-animating advent of the morning sun, the prisoner was to be seen carrying, at his own request, his bundle of blankets, and scrambling down the stony kopje side between files of his armed guard, to the open grave-side in a sheltered hoek, where, before the partial disrobement, necessitated by the regulations, took place, the condemned man calmly asked for a pencil and paper upon which he wrote with a steady hand an address in France whither he wished forwarded his personal belongings—a few silver coins, a cheap metal watch, and a pencil-case upon which an advertisement was inscribed calling attention to a particular brand of whisky.

It will perhaps be fitting to conclude this chapter, which covers a period when so much opposition (the now famous "Armed Protest") was exhibited to the Government's resolve to institute a campaign against German South-west Africa, with some observations made by me on my return from the Protectorate concerning German designs against the Union, from evidence I noted at points in the south which I especially made it my business to visit.

There are many variations of country in the newly-acquired Protectorate hitherto known as German South-west Africa, and while that portion from Rehoboth northwards affords splendid pasture, south of the town named the territory merges into what is apparently an extension of the Karoo. And yet it was not in good grazing areas that our German neighbours sought to establish their largest military posts. Strangely enough, there was quite an elaborate system of railways, barracks, telephones and telegraphs concentrated in the almost sterile portion of the country, and mostly dotted along the border, whereas in the northern districts, where the best farms are to be found, and cattle at least appear to thrive most successfully, military stations are few and far between.

Militarism was every bit as much the alpha and omega of this late German possession as it was of the Fatherland, and a tour through the country should convince the most sceptical of the intentions of the Germans, had not the assassinations of a year ago precipitated Germany too suddenly into a war which she was undoubtedly preparing to wage preferably a few years later.

Germany was prepared as no other nation was prepared for war (though it is generally admitted that her time was not quite ripe to shatter the world's peace), and if this has been realised in Europe, her preparations and designs in South-west Africa now lie fully exposed.

For so undeveloped a country the railway system is somewhat remarkable, and can only have been constructed for military needs. But what were the needs existing in South-west Africa for so colossal a system? They would have one believe that their millions of pounds' worth of railways, military stations, and workshops have been created for protection against the possibility of further native risings. If this were the case, then why, it may reasonably be asked, has the bulk of the wealth been expended on a series of important stations, mostly situated in the southern and almost uninhabited portion of their territory? The facts, however, will speak for themselves. At the commencement of the war the broad-gauge line, which runs through the heart of the country and is linked up with the two coast ports of Lüderitzbucht and Swakopmund, had its southern terminus at Kalkfontein, approximately only seventy miles from the Union border at Raman's Drift, and there is little doubt that the line was to have been pushed on to Warmbad, which is only forty miles from Union territory, and which, owing to its abundant spring water supply, would have made an ideal concentration and "jumping-off" place for a military expedition. As it is, the extent of the German military post at Warmbad, with its many stone and cement offices, barracks, stables, kraals and lazaretto, is out of all proportion to the obvious requirements of the district.

But the principal evidence lies at Keetmanshoop, where the military works, though on a smaller scale, are of the character of a Woolwich Arsenal. The whole of the stores and workshops are fenced in, and during the German régime no civilian was ever permitted to enter the enclosures. Some of the stores for clothing and supplies measure 140 ft. long by 40 ft. wide, and it is estimated they could hold equipment and supplies for an army of 10,000 men at least.

A rail line from the station passes through the yards, between the sheds, to facilitate the handling of large quantities of goods. Many of the buildings are of cut stone, while others are of a portable iron nature. In the machine shops there is a variety of valuable plant, including a cold-tyreing contrivance (as used in the Woolwich Arsenal), hand-lathes and drills, hand-saws and gauge-tables, planing machines and circular saws, machines for rolling metal, a quadruple forge, electric light plant, and a horizontal driving engine (curiously enough the product of a British firm) which creates the power throughout the shops. In one store alone there were racks for over 6,000 rifles, and four magazine stores which are calculated to hold two or three million rounds of ammunition apiece. Keetmanshoop, therefore, formed the base for the many stations congregated in the southern area. At Narubis, only sixty miles south-east of this base, there are artillery barracks. At Kabus, another military station, eighteen miles north-east, there are horse lines for 500 horses. At Ukamas, only a few miles from the Union border, two companies were stationed before the war, and at Namus, towards Kalkfontein, exception-

Inspection of 2nd I.L.H. by General Smuts, who is calling for "Three cheers for the King."

BRIDGING THE ORANGE RIVER.
The first Bridge, with Government supply train passing over to a large island in the centre of the river, on the Prieska-Upington Line The floods almost washed the bridge away

Rail Head Approaching Upington.

Lieut.-Col. G. CRESWELL CLARK, C.M.G., V.D.,
Commandant Railways (Johannesburg Division) Defence Rifle Corps.

Record Railway Construction.
Prieska to Upington.
130 Miles Completed in Record Time.

Field Telegraphs along Railway Line.

Col. J. P. COLLYER, Chief Staff Officer.

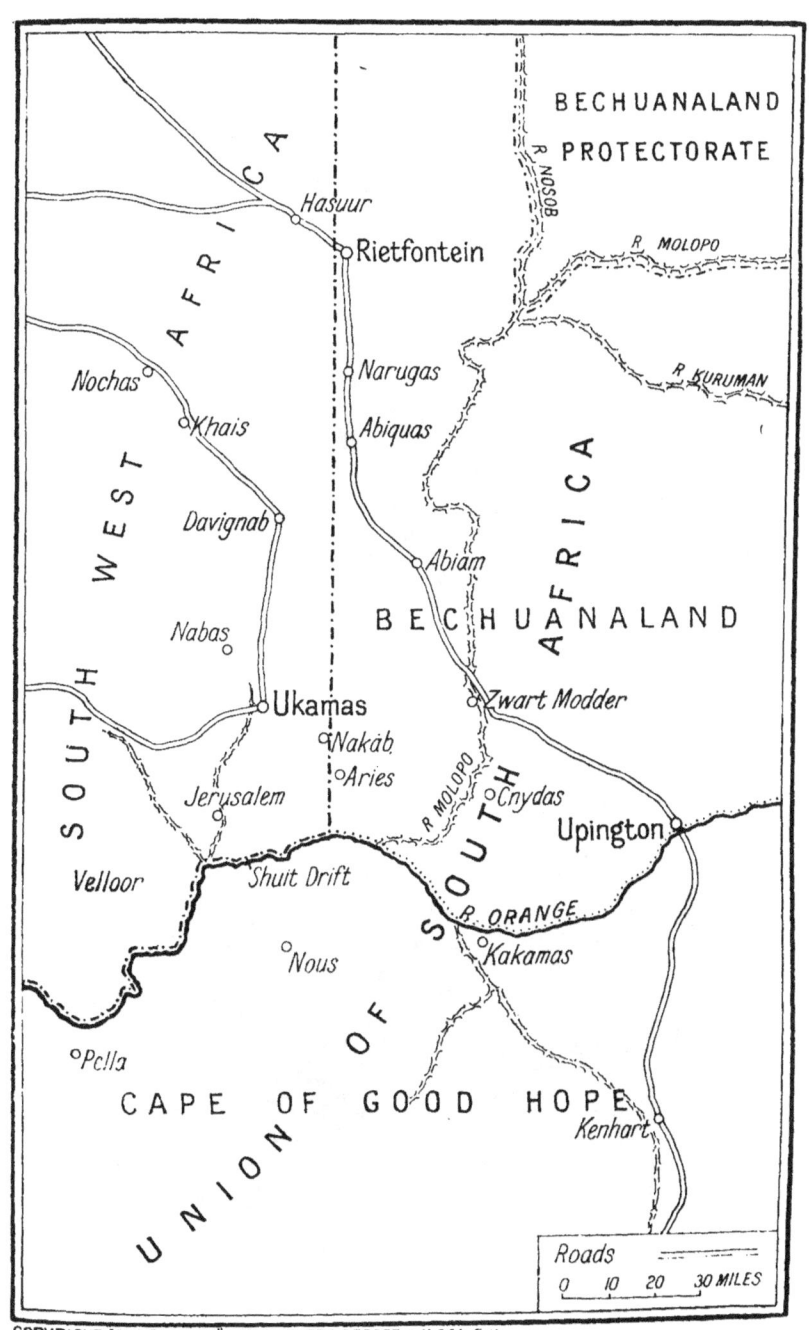

A Waterhole in the Desert.

Transport Difficulties.

Lieut. Botha driving a captured German Motor Lorry on the Railway.

Campaigning near the Orange River.

Miss Frances Botha bids farewell to Despatch Riders.

Bringing in British after Kakamas.

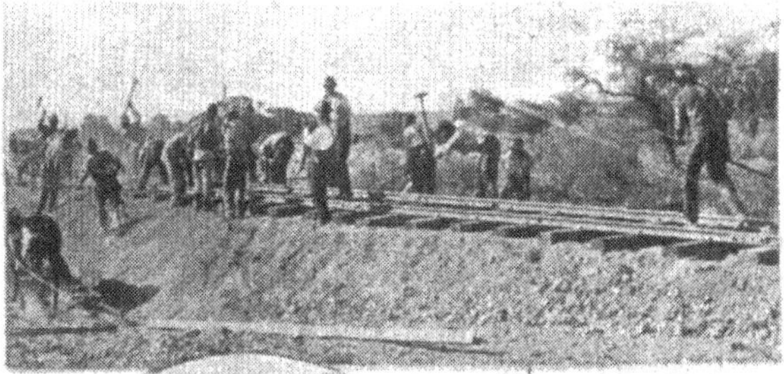

SPIKING RAILS TO SLEEPERS

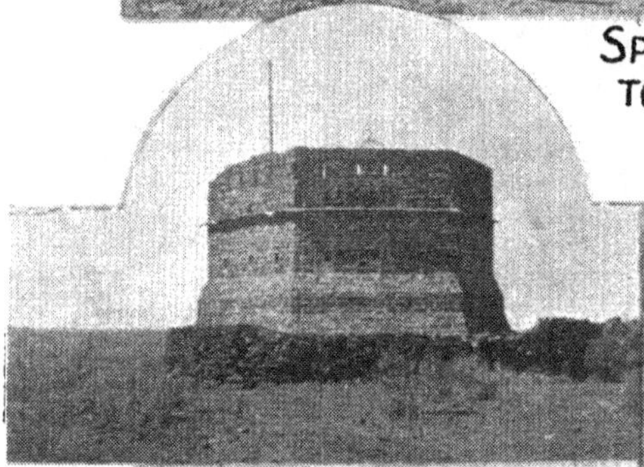

BLOCKHOUSE AT PRIESKA

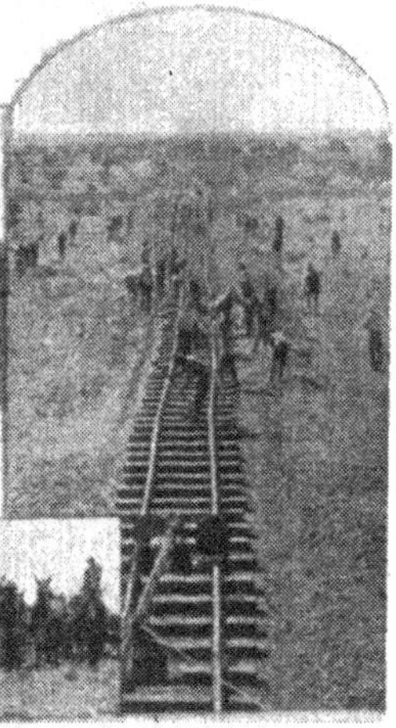

LAYING THE TRACK

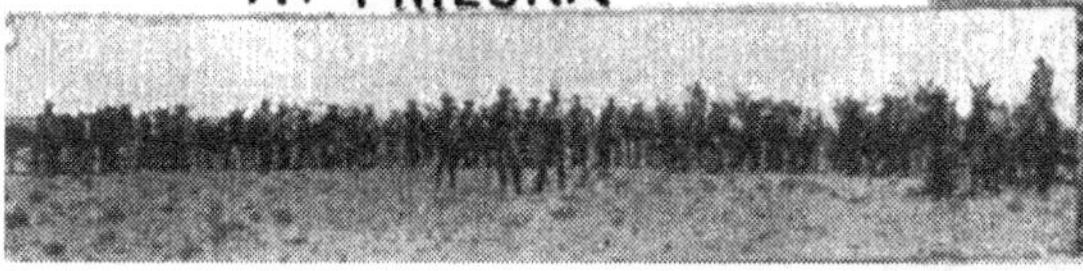

MULE TRANSPORT

HAULING RAILS.

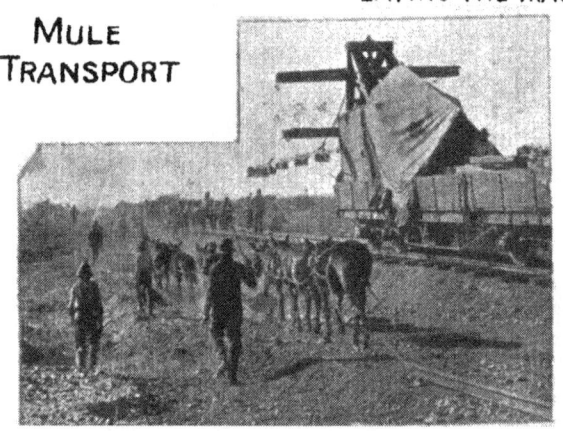

RAILWAY AND PONTOON SLIPWAY

BUILDING THE TEMPORARY BRIDGE

FIRST TRAIN CROSSING THE RIVER

ally good barracks have been erected, and here three companies were in occupation in normal times. At the outbreak of war the 8th Company was at Warmbad.

Amongst other stations which are in addition to, though quite distinct from, the ordinary police posts, and which revolve, as it were, upon Keetmanshoop, are Chamis, Arahoab, Churutabis, Chabis, and Gochas, at the last-named of which the 7th Camel Corps was posted. All the posts and stations are linked up by telegraph and telephone, and the roads lend themselves to fairly rapid motoring. Keetmanshoop is by no means the old-established town that its solid appearance suggests, and it is easy to see that it has been almost entirely fostered by the young Woolwich of German South-west Africa which reposes in its midst.

CHAPTER II.

AT WALVIS BAY.

At Cape Town I found fresh instructions awaiting me concerning a new sphere to be associated with a sea voyage, tropical climes, and an expedition to be known as the Northern force. Indeed, there had been much speculation before our embarkation on December 21 as to our precise destination, and the element of uncertainty added a charming air of mystery to the importance already attaching to the Northern Force.

For days past the troopships had been growing grimy with their long hours of loading, and uncomplainingly settled their big hulls further and further into the obliging waters, as the steady stream of men continued to flow from shore to ship. There is an end to most things, however, even to the capacity of a liner, and by sunset on a day in December, which will remain a memorable one to many, the last man had come aboard (albeit by swarming up a friendly rope at the last moment), and our particular troopship, in conjunction with others of the flotilla, cast off to the accompaniment of a spirited rendering of the inevitable "Tipperary" by the band of the Irish on the ship, and a fluttering of diminutive handkerchiefs from the quay. Slowly we wended our way to our allotted station in the Bay, there to await the dawn, and in the stillness of the night, when all lights had been obscured and our companion vessels were hardly discernible a length away, there were not a few who discovered a pretext to steal on deck for a last view of the twinkling lights of Cape Town lying sheltered beneath its giant protector.

Packed were the transports from bottom hold to upper deck with what might excusably have been taken by the uninitiated for a hopeless conglomeration of men, animals and equipment. But neither chaos nor confusion prevailed, all was as well appointed as the circumstances and the space permitted, and it soon became evident that this section, at least, of the Expeditionary Force to G.S.W.A. had been efficiently organised. All was carried on quietly and in an orderly and dignified manner, and in these days of wireless telegraphy who will deny the necessity for privacy of procedure?

Well before sunrise our flotilla was marshalled in an imposing double line, flanked by an escort of sombre though formidable men-o'-war, and before the average citizen of Green and Sea Point had awakened to an intelligent realisation of another day, Robben Island already lay far in our wake, and we were throbbing our way north to the unknown. The voyage was entirely devoid of incident. No enemy ships were seen and none was imagined. On Christmas Eve we drew away from the slower-going transports and steamed ahead, not for the Fiji Islands, but, as had cleverly been deduced by the more intellectual amongst us, for Walvis Bay. Early Christmas morning found us within the Tropic of Capricorn, negotiating the intricacies of the entrance to the Bay around Pelican Point, with the settlement showing up like a neglected Hudson Bay Company's village in the frozen North. There was a noticeable air of peace, appropriate to the day, as we dropped anchor a mile or so off the shore. But what lurked behind this suspiciously calm atmosphere? Would the enemy oppose us? There was only one way to settle the debatable point, and that was to step ashore and "make inquiries." For perhaps their knowledge of quaint tongues, the South African Irish were chosen to form the landing party at the settlement, and as a compliment, presumably, to Johannesburg, the Rand Rifles were towed in the ships' boats in the direction of the Whaling Station, some two miles further up the coast.

Those who remained on board the transports eagerly watched through their glasses the fortunes of the two parties as they drew nearer and nearer to the shore, and many an ear was strained to catch the expected report of rifle fire. But only the megaphone voice of the Naval Transport officer who supervised the parties could be heard across the placid waters of the Bay.

The jetties were already reached, and in a few moments more our troops could be seen swarming towards the town on the one hand, and the Whaling Company's property on the other. Semaphores, flags, and helios were soon in excited motion conveying the glad tidings of a bloodless victory in the reconquest of Walvis Bay.

Miles and miles and miles of unutterable desolation, to misquote an observant trooper, adequately described Walvis Bay and its environment on Christmas Day, 1914.

The township (save the mark!) consisted of a disordered array of ramshackle wooden structures, mostly in the last stages of decay, and conveying a general impression of having been deserted at least a century ago. Certainly a grim struggle for supremacy has been carried on for years between the forlorn buildings and the restless sand, and it is equally certain that the latter, up to the time of our arrival, was many points up in the desperate game.

Behind the settlement, as it was more appropriately termed by the inhabitants, the country is, as already described, dreary and illimitable stretches of sterile sand-dunes fading away to dim and misty blue mountains far back in the interior. Of the Bay itself, too much cannot be said in its praise as affording one of the finest harbours on the African coast, well accounting for the tenacity of purpose with which it has been held as a British possession for so many years.

Although situated just within the Tropic of Capricorn, Walvis Bay enjoys an astonishingly equable and pleasing climate, the temperature, according to local opinion, seldom advancing beyond 87 degrees in the shade. This advantage is attributed to the proximity of an Antarctic current which is incidentally responsible, also, for frequent fogs and heavy mists, not altogether beneficial, by the way, to those with rheumatic tendencies. The beach almost rivals that of Muizemberg, in the Cape, and was taken full advantage of by the troops for bathing and other aquatic diversions.

Col. Skinner was in charge of this Expeditionary Force (until such time as General Botha could take command), and his personal staff comprised Major Mitchell Baker, Capt. C. F. Stallard, K.C., Capt. Piet v.d. Bijl, and Capt. Christian. The combatant sections were: 1st Imperial Light Horse (Col. Ligertwood), Grobelaar's Scouts (Major Grobelaar), Machine Gun Section (Major Giles), and Heavy Artillery Brigade (Col. Rose).

The 3rd Infantry Brigade, under Col. Burnside, with staff officers Major Harvie and Capt. Reginald Schwartz, consisted of 2nd Transvaal Scottish (Col. Kirkpatrick), Kimberley Regiment (Col. Rogers), and 1st Rhodesian Regiment (Major Warwick, *vice* Col. Burnside commanding the Brigade), and was responsible for the area around the Whaling Station.

The 4th Infantry Brigade was under the command of Col. Wylie, with Major Taylor and Capt. Judd as staff officers, and this brigade consisted of 1st Durban Light Infantry (Col. Goulding), South African Irish (Col. Brennan), and Rand Rifles (Col. Purcell).

The landing was effected, as already stated, on Christmas morning, and once ashore preparations for defence against attack from the interior were made along the whole two miles of sand-dunes from the Port to the Whaling Station, the troops so employed experiencing a Christmas Day under novel, if not altogether too pleasant, circumstances. Bully beef and biscuits, the latter apparently conforming to no particular recipe, were hastily issued aboard the transports, before the landing parties tumbled into their boats. Each man's water-bottle was required to provide him with sufficient liquid for at least twenty-four hours, during which period it was campaigning with a vengeance, coming so suddenly upon the tranquil and comparatively luxurious life on board ship. Nevertheless, all were as keen as the proverbial mustard, and if in one instance, at least, the officers had had the intelligent foresight to provide themselves with tit-bits from the ship's larder, it was the subject for amusement rather than envy with the rank and file. It was while these "delicatessen" were being seriously discussed by a party of young subalterns behind a convenient sand-dune that a private, wearing an identification disc as a substitute for a monocle, suddenly popped his head over the engrossed officers and shouted: "Any complaints, what?" and as suddenly disappeared.

Serious business commenced with the dawn, when a small patrol of Germans, riding along the beach from the direction of Swakopmund, and apparently unaware of our landing, owing to the mists so prevalent at that period of the year, found themselves suddenly confronted by a party of entrenched Rand Riflemen beyond the Whaling Station. There were only two of the enemy, one being wounded and captured with his horse and equipment, while the other, believed to have also been wounded, escaped in the mist, beyond which it was impossible to see more than a few yards ahead. "First blood," therefore, in the new sphere of action correctly fell to the Rand Rifles.

First and foremost among the responsibilities of the Staff was the question of water. The "Settlement" had been supplied with water, in normal times, from wells sunk in the bed of the Kuiseb River, about four miles out, at a spot called Sandfontein. These wells, however, had been polluted by the enemy, and required time to be restored. In the meantime the matter was a vital one, and provision had been made for such an emergency. Water had been brought up by thousands of tons from Cape Town in the ballast tanks of the transports, and this supply was rapidly transferred to the shore. And from the moment of landing began strenuous times for the South African Engineer Corps (Col. Collins). Multifarious were the duties which fell under the scope of this extremely useful unit. While some were levelling the drift sand in the streets with dam-scrapers drawn by teams of mules, others were hauling ashore material, too heavy to be handled at the crazy little jetty, over hastily improvised slipways. The carpentry section were hard at it building stout lighters with which to convey the enormous quantities of cargo from the ships to shore, the electricians were busy installing electric light into the principal headquarter offices, and a demolition gang was employing itself razing a portion of a building to the ground to make room for an additional tramline from the jetty to the Supply and Ordnance Stores. These were but a few of the works upon which the Engineers were speedily embarked. With the exception, at the outset, of the Pay Department, nobody can fairly be stated to have been idle. The next heavily taxed Departmental Unit was assuredly the supplies, which fell under Col. Ross-Frames, A.Q.M.G., and in the intervals of keeping watch in the trenches the infantry responded with willing alacrity to the call from the Service Corps for manual labour at the jetties, off-loading lighters into trucks, and hand-pushing these burdens to their respective destinations, with a spirit as commendable as the work was arduous. This was before native labour was available, the few local Damara natives who had come in from the district for food and protection being quite unsuited to the particular work required of them.

Immediately around the Walvis Settlement, which is really situated in the generous mouth of the Kuiseb River, the ground is firm between the drifted sand-dunes and of a clayey consistency. This being the case, and with possibilities of aeroplane raids to come, the infantry created dug-outs for themselves of such ingenious burrow-like construction that Major Creswell dubbed the S.A. Irish the " Troglodytes " while passing through their lines on one occasion.

With the aid of a chain of blockhouses and barbed-wire entanglements, the country outside of which was patrolled by the Imperial Light Horse, the place was put into an excellent state of defence, while the water-holes at Sandfontein were equally well protected by blockhouses, a company or so of one or other of the infantry regiments taking turn and turn about at garrison duty at this desolate spot. I have made mention of aeroplanes, and in the light of after events it is amusing to recall the ignorance displayed concerning this new engine of warfare, and the consequent needless alarms occasioned by the want of knowledge of the subject throughout the Union. The Germans possessed only two aeroplanes, and these of none too recent pattern, and during the whole course of our stay at both Walvis and Swakopmund, never a sign was seen of either of these machines at the coast. The reason for this was, as the Germans themselves afterwards explained, that their aeroplanes were unfit to cope with the variable winds from the sea, and their greatest non-stop flights were from the aerodrome at Karibib to the neighbourhood of Rossing Mountain, a double journey of roughly 150 miles. Their petrol capacity did not warrant them indulging in trips of very much greater distance than the one quoted. But here is the extraordinary part of the "Plane Panic" (as it might well have been termed) which existed throughout the Union when the whole world started to go to war.

In Cape Town, one evening in September, 1914, an otherwise sane and sober individual confided to me that he had just arrived from Sea Point, and had observed, with his own eyes, a monoplane, in which was seated a solitary person, "German in appearance," swoop down over each of the forts situated around that coast, and finally make off in the gathering gloom. This was only one of many such hallucinations with regard to enemy aeroplanes—all told with a degree of circumstantial detail difficult for one not present on the particular occasion to refute.

On Friday, January 8, Colonel Skinner, accompanied by his staff and a strong escort of Imperial Light Horse, made a night reconnaissance to Ururas, a German Police Post situated on our south-eastern border (Walvis territory), about 20 miles distant. The station, however, was found to be deserted, and the patrol of the enemy, which it was hoped we should encounter, had already left the neighbourhood. Our force returned to camp the following day, without having sighted a single German. This reconnaissance represented the initial entry of the Northern Expeditionary Force into the enemy's country, and established the fact that our immediate front was clear of the enemy for some many miles inland, and patrols of Imperial Light Horse continued thereafter to maintain information on this point.

It was a few days after this brief survey of the enemy's territory that an occurrence of a phenomenal character was experienced at Walvis Bay, in the shape of thousands of soles cast up on the shores by, it is alleged, a mysterious sort of eruption, of presumably volcanic origin, which annually takes place somewhere within the confines of the harbour any time between January 1 and 15. Somewhat reminiscent of manna from Heaven, it is a unique sight to observe the shores littered with a fish of such universally pronounced delicacy, yet all too unfortunate rarity. Besides the soles, which are alive when caught, and of perfect freshness, many other denizens of the deep were likewise brought ashore at high tide, and included rays, gurnet, harders, sharks, and swarms of smaller fry, mostly in a semi-stupefied state. A strong odour of sulphur was distinctly noticeable in the atmosphere during the night preceding the first wash-up on the beach, while the sea itself assumed a particularly greenish tinge in the day time. The men thoroughly enjoyed the novel experience of picking up soles, merely for the "asking," and all of good average size, with occasional hefty samples. When the supply on the shore came to an end there were many competitors, and many half-sackfuls at least represented an individual collection. A raid into the retreating waters was made by the men with bayonets and a variety of improvised spears, including mess-forks tied to broomsticks, and further heavy supplies were bagged amid much excitement and good-humoured banter.

This remarkable "windfall" lasts, as a rule, for several days, and, in spite of our numbers, soles figured largely and frequently on the menu of the meanest, and bully beef was relegated to a back seat.

The event had been foretold by an inhabitant fortunate in the possession of agreeable memories of previous upheavals, but I am afraid that confidence in his powers of veracity was a quality sadly lacking at the time among his hearers. Later, however, he pursued the even tenor of his way with a pardonable little smile of self-satisfaction.

All this time works of wondrous capacity were being executed by the Engineer Corps, the "S.A.E.C." Railway engine parts, condenser plant, rails, sleepers, giant packing cases, tubes, and trucks (to mention only a few of the more cumbersome impedimenta required for the desert war) were being transported ashore on locally constructed lighters. While piles were being driven in, as well to strengthen the old wooden jetty as to create more accommodation for the erection of heavier cranes, the first sods were being turned, and rails and sleepers laid for the new broad-gauge line to Karibib and Windhuk, and the foundations established for a capacious condenser plant.

Both ground and aerial telephone lines between Walvis and the Whaling Station, as well as from office to office, were among the earliest works of Colonel Collins' command—works that evoked the admiration of the professional and layman alike. The Supplies, too, were feverishly at work, accumulating veritable mountains of "bully," biscuits, and groceries, not to mention colossal stacks of fodder for horses, transport mules, and the oxen employed to haul the "Cow" guns; for it must be known that the country, as far as the eye could reach, was entirely devoid of any form of animal sustenance—the true desert area—and, in consequence, every atom of food *and water* for both man and beast had perforce to be conveyed over 800 miles by sea from Cape Town. Such were the difficulties in the initial stages when we were still at the coast in touch with the shipping. But who was to be the genius who would maintain supplies and transport further into this appalling stretch of country! Personally, if the transport must be by road, I considered that for the successful accomplishment of such a task, the Age of Miracles would, indeed, require to be at hand. What actually transpired we shall see in the subsequent chapters. Anyway, if an exceptional sort of genius was not forthcoming, a very harassed A.Q.M.G. presented a fair imitation of the ordinarily accepted variety.

All work and no recreation must soon have spelt disaster to health and consequent strain upon the Medical Department. Therefore, certain time was devoted to sea-bathing, fishing, and sports, with an occasional evening concert, and the troops generally enjoyed complete health of both body and mind; while the doctors experienced comparative leisure.

And referring to sports reminds me of a curious feature which is noticeable during most campaigns conducted by Britishers: the extraordinary facility with which sporting accessories are mysteriously produced from apparently nowhere, whenever and wherever required. Should a Rugby match be resolved on, the orthodox ball is suddenly brought to light, from Heaven knows where. Should a trawling expedition be arranged, somebody immediately contributed (presumably from the lining of his helmet—there is no other apparent place of concealment at the time) a complete fisherman's net. And so it carries on, almost indefinitely, till one is forced to the belief that if it were desired to give a musical comedy performance among the sand dunes, someone is sure to be found ready with the necessary accompaniment of ladies of the chorus concealed in his haversack.

Certain restrictions were placed by the General Officer Commanding upon the facilities for the acquisition of alcoholic liquor, which gave rise to much choler among the larger section of the force, to whom, apparently, alcohol was an essential form of daily nourishment, and which caused some wags to construct a small grave in the sand wherein might be seen, peacefully reposing beneath a glass cover, a receptacle having obviously once contained a beverage known to the connoisseur as beer. At the head of the grave a simple wooden cross was erected, the inscription upon which recorded the following:—

"To our lost Beloved Beer.
"Died of consumption,
"December 29, 1914."

A pathetic-looking wreath of corks, with tags attached, conveyed sympathetic messages in the form of "Deeply mourned" and "In loving memory of our Beer Departed."

One of our men-o'-war in the Bay frequently succeeded in intercepting wireless messages from Windhuk, which the German authorities were evidently under the impression our machinery was not properly attuned to catch. On one occasion Windhuk was endeavouring to acquaint Berlin with the death by misadventure of their Commander-in-Chief, Colonel Heydenbreck, and seeking instructions for the appointment of a successor. This was a tit-bit of news not to be missed in such dull times as we were then undergoing; but it was undesirable that the Germans should learn that we were tapping their communications, and as by some means, probably quite simple, the daily Cape newspapers were filtering through to Windhuk, a little thought was necessary before launching this interesting piece of news. The information, as it appeared in the Press, read that a rumour was current in Portuguese Angola that Colonel Heydenbreck, commanding the enemy's forces in German South-west Africa, met his death recently while examining hand grenades at Windhuk, one bursting in his hand.

With reference to the sudden death of Colonel Heydenbreck, Commanding the German Forces in the Protectorate, the Windhuk journal published the following obituary notice, which served to confirm the report referred to above:—

"On November 12, died at Kalkfontein South, as the result of a severe wound received during experimental practice with grenades, the Imperial Lieut.-Colonel in Command of the Forces in South-west Africa.

"Joachim Van Heydenbreck.

"Officers and men of the Imperial Forces, we lose in him who has so suddenly been called to the Great Army a great personal friend of mine and a benevolent superior; a man who has been tried in Peace and War, and to whom we all looked up with confidence. For seventeen years he was a Member of the Forces, a shining example of soldierly virtues—now he is dead. His last care was for the Army of the Protectorate and its task; his last thought was for his Almighty War Lord.

"Officers and men mourn for him. The period of his successful command will constitute a glorious page in the history of the Protectorate Army, and his memory will remain as that of a hero held in high honour.

"(Sgd.) FRANCKE,
"Major and Acting Commander of the Imperial Forces
"in the Protectorate.
"Windhuk, November 18, 1914."

Prior to the operation which it was found necessary to perform upon Colonel Heydenbreck, he issued the following order to the troops:—

"I send to all members of the Imperial Army my best farewell wishes, and I confidently hope that the Imperial Army will continue its march to victory. His Majesty the Kaiser, Hurrah!"

The following are particulars concerning the career of the deceased in Africa:—

"Colonel Heydenbreck came out to German South-west Africa in 1896, as a Senior Lieutenant. In 1897-8 he took part in the campaign against the Topnaar Hottentots and the Hereros in the north-west. He was promoted to Captain in

1898, and during 1903-4 he was in command of the Artillery. He left German South-west Africa for a while for reasons of health, and in 1905 he became Military Adviser to his Excellency the German Governor. In 1906 he went back to Germany, but returned as a Major in the following year in order to organise the Police Force. Since 1910 he was in command of the Protectorate Troops. He was gazetted Colonel on October 1, 1913."

The gentleman operating the Windhuk wireless station certainly appeared to possess the instincts of a cheery sportsman, and employed most of his spare time in transmitting gentle gibes to the Union troops, wherever they might be situated. His favourite call into the wild was, "I say, Mister," etc., etc. On one occasion he playfully recommended a particular force to abandon football and to resort to the more serious game of war. On the following day, curiously enough, this same force encountered a force of the enemy, killing two and capturing three. Whereupon it is related that a reply was despatched to the facetious one that his advice had been taken, and that a score in the new pastime had been promptly notched, amounting to " two goals and three tries."

The following ode to Walvis Bay was composed by Captain Jeoffreys, of the S.A. Irish Regiment :—

WALVIS BAY.

(To the tune of "Mandalay)

I.

There's a mist and mirage floating
   Over sea and over land,
And the carrion-crows and pariahs
   Seek their food from out the sand ;
And I feel a bit downhearted
   As my close-cropped head I lay
On the ever-shifting sand-dunes
   To the east of Walvis Bay.

Refrain :—
   To the east of Walvis Bay !
      To fatigue-work every day !
   For there's lighters and there's coaling,
      And there's many rails to lay.
   To the east of Walvis Bay !
      There's now no Huns to slay,
   And the biscuits kill the dog-fish
      On the shores of Walvis Bay.

II.

As I snooze beside my blockhouse
  With my " bully " still intact,
I have dreams of fighting Germans!
  Then I wake to solid fact.
For the bugle sounds reveillé
  Long before the dawn of day,
And I wonder what's a soldier
  When he lands in Walvis Bay.   Refrain.

III.

Oh, I hope the day is dawning
  When the order is to go
Towards the scenes of fighting
  With the looting German foe.
I will praise the hardest biscuit,
  I will bust my princely pay,
Where I humped the rails and sleepers
  In that dry old Walvis Bay.

CHAPTER III.

AT SWAKOPMUND.

On the afternoon of Wednesday, January 13, Col. Skinner left Walvis Bay on a reconnaissance towards Swakopmund, taking with him the Imperial Light Horse and Grobelaar's Scouts.

Halting some distance beyond the Whaling Station, our force bivouacked till about 11 p.m., when the march was resumed in darkness along the foreshore, between a series of unmistakable sand-dunes on the right and noisy surf to the left. All went silently and well till the town was dimly sighted about a mile ahead in the first grey streak of dawn. At this point the beach path narrowed to such slight dimensions that advance was only possible in single file, and to accelerate matters a portion of our force deployed to the right around the dunes, with instructions to push on and cut off any possible retreat from the town on the right. These movements involved some slight dissection of the force. An advance party had already negotiated the small defile, and had drawn up some distance ahead, when a violent explosion rent the air about 200 yards behind them, and, mercifully, in advance of the oncoming force. Several horses took fright and raced about in the semi-darkness, many men being unhorsed. No harm was apparently done, and the slight confusion occasioned was only temporary. While those ahead, among whom were Col. Skinner and his staff, quietly remained where they were, it was deemed advisable that the remainder should withdraw around the sand-dunes; but before the plan could be put into effect another fearful concussion took place, and odd bits of nuts, bolts, rock and lead fell in showers, together with volumes of sand cast up by the exploded mine. Miraculously enough, no one was hurt, but a few yards farther on a third mine was exploded immediately beneath two of our horsemen, killing them outright.

It would be absurd to deny that our force was completely taken by surprise at this method of warfare, but their behaviour under such an entirely unexpected and trying ordeal was nothing less than admirable, and only a few moments were occupied in re-forming and continuing the advance right into the town, no other formidable obstacle being encountered.

A retreating party of the enemy, numbering about twenty-five, in their flight, fired a few shots at our patrols, and unfortuately succeeded in inflicting a casualty in one man wounded, though not severely. The personal sensations as described by some of those who so providentially escaped the results of the Swakopmund land-mine explosions, are interesting, if variable. A member of the staff narrated how he was only 100 or 200 yards away from the first explosion, and in the dim light of early dawn he saw a column of fire ascending heavenwards, to the accompaniment of a terrific report and showers of broken metal, stones and sand. His horse was slightly wounded in two places by flying fragments. He afterwards examined the scene of the upheaval and found a hole in the sand as deep as an inverted bell-tent, though with a much greater circumference. The second and third explosions soon convinced all of the real source of danger. One veteran soldier, a popular commanding officer, frankly admitted that he bore numbers one, two, and three concussions with a certain amount of (to himself) surprising if fast diminishing *sang froid*, but thought that a fourth would have converted him into a "jabbering idiot."

Many had remarkably narrow escapes, and that our casualties were so few may be attributed alone to the fact that our arrival was timed just before dawn, and our movements in consequence obscured from the observation of those operating the mines.

A written message was picked up a few days later in a conspicuous spot in the desert frequented by the German patrols, to the following effect: "Trust you enjoyed your reception, and desire to inform you that warmer ones are in store for you. (Signed) Swakopmund Entertainment Committee."

It would appear to have been one of those occasions when one may be permitted to respond with: "He laughs best who laughs last."

A precautionary measure was taken against further surprise from observation mines by the early despatch of a plough through the sand encompassing the town.

Although it was at first stated, with reference to the mines exploded by the enemy during our entry into Swakopmund, that they were operated from a position somewhere in the town, it has now been definitely established that the operator was concealed in a sort of large packing case let into the sand on the beach close to the high-water mark. Some time elapsed before the dug-out was found, the entrance, through a small manhole, being cunningly strewn about with seaweed and scrub, so effectively veiling the position that many of our people afterwards recollected that they had passed within an ace of the spot. It has also transpired that the operator, after having set off the mines, remained in hiding throughout the day and decamped under cover of darkness about nine o'clock in the evening. In the vacated cabin were found the mechanical starting apparatus, a mattress, a partly emptied bottle of peppermint liqueur, a candle, and some literature. These contact mines, which figure so prominently during the campaign, appear to have been prepared by what might well be termed a connoisseur in infernal contrivances. First laying a box containing anything between thirty and forty sticks of dynamite in a cavity made in the ground, an inverted T piece of piping, closed at both ends of the cross section, but with an aperture in the middle to connect with the explosive underneath, is arranged to rest upright upon the dynamite. Suspended from cork supports, within the cross tube is a small glass cylinder about the size of a clinical thermometer, and containing a liquid agent. Around this cylinder is placed a quantity of a powdered substance. The iron rod already referred to, which is barely visible above ground, rests upon a piece of putty within the perpendicular portion of the piping, and immediately above the glass tube. The slightest jar upon the rod dislodges the putty and allows the weight of the iron to fall and smash the glass, which thus releases the liquid amid the powder. The result of this particular combination of ingredients has been known for some time to most students of chemistry, and more recently, unfortunately be it said, to some members of the Northern Force.

Although Swakopmund may be aptly termed a monument of bluff, inasmuch as it suggests in many respects a " White City " perched on the edge of a desert, vaingloriously overlooking a foreshore more adapted by nature to surf-bathing than shipping, a big contrast is afforded between it and the humble and apologetic little Walvis Settlement.

The general style of the residences and stores breathes the cult of the Teuton, and the lavish mode in which most houses are furnished, and the high quality of the goods still remaining in a few of the leading shops, suggest a well-paid and correspondingly liberal community. Channels for the speedy dissolution of superfluous wealth are represented by numerous attractive-looking hotels, beer " gardens," cinematograph theatres and a music-hall. That Swakopmund was inclined to be a gay city there is no gainsaying, and suddenly to come upon it from an ocean of water on the one side and an ocean of sand on the other is an experience as extraordinary as it is unique.

I was shown round several of the buildings and noted evidence of some ruthless looting and wanton damage committed, prior to our occupation, by Hottentots.

Several houses contained mementoes in the shape of pieces of the shells fired by H.M.S. "Kinfauns Castle" during her visit in September. In some cases the departure of the inhabitants appeared to have been extremely hurried, remnants of interrupted meals remaining on the tables; a half-cup of coffee and some very stale rolls on a fully laid-out breakfast table in one place; a partly consumed glass of wine and a crumbled rusk in another. But never a ha'porth of food in any bulk.

The principal thing considerately left behind by the enemy was a decidedly ingenious but thoroughly infernal device, locally improvised and obviously intended to be launched as a torpedo against our warships whenever they might be lying off the shore. How far, if at all, it would have succeeded in its object is impossible to say. Either the wretched thing contained nothing or it carried enough explosive to remove the whole of Swakopmund to a nameless locality. On eventual examination, in place of the expected gun-cotton, only sand was revealed, and this left, not exactly in a spirit of "spoof." Indeed, if any humour was ever associated with the invention, it was of a very grim kind. The detonator, on the same principle as those used in the land mines, and previously described, was already in position, and the sand was merely to be employed in a preliminary trial, as a guide to the weight of explosive required to accord with the balance and other features.

Our unexpected arrival upon the scene apparently interrupted further research in this direction. I understand this contrivance now reposes peacefully and appropriately in the Naval Museum at Simonstown.

As was pointed out at the beginning of the chapter, Col. Skinner's movement towards Swakopmund was originally intended merely as a reconnaissance, but due to the poisoning of the water supply and the laying of mines, together with the complete abandonment of the town by the enemy, it was deemed advisable to retain what he occupied, although the moment was altogether unpropitious for creating lines of communication, and so adding in any way to the existing difficulties of transport and supplies. To have withdrawn our forces could only have resulted in the enemy gathering more courage, together with more material for further mines, and who could say that the luck, which with the exception of the two unfortunate signallers was nothing less than extraordinary, would hold good in a second similar experience?

The decision, therefore, to occupy Swakopmund forthwith, though it involved some risk, eventually resulted in considerable saving of time, enabling railway construction to be pursued simultaneously from both ends, while the water supply, landing facilities, etc., were being improved at Walvis.

Landing Locomotives at Walvis Bay.

Building the Desert Railway from Swakop.

Landing Horses at Walvis Bay.

An Armoured Car.

Mrs. Botha on Railway near Swakop.

An Ammunition Wagon in an awkward part of the road.

General Botha and Staff near Salem.

Outspan in the Bush.

Outspan in the Veldt.

General Botha at Karibib.

Until the poisoned wells, which represented the town's sole water supply, could be restored to a normal state, it was impossible to keep the mounted men as a garrison, and the transference by sea was immediately made by the 3rd Infantry Brigade, under Col. Burnside, who was placed in temporary command at Swakopmund, enabling Col. Skinner to remain longer at the over-tried base at Walvis.

The railway had had no time to make any considerable headway, owing principally to the primitive means available for landing material, and in this process rails and sleepers must, of course, give way to the more vital foodstuffs, during the early stages at least. Consequently, it will be seen that the transportation over the seashore of sufficient supplies to maintain the requisite garrison at the newly-occupied town was at that time a physical impossibility. There was the sea to fall back upon as a channel for the conveyance of supplies from Walvis to Swakopmund, but this too was a precarious method, owing to the fact that the off-loading on to the ocean jetty at Swakopmund was entirely dependent on the caprice of the sea, and often, for days at a time, it was rendered impossible for lighters to come alongside. The obvious plan was to have awaited the construction of the railway to Swakopmund before venturing on the occupation of that town, and had not the beach reconnaisance resulted so successfully, such would undoubtedly have been the wisest plan to pursue—hustling methods being entirely out of place in this desert warfare.

It is a noteworthy fact that our harmless Teutonic neighbours were not content with defending their hearths and homes from attack on the confines of that home, but sowed their diabolical land mines on the Walvis side of the Swakop River mouth, and therefore in Union territory. Curiously enough, it is not the enemy himself, but his alien friends, who so strenuously deny that he was equally prepared to attack as to defend. What eventually decided his course of action was the strength and vigour with which the Union Government took up the campaign after the Sandfontein disaster. That he was early in the campaign and prepared to attack, the reference in Chapter I. to German guns supporting Maritz at Keimoes and Kakamas, and later at Upington, should form ample evidence of his intentions. While our enemy disclaims hypocrisy, his supporters in the Union would thrust the objectionable cloak upon him.

On January 16 Colonel Skinner proceeded to Swakopmund when the official annexation of that town to the Union of South Africa took place, the Union Jack being hoisted at the Signal Station, to the accompaniment of three British cheers.

The water supply was the first consideration, and the troops were employed, in the intervals of other duty, in assisting the engineers to cleanse the wells of their poisonous impurities. The wells were situated to the south of the town in the bed and at the mouth of the Swakop River, and the sheep-dip with which the water was contaminated by the enemy was soon dissipated by the celerity and energy of the infantry, assisted by the slower agency of the constant underground flow.

Now we come to the defences of the town. Admitted that the mounted, and therefore more mobile, section of the force was limited to a few squadrons of the Imperial Light Horse, and that the strength of the enemy encamped a few miles out at Nonidas was an unknown quantity, surely the G.O.C. was ill-advised in establishing his outer defences on the confines of the town's backyards.

A more critical history than this pretends to be may offer some explanation in extenuation of this curious mode of action during the early days of the occupation of Swakopmund.

Until General Botha arrived and established more confidence, the liability of being spitted at night on a sentry's bayonet at street corners was a constant source of danger as well as of irritation to all.

But dug-outs, bomb-proof shelters, and a maze of trenches were, metaphorically, thrown to the winds when the Boer General marched out, soon after his arrival on the scene, to clear his immediate front and to provide the troops with breathing space between Swakopmund and the enemy.

While the Rhodesians were constructing these entrenchments several suspicious-looking metal drums, full of a liquid into the nature of which none was sufficiently curious to inquire (the poisoning of the wells by the enemy having produced a dampening effect upon the ardour of the more inquisitive ones), were pressed into service as supports to the loose sandy sides of the excavations. Men record to-day in sorrowful tones how they unconsciously slept against these casks for nights on end, and it fell to the lot of a private of a relieving regiment, guided presumably by instinct, to thrust his bayonet unerringly into the heart of the nearest barrel, producing a fountain of—German beer!

By February a portion of the Rhodesian Regiment had been pushed out to occupy the sand-dunes guarding the approach down the Swakop River bed. The sand-dunes here run inland in long series from north to south for a few miles only, when the ground becomes firm and pebbly with a gentle undulation towards Nonidas. The Rhodesians held the last ridge but one of sand-dunes, daily sending forward a few men as outposts in the early morning to overlook the open country and returning them back at nightfall nearer to the main picket. Such was the position when on Sunday, February 7, Colonel

Skinner moved out before dawn with the I.L.H. and a detachment of his only available artillery (the Heavy Artillery Brigade) to reconnoitre the enemy's position beyond the Rhodesian outposts. By a strange coincidence it transpired that the enemy had also despatched a reconnoitring party, who, during the night, occupied the last sand-dunes already referred to, and at daybreak, as the Rhodesians were crossing the open space dividing the ridges, opened fire upon the surprised men, killing two outright. Simultaneously, Colonel Skinner and staff, who had gone ahead and taken a direction to the right to higher observation ground, saw the enemy's horses revealed behind the dunes in the growing light. Although the distance was probably over 1,000 yards away, some of the staff could not restrain a few enfilading shots with their revolvers at such a tempting bait, and away went the Germans back to their camp at Nonidas.

The I.L.H., under Major Panchaud, were due to arrive at the Rhodesian outpost at 7 a.m., and actually reached the spot a little before that hour, by which time, however, the "game" had been scared away.

The enemy, in their hasty retirement, left one of their number behind, who was promptly taken prisoner. Later, a small party of the Germans returned under a white flag requesting permission to seek their wounded. As there happened to be none this incident was treated with suspicion, though unfortunately not at the time, and the bogus ambulance party was permitted to depart. A detachment of I.L.H., working along the north bank of the river, came upon four powerful contact mines in a railway cutting in the line of advance of our troops, but these were all safely removed by the attendant engineers.

Information of considerable value was stated by the staff to have been gained by this reconnaisance.

As the I.L.H. Cossack posts, chafing to be out and doing, were retired each evening from the first rise out of town, the enemy patrols habitually rode up and occupied the vacated ridges well within sight of the signallers on top of the Damara Tower, situated only a few hundred yards from the beach. In such neighbourly proximity were the two armies that the enemy took to practising little amenities. One sunny day a party of I.L.H. found a note in a conspicuous spot, held down by a stone and accompanied by a bottle of genuine German beer. The note counselled the Force, in vulgar parlance, to " chuck it," in view of the fact that they, the Germans, " had surrounded Paris, and had our Fleet bottled up." A postscript begged for cigarettes in exchange for the malted offering, and although the latter request was acceded to, the enemy became a trifle too playful when he later substituted mines for "Münchener."

So uneventful were the days spent at Swakopmund that the smallest incident stands out well in the memory. I recollect the jubilation of the Scots (the 1st Transvaal Scottish) when a German scout, venturing too near their well-concealed trenches early one morning, was brought to earth by quite a shower of lead. Curiously enough none of the many wounds occasioned proved fatal, the most serious necessitating the amputation of several finger joints.

Perhaps it happened in Swakopmund, perhaps in Flanders; anyhow the story seems a good one and worthy of repetition. The Orderly Officer was going his usual rounds at meal-time, and, after investigating a complaint about a certain article of the daily dietary and rebuking the men for an unworthy accusation against the company "chef," added "It is excellent soup." "Yes, sir," responded the spokesman, "that's what we say, but the cook insists that it's tea."

A good deal of irresponsible nonsense has been talked concerning the so-called looting which took place at Swakopmund, and it may do some good, certainly no harm, to ventilate this matter. With such atrocious examples in Belgium and the invested portion of France it was nothing short of an absurdity to apply the term " looting " to the insignificant pilferings at Swakopmund. Apart from the solid and therefore more cumbersome forms of furniture, the enemy had carefully removed every portable article of value, and if a wash-basin, a Chinese lantern and a lady's discarded straw hat can fairly be stated to enter into the category of plunder, then Swakopmund was, for a short while, exposed to much "frightfulness" of this character.

The inhabitants of Swakopmund deserted the town during the month of September, and in the Windhuk paper *Sud-West* of November 27 the following appeared : "Brought in as prisoners yesterday were four whites, who are seriously suspected of having initiated, aided, and directed the robberies at Swakopmund carried out by Walvis Bay Hottentots. They are two South Africans, Potgieter and Botha, a German named Kessler and a Portuguese. If investigation and trial justify the accusations, the four will hardly fail to end on the gallows, as they deserve."

In December the Germans, I understand, summarily shot some fifteen Hottentots for looting and wanton damage in Swakopmund. Further, between September and the date of our occupation in January, German patrols constantly visited the town.

There is a piquant little story which may appropriately be introduced at this point. A certain trooper, whose duty it was to prepare the day's sustenance for his particular section, was stealthily emerging from a house in a side thoroughfare with a cheap paraffin stove under his arm, when he found himself suddenly confronted by an indignant officer, who roundly reprimanded him for his lack of decent restraint. "Ssh, sir! Ssh, sir!" soothingly whispered the man, as he gently closed the door, "have you forgotten Louvain?"

Then there was the isolated incident of a piano, which was bodily removed from one of the newly-occupied coast towns, but the recorder sacrificed veracity for a good story. Four stalwarts from a tug in the bay decided to remove a grand piano from a house in the town, and straightway proceeded to carry their intention into effect. Covering the bulky instrument with its own blue dust cover, the quartette, each shouldering a corner, stepped solemnly down the street to the quay with their burden. None questioned their behaviour, and those who happened to be about stood aside in respectful and reverential attitudes, mistaking the demonstration for a funeral party.

About this time an adventure, due entirely to his disregard of personal danger, happened to Colonel Skinner, which perhaps amounted to an exceedingly narrow escape of his life. It was in the course of a small reconnaisance outside Swakopmund, in the neighbourhood of Eier Farm, that Colonel Skinner and his staff exposed themselves at too close range to the enemy's fire. Colonel Skinner's horse was shot beneath him. He seized Captain van der Byl's stirrup leather and ran alongside the galloping horseman until well out of the danger zone.

Apart from the more solid "comforts" so regularly and generously despatched to the troops in the field by the people of the Union, the Loyal Women's Guild and other thoughtful feminine institutions especially devoted their energies to the making of veils for the unfortunate soldiers whose duties confined them to the heart of the pitiless desert area, where sandstorms reigned supreme. To those lounging at the bases a gossamer veil was indeed as superfluous a decoration as, in their case, a war medal would be, but it was chiefly from this ubiquitous class of individual that the first uncouth complaints arose as to the unserviceable nature of these particular gifts. It is pleasing to record, however, that the soldier performing the hazardous work at the front was only too fully appreciative, not only of the splendid spirit of sacrifice which animated the gentlewomen of the Union, but of the great comfort and convenience the result of their energies afforded.

We were an odd assortment of humanity in the Northern Force. There were men from Delagoa, men from Rhodesia, others from the malarial swamps of Central Africa, one hard-bitten warrior from Lake N'gami, and a wiry contingent of

Swazies (all quite white, but occasionally heard to discourse in wild and wonderful tongues). Then, too, there were men who called a " dixie " a " billy," and prated of the " swag " and " humping the bluey," while others from the rugged Rockies " guessed and calc'clated " as to the duration of the campaign, in company with the bronzed, bearded and " happy-go-lucky " denizens of the illimitable veld. Intermingled with these woolly veterans were lawyers, doctors, magistrates, bankers, editors, farmers, and a whole " Empire "-full of actors and singers from whom the material for our concerts was drawn.

Such, for the most part, was our composition, and a more formidable force it would be hard to find.

With the majority campaigning came as naturally and gracefully as (to use a colloquialism) " falling off a log," and a camp on the unutterable sand-dunes, or the luxury of being billeted in a furnished domicile in Swakopmund was all one and the same to the old stager. Nothing came amiss. It is ever a feast or a famine in times of war, and on most mail days the former came under discussion. One has a cake from his mother, another some potted tit-bits from his wife, and the rations, good in themselves, were greatly supplemented on these occasions. There are some men possessed of the enviable faculty of never being " left." Where the average man might reasonably be expected to expire for lack of anything in the nature of sustenance, others trek through triumphantly with ever-increasing avoirdupois. As an instance, a certain mess-president, famed for his untiring energy and resource, was out on patrol in a portion of what is known as the Namib Desert, where even a hunger-striking suffragette would have cause to blanch at the prospect. After a few days in this awful wilderness he returned with a sack containing, among other things, cabbages and a haunch of venison ! The latter was the result of a good shot near Gvanikontes at a springbok, by one Lloyd, of Swazieland. and was the first head of game to fall to the Northern Force in German territory.

CHAPTER IV.

GENERAL BOTHA TAKES COMMAND.

On February 11 General Botha arrived to take active command of the Northern Force, and with him came the burghers, under Brigadier-General Brits, mostly jovial men of huge proportions, who were possibly as much at home in the saddle as on their own farms.

General Botha was accompanied by the following staff:—Colonel Collyer, Chief Staff Officer; Major Bok, Military Secretary; Major D. de Waal, Provost Marshal; Colonel Odlum, Medical Staff Officer; Major Stopford, Principal Signalling Officer; Major Trevor, O.C. Headquarters Transport; Capt. Esselen, A.D.C.; Capt. Louis Botha, A.D.C.; Capt. Collender, O.C. Topographical Section; Capt. Ribbinck (in charge war dogs); Lieut, Wagner; Lieut. Cook, field telegraphs; Lieut. Jantje Botha.

Intelligence Department: Major Leipoldt and Lieuts. Nobbs and Richter (afterwards promoted Captains).

Bodyguard: Major Trew, O.C.; Capt. Fulton and Capt. Donald.

The completion of the railway from Walvis to Swakopmund synchronised with the advent of the soldier statesman, and formed the occasion for much local satisfaction.

Monday, February 15, was a memorable day in German South-west Africa, when, after a lapse of over ten years, the Swakop River came down in flood, bringing with it the accumulated refuse of those years, and discolouring the sea for miles for many days after. The railway, which had been lightly run across the flat mouth of the river, was washed away for some hundreds of yards, and caused a temporary suspension of traffic. The coming of the flood was indicated many hours beforehand by the rising of the water in the wells, caused by the pressure through the saturated sand of the river bed from many miles up country.

It was during the early part of February that the monotony of garrison life was broken by the arrival in our midst of four exhausted tatterdemalions, who stated that they were our own men escaped from the custody of the Germans from a spot in the far interior called Franzfontein.

A most remarkable story was unfolded of a 200-mile trek on foot over formidable mountains, waterless desert, and dreary seashore, covering a period of ten days, during which time the undaunted quartette endured hardships and escapes of a stirring and dramatic character.

Happily for them, they were alive to tell the tale of an unprecedented journey, mostly through forbidding desert country, in which no rain had fallen for years. Strangely enough, rain set in on the very night for which their escape was planned, and, but for this fortuitous circumstance, the bones of the four would to-day be lying bleaching in the great Namib Desert. The names of the adventurous ones were Sergt. A. Mackenzie (Upington Commando), Rifleman O. C. Maritz (1st S.A.M.R.), Rifleman F. M. Franzsen (Veteran Reserve Corps), and Corporal H. J. McElnea (1st T.L.H.).

The story of their hardships and privations was simply told by Franzsen, who was the leader of the expedition.

With only a few dozen chupatties, two canvas water-bags, and three water-bottles, the plucky little party effected their escape from their prison camp on the night of January 30, and with the aid of a compass steered a course eastward for the coast.

The rain, which commenced to fall as they emerged through a hole in the wire entanglements and thorn bush, fortunately hid their spoor, and by the second night the party had arrived at mountainous country where pursuit was no longer to be feared. The difficult nature of the country now arrived at convinced them that it would take seven, instead of five, days to reach their destination, and it was, therefore, resolved that they must go on half a chupattie apiece for each meal instead of a whole one. " We attempted to sleep that night in the rain," said Franzsen, " and sucked up the water in the little pools among the rocks, and so filled our bottles." He added, " We all suffered with rheumatism after the rains." Then followed days of increasing distress owing to the shortage of water, shrinking of provisions, and blistered feet, but, particularly because of the growing scarcity of supplies, it was impossible to dwell too long by the roadside.

From time to time they came across fresh lion spoor, and the spoor of other wild animals, " which we weren't keen on meeting." After the mountains followed bare desert country without a particle of vegetation. There is a simple human touch in the laconic remark which was introduced at this point : " McElnea's feet gave in, and Maritz gave him his own boots to wear." Eventually they arrived at Cape Cross Lighthouse, which, though deserted, yielded up a cooking pot and half a bottle of seal oil with which they managed to cook some limpets gathered along the beach. McElnea had gone astray from the others a few miles from the coast, and although his companions delayed another day in the hope of his turning up.

they were at last reluctantly compelled to resume their journey towards Swakopmund. Much to their relief, the following day they came upon McElnea's spoor along the beach, and later encountered him in a greatly exhausted condition, having been without food and water for two days. A drink of water revived him, and after continuing their way slowly along the seashore, Maritz, with a stick, killed a half-dead seagull. "We skinned the bird and put him in the pot which we had brought from Cape Cross, and cooked it in salt water. After boiling the bird for about fifteen minutes, we ate it, and very nice it was." "This," said Franzsen, "saved McElnea's life." And after walking, without a halt for sleep, from the Friday morning until the Sunday night, the courageous fellows arrived at Swakopmund. McElnea had to be assisted into camp on a horse. "On taking us over from the outposts, a stolid military policeman told us not to wander about!"

By February 22 General Botha was ready to make his initial demonstration against the enemy in anticipation of the first phase in the grand operations. General Botha had been on the scene exactly eleven days, and in that time an incredible amount of preparation had been set in motion.

The burgher commandoes, in brigades of 2,000 to 3,000 each, had, during this time, been arriving, at intervals, at Walvis Bay, where vast work was entailed watering and feeding their horses. Some idea of this task may be gathered from the fact that the water for the animals was pumped from the Sandfontein wells, four miles away, and, owing to its too brackish quality, required a reasonable mixture of fresh water brought by ship from Cape Town.

Supplies had been accumulating as fast as the arrival of shiploads would permit, and although there was much in hand, a big strain was put upon the Commissariat, in the daily provision of a full ration for thousands of horses and transport animals. Each shipload of horses required a rest ashore before the animals could be transferred by the beach route to Swakopmund, and owing to the limited water supply at Walvis, it was necessary to send away one batch before the next lot could safely be handled ashore. All this time the railway was kept busy dumping supplies into Swakopmund, and on the single line some astonishing records were created by a determined and efficient Supply Staff. These were some of the more strenuous works upon which the army was employed at a time when the Union was clamouring for news of its forces, and it was just these preparations which it was desirable to hide from the enemy, whose knowledge of our movements amounted to even less than our acquaintance with either his immediate strength or his exact position. This dearth of information should not be reckoned as a reflection upon our Intelligence Department, as then constituted. Before the arrival of General Botha and his own immediate staff, Captain Nobbs (1st Rhodesian Regiment) had conducted this branch of the service at Swakopmund in as thorough a manner as the available information permitted. In the exposed desert country it was quite impossible surreptitiously to overlook the enemy's camps—even one solitary figure standing out in conspicuous relief against the sheen of the sand—and native intelligence, which plays such a prominent part in all South African campaigns, could not be utilised, the country for many miles inland being purposely denuded of natives by the Germans. In spite of these difficulties, a fairly comprehensive system of intelligence was inaugurated by Capt. Nobbs, and afterwards carried on by Major Leipoldt, in conjunction with the originator, and Captain Richter. The system was chiefly to be recommended for its simplicity, and it cannot be giving away too much to explain that it amounted to nothing more than the collection and collation of every atom of information from any and every source—scraps from German newspapers, carelessly discarded correspondence, and even picture postcards bearing upon the particular subject. By this means the Intelligence Department under Major Leipoldt was enabled to publish, for the information of the troops, an almost complete list of officers and their commands serving with the German forces, from details culled from a variety of sources, which fitted together in a manner suggestive of a jig-saw puzzle.

With this system to go upon, General Botha directed his first effort against the enemy, with the intention of extending his scope before launching the bigger operations towards the capital. On the night of February 22, therefore, all the available mounted men, which included, besides the brigades under General Brits, the 1st Imperial Light Horse and Grobelaar's Scouts, were despatched to make wide enveloping movements north and south of the Swakop River in the direction of Goanikontes farm, where the enemy were believed to be congregated in some force. Some hard travelling through the night over unknown country was necessitated to enable the columns to arrive at their destination before dawn. Grobelaar's Scouts accompanied the Imperial Light Horse on the left flank, but this column failed to materialise at the appointed spot; as also did one of the burgher commandoes. Before dawn General Botha, with the 3rd Infantry Brigade and Artillery, advanced in the centre, directly upon Nonidas, H.M.S. "Astrea," with her 6-in. guns, standing upon the mouth of the Swakop River in support of the movement.

Daylight the next morning found the centre force, which included the 2nd Transvaal Scottish, 1st Rhodesian Regiment, and the 1st Kimberley Regiment, in extended order overlooking the wide hollow in which the Nonidas farm is situated. With the first streaks of light a tremendous fusillade broke out at a point many miles farther up the rugged river valley, and continued intermittently throughout the morning, accompanied by an occasional boom as of cannon echoing through the sombre gorges. The Germans had early vacated their advance camp at Nonidas, the foremost men of the Scottish encountering their abandoned posts in the dark, and a flare in the direction of Richthoden, a siding on the old railway line, denoted that the station had been set alight by the enemy in their retirement on Goanikontes.

The Headquarters Staff, with the infantry, halted at Nonidas, and awaited for hours some news of progress forward. The sharp crackle of rifle fire, intermingled with the duller roar of heavier weapons, resounded across the miles of broken country, and dense volumes of smoke arose at different points in the neighbourhood of the farm. At the least, it seemed that the Germans had been surrounded, and only needed to be impressed with the fact before yielding themselves into the hands of the Union troops. But the surmise was unfortunately incorrect. The Germans escaped the attempt to ring them in, and made off in apparent alarm towards Riet before our mounted forces could rectify their errors of direction and join hands across the valley. Several Germans remained behind at Goanikontes to ignite, blow up, and otherwise destroy as much of the camp equipment as could not be got away, and the desperate rifle and gun fire heard back at Nonidas reduced itself to harmless noise created by the destruction of thousands of rounds of both small arm and artillery ammunition. The advance parties of burghers arrived on the scene in time for a brush with the enemy's rearguard, of whom they captured nine, including one wounded. A large quantity of ammunition, clothing, and other military stores, together with transport, was rescued intact from the general conflagration.

That it was a close call for the enemy was evidenced by the statements of some of the prisoners, who paid a high tribute to the extraordinary mobility of the burghers, and expressed astonishment at the utter boldness and dash which characterised their movements. Only their better knowledge in the dark of the rough gorges in their line of retreat enabled the German main body to escape from the threatened embrace of the South African horsemen.

The prisoners confirmed the opinion formed at the time—that the Germans encountered during Col. Skinner's reconnaissance on Sunday, February 7, were, by a curious coincidence, on their way to attack Swakopmund in ignorance of our strength.

The drinking water at Nonidas was believed to have been deliberately poisoned, bottles containing chemicals of a suspicious nature being found in the well. The contents of these were sent to the Union for analysis, and General Botha again had occasion to direct the attention of the German Military Commander (Col. Francke) to this shameless flouting of the Geneva Convention. This appeal to the Teutonic mind to conduct the war on the humanitarian lines agreed to by the convocation of representatives of European nations (including Germany) met with the same lofty indifference as was conveyed in the response to the earlier communications on the subject. Col. Francke pointed out that the Geneva Convention provided for the pollution of drinking water so long as a written notice stating "This water has been poisoned" was posted in a conspicuous position on the spot. This, he contended, he had done, and if people chose to disregard these warnings, it was their own look-out, or words to that effect.

The only occasion on which any kind of warning was given was at Kubas, where a piece of cardboard imprinted with the word "Poison" was found partly embedded in the sand close to a water-hole.

In each of General Botha's notes it was pointed out that if the ignoble practice were persisted in he would reserve the right to exact any form of reprisal he deemed suitable, and that Col. Francke himself would be held personally responsible at the conclusion of hostilities. In spite of the bluster displayed at the outset, it was nevertheless a significant fact that, shortly after the exchange of the correspondence referred to, the poisoning of water lost much of its attraction in the eyes of the German military authorities.

With the occupation of Goanikontes a farm situated in the rich valley of the Swakop, an excellent supply of fresh water became accessible, and the Engineers, under Captain Muller and Lieut. Wauchope (both deservedly promoted Majors at a later stage) successfully employed their energies in improving the facilities for its better distribution for animal-watering purposes. Large fields of green lucerne were also found here, and made full use of by the burghers and the Imperial Light Horse for their appreciative steeds.

Patrols followed the track of the departed Germans through Heigamchab on past Husab to within a few miles of Riet, in front of which the enemy appeared to have concentrated.

At Husab, as elsewhere, petrol engines were erected in the river bed, and as soon as the watering arrangements were adequately adjusted to enable hundreds of animals to be watered simultaneously, this spot on the map became the advance commissariat depôt in anticipation of the next forward movement.

Subsequent to the occupation of Goanikontes, Lieut. Wauchope was responsible for the discovery of no less than thirty-seven cases of dynamite, arranged in sinister proximity to a case of old horse-shoes, a case of flanges of pipes, and a quantity of detonators, close to a newly dug trench in a narrow pass between rocky kopjes. Electric wires were laid from the trench to an observation post just behind the hills, and it is quite evident that the enemy was preparing another surprise packet for our troops when our rapid advance prevented the perpetration of further mischief.

In a building at Goanikontes a quantity of the small tubes already described in a previous chapter as playing an important part in the construction of land mines was also found.

A copy of the Windhuk newspaper *Sud-West* of February 9, picked up at Goanikontes, contained, under the heading of "How the British were Received at Swakopmund," an amusing, if inaccurate, account of what took place on the occasion of the explosion of the land mines. After giving a description of the manner in which the mines were laid (each one contained five cases of dynamite, surrounded with a cartload of bolts, screws and nuts, and filled up with gravel and stones), the writer relates how a man named Woker, on the approach of our troops, set off the mines. "At the same moment took place such a terrific explosion that only he who has actually heard the terrific din can have any conception of it. A noise, a shouting and roaring, a chaos of men and animals, smoke, sand, and fumes. Now everything that had not been blown into the air in bits tumbled towards the mouth of the Swakop, but Messrs. the Englishmen had reckoned without us. With iron nerve Woker had in the meantime detached the wires of the exploded mine and switched on the second mine. Again the same deafening cracking, shouting, and roaring. Everybody flew on the path leading towards Walfish Bay, when they naturally came to our principal mine. No sooner did they arrive there than that also went off. From the lighthouse Corporal Neckel, as well as I, could see how several men were thrown right on top of the dunes, about 15 metres high. After the last mine had exploded everybody retired, and the place was clear of the enemy. Only two men tried to follow the wires of the second mine, but were fortunately called back, and disappeared behind the dunes. Everybody was joyful because our work had been crowned with success. According to a prisoner, captured later, the mines must have caused terrible havoc. Pieces of saddles, men, and animals were lying around. In addition, half of the hostile troops rode back to Walfish Bay in panic. One of them died shortly afterwards, while another was seriously wounded. According to the statement of the prisoner, the Antonius Hospital in Swakopmund cannot hold all the enemy's wounded in that town, and the post office had to be pressed into service as a hospital. It will interest you to hear that Woker was deservedly promoted at once to the rank of corporal."

Thus ends a narrative not exactly unique in its possession of a grain of truth with a superstructure of fiction, for which alone Mr. Woker would have been entitled to his advancement and his friend, the recorder of events, to an Iron Cross.

The grain of truth lies in the fact that three mines were exploded and two of our men with their horses blown up. No further casualties occurred, and the suggestion that even the post office was "roped in" for the accommodation of the mutilated is a pretty piece of editorial fiction of the kultured variety.

In spite of our tropical situation, the climate on the return to Swakopmund was actually assuming such a damp and chilly character that, pursuing the form of nomenclature in popular use by the Central Force, there was a growing inclination to scrap the Teutonic-sounding appellation of Swakopmund for one more appropriate, if, in view of our geographical position, a trifle paradoxical, in that of "Koldaszell." We were spared the necessity for anything so premature. The task had hitherto been to overcome the desert, but during Monday and Tuesday (March 8 and 9) the Namib desert made a very creditable effort to reverse this order of things. For the first time since the arrival of the troops in those parts the wind blew directly from the sweltering interior, and the mountain indeed came to Mahomet, projected by a 50-knot gale of sirocco-like intensity. Scorching and suffocating winds, accompanied by clouds of fine sand and myriads of flies in the daytime, and followed by a plague of moths and mosquitoes at night, made life almost unbearable for the days it uninterruptedly continued. Apart from several cases of sunstroke occasioned by the excessive heat, the occurrence served to furnish some rather surprising revelations of the intimate knowledge enjoyed by certain members of the Northern Force of the conditions prevailing in the nether regions. For instance, one grizzled warrior, who had baked in Egypt and stewed in Ceylon, volunteered the opinion that these days had been like "hell with the lid off." And it is supposed that he spoke from experience.

Unfortunately for the 3rd Infantry Brigade, presumably to avoid the possible growth of herbage beneath its feet, manœuvres on the plains of Nonidas had been arranged for the memorable Monday—and the manœuvres it had to be, in spite of terrific heat, blinding clouds of sand, and increasing cases of sun affection throughout the demonstration. The indomitable perseverance and grim determination with which the manœuvres were enforced by the Colonel Commanding the Brigade was only equalled by the attitude of the driver of a certain municipal water-cart, who, taking for his motto: "Duty must be done though the heavens pour and the skies weep," continued to spray the thoroughfares with water during the programme of a particularly heavy thunderstorm.

Preparatory to the advance upon Windhuk, a military genius was smitten with a brilliant idea. In view of the possibility of the recurrence of contact mines, the notion was evolved that herds of goats should be driven ahead to tread upon the offensive projections, and the proposal commended itself to all except those who could not see just how the goats were going to be steered—in short, who would be the V.C. heroes willing to drive the unsuspecting animals forward? Meanwhile, hundreds of goats had been sent up to the front and were being grazed for some time in the river bed at Nonidas, in addition to receiving a liberal amount of imported fodder, running into tonnage, as a daily ration! Some difficulty was experienced in the assignment of the goats to the proper custody. The Engineers, upon whom it was hoped to foist the sacrificial animals because they were to be employed as an instrument to explode mines, and, therefore, so it was considered, were entitled to be classified as, perhaps, a "demolition gang," fought strenuously against the duties of herd which it was sought to impose upon them. The Scottish, too, rejected the proposition with enemy instinct, while the Remounts took it as quite an affront. There was nothing else for it; it was one of those occasions where a special appointment was called for among the already overloaded ranks of "Captains all," and so a three-starred, if not ill-starred, individual was created "O.C. Goats." Eventually the tender-hearted burghers volunteered to herd the universally scorned goats while concentrating at Nonidas for the advance. But by the time it was required to set out across the desert the burghers had evidently made up their minds to relieve the goats of their dangerous duties, for there was no answer to the roll call—only a steady frizzle from innumerable camp fires broke the stillness of the night, and an odour, quite impossible to associate with the bully beef ration in vogue at that period permeated the warm desert air.

CHAPTER V.

BATTLE OF RIET.

What is officially termed the first phase in the Northern Campaign, and which culminated in the occupation of Jackalswater and Riet, both strong strategical positions, would best be described as a brilliant swoop through country which, for its utter desolation, is probably without parallel in any other corner of the world.

Even the arduous Egyptian campaign could scarcely have presented greater difficulties than those with which the Union Forces were here confronted; interminable miles of dreary desiccated wastes—*sans* vegetation of any kind—out of which arise in a variety of heights and a confusion of order, unscaleable granite rocks of massive proportions, intermingled with smaller series of serrated and barren ridges. Not a drop of water, not a sign of life—a truly forsaken wilderness.

Through this extraordinary territory meanders the dry course of the Swakop River, between wondrous gorges of such awe-inspiring character that the voice is instinctively hushed at the terrible grandeur, as if in fearful expectation of a sudden encounter with the " Old Gentleman " himself, armed with horns and trident complete.

In spite of these discouraging conditions, however, the operations in this area resulted in the confusion and rout of the enemy, and the capture of a large proportion of his force with guns and other booty, together with the acquisition of some 70 miles of German territory from the coast inland.

General Botha made his dispositions as follows :—On the night of Friday, March 19, Col. Comdt. W. R. Collins, with the Left Wing of the Second Mounted Brigade, was sent from Husab to the north of Pforteberg and north of the Government Railway, to move between Jackalswater and Kubas, and also to attack Jackalswater at dawn on the following morning. At the same time Col. Alberts, with the right wing of the 2nd Mounted Brigade, under Col. Comdt. L. P. J. Badenhorst, was sent to attack Pforteberg at dawn on Saturday morning (March 20), at a spot where the railway and the Kubas road pass over the berg.

Colonel Collins succeeded in cutting the enemy's communications, capturing a train in the process, and attacked Jackalswater at dawn. The enemy were, however, too

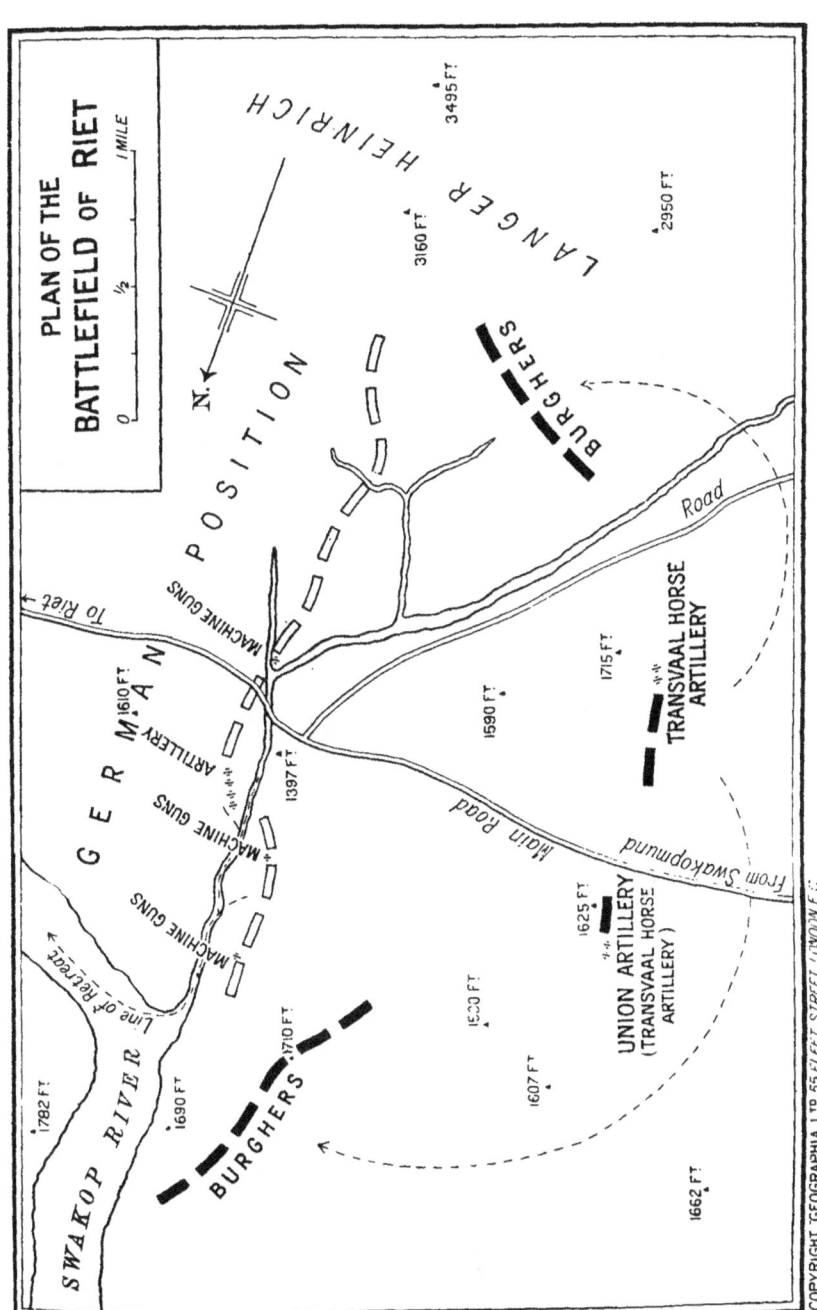

Motor Cyclist Despatch Riders near Riet.

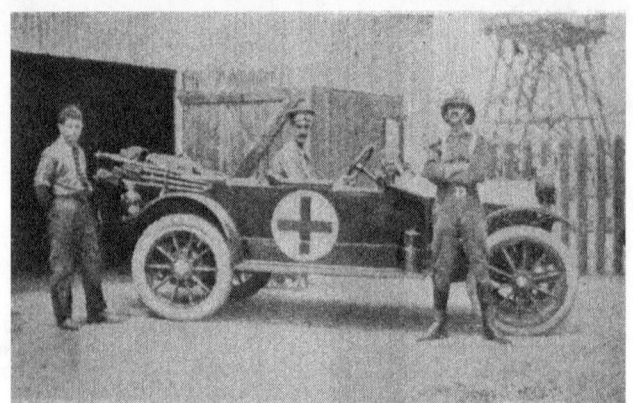

A Motor Car on Ambulance Service.

Two Types of Light Ambulance Wagons.

German Camel Corps Patrol.

Souvenirs of a German Camp.

German Camel Ambulance.

Colonel Francke and Governor Seitz leaving Windhuk.

The late Colonel Von Heydebrek and Major Francke at a War Council early in the Campaign.

strongly entrenched to be dislodged from this position, although Col. Collins undoubtedly prevented any assistance being sent by the enemy to Pforteberg, which was simultaneously being attacked by Col. Alberts and Col. Comdt. Badenhorst.

The 1st Mounted Brigade, under Brig.-General (then Col.) Brits, with the Transvaal Horse Artillery, moved from Husab on Friday evening to attack Riet at dawn on March 20, the Bloemhof Commando, under Commandant Bezuidenhout, being detailed to move round Langer Heinrich by Klein Tinkas and Mittel Tinkas on Schwarze Kuppe. General Botha accompanied this brigade.

The engagement at Riet practically resolved itself into an artillery duel between four guns of the Transvaal Horse Artillery and six German guns of similar calibre to our own.

So admirably were our guns disposed that the practice made by the enemy never once bothered them throughout the day, and a stray shrapnel bullet which struck the hindquarters of a battery horse, ridden at a point far behind, being the only casualty incurred by the Artillery. A different story is to be recorded of our gunnery, which never failed to find the mark, as was amply demonstrated when the gun emplacements of the enemy were afterwards examined, and found to be considerably battered about. It was very evident that here the Germans intended to make a firm stand, and they were much favoured in this determination by the peculiarly rugged nature of the country, of which I have already endeavoured to convey some impression.

The overture started about 7.30 a.m. with a shell from the Germans which fell away to the right over the steep and unoccupied slopes of Langer Heinrich Mountain. Sharp and frequent exchanges followed, and were carried on intermittently until midday, when the enemy's fire showed signs of flagging. For a couple of hours the enemy's batteries were silent, but towards 2.30 p.m. Major Taylor observed a movement to the right of the gorge in which the German guns were concealed, and rightly conjectured that the enemy were attempting to bring round their gun-teams. A shell was promptly despatched over the indicated spot, with such accuracy that a team of mules was straightway destroyed. A limber, fully stocked, and perforated by a shell, was found the following morning, still harnessed to the dead animals, besides two artillery wagons abandoned by the enemy in their flight. Desultory firing continued until dusk, when the enemy, completely routed, evacuated their position and camps under cover of darkness in much haste and confusion. In their retreat, the Germans blew up several railway truckloads of ammunition and general stores, while the line of their retirement eastward up the Swakop Valley was littered with hurriedly discarded great-coats, water-bottles, haversacks, and other infantry equipment.

At their artillery and infantry camps bivouacs were left standing with the men's kits, unpacked, lying around.

The German casualties amounted to eight dead found in proximity to their gun positions, eight others left behind wounded, and twenty-eight prisoners. Several newly dug graves were also seen in their lines, and many wounded were reported to have been removed by the Germans themselves.

The enemy were prevented from blowing up the water-holes at Riet by a small body of burghers under Capt. Lemmer, who successfully sniped a party of the enemy attempting to approach the wells. A large quantity of dynamite was found close to the spot the following morning.

When our troops were gathered round the water-holes at Riet an individual, partly concealed by bush a few yards away, attracted attention by his agitated attempts to dislodge some object from the ground. For several minutes he was the source of almost amused interest to the burghers awaiting their turn at the water, till it occurred to one of them to step over and satisfy his curiosity, when a real live German was found, ineffectually tugging at a wire which led to a mine situated immediately beneath the place where our horsemen clustered. Fortunately the Engineers had previously observed and cut the wire. The irrepressible one was promptly made prisoner.

While the artillery were effecting their coup at Riet, Col. Alberts' Brigade of Burghers, aided by the 4th Battery (S.A.M.R.), under Capt. Wolmarans (who had gained a prior reputation in the old Transvaal Staats Artillery), had been heavily engaged at Pforteberg, over 20 miles away to the north, and had early accomplished a very satisfactory performance in the capture of 210 prisoners with two field guns and a couple of maxims.

Here the German position, though a strong one, was early rendered untenable by the flanking movements of the mounted men, and after a desperate attempt at resistance the German force, to avoid utter annihilation, was compelled to surrender. One portion of Col. Alberts' men made a frontal attack and others charged spiritedly towards the guns, firing from their saddles, to the added bewilderment of the Germans, who were by now practically surrounded.

On seeing the burghers converging on horseback from all points of the compass a German officer is reported to have ejaculated: "But this is not war; it's a hippodrome."

The Machine Gun Section, under Lieut. L. Campbell, did good work, and a deadly hail of shells and bullets from all sides completed the discomfiture of the enemy, whose efforts to re-man their guns were rendered futile by the exactness with which our artillery persistently located the positions. Already a pile of killed and wounded were lying round the German guns intermingled with dead and dying mules—a sight sufficient to impress on the mind the real horrors of war. One body was found with the top of the head blown clean away, while another man had his lower jaw completely shattered by a shell. The enemy eventually put up the white flag after a game fight lasting several hours.

After the fight a wounded burgher stated that the Germans had set out first of all to shoot the burghers' horses as they dismounted, not anticipating that the Boers would storm and capture their position on foot. Another described how Commandant Piet Botha, of Heidelberg, unsuspectingly walked into a party of German soldiers. It was too late to retreat. He determined to "bluff." Keeping his head, he called upon the officer in command to surrender. The officer laughingly replied that that ruse would not do—the Herr Burgher must consider himself a prisoner. Commandant Piet Botha quietly but firmly assured the German that he really had come to take his surrender, "and," said he, turning round to see another straying burgher, who, luckily, just then made his appearance, "Here is one of my men coming to find out why you are detaining me." The Germans wavered before this delightful piece of audacity, but were unconvinced. At that moment, however, one of our shells burst over the position. In the confusion that followed Commandant Botha and his companion rejoined their comrades, and eventually captured their would-be captors.

German prisoners stated that Windhuk was constantly in wireless communication with Berlin, although they admitted that messages were more easily received than transmitted. They continued to believe that the Germans were in occupation of Paris, and that the Kaiser would shortly send reinforcements to their succour. Correspondence picked up on the battlefields at Riet and Pforteberg indicated a better realisation of the true state of affairs among the more educated classes in German South-west, who frankly admitted among themselves that the situation in the Protectorate, at any rate, was fast becoming hopeless.

No one could definitely say at the end of the day what was the measure of our success, until a tremendous explosion during the evening, reverberating among the hills for miles around, suggested to the Staff that the water supply at Riet had been blown up, and, consequently, that the enemy were retreating. Most of the horses and the mule teams of the guns had been sent to water at the nearest point in the Swakop River, many toilsome miles back along the road they had already traversed. Daylight disclosed a vacated position, and our troops were early making their way to Riet, a farm situated in the river valley a few miles farther on, where the waterholes were found to be secure. Near by, around the railway line, specially built by the Germans to feed the position from Jackalswater, were the smouldering remains of several truckloads of military stores, including ammunition, the actual result of the overnight explosion.

The sudden collapse of the real German line of defence at Riet tempted General Botha immediately to undertake the advance, there and then, to Windhuk; but the demand upon the Defence Department for an adequate supply of wagons failed to be met. Consequently, General Botha, much to his personal chagrin, was compelled to retire to Swakopmund with the bulk of the burgher forces, there to await the completion of preparations for a re-start under better auspices.

The explanation tendered by General Smuts, in the course of a speech at Cape Town, at the termination of the campaign, was that they had really been prepared for the Northern Expedition to follow the line of the Otavi railway. (Such an advance could only have been according to the rate of progress maintained by the railway engineers in the process of reconstructing the line to the standard gauge. But how one solitary line could have borne the burden it was contemplated to impose upon it was a point which could never have been adequately studied. As it was, some anxious moments were caused to the authorities at Swakopmund in keeping the comparative handful of troops engaged in guarding the line supplied with water, food, and fuel, and at the same time forwarding supplies to Kilo. 13, and construction material to railhead.)

General Smuts further explained that the additional transport necessary for an advance up the Swakop Valley was not obtainable in the Union, and even had it been so, there were not sufficient ships available at the time to carry it to Walvis Bay.

As the food requirements of the infantry were considerably less than those of the Mounted Section, the 4th Infantry Brigade was sent out to occupy Riet and its neighbourhood, and a few mounted patrols were left to work up the Swakop Valley and south-east along the Otjimbingwe road. By this means some opportunity was afforded the commissariat to amass mountains of supplies well forward at Riet, albeit the method of transport rendered the process slow and laborious. The train from Walvis Bay, running over the newly laid broad-gauge line, brought the supplies to Kilo. 13 (roughly eight miles beyond Swakopmund), where they were off-loaded on to wagons which trundled them across to the old transport road on the other side of the Swakop River. Here the loads were transferred on to motor-lorries, which, somewhere in the neighbourhood of Heigamchab, owing to the heavy sand, again gave place to mule wagons to Husab and Riet.

The South African Engineer Corps were kept busily employed improving the watering arrangements at Riet, Husab, and other points in the Swakop River, where petrol pumps were erected to cope with the heavy demands of the transport animals and others during this period of detention, and the thousands of horses still to come as soon as the reserve of supplies warranted the army setting out again.

All this time the Otavi line away to the left was being slowly replaced, mile by mile, by the broader Cape gauge, Colonel Skinner advancing the 3rd Infantry Brigade (with whom were the 1st Imperial Light Horse) along the old track in sympathy with the rate of progress of the new construction, and always leaving protecting blockhouses at intervals along this waterless desert route.

And what a difficult problem the watering of this large body of men, horses, and native labourers on the line became. There was only one possible way of doing it, and that was to bring the water from the coast. And a daily water-train, sandwiched in between the equally urgent supply and construction trains, was inaugurated at the outset to deliver water at the blockhouses and sustain life in the troops forward. This system it was found necessary to maintain even as far as Ebony Siding, close upon 70 miles from Swakopmund, and still more trains were required, solely for the conveyance of water, as the distance increased. From Ebony onward it was afterwards possible to supply water from Usakos. The monotonous character of these lines of communication duties was relieved to some extent by the visits which now began to be paid by the German aviator, and in spite of the fact that he left cards in the shape of bombs on each occasion, much interest and keen excitement was aroused by his "calls." The bombs all fell harmlessly many yards away from their objective, and, far from creating panic and sending the troops scuttling for cover, every one (including appropriately enough the mess cooks) found the chance of a "pot" at an aeroplane far too good to be neglected, and so the intended terror-striking visit was usually converted into an all-absorbing entertainment by the "boys." Several times the machine, following upon a volley from the rifles, was seen to bank suddenly, the aviator apparently finding our unorthodox reception of German frightfulness extremely disconcerting. On one occasion our anti-aircraft gun, which had been inscribed in white paint with the name "Skinny Liz" (and was afterwards irreverently dubbed "Lizzie Skinner") forwarded a few samples of shrapnel in such close proximity to the aeroplane that she suddenly appeared to take fright, and, with the propellor between her teeth, as it were, bolted back on top gear in the direction of Karibib.

Another elevating diversion which engaged the attention of the troops was mine-sweeping in the wake of the enemy, and between Trekkopjes and Ebony Siding alone detonators were discovered connecting with eighty mines. On the Khan Copper Company's property sixteen mines were found in the "spoor" of passing wagons, and when exploded by the Engineers blew in every window in the buildings. Immense quantities of dynamite were also found at the Khan Mine, far more than could possibly be needed for ordinary mining operations; and this was a noticeable circumstance all over the country, quantities of discarded dynamite positively littering the trail of the retreating foe from Swakopmund to Otavi.

What with the necessity for keeping on the alert for mines from below and bombs from above, and carefully examining all water sources for traces of poison, the Northern force, although seldom engaged in bloody battle, were nevertheless doing men's work, and none performed a more irksome task than the infantry, who manned the lonely blockhouses along the dreary lines of communication. Everyone was fully appreciative of the extraordinary achievements of the mounted forces; but few of the horsemen, I venture to think, would have been willing to exchange their varied duty for the utter monotony of sentry-go in the middle of the desert. And afterwards, when the infantry, under Brigadier-General Beves, were strongly represented up north at the final surrender, who would deny that their march of close upon 300 miles on foot in a tropical zone, often short of water and on reduced rations, was an accomplishment not only worthy of the greatest admiration, but one which is reflected in few, if any, equivalent performances.

CHAPTER VI.

TREKKOPJES.

The engagement at Trekkopjes, a siding on the Swakopmund-Otavi railway line guarded by the 3rd Infantry Brigade, afforded a remarkable and not altogether impressive demonstration of the military strategy of our opponents, although, had it not been that their intentions became known to Colonel Skinner by a mere chance, recalling a similar coincidence at Swakopmund on Sunday, February 7, the enemy might have furnished our troops with an unpleasant surprise.

On the night of Monday, April 25, Colonel Skinner, accompanied by the Imperial Light Horse, proceeded on a reconnaissance in force along the south of the line in the direction of Ebony. The troops left behind at Trekkopjes were the Scottish and Kimberley regiments, with the Naval Armoured Motor-car Section, recently arrived from England, and incidentally the Continent, where they had already seen active service.

For several hours the column trekked onward past Karub Siding, the moon casting a deceptive light over the wide and undulating expanse of the desert, without, however, revealing anything materially disquieting. At about 1 a.m., when near Ebony, the advance guard of the Imperial Light Horse reported a strong body of the enemy, with guns, moving parallel with the railway line on the opposite side. The steady rumble of the gun carriages travelling along a ridge, running from the Palgrave Mine to Trekkopjes, could now be distinctly heard by the main party.

So close did one of the I.L.H. troopers get to the Germans, in an endeavour to ascertain their strength, that in the dust-laden air he was suddenly passed by a horseman, who peremptorily ordered him in strong gutteral tones to "keep in line."

After such a close call our intrepid scout chose in preference a bee-line back to his regiment.

Some critics have pertinently asked why Colonel Skinner did not immediately arrange for an ambuscade across the German line of advance. Such a hastily-planned ambush against an unknown force might or might not have succeeded, although it is difficult to believe that confusion and upset of the German plans would not have resulted in (who knows?) a few guns to our credit. Colonel Skinner decided on the alternative and retired at some speed to prepare the camp at Tiekkopjes against surprise. The Rhodesians were hastily summoned by train from Arandis Siding, about twenty miles back on the line, and the Scottish and Kimberleys were promptly set to work striking tents and extending the entrenchments around the camp.

The Scottish occupied the right flank along the semi-circular line of trenches covering the point from which the attack was expected, the Kimberleys being disposed across the centre, and the left flank was reserved for the Rhodesians, who arrived at 7.30 a.m., in time to close up the line before the attack commenced.

At 5.45 a.m. the near approach of the enemy was proclaimed by an explosion on the railway line. It afterwards appeared that the enemy blew up the line east of the camp with the intention of preventing the arrival of reinforcements by rail, on the supposition that it was south of our position.

At 7.40 a.m. the enemy began shelling the camp from the ridges south-east of Palgrave Mine, at a range of about 5,000 yards, advancing and retiring their guns by half batteries.

Certain of the tents had been left standing, and in the half light the Germans energetically directed their first deluge of shrapnel solely over the deserted canvas. Unfortunately, apart from the anti-aircraft gun, the camp was without a single field-piece with which to respond to the ceaseless shower of shell, and " Skinny Liz " came in for far too many flattering attentions at the hands of the German gunners to enable her to be utilised during the attack. A further unlucky circumstance was the removal, only a day or two before, of two guns of the Heavy Artillery Brigade, recalled to participate in the general advance commencing the same day from Swakopmund.

As the morning advanced the enemy began to develop an attack on foot with fixed bayonets, securing good cover among the rocks and melk-bushes, which here abound.

Owing to the rocky nature of the ground it was found impossible in the time available before the arrival of the enemy to deepen our trenches to any appreciable extent, and in consequence many of our casualties occurred through the lack of sufficient cover, several of the men being wounded in their legs, which projected behind them.

The brunt of the attack was borne by the 2nd Kimberley Regiment, though all engaged underwent an experience which, if brief by comparison, yet in its fierce intensity was not dissimilar to European warfare as practised to-day.

Probably the principal rebuff to the Germans was administered by the Naval men with their armoured cars, which, moving to and fro on the south of the railway, sprayed the cautiously advancing Germans with Maxim fire as they flitted for cover from bush to bush. These newly-acquired war-machines came as a rude and unexpected shock to the Germans, whose aviator had mistakenly listed them in his report as field kitchens! The cars might have offered them a further revelation had it not been that the railway embankment proved insurmountable and prevented the armoured cars from getting to closer quarters with the enemy. So well are these cars protected that a rifle bullet, fired at point blank range, fails to penetrate the armour.

Lieut. Hollingsworth, in charge of the Machine Gun Section with the Rhodesian Regiment, was early shot dead while counselling his men to take better cover.

The firing was heavy and continuous until 10.30 a.m., when the German rifle and machine gun fire began to slacken.

As it appeared that the enemy were about to retire, the Kimberley and Transvaal Scottish battalions were ordered to counter-attack, and shortly afterwards all the available Imperial Light Horse, consisting of a squadron and a-half, were sent forward on the outer flank towards the north-west; but small progress could be made against the German artillery, which vigorously renewed its energies to cover the retirement. An hour later, at 11.30, the German batteries limbered up and withdrew, whereupon "Skinny Liz" rapped out a few retorts in return for the forward advances made by the Germans throughout the morning.

Our casualties were three officers and six men killed, and two officers and thirty men wounded. The Germans left on the field two officers and five men killed, and two officers and twelve men wounded. We also captured one officer and twelve men. The diary of a German doctor found in Windhuk gave the total German casualties as fifty-four. The official German report of the fight makes interesting reading :—

"Major Bitter attacked the enemy at daybreak on April 26. The enemy held a well-fortified and favourable position along the Otavi railway, and in spite of our having destroyed the line at the beginning of the action, they were able, after a very short time, to pour in reinforcements by armoured motor-cars, together with artillery from Arondis, Rossing, Khan and from the north. We subjected their camp to artillery and rifle fire for a considerable time, but at 10 a.m. our troops were compelled to withdraw, as still more reinforcements were reported to be approaching. Our losses are not yet definitely ascertained, as a number of our wounded fell into the hands of the enemy. Amongst our wounded are Hauptmann (Captain), Von Watter, Baron Bentheim and

Dr. Mahnz (Chief Medical Officer), in the hands of the enemy. There is still uncertainty as to the fate of twenty-six other wounded men."

It may be explained that the Germans, in mistake, blew up the line ahead of Trekkopjes instead of behind, as actually intended, to prevent the arrival of reinforcements.

With regard to the strength of the enemy force engaged, it was difficult to estimate accurately the numbers owing to the dust and their good cover. Prisoners admitted they had 700 mounted men with two batteries of quick-firers, but an Imperial Light Horse officer, whose specially good position to the west of Trekkopjes enabled him to gauge the number of Germans, thought that 1,500 was probably a truer reckoning. The prisoners also stated that another force with guns should have attacked our camp from the east, but failed to materialise.

The severity of the artillery bombardment was demonstrated by the riddled condition of the tents which had been left standing, shrapnel and shell splinters being found in exuberant plenty, embedded in kits and lying about the camp ground.

A curious feature in the German commissariat was noted that day when the water-bottles of the majority of the prisoners and wounded men were found to contain rum in varying quantities. Later we ascertained from natives that the officers of the force set out from Usakos to Trekkopjes on a wave of enthusiasm and champagne, and returned on a back-wash of depression.

CHAPTER VII.

ADVANCE TO WINDHUK.

Before proceeding with the details of the advance too much cannot be written of the almost insuperable difficulties attending General Botha's Army across wastes of the desert belt. In a country boasting about as much sustenance as the Polar regions, every mouthful of food for man and beast had in consequence to be transported, mile upon mile, along loose sandy tracks, through steep ravines and over rocky mountain passes, and if it is remembered that each load must include fodder for the draught animals themselves, for the forward journey as well as the return to the base, some conception of the magnitude of the task upon which the commissariat was engaged may possibly be conveyed to the lay mind.

To the average man it all appeared a hopeless proposition, even with the best of facilities; the Germans, too, believed an advance through the desert from Swakopmund to be beyond the bounds of possibility, and in a December issue of the Swakopmund newspaper the editor voiced the general opinion as follows:—"We do not, however, think that the British will permanently establish themselves in Swakopmund. There is nothing to get here, and to make Swakopmund the base for an invasion of the interior seems, to anyone who knows the country, to be a step without any prospect of success. The British Commanding Officer will therefore probably content himself with hoisting the Union Jack here and steaming away."

Yet we progressed intrepidly into the enemy's country, and the officers responsible for supplies and transport pursued a herculean undertaking, undaunted by the discouraging conditions of a forbidding country and an insufficiency of vehicles. Though, metaphorically, more kicks than ha'pence of credit were inclined to fall to these vitally essential arms of the service for the smallest of supposed shortcomings. Rations of a quality and quantity hitherto unknown by the veteran soldier were available, at the outset, without interruption, right up to the most advanced posts, and it would be nothing less than ungracious to withhold proper recognition of such invaluable services in a campaign unique for its difficulties. We were fighting the desert first and the enemy afterwards, and while the latter was brilliantly accounted for at Riet and

Pforteberg by the combatant section of the force, the steady progress against the former by the departmental corps was an equally meritorious performance.

Brigadier-General Coen Brits, with his A.D.C., Lieut. Muchaelian, left Swakopmund on the afternoon of April 26, arriving at Nonidas, where his brigades were encamped, that same evening. Towards the end of the following day the column moved out on the Riet road, and after trekking through the night in bright moonlight, arrived at Husab at 5 a.m. We had now left the mist belt far behind, and were within the field of operations of the enemy's aeroplane. In the absence of an anti-aircraft gun, Major Taylor (Transvaal Horse Artillery) sunk the trail of one of his 13-pounder quick-firers into an excavation in the sand, creating a tilt sufficient to secure the aviator a morning greeting. The column left that same afternoon without a call from the aerial visitor, so the efficacy of the improvised anti-aircraft gun was never tested. The precaution, however, was a sound one, the aviator having only a day or so before hovered over the supply stacks at Husab. Riet was reached at 2 a.m., and after a rest and watering the animals, the march was resumed at 2 p.m. along the river valley to Salem, where a Field Hospital was already established in the evacuated farm buildings. Here we saw some neglected lucerne fields which had been eaten almost down to the roots, but during the few hours' halt the horses patiently busied themselves in an endeavour to obtain even a microscopic nibble at the first green fodder some of them had seen for months. The road past Salem farm, by which route Brig.-General Brits had been preceded by General Botha and the 3rd and 5th Mounted Brigades, under Brigadier-Generals Myburgh and Manie Botha, was by now churned up into deep black powder, which rose like a thick, choking fog, obscuring the teams from the drivers and transforming white men into the semblance of nigger minstrels. Sir Walter Hely Hutchinson (one-time Governor of the Cape Colony) is credited with the saying, in reference to South Africa, that where there were good roads there were bad farms, and where the roads were execrable the farms were good. If this is truly the case, then the Salem farm well proved its claim to recognition as a valuable property.

At 1.30 a.m. the column arrived at Dieptal, another farm property in the Swakop Valley, and encamped in bivouac until 4.30 a.m. The next day, and for several days following, the advance was along the dry, sandy bed of the Swakop River, which is hereabouts flanked on either bank by picturesque stretches of green and well-wooded bush, containing some giant timbers, and affording distinct relief from the utter monotony of the surrounding desert country. On either side, beyond the bush, rose, barren and austere, mighty ridges of solid rock spreading away to the Chuos Berg on the north flank, and in the south to what are known as the Great Granite Mountains. The beauty of the river valley compensated in some slight measure for the more obvious drawbacks represented by the scarcity of water, half rations and the uncomfortable knowledge of the presence of contact mines, considerately planted about the river bed by an excogitating enemy, and which were no aid to poetic flights of fancy.

On Friday, April 30, an explosion was heard ahead of the column, and the news came back that three scouts of the Middleburg Commando had been blown up by a mine in the river bed near Dorstriviermund. The mine was of the observation kind, and was operated from a distance by a party of the enemy, who, after the explosion, hurriedly took their departure, leaving the mechanical starting-box behind in their concealed position. The unfortunate men were literally blown to pieces, and portions of their horses were found a hundred or more yards from the cavity made in the sand by the explosion. Thereafter the column proceeded cautiously, ever on the look-out for a protruding rod of iron.

The idea of the enemy in sowing mines was, of course, to demoralise our troops, but like "the Great Blockade" against England, it was a miserable failure, although it must be admitted that the sensation of riding over a possible minefield was as novel as it was disconcerting.

The water question was found to occupy the mind to the exclusion even of mines, especially in view of the large number of men and animals to be catered for. At the various outspans numerous parties of men, armed with spades, set to work digging for water in the river bed. At the depth of a few feet it was generally found, and the seemingly impossible task of watering thousands of men, horses and mules from these miniature wells was oft repeated.

At intervals the column arrived at a regular water-hole, usually associated with a farm, the pump at which, however, had been almost invariably disabled by the enemy, and the supply being insufficient for all, fresh wells had perforce to be dug.

The transport and gun-teams experienced a hard time, ceaselessly hauling their heavy loads through the deep river sand, and it was only because they had started off in splendid condition from the base, that few signs of distress were as yet manifested among them.

Passing the mouth of the Gamikaub River, the column was halted for a few days in the neighbourhood of a farm called Bulsbout. General Botha, with his staff and bodyguard, who had worked across country from Itjimbingwe, stopped a few miles further on, round a bend in the river at Pot Mine. Here Brigadier-General Brits spent most of the time, in company with General Botha, awaiting news of the 3rd and 5th Brigades, which had been sent to cut the line between Karibib and Windhuk.

General Smuts arrived on a visit from the Southern Force, having motored over from Swakopmund in our trail, and left again on his return journey on May 4.

About this time subtle efforts were being made throughout the Union, by a certain section of the community, to create embarrassment to the authorities wherever possible, and a particularly malignant kind of rumour reached Swakopmund shortly before the Windhuk advance to the effect that relations between General Botha and General Smuts had become strained. General Smuts, it may be explained, was at the time supervising, in person, the operations in the south, and the impression it was apparently desired to convey was that General Smuts had grown jealous of the Prime Minister's increasing popularity. If it was ever necessary to give the lie to such a ridiculous report it was early dissipated by General Smuts' arrival from the south on a visit to General Botha at Pot Mine. The meeting was altogether a cordial one, and on General Smuts' departure from Karibib, some days later, the farewell between South Africa's two great men was almost boyish in its open sincerity.

From Dorstriviermund General Brits had despatched Colonel Lemmer with the 1st Mounted Brigade across to Kubas to reconnoitre a strong natural position on the old Government line to Karibib, and this the burghers occupied without opposition on May 2. News having come through that General Myburgh and General Manie Botha had succeeded in cutting the line as directed, General Botha, taking with him General Brits, with the 2nd Mounted Brigade, the Transvaal Horse Artillery, and a detachment from the Heavy Artillery Brigade, left the river at 1 a.m. on the morning of April 5 and struck out directly for Karibib, the important junction of the lines from the north, south, and west. Colonel Wylie, with the 4th Infantry Brigade, composed of the 1st Durban Light Infantry, the S.A. Irish, and the Rand Rifles, was in the meantime working up the railway from Riet towards Kubas and Abbabis, to secure the line through to Karibib. From the Swakop Valley to our destination there was a trek of close upon forty miles to be performed in one unbroken journey without water, with the prospect of opposition and consequent delay en route, and the uncertainty as to whether the town water supply at Karibib would be found to be preserved. The few water-holes encountered on the way were, as had been rightly surmised, destroyed, and the windmills lay in a tumbled mass upon the ground at each of the farms. And it is worth pointing out here that no enemy could have damaged some of their farm properties more than did the Germans themselves in the vain hope of arresting our advance.

On and on the column trekked over a seemingly neverending trail, without a sign of water or a glimpse of the railway town, the labouring mules and drooping horses patiently toiling on through the tropical heat of the day and the suffocating dust of the track.

At last the town could be discerned a few miles ahead, lying in a hollow between low scrub-studded kopjes, all widely encircled by heather-coloured ranges of weather-beaten granite mountains. At this point General Botha sent in a messenger with a white flag demanding the immediate surrender of the town. In the meantime General Brits took the 1st Brigade well forward, backed by the guns of the Transvaal Horse Artillery, in readiness for an attack if such were called for. Would our entry be opposed? Immediately arose the dreaded question of water. To be held up within sight of a plentiful supply, for who could say how long, was a thought one scarcely dared dwell on. For we represented only a portion of the Northern Force, whom a concentration of the enemy might hold at bay for a sufficiently long time to render desperate the parched condition of our animals. Had we met with opposition it was the intention, so I am informed, to send back half the animals during the night to the Swakop River, and await their return before releasing the remainder for the same process.

In theory the idea was picturesque, though it is a little difficult to conceive how the notion would have operated in practice. The animals had already performed a march of over forty miles without water, and forty miles back would have been necessitated to the river, with a return over another forty-mile waterless stretch. Presuming that Karibib had not fallen by that time, the pilgrimage would supposedly have been repeated—always provided that the animals still retained their powers of locomotion.

However, at about 3 p.m., with the aid of our field-glasses we could see the officer, who had been despatched with the white flag, returning, and the uncertainty prevailing as to the nature of the reply was soon brought to an end when it was announced that General Botha's demand had been complied with.

Accompanied by Brigade-Major Brink and others of his staff, Brigadier-General Brits preceded the troops, and was received on the outskirts of the town by a few of the leading citizens bearing a white flag. Prior to the arrival of this peaceful party one of our scouts had galloped back from the north of Karibib to report that he had come under fire from the town itself. As the German forces were observed making away in a cloud of dust northward, it was concluded that the shots emanated from their rear-guard, who probably feared further pursuit. It was stated at the time that a female inhabitant of the town received a bullet in her shoulder, and under the circumstances it would be unfair to bestow blame upon anyone on either side for the unfortunate occurrence.

The Transvaal Horse Artillery, of Riet fame, under Major Taylor, and a detachment of Howitzers, under Captain Pickburn (H.A.B.), maintained their places steadily with the column throughout, as did the Machine-Gun Section of Maxims and rifles, under Capt. M. J. Wolmarans. So for the sake of our dumb friends at least, it was a relief to find the town evacuated, and the poor fatigued beasts were watered with all expedition. The entry into Karibib was greeted by the sight of clear crystal water running into a commodious cement trough, from which it was impossible to restrain the horses once it was scented, and long and deep were the draughts of which they greedily partook before permitting themselves a pause for a sigh of profound satisfaction.

With the exception of a few native servants the streets were deserted, though several anxious faces were to be seen peering cautiously through curtained windows in most of the houses in the main thoroughfare. Our peaceful demeanour soon, however, inspired confidence, and realising that it was apparently not our intention to convert the town into a second Louvain, the population of both sexes boldly began to emerge from its concealment to view the khaki army. All was quiet and orderly; Colonel (then Major) de Waal, Provost-Marshal to the Northern Forces, promptly entered upon the duties of his office in consultation with the Mayor and leading citizens. There were no supplies in the town except what was left by the military for the maintenance of the inhabitants—a supply sufficient to last everyone for two months. Our position was less comforting. We had outdistanced the supply " trains," and rations for men and animals were for some days down to the irreducible minimum, and the long-promised grass country was still conspicuous by its absence. It is true that in the near vicinity of Karibib sparse grass was met with, growing in isolated and parched tufts, but after their long enforced abstinence from grass the animals almost failed to recognise their natural form of diet, and required to be educated up to a proper appreciation of it.

A large quantity of rolling-stock of both the narrow and broad gauges was found in the station yards, as well as a small engine or two which usefully supplemented those already being employed to link up the force by rail with the base.

British Prisoners from Sandfontein leaving Windhuk Station.

German Artillery in South West—Ox Transport.

Obstructing the Railway south of Windhuk during German Retreat.

1st Imperial Light Horse Skirmishing.

General Botha with his Staff directing a fight during the advance from Swakop.

General Botha at Windhuk Station with his A.D.C., Lieut. Jantje Botha, and Lieut.-Col. Mentz, Military Governor of Windhuk.

Burgher Forces entering Windhuk.

Captured German Wagons at Windhuk.

General Botha enters Windhuk by motor car.

It is here that the 3-ft. 6-in. gauge from Windhuk meets the 2-ft. gauge from Swakopmund and from the North. Unfortunately, the old Government line, via Jackalswater, which it was hoped to utilise for the quick conveyance of supplies to Karibib signally failed to realise the confidence reposed in it at the outset, owing principally, it was stated, to the incapacity of the engines and the action of the water on the boilers. Although sound engines of the narrow-gauge variety were sent round from the Union, a few old engines discarded by the Germans had also been brought into action after undergoing treatment at the hands of the Engineers. The engines really capable of performing the work were in possession of the Germans. So the longer and more laborious route via Usakos and Onguati had to be resorted to.

The Army was meanwhile on the verge of starvation for the want of everything but fresh meat, of which there was luckily an abundance in the neighbourhood, and the urgent requests to the base were for biscuits and fodder only, until further orders.

Of bread there was none to be had in the town, the inhabitants using a substitute made from mealies, of which they had only sufficient for their own needs.

Only a few days elapsed before Colonel Wylie arrived with the 4th Infantry Brigade, which had marched over sixty miles in a column parallel to the Mounted Brigades from Riet to Jackalswater, and up the old railway line, through Sphinx, Drostriviermund, Kubas and Abbabis.

They too had failed to see anything of the enemy except his land mines and polluted water-holes. Around Kubas, where miles of entrenchments and many gun emplacements were discovered to have been hastily evacuated, almost one hundred contact mines were found, and rendered harmless. The casualties caused by land mines were altogether miraculously small in comparison with the large number of these devices with which all roads to Windhuk were uncomfortably bestrewn. At Kubas, days after the removal of the mines, already referred to, had been effected, one was found close to a water-hole, around which men and horses had trampled for days. The mine was constructed on the trap-door principle, and by some remarkable stroke of fortune the lid had been broken without setting off the detonator beneath. Another providential escape was that of Colonel Brennan and Captain Goldberg, and with them probably the entire regiment of South African Irish, who were the leading battalion with the 4th Infantry Brigade on the march to Kubas. Col. Brennan had taken a seat in a motor-car of the Machine Gun Section, driven by Captain Goldberg, and proceeded in advance of the column, the better to gain a knowledge of the country in case of an attack by the enemy. When in the neighbourhood of Sphinx Siding the car, in passing through a narrow dip in the roadway, was observed to have run between several points of iron of a now familiar type. The column was immediately halted, and precautions against surprise having been taken, examination of the mined area brought to light the boxes of explosives containing in all some four hundred and fifty sticks of dynamite and blasting gelatine, above which ten contact points had been arranged across the eight-foot width of roadway. Two of these points had been brushed by the wheels of the motor-car.

Experts stated that the mine was powerful enough to have ensured the death of all within a radius of a hundred yards.

Colonel Wylie had a similarly unpleasant experience the following day. And Col. Rogers (Kimberley Regiment) and Capt. Hayes (I.L.H.) also narrowly escaped annihilation at the Khan Mine. These two officers were riding away from the mine property when Capt. Hayes' horse struck its shoe against a projecting piece of metal in the roadway, and from the spot in the ground smoke immediately began to issue. It is perhaps superfluous to add that neither of them found his natural curiosity sufficiently strong to detain him a moment beyond the time necessary to apply spurs. Curiously enough, no explosion took place, though subsequent examination disclosed a rich deposit of dynamite. Yet a further instance was reported of a man who actually trod upon a mine, and got off with only a slightly injured toe and a scarred leg, the detonator alone exploding. In the Dorstrivier a native wagon driver, seeing a mine in front, jumped off his vehicle right on top of another mine, which exploded with just enough force to kill the boy, though it left the wagon and team undamaged.

The uncertainty as to when one might involuntarily be projected heavenward was a nerve-racking experience for all, but the majority of the native wagoners became absolutely " panicky," after having witnessed the result of the explosion at Dorstriviermund during General Brits' advance. As the column continued on its way up the river bed, wagon boys, anxiously searching with their eyes the ground, would suddenly and excitedly sing out in warning tones, " Pas op, Baas! " and point with their whips to what usually resolved itself into a small black twig sticking straight up out of the white sand. It was about this time that Capt. Harris' native servant, one evening taking his master's revolver, shot himself dead only a few yards away from his astonished " baas." The explosions had evidently preyed on the boy's mind, though it is an unusual occurrence for a native to take his own life.

The plan of campaign pursued on the eventual advance to

the capital was in principle precisely the same as was intended when the check arose at Riet, due to the shortage of transport. Colonel Skinner was to hold the left, and therefore northern, flank along the Otavi railway with the 3rd Infantry Brigade and 1st Imperial Light Horse moving steadily along to Ebony and Usakos in sympathy with the other columns. Colonel Wylie, with the 4th Infantry Brigade, took the left centre route along the old Government line, between the Swakop Valley and the Ceros Berg, converging with Brig.-General Brits and the 1st and 2nd Mounted Brigades, who followed the course of the Swakop River, upon the town of Karibib. General Botha himself took the 3rd and 5th Mounted Brigades away to the right flank via Tsaobis and Otjimbingwe.

From Otjimbingwe Colonel Alberts was despatched with a portion of his brigade to ward off anything unexpected from the direction of Windhuk and the extreme right, while Brig.-General Myburgh proceeded out in broad daylight upon the Windhuk road with the balance of the force, as a blind to the enemy, whose scouts naturally reported that our designs were immediately upon Windhuk. After proceeding along this road for about ten miles, as far as Uitdraai, General Myburgh swung suddenly to his left and made directly across country for Wilhelmstal, situated on the main line between Karibib and Okohandja. This was the force with which it was intended to attack Karibib from the north, but General Myburgh's masterly execution of his particular mission to cut the line at Wilhelmstal gave the Germans food for reflection which resulted in the hasty evacuation of the railway town.

CHAPTER VIII.

OCCUPATION OF WINDHUK.

Conversations over the telephone at Karibib with the Mayor of the capital having resulted in the assurance that the entry of the Union troops into Windhuk would not be opposed, General Botha, taking with him only a few of his Staff and a small detachment of the Bodyguard (South African Police) under Major Trew, decided to make for Windhuk with all speed.

Seventeen of the best motor-cars were pressed into this special service, and included a motor section of the Machine Gun Corps with a Maxim and Rexer guns. Contenting himself with such a small protective force, General Botha adventurously set out on a journey of close upon one hundred and twenty miles.

Leaving Karibib at 2 p.m. on May 11, we arrived and bivouacked that night in proximity to the small wayside station at Okasisse.

The route led eastward, parallel to the railway line, through thick thorn-bush country and on past the blue towering heights of the Ombutosu Mountains far away to our left. The virgin bush yielded ample dry wood for the few small fires needed to cook the simple fare of fresh goat and coffee, in which the General participated with the rest, personally assisting to maintain the blaze with an occasional hefty branch procured from a near-by tree. Pickets were duly posted in the event of an unsolicited call from a prowling German patrol, and Captain Wolmarans kept the comforting machine guns ready for action. But nothing untoward occurred, and at the first sign of dawn we were up and away; the apology for a road meandered through bush of varying density to within a few miles of Okahandja, where the unkempt trees gave way to charmingly wooded natural parkland, which converted the track into a shady avenue leading directly into the small though picturesque town. Here a halt of several hours was made, General Botha conferring with Brigadier-General Myburgh (the bulk of whose command was already on its way to Windhuk), and also, by telephone, with the Mayor of Windhuk, relative to the time of our arrival at the capital the next morning.

From Okahandja to Windhuk the road can only be described as execrable, and that our fleet of motor-cars negotiated its appalling intricacies without a single mishap spoke as highly for the present-day efficiency of motor traction as it did for the proficiency of our drivers. Our old friend the Swakop River wound tortuously across the track, and all too frequent were the crossings to be made through the deep, sandy bed. Much strenuous work devolved upon all on these occasions, General Botha himself, Staff Colonels, Staff Majors, and others all pushing vigorously and perspiring freely in the broiling sun to gain the opposite banks.

Progress, under these circumstances, was, as may be imagined, none too rapid, and another night in the bush was necessary about 20 miles from our destination. At one point on the road, in a clearing in the bush, we came upon four wagons and teams of mules abandoned by the Germans. The animals had been killed in their traces, and the wagons were partly destroyed by fire.

Daybreak again found every car jolting away over the last lap to the long-desired goal, and by 10 o'clock in the morning the church spires and the tall and attenuated masts of the wireless began to show up above the sea of bush; a halt was made in sight of the red-roofed town itself, to await the arrival of the Burgomaster. Owing to the difference in time (our army keeping the Cape time), some delay was occasioned, but eventually the Mayor, dressed in immaculate white duck and driving a smart brown phaeton, arrived on the scene, and a long conversation ensued between this official and General Botha, in the course of which the town was formally and unconditionally surrendered.

The scene was worthy of perpetuation at the hands of an artist. There, in the middle of the path, in bright sunshine, stood the khaki-clad form of General Botha, his great bulk positively overshadowing the—by comparison—almost diminutive proportions of the Burgomaster, and, with a stern and dignified expression upon his features, he conversed in earnest tones with the town's representative. At a respectful distance behind the two central figures stood the members of the Staff—just a little in advance of the long trail of motor-cars. Drawn up on either side of the road were Brigadier-General Myburgh's advance guard of burghers, accompanied by the 4th Battery (S.A.M.R.) Artillery, under Captain J. F. Wolmarans. Both General Botha and the Burgomaster spoke in English. The conversation being concluded, the Mayor drove back to town, and then began the march into what has now become the historic capital of the South-west African Protectorate.

The Mounted Brigades, under General Myburgh, here formed procession with the Headquarter motor "column," which comprised, in addition to General Botha, the following officers :—Colonel Collyer (Chief Staff Officer), Major Bok (Military Secretary), Major de Waal (Provost-Marshal), Major Trew (Commanding Bodyguard), Major Leipoldt (Chief Intelligence Officer), Captain Esselen (Personal Staff), Captain Muller (S.A.E.C.), Captain Dingwall, and Lieutenant Cook (Field Telegraphs), Captain Collender (Topographical Section), the Machine Gun Section, commanded by Captain M. J. Wolmarans, with Captain Goldberg and Lieut. Snow.

The long and imposing cavalcade proceeded directly to the Rathaus, on the stoep of which General Botha, with his Staff, and the Burgomaster were already assembled. The burghers, mounted on their horses, were drawn up several deep in a semi-circle facing the entrance. A large number of the inhabitants were congregated on either side of the steps, and followed the proceedings with grave interest.

The Union Jack was hoisted over the building amid cheers from the troops. A Proclamation was then read in English, Dutch, and German, declaring martial law over the whole of the area bounded in the north by the Swakopmund-Karibib-Okahandja railway line, and thence eastward along latitude 22° to the Bechuanaland border.

After impressing upon the inhabitants, who, with refugees from Swakopmund and Lüderitzbucht, numbered over 3,000, that so long as their conduct warranted it, so long would they enjoy exemption from any vexatious restrictions, the troops were dismissed to camps on the outskirts of the town. Owing to the jaded state of the horses, the town for the first few days was patrolled by military police in motor-cars.

Colonel Mentz and Colonel de Waal were temporarily installed as Military Governor and Provost Marshal of Windhuk respectively. There was, however, little need for any special vigilance. An air of calm serenity pervaded the town, and even feminine expeditions, with their inseparable interludes for tea and gossip at the cafés, continued uninterruptedly, and war appeared to be, for the time at least, far from the minds of the residents. Before the occupation it was generally believed that Windhuk was suffering severely from the shortage of food, but, apart from the entire absence of luxuries (the prices of which were naturally inflated), nothing like famine conditions prevailed. Of fresh meat there was an abundance ; the bread, composed principally of mealies (maize), under the special treatment employed, was quite palatable; and sugar, tea, and coffee, though scarce, were obtainable in limited quantities at the hotels and restaurants. Jams and condiments generally had long since given in, but not being indispensable articles of diet, their absence failed to incommode the inhabitants seriously. Altogether, Windhuk had not fared too badly, and continued to live well under the circumstances.

The country from Windhuk northward affords excellent pasture for cattle, herds running into thousands of head, and in splendid condition, fortunately being available. The "Promised Land" thus far appeared to be fulfilling some of the expectations held out by those with a previous knowledge of the country, though it was hard to realise, during the trying march through the Namib Desert, that conditions could ever improve.

After such a period of unusual privations across country unequalled for its amazing austerity and altogether forbidding aspect, it took a little while to realise thoroughly that we had at last arrived at our primary goal—Windhuk, the capital of German South-west Africa! The home of the second largest wireless apparatus in the world, which so recently had been in direct communication with Berlin, over 5,000 miles distant.

A visit to the wireless station, situated a short distance from the town, revealed the presence of a surprisingly large and powerful electrical plant, housed in a substantial stone and iron structure, from which radiated cables to several steel masts, each 360 ft. in height, resting upon large glass insulators, and disposed over an area of many acres. The machinery in the power-house, which consisted of two engines each of 290 h.p. and two of 70 h.p., remained intact, as also did a complexity of accumulators and other electrical contrivances. The instruments in the operator's room had, however, been removed. The total cost of this colossal wireless station is stated to have exceeded a quarter of a million sterling.

None had doubted General Botha's ability to accomplish successfully the colossal task which lay before him when he set out from Swakopmund only a short sixteen days before. The event, indeed, showed that only indomitable courage and a perseverance bordering upon the obstinate, on the part of our remarkable leader, could have seen the campaign through to such a satisfactory issue. It is true that no big battles were added to history, but this was due solely to the clever strategy and wonderful marching inspired by General Botha, who so successfully followed Napoleon's principle of expending the sweat of his men instead of their blood. The bold resolve to push through to Windhuk at all costs, leaving supply "trains" hopelessly in the rear, was reminiscent of Lord Roberts's courageous decision in 1900 to sacrifice over 200 wagons full of supplies at Riet River, in order to hurry forward and ensure the investment of General Cronje's force at Paardeberg.

And what redoubtable marching had been done! Columns traversing hundreds of miles of the enemy's country for days at a stretch, often without food and water, and mostly on a little fresh meat for the men, and a handful of grass for the animals, gathered with difficulty from odd clefts in the rocks! The 3rd and 5th Mounted Brigades subsisted for as many as eight days on meat alone, without even the desirable concomitant of salt, and all the time pressing rapidly forward. The feat can only be described as splendid, and worthy of the best traditions of both Boer and Briton.

While the 3rd and 4th Infantry Brigades were being absorbed along the ever-increasing lines of communication, the Duke of Edinburgh's Own Rifles (Colonel Gregory in command), who had been guarding the blockhouse line between Walvis and Swakopmund, were moved up-country over the big chess-board, and eventually relieved the 1st Durban Light Infantry at Karibib. The Southern Rifles were transferred directly from Walvis to Swakopmund, Lieut.-Col. Weir, the officer commanding, assuming the duties of Officer Commanding Troops at the latter town in the place of Lieut.-Col. Dick, who, with his regiment, the 2nd Durban Light Infantry, had followed the advance.

The occupation of Windhuk and the retirement of the enemy northward, obviated the necessity for the further retention of infantry in the southern field of operations, and a transference was accordingly made, amongst others, of the 1st Infantry Brigade, under Colonel P. S. Beves, from Lüderitzbucht to Swakopmund, by sea. The regiments so transferred were 1st Transvaal Scottish (Lieut.-Col. Dawson Squibb), Witwatersrand Rifles (Lieut.-Col. J. Smythe, V.D.), and Pretoria Regiment (Lieut.-Col. Freeth).

On the promotion of Colonel Beves to the rank of Brigadier-General, his command was reorganised to comprise 1st Durban Light Infantry (Lieut.-Col. Molyneux), 1st Transvaal Scottish, Pretoria Regiment; 1st Rhodesian Regiment, and the 2nd Kimberley Regiment. With this augmented brigade Brigadier-General Beves accompanied the final advance to Otavi.

The South African Mounted Rifles, under the command of Brigadier-General Lukin, D.S.O., were also brought round from the Southern Army, and, with the 1st Imperial Light Horse, formed the newly constructed 4th Mounted Brigade. Sir Abe Bailey acted as D.A.Q.M.G. to this brigade, with the rank of Major.

Colonel Skinner was appointed General Officer Commanding Lines of Communication.

The following extract from a private letter of a German soldier, picked up at Riet, provides an amusing contrast to the last editorial published in the *Sud-West* prior to our entry into the capital :—

" . . . He (the writer's brother) has at Stolzenfels met, not the English, as he hoped, but has made the acquaintance of the Boers, as he had to work together in parts with Maritz and his commando. You will probably be interested to hear his opinion about them. He thinks they are an appalling piggery. He considers the average Boer does not stand much above the native, and he thinks it impossible for Boers and Germans to work together, or even to co-operate, as a Boer has no idea of obedience or discipline. If it strikes a Boer to do so, he will leave his work, go out of the firing line, and boil some coffee, even if his superior stands next to him and swears, unless his officer has a good sjambok and a strong arm. It is sad to have such allies. My brother thinks also that we cannot trust the Boers. . . ."

The editorial reads :—

"The occupation of Windhuk must at present be taken as unavoidable. Days, perhaps even only hours, separate us from tha moment. It is our duty to bear the inevitable with dignity. We need not say that the approaching forces will not be opposed in any way on their entry into the town, and, under the circumstances, we may rely with complete assurance that not a hair of a head of a single citizen will be injured by the enemy. General Botha's troops are neither Russians nor undisciplined French, but are men of a kindred race, of the same Teutonic extraction as ourselves, whose leader would never countenance any improper conduct against members of a fellow-cultured nation. Wherever the enemy have thus far occupied any portion of our territory they have behaved themselves as civilised soldiers. Men, women, and children have been treated by them with the utmost respect and consideration. They have not only respected private property, but have even placed guards over private residences, and we are certainly entitled to say that the troops now approaching us will be equally considerate.

"News reaches us from Keetmanshoop that our womenfolk left behind there have been treated with every possible respect, with great courtesy; and similar reports come from the farms to the north. The enemy have paid in cash for all foodstuffs requisitioned, and in every case their personal bearing towards the farmers and their families has been thoughtful and friendly. We, therefore, repeat with emphasis that the citizens of Windhuk may await the advent of the enemy free from all anxiety, and we are certain that the opposing forces within our gates will extend to us the same kindly treatment that they have displayed elsewhere."

The article concluded with an appeal to the inhabitants to do nothing to excite ill-feeling, but, on the other hand, enjoined upon them to preserve their dignity, and to abstain from fraternising with the enemy.

A further article stated: "The occupation can, at the most, only last a week or two, as dire calamity has undoubtedly overtaken the Allies in Europe. Calais is practically in our hands, and with Calais we have our hand on the latch of the door to England. British Statesmen are not going to wait until we have entered their prosperous land, and will assuredly offer us the hand of peace in order to save their country from invasion. It goes without saying that the Fatherland will not conclude peace which leaves German South-west Africa in foreign hands, and we may say with confidence that the enemy's banner will not long wave over us."

A tribute to the work of the troops was published in Special Field Orders at Karibib on General Botha's return from Windhuk: "The General Officer Commanding-in-Chief desires at this stage of the campaign, when the enemy's capital and principal towns, seaports, and the bulk of the railways have fallen into our hands, to express his very high appreciation of the splendid spirit shown by all the troops under his command. The work just completed has been performed under conditions which only those who experienced them can properly appreciate, and the country has every reason to be grateful to and proud of the men who have accomplished the task. It has fallen to the lot of some of the troops to be compelled to undertake duty of a more monotonous nature than that allotted to their comrades in the front of the advance, and the work done was impossible without the uncomplaining services rendered by the troops on lines of communication, who performed their part of the general work with cheerfulness and readiness, of which the General Officer Commanding-in-Chief desires to record his admiration. All troops were not fortunate enough to engage the enemy, though in several instances they had done so with conspicuous success."

Simultaneously with General Botha's departure for Karibib came the news that a German convoy, about 20 miles to the east of Windhuk, was endeavouring to rejoin the main body in the north. Col. Mentz hastily collected his command, which included Hunts' Scouts, and, with the battery of artillery which had silenced the German guns at Pforteberg (the 4th Battery S.A.M.R.), hurried out to intercept the prize. After the exchange of a few shots the convoy of some fourteen wagons, loaded with ammunition and supplies (including a large consignment of rum), fell an easy prey to our superior force, and was brought into the capital together with more than a hundred prisoners.

Taking advantage of the lull in the operations, I made a trip back to Swakopmund from Windhuk, viâ Karibib, Usakos, and Ebony, and thence by the broad-gauge line to the coast. The journey cannot truthfully be described as having savoured of the *de luxe*, the first part being performed perched on the top of a tender from Usakos to Ebony, over the original diminutive line, behind a wheezy little engine, which recalled the model variety associated with Yuletide and the nursery floor. The miniature train, however, bravely tackled the long and steep climb to Ebony, bidding farewell to the mountainous country lying immediately behind. Aukus, a signboard doing duty for a station overlooking the well-wooded Khan River Valley, where twinkling fires denoted the camps of the 1st Mounted Brigade, was reached with comparative swiftness, and it was not until after the re-start from here that our little coffee-pot of a locomotive began to develop irritating asthmatic tendencies. Every few miles a halt on the moonlit desert was caused by a violent bronchial attack on the part of the engine, preceded by shrill, suffocating gasps dying gradually down to low, moaning sobs, as if it only too well comprehended its own incapacity. On each of these occasions the fires were drawn from the engine, and a fresh cooking of water was required before courage enough could be instilled to propel us a few further miles onward. Ebony, where the tents of the Headquarters of the 3rd Infantry Brigade showed up in the bright but chilly night, was eventually reached in the small hours, and a transference to the broad-gauge train in waiting was immediately made. Flat open trucks were now our portion, and, together with the many burghers homeward bound, some attempt was made to bed-down for the remaining hours of darkness, as far from the unprotected sides of the truck as the limited space and large numbers would permit. But it was war time, and the accommodation in the circumstances nothing more than could be expected.

War teaches one many things, and it particularly inculcates a spirit of contented philosophy. Consequently, there was never a murmur at the delays, which in ordinary times would be classified among the soul-destroying incidents of life. Had anything been needed to still impatience, the occasional glimpses of solitary figures at lone blockhouses, separated from each other by miles of maddening monotony, would have proved more than sufficient to shame one into a state of composure. Not a blockhouse we passed but cheery farewells were " semaphored " to the returning troops from groups of men silhouetted against the skyline alongside their little sandbag homes on the desert plains, evoking hearty response from the burghers.

Trekkopjes, the scene of the fight of April 26, was passed without a stop, though the pace allowed ample opportunity to view the graves of the unfortunate men killed in action, several mounds with neatly constructed crosses marking the burial place close to the station.

On the train, homeward bound on furlough, were a few of General Botha's despatch riders, a corps of necessarily hardy men who performed miracles on their motor-bicycles, and maintained communication across weird and wonderful country, where even signalling was at a disadvantage. Both the men and the machines had thoroughly proved their mettle, but it was not surprising that such strenuous and nerve-racking work had its limitations for even the vigorous young men employed, and so a brief respite had wisely been granted.

Swakopmund and the end of the journey was reached at midnight of the third day after leaving Karibib, less than 180 miles away.

CHAPTER IX.

THE FINAL ADVANCE.

The day following the occupation of Windhuk a message was transmitted from Karibib that Governor Seitz and the military commander, Colonel Francke, had intimated their desire for a " conversation " with General Botha. Accompanied by the Chief Staff Officer, General Botha motored back to his headquarters, the majority of the staff having to be left behind at Windhuk owing to the shortage of petrol. The return trip to Karibib was an eventful one and came near to disappointing the Germans of an important figure at the coming conference. It was while the motors were humming along the track through the bush that a khaki-clad horseman, whose commando shall be nameless, was suddenly observed in the middle of the path in front levelling a rifle directly at General Botha. Lieut. Snow, who was driving the General's car, swerved round the swaying figure and made an unsuccessful grab to dislodge the desperado; whereupon Captain Esselen (A.D.C.) sprang out and brought the horseman to earth, and to a realisation of the enormity of his offence. Staggering to attention the would-be assassin hiccoughed his apologies to the General, whom he explained (with just a suspicion of brogue) he had mistaken for Governor Seitz, and scrambling hastily upon his horse, zigzagged away into the bush.

The remainder of the journey was accomplished without further adventure, and several succeeding days were taken up with the interchange of correspondence between General Botha, from his headquarters at Karibib, and the German authorities at Omaruru.

An armistice of forty-eight hours was eventually declared to be in force from midday on May 20, and early the following morning General Botha, with an escort, proceeded to Giftkop, an agreed upon rendezvous, on the main road about thirty miles north of Karibib. Here were already assembled H.E. the Governor Seitz and Colonel Francke, with several of the staff. Military salutes having been exchanged all round, the principal officers on both sides adjourned for the conference to the shade of a thorn-tree by the roadside.

The purport of the German peace proposals, which were nothing if not cool, was that the northern boundary line defined in the Windhuk Proclamation should form the division between our separate possessions. In other words, that both armies should call a halt, the Germans retaining all the territory north of the line, and the Union forces the whole of the country lying to the south, which, of course, included the capital. The contending forces should then "mark time" in their respective spheres, and await the conclusion of hostilities in Europe to decide the ultimate fate of the Protectorate.

The Governor Seitz added that, of course, a neutral zone would have to be established between the parties. At the mention of the term "neutral zone" General Botha requested the interpreter to explain to his Excellency that, as his knowledge of English unfortunately suffered limitations, he would be glad if the meaning of this expression could be explained. The interpreter was about to transmit the request when, with well-feigned innocence, General Botha quietly interjected: "Oh! I think I understand now what 'neutral zone' means. That was Belgium's position before Germany invaded her." As was afterwards reported by an eye-witness, Governor Seitz indulged in a few moments of "morning hate" before the conference could be resumed.

The result of the negotiations was manifested that same day when the armistice was declared off at the expiration of the original time.

Many incidents sadly lacking the quality of truth have been based upon the meeting at Giftkop, and one such fictitious narrative depicted Colonel Francke's personal attitude towards General Botha as melodramatic in the extreme. It relates how the Commander of the German forces frequently arose from his seat throughout the conference, and paced up and down "the tent" in high dudgeon. As a matter of fact, the only occasions on which Colonel Francke arose from his seat were in response to signals from his second-in-command to partake of liquid refreshment at an adjacent wagon.

The delay occasioned between the occupation of Windhuk and the final advance no doubt appeared inexplicable to those in the Union whose supplies are at their own doors, and to whom anxiety on that particular score has been an unknown factor since birth. But with an army bordering (for South Africa) on the vast, planked down a thousand odd miles by sea and rail from its main supply base, there was much to be done and much time obviously to be consumed in the preparations for another bold advance, leaving commissariat depots again far behind, until such time as the railways could be restored. It must also be borne in mind that it took the animals some considerable time to recover from their astonishing and exhausting dash on the capital, and their recovery could only be effected by liberal rations of fodder, toiled up on a single line of railway from the coast; first by broad gauge to Ebony, there to be transferred, bundle by bundle, to the lighter railway which carried it beyond Usakos to where a bridge over a deep gully had been blown up; from this point, consequently, it was necessary to employ wagons to convey the once more man-handled supplies to the opposite side to re-load on to the continuation of the narrow gauge railway through Onguati Junction to Karibib. And while it was desirable to accumulate as expeditiously as possible huge quantities of supplies for the next advance, it should be understood that the waiting and re-organising Army had meanwhile to be fed, and the stupendous task of not only keeping pace with the daily demands, but of piling up a reserve to go forward with the troops was a feat in itself.

The damage caused by the enemy to the line between Windhuk and Karibib having been rectified, the first through train arrived at the latter station on May 18, from which date a regular daily service either way was inaugurated. Several engines and much rolling-stock of the broad gauge were found at Windhuk, and with the ready and paid assistance of German railwaymen, hidden parts were unearthed, enabling dismantled engines to resume their wonted usefulness.

By the middle of June sufficient supplies had been amassed at Karibib to warrant the continuation of the march against the enemy forces, now congregated to the north. The advance was simultaneously commenced by three separate columns on June 18.

Brigadier-General Myburgh was made responsible for the right flank with the 2nd Mounted Brigade, under Colonel Alberts, from Okasisse, and the right wing of the 3rd Mounted Brigade, under Colonel Jordaan, from Wilhelmstal.

Brigadier-General Brits, with the 1st Mounted Brigade, under Colonel Lemmer, proceeded in advance to Omaruru, which town he occupied on June 20, before assuming charge of the extreme left flank.

General Botha and the Headquarter Staff accompanied the main force, which was composed of the 5th (Free State Volunteer) Mounted Brigade, under Brigadier-General Manie Botha, and the 4th Mounted Brigade (South African Mounted Rifles and 1st Imperial Light Horse), under Brigadier-General Lukin, D.S.O., the 1st Infantry Brigade, under Brigadier-General Beves, and a detachment of Heavy Artillery, under Lieut.-Colonel Tripp.

Omaruru, at which point a pause was made while the aviators reconnoitred the German position forty miles north at Kalkveld, may be described as a pretty little village situated on the Omaruru River, which, at this period of the year, was reduced to a mere trickle of water—a sight, however, to gladden the hearts of all, after the waterless expanses of the Namib.

We were now well into bush and grass country, similar in appearance to parts of Rhodesia and the northern Transvaal, with occasional reddish ant-heaps peaked up to ten and twelve feet in height. The climate unhappily savoured more of the High Veld in mid-winter, and with cold biting winds through out the day and white frosts at night, Balaclava helmets, Cardigan jackets, greatcoats and mufflers were greatly in evidence in this torrid zone!

It had often been stated that the enemy had brought away from Swakopmund several large boats with which it was their intention to retreat across the Kunene River on their northern border. Whatever the purpose for which the boats were destined, all doubt of their existence was removed at Omaruru by the novel sight of six heavy surf boats, each about 50 ft. in length, jacked-up in a long line close to the railway, from which they had apparently been off-loaded.

With the exception of the partial destruction of a three-span bridge over the river close to the town, the railway line was in good order and enabled the service from Onguati to Omaruru to be continued.

Many of the inhabitants of both sexes remained behind in the town, as at Windhuk, Karibib and Okahandja, and a pathetic story was related by a staff officer, whose attention was directed to a forlorn little girl of the "flapper" age who was standing outside a house, not far removed from Headquarters, sobbing hard and ceaselessly. Friendly inquiry elicited the information, volunteered between choking sobs, that " so *very* many British troops were passing, and the German troops were so few, and—her sweetheart was with the unfortunate minority." Her weeping was vigorously renewed as each new unit passed, until the sad little figure was at last gently led away by a sympathetic bystander.

From Omaruru the advance developed into a pursuit of the enemy, who had relinquished at Kalkveld the only likely position they could have attempted to hold on the route to Otavie. By June 27, when the main force reached Otjiwarongo, a small town on the railway line, General Botha had already created fresh records in marching, coupled with a further exhibition of his astute and telling strategy. Even the historic dash to Windhuk threatened to be excelled, and our experiences were certainly noteworthy. The chief disability was again the dearth of water, and it was almost miraculous to find thousands of men and horses watering at single wells, often by means of buckets and a rope only, and at

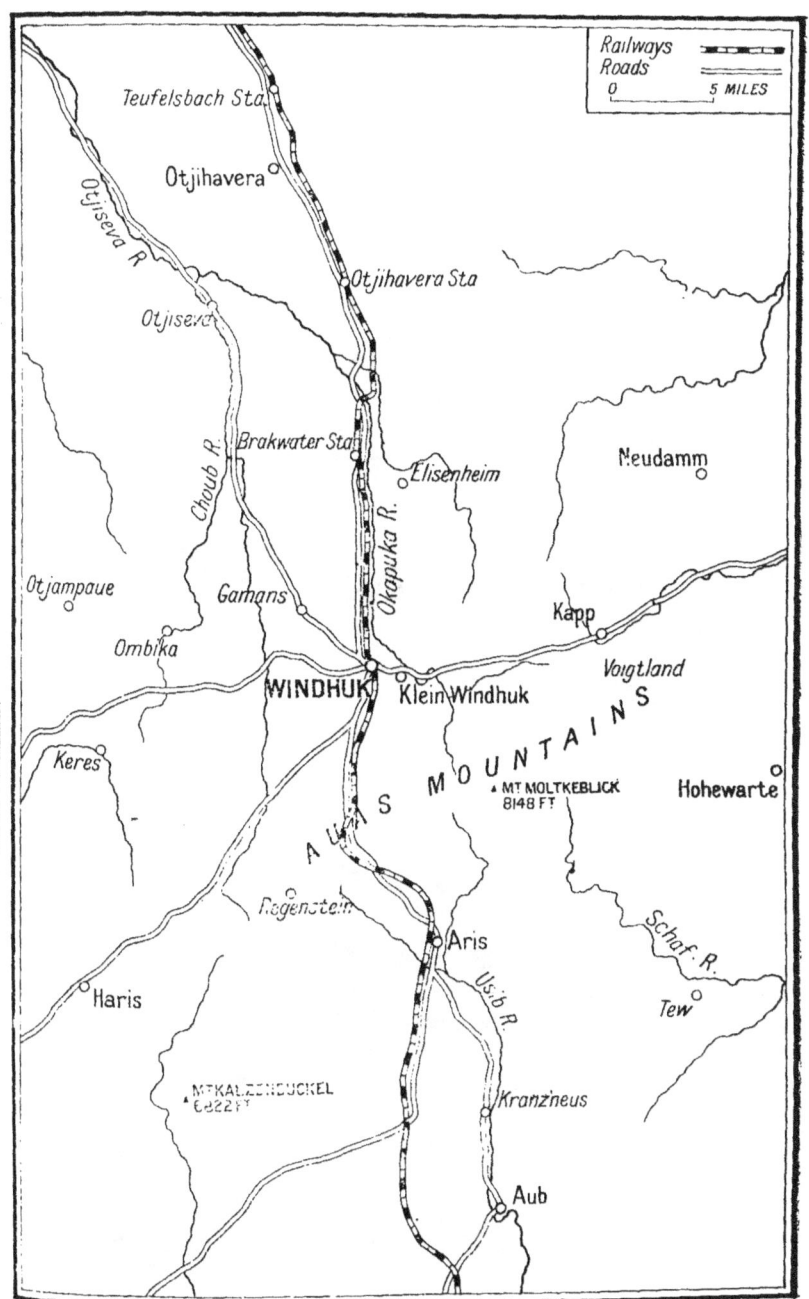

Windhuk War Monument with two captured British guns.

Hotel Kaiserhof, Windhuk.

Ebony Siding, on advance to Otavi, where wide and narrow gauge meet.

Some of the Captured German Guns at Windhuk.

Engine Room of the Great Wireless Station at Windhuk.

View from Military Barracks, Windhuk.

General Botha at Windhuk.

After the surrender at Windhuk. General Botha at the Town Hall.

All that was visible of the Great Wireless Station at Windhuk.

Union Motor Cars at Okahandja.

Typing Staff Orders in the Field (German South West).

German Prisoners after Otyimbingwe.

Taking the Surrender of German Troops near Otavi.

Mauser Rifles Surrendered at Otavifontein.

German Prisoners brought in by Motor.

German Howitzers surrendered at Otavifontein.

the same time maintaining a rapid pace hard on the heels of the enemy.

Near Erundu a motor despatch rider too far in the van, turning a corner in the narrow lane through the bush came suddenly upon the enemy's camp, so lately deserted, that he caught sight of the rear-guard disappearing less than a hundred yards away, and a neglected "dixie" steaming temptingly upon a fire.

The wells, which varied considerably in regard to their yield of water, were few and far between, and the probable condition of the next provided an element of precariousness with which we could well have dispensed.

To linger and institute minute investigations would be merely to play into the enemy's hands, and favour the security of their retirement. For delay would involve extra consumption of rations, and we were now far from the nearest base, and carrying only sufficient to see us through to our destination—the end of the railway line. Also it would prove an undesirable prolongation of a campaign upon which, all instinctively felt, the curtain was about to be rung down.

In less than a week the bulk of General Botha's army had traversed a distance of over 120 miles from Karibib to Otjiwarongo, practically on two waterings only from Omaruru; for, owing to the congestion of animals at some of the wells, it was often necessary to push on to the next, and trust to Providence that it would be found intact.

Since the enemy offered no resistance, the third and final phase of the campaign resolved itself into a "drive" on an unprecedented scale, the columns employed marching almost night and day through country totally unsuited by Nature to the pursuit of military operations of such proportions.

Our particular unit, after leaving Omaruru, trekked through to the first water at Otjua, and thence on through the night to Kalkveld (Police Post), where we caught up with Headquarters. Here we outspanned our team at about 3 a.m. amongst a host of camp fires and a slumbering army. A short sleep until daylight and up to water the animals before resuming the trek. But a disappointment awaited us. There was water, but the supply was limited, and General Beves had his whole brigade of infantry to consider. A few miles on, at Kalkveld Station, there was, we were told, another well, at which the animals were being watered. Arrived there, we came upon a mounted brigade of Field Ambulance endeavouring to assuage the thirst of their many teams of mules with buckets of water laboriously drawn from a well, whose supply was fast diminishing. So desperate had the state of the animals at this stage become that, as each team was drawn towards the well, the mules took charge, and, in their mad rush, one or two would tumble headlong across the trough into which the water was being tipped. The officer in charge said he hoped to complete the task in five hours more (they had already been busy for three hours !) Such a delay was not in accordance with our programme, and Headquarters had again got a start.

The next water was four or five miles on, and the supply was stated to be much better. It was decided to trek on, and by dusk we arrived at the farm Omuronga, where, by inspanning two of the mules to a beam attached to a pump in the well, a small flow of water was projected into a stone trough. The Imperial Light Horse were, however, in possession before us, and we had to await our turn. There was one squadron more to be watered, and this occupied nearly three hours; such was the force of the pump and the limited extent of the receptacle—one hundred horses in three hours ! All around the well was assembled a large herd of cattle (evidently the property of the owner of the farm) clamouring for water at their accustomed place, and while our mules and horses were enjoying their turn, we were all kept busily occupied in the dark warding off with sticks the desperate rushes of those beasts. Before leaving the well we noticed a discarded troop horse pathetically licking a joint in the water-pipe, and saw to it that he had the drink he was longing for.

With the moon close upon the full, our road was clearly defined through the heavy bush, and on we made for Okanjande, 25 miles away. The pace was necessarily slow with a wagon team, and compelled us to ride at a walk.

The nights were bitterly cold and frosty, and encouraged a strong and growing desire for sleep, and when the noddings became too frequent, threatening precipitation into the roadway or a thorn bush, we would walk and lead our horses, and incidentally set the blood into better circulation.

We intended to water and sleep at Okanjande, but it was well on into another night before we came up to this hamlet, where the political prisoners had been released.

What strange fancies assail the mind when sleep has been denied for unaccustomed periods ! It was, we found, the experience of most of those accompanying the advance. In the moonlight, harmless bushes will assume most fantastic shapes, and a roadside camp fire at comparatively close quarters will, by its glow cast against the branches of a tree, serve to conjure up a variety of objects quite irrelevant to the circumstances. As an instance, three of our party riding together during the night simultaneously commented upon the strange fancy which had prompted someone to erect a large marquee tent, well lit up, in the middle of the bush miles from anywhere. Closer inspection led to the gradual dissolution of the circus-like structure, which melted away, leaving a camp fire, a transport rider, and a wagon.

At last we creaked into Okanjande in the middle of the night, to learn that the main water supply had been destroyed by the enemy, who had left only one well with a primitive pump, which, in response to much hard work, grudgingly doled out water with as much force as may be associated with the last cup from a teapot.

Animals were waiting here by the hundred, and our chance was a very remote one. Six miles ahead, according to a returning transport conductor, was Otjiwarongo and plentiful water. Water we must have, and sleep must wait, and again, with dangerous swayings in the saddle and long stretches on foot to counteract the soporific effects of unbroken night trekking, we continued the march to the railway town, arriving well within its vicinity by daylight. Another rude shock awaited us, for the water supply was totally inadequate for our purposes, so a passing soldier testified. What a dilemma! We must ride on into the town and seek better authority. It was true that the town supply was meagre, but, wonderful to relate, there was a huge dam of water a few miles south, at which the Headquarters and main force were camped. Sleeplessness and exhaustion were forgotten with such a prospect in store, and the few further miles were accomplished with alacrity by all.

We will now follow the fortunes of the main body from Otjiwarongo onward, and leave the details of the advance of the brigades on the wide-flung flanks until such time as we again get into touch with them.

The Infantry Brigade was toiling patiently on somewhere in the rear, not a bit discouraged that the mounted men would persist in making the pace so sultry, and, as will be seen later, the foot-men rendered a most creditable account of themselves in the arduous marching they were called upon to perform.

Leaving Otjiwarongo on Sunday, June 27, General Botha pushed on to Omarassa, a farm and railway halt 30 miles away, where a moderate water supply from springs in limestone formation was obtainable. The next watering-place to Omarassa was Okaputa, only five miles further on, while between that farm and Otaviefontein there was a waterless gap of 45 miles. Having watered at Omarassa, the animals were not prepared to repeat the experiment after such a short interval; hence the next march became extended into one of 50 miles, which was brought to an end during the last night in June.

Shortly before sunrise on July 1 Brig.-General Manie Botha. leading the advance with the 5th Mounted Brigade, reached the western extremity of the Elephant Berg, still six miles off water and the Military Station of Otaviefontein. Here the first effort at opposition was made by the enemy, who at daylight opened fire upon our men from schanzes, hidden among the thick bush, with which the low berg was liberally covered. The guns of the 2nd Battery (S.A.M.R.), under Capt. Lorch, quickly succeeded in shelling the Germans from their obviously ill-prepared position, and, in spite of the disadvantage of having just completed an exceedingly trying march, a desperate running fight, extending over several miles through relentless thorn bush, against a force of about 800 of the enemy was keenly engaged in by the eager Free Staters. With the assistance of the 2nd Battery and the Machine Gun Section under Capt. Blaine, they succeeded in forcing the retirement of the Germans from Otaviefontein back on to their main position in the Sarg Berg, south of Khorab Siding.

The gunners shelled the fast-disappearing German convoy to such good purpose that two wagons and a Scotch cart loaded with ammunition and other stores fell into our hands. Here two of our men, while misguidedly attempting, without aid, to cut off these vehicles, were killed by our own shell fire. Our total casualties were four killed and seven wounded, the German losses amounting to two killed, eight wounded, and twenty-four prisoners.

In the meantime the S.A. Mounted Rifles and Imperial Light Horse, on approaching the Elephant Berg, were deployed to the right by Brig.-General Lukin in the direction of Eisenberg Nek, where, from information obtained, he suspected that some particularly powerful mines had been sown. Under Capt. Judd, the 3rd Squadron, 1st Regiment S.A.M.R., were dismounted and extended through the bush to search for likely wires connecting the mines in the trek with an observation post. The wire was fortunately found and promptly cut, and, following it up, the S.A.M.R., proceeding cautiously through the bush up the slopes of the Elephant Berg, came suddenly upon the enemy's observation post, and surprised three Germans in the midst of a puzzled endeavour to create a contact with the aid of the usual electrical contrivance.

The roadway through the Nek—a tempting route into Otaviefontein—was found to be heavily mined for a distance of 150 yards in a snake-shaped trail, and when, subsequently, exploded by Major Wauchope (S.A.E.C.) ploughshares, bolts, nuts, and specially cut scrap-iron hurtled through the air for hundreds of yards around, a flying fragment of iron unhappily wounding Capt. Nobbs (Intelligence Officer to General Lukin's Brigade), who was witnessing the result of his own investigations at a distance of over 40 yards away.

A further series of mines, both contact and observation, was understood to be awaiting us around the enemy's next position, and, after the cessation of hostilities, this was confirmed by the Germans, who busied themselves in the destruction of their own mines.

With the occupation of Otaviefontein and its inexhaustible supply of spring water, together with the railway junction of Otavi a few miles to the west, the principal difficulties in the path of the final advance were overcome, and it only remained to hasten forward supplies before launching a blow at the enemy now concentrated at a position about 10 miles north on the lines to Tsumeb. We had out-distanced supplies, and fresh meat acquired " on repayment " at the farms *en route* had for days represented the only available ration. Biscuits and groceries were at a premium, and tobacco and cigarettes had dwindled to microscopical proportions, but we put our trust in those who sit in high places, and were not disappointed.

Three days later the 1st Infantry Brigade swung into Otaviefontein, erect but dust-begrimed, at the conclusion of a march which called forth from General Beves the following well-earned appreciation :—

" On our arrival at Otaviefontein I take the first opportunity of expressing to you my keen appreciation of the work performed by you. You covered 245 miles, and those from Ebony 270 miles, practically without a break, the last 80 of which have been accomplished in four days, with a final burst of 45 miles in thirty-six hours, a feat which in ordinary circumstances would be exceptional. Under the conditions of this country, however, where water is difficult to obtain, heavy dust is the rule and not the exception, and difficulties of transport necessitated your receiving half, and for six days quarter rations, I look on the performance as one that reflects the greatest credit on all who have taken part."

After referring to the honour he felt in commanding the 1st Infantry Brigade, General Beves concluded his message with thanks to all ranks for the pluck, perseverance, and tenacity displayed under most trying conditions.

Subsequently, Col. Francke, on being informed that infantry had arrived at Otaviefontein, paid them an unintentional compliment when he remarked : " Of course, they travelled most of the way by train? "

It was a little discouraging to the infantry to find that their arrival coincided with the declaration of an armistice between the two opposing forces, though a rest was both merited and essential.

The ambitious sentiment of " Deutschland Uber Alles " was faithfully portrayed in an elaborate map of the world in coloured chalks which adorned the whitewashed wall of a room in the German barracks at Otaviefontein. The re-shuffling of the world's territorial possessions has, of course, been done with a lavish hand, so far as the Fatherland is concerned. The principal features of the reconstructed universe were highly instructive. The British Isles became straight-away "Deutsch Brittannien." Belgium was wiped off the earth; and Germany extended to embrace the northern half of France, leaving only Holland intact within this sea of German territory. Italy was overrun by Austria down to one-third of her "top-boot" shape, while Spain obliterated Portugal entirely, and received, presumably for her observance of neutrality, the whole of Australasia.

Germany reserved to herself the trifling little proposition of India, and arranged for Austria to act as a buffer between that and the Chinese Empire. Austria, on the map, was again employed in the same capacity in the extension of her present territory northward in an elongated point between Russia and the German Empire, and Sweden was permitted to expand half-way across the Russian northern seaboard. Canada had vanished, and the whole of that continent was designated the United States of North America, and automatically attached to itself "Greenland's Icy Mountains."

Africa was sub-divided simply and expeditiously. All south of the Equator down to the Cape of Good Hope, roping in Madagascar in its liberal sweep, fell to Germany, together with a generous slice of the Moroccan coast. Of the rest. Turkey was allotted one-half, comprising Egypt and the Suez Canal, and Austria, the remainder down to the Bight of Benin.

A notice on a side wall read as follows: "Nicht mehr existierende staaten: England, Portugal, Belgium, Japan, Servia, and Montenegro."

Altogether a pretty flight of fancy!

CHAPTER X.

SURRENDER.

The armistice was preceded by an exchange of messages forwarded under the protection of a white flag, and on Tuesday, July 6, it became known that a peace conference was taking place at kilo. 500, between General Botha and H.E. the German Governor and Colonel Francke. The intervening days until peace was declared were days of unutterable tedium to the eagerly impatient troops; but the fiat had gone forth for all, in military parlance, to remain " as you were." Perhaps the Headquarters Staff suffered less exasperation, due probably to their privileged cognisance of the trend of affairs in general.

They, at any rate, were early acquainted with the doings of our flanking columns, doings which, taken in conjunction with the existence of an armistice, provided news of an all-absorbing kind.

Although the armistice stipulated that all movements were to be suspended so far as our main force was concerned, a necessary understanding fortunately appeared to exist as to supplies for our famishing troops.

The Mechanical Transport Corps, under Major Hope, though setting out in the track of the army many days after its departure from Karibib, attained well-earned distinction by catching it up at Otaviefontein with welcome supplies. In six days the fleet of forty-three motor lorries, each conveying two tons of supplies, covered the 270 miles between Usakos and its destination without a single mishap—a praiseworthy performance, in view of the exceptional drawbacks of the country.

The news which came to hand from General Myburgh, viewed in correlation to the position existing between the main opposing forces, savoured acutely of the burlesque. He had brought an astonishingly rapid march to a conclusion with the occupation of no less a place than Tsumeb, the terminus town of the line to the north, thereby completely cutting off the enemy's retreat. The situation was probably embarrassed to some extent by this surprising movement, although the armistice clearly applied only to the forces with which General Botha was in contact.

It will be appropriate at this juncture to recount the experiences of General Myburgh from the time he set forth into the wilderness of sand and bush with the 2nd and 3rd Mounted

Brigades from Okasisse and Wilhelmstal respectively. The route lay over the great Waterberg Plateau, which was reached on June 26, a few prisoners being taken at the military post of Okosongomingo, where delightful gardens of bananas, pawpaws, and other tropical fruits flourish under irrigation from a spring in the mountain side.

A long march brought the force to Otajewita on June 29, but the wells here were found to be destroyed, and the position appeared to be a critical one both for animals and men, until, as the result of a prolonged search in the mountains and kloofs, a small spring was discovered among the rocks and opened up by the Engineer detachment, who pumped the water into canvas troughs. This spot was left on June 30, and a course followed diagonally up the rugged slopes on to the top of the plateau, the thick bush of the plains being superseded by heavy sand, and such was the nature of the roadway up the mountain pass that the burghers had to lift the wagons bodily over intervening krantzes.

The crossing of the plateau was laboriously weary work for the wagons through a stretch of 15 miles of sand. The well at Omboamgombe, on the other side of the berg, was eagerly looked forward to. On arrival, however, on July 1, it was found that Col. Jordaan, working with the right wing of the 3rd Brigade to the west, had already touched there and exhausted the water supply. This compelled the 2nd Brigade to move on another 10 miles to Esere. The animals had then been without water for over two days, and were sadly feeling the strain of the heavy forced marching. The whole night was occupied with watering at Esere, where facilities were most primitive. The force here experienced bitter cold. The water in the General's basin was frozen solid before midnight, while milk obtained on the way was doled out in lumps in the morning.

When in the vicinity of the Otavi-Grootfontein line, the General received information that a force of about 800 Germans was occupying a position in a port at Guchab. Making dispositions overnight by sending Col. Jordaan with the right wing of the 3rd Brigade and the Heavy Artillery round behind the enemy on the left, via Asis, and the right wing of the 2nd Brigade to encircle the enemy's position from the right, General Myburgh, with the left wing of the 2nd Brigade, advanced at dawn, only to find that the position had been evacuated during the night, and that the enemy were retiring in the direction of Tsumeb.

Col. Collins was sent on with his wing of the 2nd Brigade, and at Gaub, on July 4, came into contact with a body of 500 of the enemy under Major von Kleish. A sharp engagement ensued, lasting about an hour, during which our artillery, under Captain Wolmarans, got in some effective work and assisted in bringing about the capture of seventy-six of the enemy, with twelve wagons of supplies. Our casualties were one killed and three wounded. Three wounded Germans fell into our hands. The enemy were hotly pressed by our men in their retirement through bush and mountainous country on to the main body at Khorab. The whole brigade then moved on towards Tsumeb, and at nightfall were only eight miles off. Colonel Jordaan left to attack the town before daylight next morning, and when he was about four miles off, a German officer approached with a white flag, stating that an armistice existed between the forces. The conversation which ensued was rudely interrupted by several shells, which came screaming across from a German battery concealed in the hills, and, without wasting further words on the genuinely perplexed Teuton, Col. Jordaan immediately took possession of some favourable ridges near by. After a slight pause, eight more shells, in rapid succession, arrived overhead, as a result of which one of our men was wounded.

General Myburgh, who had in the meantime reached this scene of extraordinary occurrences, despatched Col. Collins to Tsumeb, under a white flag, to endeavour to get into communication with General Botha at Otaviefontein, with a view to ascertaining the exact position of affairs. But before Col. Collins had returned from his mission, Capt. Esselen, A.D.C., turned up in a motor-car from Headquarters, and explained that the armistice was simply a local one, with which other forces than those at Otaviefontein were not concerned. General Myburgh thereupon pursued his original intention, and sent in a demand for the immediate surrender of Tsumeb and its garrison, which was at once complied with by the German Commander, Captain von Weiler.

To Major Botha and his Natal Horse fell the honour of the capture, separately, of the entire battery, with its complement of officers and men, which had been responsible for the shelling of our force. The guns were undermined with dynamite in readiness to be blown up in the event of a hasty retreat being found expedient.

As our troops entered the town strains of " Rule, Britannia," and " God Save the King " burst forth from our prisoners-of-war encamped close by. Enormous quantities of supplies and valuable ordnance stores were secured here—no less than 5,000 cases of rum being found in the town, and new equipment for 10,000 men. Most of the ordnance stores were in readiness to be set alight, and several million cartridges had already been burned.

So little harm had been done to the wireless apparatus that Lieut. Lever was able to communicate direct with Slangkop the same day.

With its arrival at the rail-head, General Myburgh's column had accomplished a march of over 300 miles in fifteen days.

At Tsumeb General Myburgh was notified over the telephone by General Brits that he had, with the 1st Mounted Brigade, occupied Namutoni, the Germans' final base, 50 miles away to the north-west on the edge of the Great Etosha Pan. It will be recollected that this column left the main force at Omaruru on June 20, making off into practically unknown country, acting as the left flank of the general advance. The country traversed was somewhat similar to that encountered by the Central force, but was often devoid of grass and water for longer and more anxious periods. At one point, Etaneno, at the conclusion of an exhausting march, two wells were found yielding only a small quantity of water, one so brackish and the other so bitter, that the majority of the animals, though parched, declined to drink. The next water was understood to be at Omatjenne, 25 miles to the east, but again the supply was found disappointing, being insufficient for all. Another forced trek had, in consequence, to be made 10 miles further on to Otjitasu, in the neighbourhood of Otjiwarongo, where General Botha, with the main force, was camped at a huge dam. There the animals rushed headlong to water, one mule drinking itself to death. After one day's respite, the surrounding country providing excellent grazing, General Brits was again turned out on the left flank in the direction of Outjo, 45 miles distant. This was a small military post, with a few other buildings; it was reached on June 30, and found to have been evacuated by the Germans. So far there was no sign of the enemy. A mountain gun, minus the breech-block, was found at the barracks, and was believed to have been captured from the Portuguese at Nautila. A short stay was made at Outjo, after which the march was resumed through thick bush, the machine-gun section preceding the column as an advance screen.

On July 3 Ombika was made, 60 miles further north, when the diary of one of the officers laconically recorded "Water fair; no grass." By July 4 the force had arrived at the police post of Okakuejo, only a few miles off Etoscha Pan, and here a very large quantity of dynamite was found and destroyed. Unfortunately, one man belonging to the machine guns, in a forgetful moment, leaned over a bucket of explosives while smoking a pipe, with resultant terrible injuries from which he succumbed the same night.

The force moved onward along the southern shore of the Etoscha Pan, which, being now dry, formed good going all the way to Namutoni. The whole of this route may be described as a sportsman's paradise, game, including gemsbok, springbok, blue wildebeest, and giraffes, being met with in herds, also innumerable smaller buck, wild ostriches, and fowl. Frequently, on the march, wildebeest and zebras actually ran across the path between the motor-cars, which were occasionally compelled to halt to allow the passage of these animals, suddenly emerging from the bush.

The next outspan was on July 4, at Palmietfontein, a small water-hole at the edge of a dam, where a junction was effected with the right wing of the brigade under Col. Lemmer and Lieut.-Col. de la Rey. This wing, which General Brits had despatched from Outjo to pursue a course between himself and the Centre force, had a trying experience marching through virgin territory, without tracks of any description, and boasting only interminable thorn bush. For days they proceeded tortuously to Palmietfontein, dependent solely on the guidance of a native bushman.

On July 5 General Brits' force arrived at Rietfontein, where one of the burghers shot a lion. After leaving Rietfontein, and when only 40 miles from Namutoni, the column came up with a German soldier in charge of a small convoy with several natives and 250 head of cattle. Information gained here led to the capture of a further four Germans with more transport and cattle.

Capt. Wolmarans was sent forward with machine guns, mounted on motors, to the next water-hole, Springbokfontein. Here, shortly after his arrival, the German Commandant of Namutoni, under a white flag, appeared with a letter surrendering the fort.

General Brits, accompanied by the principal officers of his brigade, motored into Namutoni and received the surrender of 170 German officers and men, 92 wagons, 2,000 draught animals, 550 cases of artillery ammunition, over a million rounds of rifle ammunition, and a huge quantity of supplies, roughly estimated as sufficient to last the whole German force for three months.

The capture also included the motor-cars of Governor Seitz and Col. Francke. Forty-two of our officers, with sixty-four men and political prisoners, were released. Our prisoners were overjoyed at the unexpected arrival of the relieving force, many being so overcome with emotion that they could scarcely speak. Several, while excitedly shaking hands with their friends, endeavoured unsuccessfully to articulate, and appeared about to faint with the sudden stress of feeling at the glad sight of our men.

General Brits' Brigade, the mounted section of which was under the command of Col. Lemmer, with Lieut.-Col. Brink,

Brigade Major, comprised the following units: Right Wing (Lieut.-Col. de la Rey), Potchefstroom A. and B. and Krugersdorp Commandos. Left Wing (Lieut.-Col. Visser): Marico, Lichtenburg, Wolmaranstad and Bloemhof Commandos; Transvaal Horse Artillery (Major Taylor); Machine Guns (Captain Wolmarans), and 7th Mounted Field Ambulance, under Major van Coller.

This brigade covered the distance of over 350 miles from Karibib in thirteen actual trekking days.

Back at Otaviefontein the time granted to the enemy for a reply to General Botha's final message on the subject of surrender of the German forces was rapidly drawing to a close, and, in anticipation of events taking an unfavourable course, the night of July 8 witnessed a notable gathering of the Generals at Headquarters. It was impossible to prophesy definitely whether the morrow would bring peace or a desperate battle, and plans were accordingly made to meet either contingency, for, as General Botha himself remarked to a member of the Staff: " I think it will be peace, but it is just as well to be careful."

The problem as to how General Myburgh was to be apprised of the progress of events was solved by the Germans, who courteously linked up the telephone line running through their camp with Tsumeb. But the question arose as to what language could be employed in which to convey instructions to General Myburgh. English or Dutch, if overheard by the enemy, would be understood. Finally, the conversation was maintained through the medium of the Zulu tongue.

Our troops remained under orders to be ready to move out and take up previously allotted positions immediately upon the expiration of the time agreed, viz., 2.30 a.m.

The situation was tense with dramatic interest, and in the inky darkness of a moonless night the officers, heavily cloaked against the biting cold, quietly moved among the bush to awaken the troops for any emergency, bearing with them minute orders in the event of the enemy deciding to invite a final battle. In the meantime, at a lonely spot on the railway line, a few miles outside Otavi Station, a solitary Staff Officer awaited, beside a throbbing motor-car, the arrival of the expected train conveying the momentous decision.

Slowly the time ticked round to 2.30 in the morning, and as yet no sign or sound of the locomotive had been seen or heard, only the derisive howl of a lurking jackal serving to break, in disconcerting manner, the eerie stillness of the night. Not a minute after 2.30 had been General Botha's inflexible order! But at that moment a light shone out through the bush, and the puffing of an engine could be heard still some distance off. At last the little train, composed of an engine and a bogie carriage, drew up at the appointed place, and a German Staff Officer, rapidly alighting, solemnly handed over a sealed envelope. About a second's delay and the motor-car sped on its way back to Headquarters, where, after a hurried perusal of the note, the news was quickly disseminated that German South-west Africa had fallen to the British Empire.

In conversation with Lieut.-Colonel Freeth, Pretoria Regiment of Infantry, at the termination of hostilities, a German officer confessed that, had the final decision been reversed, they had considered attacking our position at Otaviefontein immediately after 2.30 a.m., on July 9, with fixed bayonets, under the false impression that they would be opposed only by burgher commandos, who, of course, are untrained in the use of this particular weapon. Their intention was to utilise the cover afforded by the dry river bed, and surprise the camp, disregarding the more patent method of attack over the hills.

This officer was somewhat taken aback to learn that this probable contingency had thoughtfully been provided against, and that they would have had the pleasure of meeting in a general atmosphere of fixed bayonets, not all possessing a saw-edge.

Due perhaps to the negotiations with the enemy having lasted over several days, and thereby encouraging the expectation that peace would be proclaimed, there was no particular outburst of enthusiasm when, after some inexplicable delay, the official announcement was eventually made to the troops.

The truth, no doubt, was that the troops excusably considered they had been robbed of the legitimate fruits of their strenuous march; also they felt some resentment that terms of any kind should have been included in the articles of surrender. And it must be admitted that to extend terms to an enemy surrounded by an overwhelming army was an act the incomprehensible magnanimity of which, it is hoped, will not be overlooked by the recipients.

There was an absence of ceremonial in connection with the surrender, the transference of the prisoners-of-war and munitions being made gradually, owing principally to the inconvenient situation of the German camp at Khorab and the lack of accommodation both at Otaviefontein and Otavi Junction.

The Germans, too, had heavily mined the country in the neighbourhood of their position, and it was deemed advisable to remove these unpleasant obstructions before permitting traffic to and fro.

The total number of prisoners surrendered during the last stage of the campaign, namely, from June 18 to July 9, was 4,740. Although the official figures as to the number of Germans in South-west Africa are not yet available, it was generally believed that the Germans entered the field with approximately 6,500 men, and the difference, therefore, of 1,760 may be taken to be represented by killed, wounded, sick, inefficient, and captures throughout the course of the campaign in all theatres. In addition, there are the casualties inflicted by the Bastards, which may never be actually known.

Besides many thousands of rifles and large quantities of ammunition, twenty-two machine guns and thirty-seven field guns were surrendered at Otaviefontein. The field-pieces included 5-in. howitzers and mountain batteries.

On the return of the troops to Cape Town General Smuts admitted that, but for the want of transport for the Northern Expedition, the campaign should have been over early in May instead of July.

Apart from the battle at Riet and the attack upon Trekkopjes by the Germans, the campaign in the north conspicuously lacked the elements of war, and resolved itself into a mighty and well-engineered trek, with few outstanding features to satisfy the public's craving for sensation. Frequently when the people of the Union considered they were being kept in the dark as to the doings of the Union troops, the strongest beam of light directed upon the operations of the force would have failed to expose an incident worthy of perpetuation in the annals of history.

And so was brought to a close a campaign devoid of great battles, yet characterised by unprecedented physical difficulties, unparalleled feats of marching and shrewd generalship. The enemy had been out-paced, out-manœuvred and completely discomfited.

A Special Field General Order by General the Right Hon. Louis Botha, Commanding-in-Chief the Forces of the Union of South Africa in the Field, read as follows :—

"The General Officer Commanding-in-Chief, on leaving German South-west Africa, desires formally to place on record what he has, as far as possible, verbally expressed to different portions of his command on his journey down country from the North—namely, his high appreciation of the splendid work performed by all ranks of all units of all armies throughout the campaign which has now terminated. It would have been quite impossible to have carried out the operations which have just concluded unless whole-hearted co-operation had been the rule. This co-operation has been in evidence throughout, and all arms have combined, each in its sphere, to give full effect to the plans of the Commander-in-Chief, who finds in the magnificent work which has been performed so uncomplainingly and resolutely, an indication of what may be expected of the citizens of the Union, who place their duty before personal feelings and interests."

Brigadier-General P. S. Beves was appointed Military Governor of the Protectorate.

PART III.

SOME OBSERVATIONS & REFLECTIONS.

By
W. W. O'S.

SOUTH-WEST AFRICA.

The South African Territories, Limited,

Are now Offering for Sale

ONE MILLION MORGEN OF LAND

In carefully selected Ranching Farms, ranging in size from 10,000 to 30,000 Morgen each. The Farms are all surveyed. Diagrams and Title Deeds can immediately be given.

ALSO 50,000 MORGEN OF LAND

abutting on the Orange River, including the well-known Farms, "Houms River" and "Girtis," large portions of which are capable of irrigation.

Prices and full particulars to be obtained at the Offices of the Company,

FINSBURY PAVEMENT HOUSE, LONDON, E.C.,

or from the General Manager of the Company, At KEETMANSHOOP, KALKFONTEIN, or WARMBAD.

General Botha meets Governor Seitz.

General Botha Discussing the Surrender

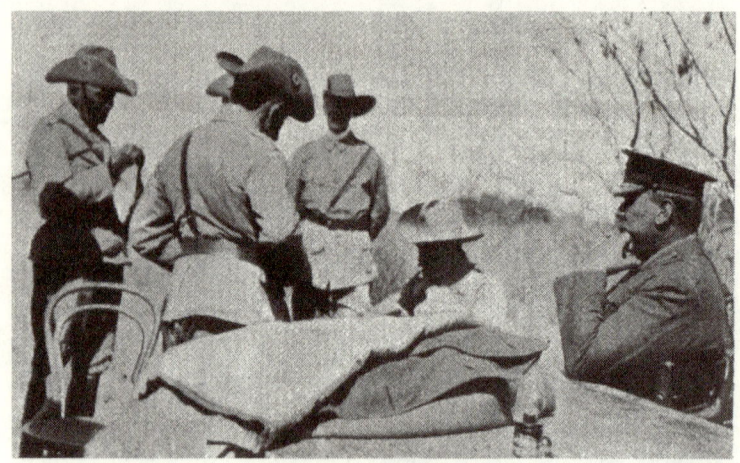

During the Surrende.

General Botha and Governor Seitz.

Discussing the Surrender at Otavifontein.

After Signing the Surrender—General Botha with Colonel Collyer and Dr. Bok.

Field Piece, Otavifontein.

Surrendered Stores at Otavifontein.

Burghers on the March.

PART III.

SOME OBSERVATIONS AND REFLECTIONS.

By W. W. O'S.

After the Germans were vanquished at Riet and Jackalswater there were few strategically sound positions left in the country which they could reasonably be expected to hold for any length of time. Kubas, where they had made preparations for a stand, was early rendered untenable by our wide developing movements. The hills of Karibib might have afforded a check to our immediate advance, but for Brigadier-General Myburgh's disconcerting movements threatening the enemy's line of retreat. While northward the only possible position between Karibib and Otavi was at Kalkveld, which could easily have accommodated an Army Corps among its rugged hills, extending in horseshoe fashion across our front. The German force, as it was then composed, might with safety and some measure of success have opposed the advance of our main column, whose mobile section was no greater than that of the enemy. General Brits and General Myburgh were by then out of touch on the left and right flanks respectively, and could scarcely have affected the position of affairs favourably for some days at least, had the enemy resolved upon the line of action suggested. Always with the comforting knowledge of the railway behind him, the German Commander could conceivably have attempted to hold our force at bay for a sufficient length of time to inflict a blow, without necessarily jeopardising his retirement.

Miles of more or less flat bush country intervened between Kalkveld and Otavi, and the only obvious course for the Germans to pursue was the one they adopted, and that was to hustle on to the next natural position, more than a hundred miles away, at Otaviefontein.

The Boer would have delighted in guerilla warfare had he been in the enemy's position (my authority for this statement was the burghers themselves), in spite of the unsuitability of the country for this particular form of warfare, but it was early apparent that the German trooper was not adapted to contend against the unconventional fighting methods of the Boers.

Detached bodies of the enemy's troops could have made things extremely uncomfortable for the straggling transport following in the wake of the army, and the thought that was ever uppermost was that assuredly the much-vaunted Camel Corps would harass our lines of communication. Only one instance was recorded of the activities of this unit. Shortly before Peace about a dozen of the enemy, mounted on camels, raided the railway line near Ebony, and succeeded in holding up a train loaded with supplies. Three " details " only accompanied the train, and were taken at a disadvantage, poised as they were on top of a pile of forage.

The engine-driver proceeded to rake out his fires, the hot coals falling upon a mine which had failed to explode in the first instance. A mild shock ensued, sufficient to lift the engine off the rails, but without inflicting any injury upon the railwaymen. Beyond relieving their prisoners of any papers they had about them, the Germans left everything else untouched, and made off again on their camels northward across the desert.

This failure on the part of the Germans to perform the obvious was demonstrated throughout the campaign. During the final phase, especially, did this neglect become more apparent. The attempts to destroy the railway line were halfhearted, while the telegraph lines remained intact along the whole route to Otavi, with the exception of the removal of the instruments and connections at the railway offices.

The destruction of water-holes would have dangerously inconvenienced our progress to Otavi, and the waterless interval of forty to fifty miles between Okaputa and Otaviefontein alone was liable to serious extension by the blowing up of a single water-hole. These things, however, were not done by the Germans, and the only reasons that may be advanced in extenuation of their sins of omission were, firstly, that the water was mostly on occupied farms, and, secondly, that the Germans expressed the belief that our occupation, though inevitable, would only be temporary.

The final position of any consequence was where the surrender took place, and no opportunity occurred to test its vulnerability.

NAVAL TRANSPORT DEPARTMENT.

While eulogising the achievements of the military portion of the expedition, the work of the Naval Transport Department, so far, at least, as it concerned the Northern force, is equally deserving of mention in a permanent record.

The transports conveying the first troops of the Northern force sailed from Table Bay for Walvis at daybreak on December 22, 1914, under escort of H.M.S. "Hyacinth" (flagship on the Cape station) and H.M.S. "Astræa." The Commander-in-Chief of the Cape Station (Vice-Admiral H. G. King-Hall, C.B., D.S.O.) was on board the former ship, which had as tender H.M.S. "Afrikander," formerly the Table Bay tug "Ludwig Wiener," now chartered by the Admiralty, re-christened, and armed with one 12-pounder and one 3-pounder gun.

The ships comprising the Expeditionary Fleet were : "Galway Castle," "Gaika," "Rufidji," "Den of Glamis," "Monarch," and "Glenorchy." In the "Galway Castle" was the 1st Infantry Brigade, under Col. Skinner, O.C. Troops, comprising the S.A. Irish, Rand Rifles, and South African Engineer Corps, totalling approximately 100 officers and 1,700 rank and file; while the 3rd Infantry Brigade, under Col. Wylie, was accommodated in the "Gaika," and consisted of the 2nd Transvaal Scottish, 2nd Kimberley Regiment, two batteries heavy artillery, two machine gun batteries, an anti-aircraft gun's crew, and a motor-car contingent, totalling 72 officers and 1,690 other ranks. The "Monarch" conveyed the Imperial Light Horse, numbering 29 officers and 541 men; the 1st Rhodesians, 21 officers and 496 men; and the Intelligence Scouts, 7 officers and 28 men. In addition, she carried 688 horses and 183 mules belonging to the Imperial Light Horse.

The "Glenorchy" was almost entirely an animal ship, having on board some 500 mules, 200 horses, and 200 draught oxen for the 4-in. "Cow" guns on the "Galway Castle." The "Rufidji"—a fine cargo ship, formerly belonging to the German East Africa Steamship Co., and which was a prize taken off Cape Point—conveyed 180 rank and file and 170 natives of the Military Post and Telegraph Administration, about 400 stevedores, and 50 sanitary natives. Rails, sleepers, and rolling stock comprised most of the cargo of the "Den of Glamis," and she also had on board 500 natives for railway construction. In addition to "live" cargo, on board all of the transports was the varied assortment of stores, equipments, and paraphernalia required by an army about to land on the edge of a barren and waterless desert. There were heavy guns and field guns, an anti-aircraft gun (mounted on the focs'le of the "Gaika," ready for use should an enemy aeroplane appear), ammunition, locomotives and other rolling stock, rails and sleepers, transport wagons, motor-cars, motor-boats, steam and rowing boats, pontoons, water-boring machines, electric light and condenser plants, water tanks, steam cranes and winches, timber and firewood, coal, petrol, bricks and building material, rations for men and animals, fresh water, and the thousand and one other items which forethought and the experience gained at Port Nolloth and Lüderitzbucht suggested might be required.

The distance from Cape Town to Walvis is approximately 720 miles, and as the speed of the convoy was the speed of the slowest vessel, i.e., the "Den of Glamis," which, heavily laden as she was, barely exceeded 8 knots an hour, it was not anticipated that the destination would be reached until late on December 25. On the afternoon of the 24th, however. "Galway Castle" was signalled by "Hyacinth" to increase her speed, and, escorted by the latter and "Afrikander," she parted company with the rest of the convoy, pushed ahead, and cast anchor in Walvis Bay in the early morning of Christmas Day.

Already anchored in the harbour were H.M.S. "Albion," H.M.S. "Armadale Castle," and the hospital ship "Ebani," besides some tugs and lighters which had been sent from Lüderitzbucht and Table Bay to assist in the disembarkation.

The responsibility for the embarkation, transport, disembarkation, and landing of troops and stores throughout the course of the campaign in German South-west Africa, and the re-embarkation after its conclusion, was undertaken by the Royal Navy. The Naval Transport Staff at Walvis, placed at the disposal of the Union Government by the Admiralty. consisted of Captain R. Kemble Lambert, R.N. (succeeded at a later date by Commander T. S. Price, R.N.V.R.), Lieut. Maurice Green, R.N.V.R., Sub.-Lieut. H. Warington Smythe, R.N.V.R., Midshipman Gerald Boyes, R.N.V.R., and C. P. O. Lamerton, R.N.V.R., with some sixty petty officers and men of the South African Division of the Royal Naval Volunteer Reserve, who carried out signalling duties on the transports and beach, manned motor-boats and steamboats, found fatigues, and assisted generally in the disembarkation.

Under protection, if necessary, of the guns of "Hyacinth," "Albion," and "Armadale Castle," the troops on the "Galway Castle" were disembarked on the morning of Christmas Day, and, accompanied by H.M.S. "Afrikander," were conveyed to the beach in naval cutters, which were towed by tugs. It was decided to effect a landing simultaneously at two points about a mile and a-half apart, viz., the Settlement and the Whaling Station, where there were jetties of a sort, and in the event of these being found to be mined or under heavy gun fire, landings were to be attempted at various points along the beach. Chief opposition was anticipated at the Whaling Station jetty, as at that point high sand-dunes approached within 50 yards of the beach, which would have given the enemy excellent cover for machine or field guns. Consequently, it was decided to make this the chief point of attack, capture the sand-dunes, entrench, and form a covering party while troops from "Gaika" and "Monarch" were being landed. As already remarked in Chapter II., no enterprise was shown by the enemy, and a most peaceful landing was effected at both points by the troops in the first "tow," consisting of the tugs "Annie," "Eland," and "Garth," towing cutters of "Albion," "Hyacinth," and "Armadale" respectively, containing about 350 officers and other ranks. The tugs "Sir John" and "Stork" followed at a few minutes' interval with 600 more troops accommodated in boats of "Armadale" and "Galway Castle." The remainder of the troops on board the latter ship were landed the same day, and those on the other transports the next day.

The landing of guns, heavy material, and stores called for much energy, resource, and ingenuity on the part of the Naval Transport Department. Practically everything had to be man-handled, there being no steam cranes or weight-lifting appliances, other than a small hand crane capable of lifting only a ton's weight every half-hour. Nor were any additional mechanical facilities afforded during the six weeks following the occupation of Walvis, if one excepts some steam winches erected on the beach towards the end of January, and which were used solely for the landing of rolling stock and rails for the line to Swakopmund, to the construction of which everything else was subordinated by the South African Engineer Corps—the sappers and miners of the Union Army.

This unit, which did such excellent work throughout the campaign, would have increased its usefulness considerably had it possessed a Harbour Company, whose sole duty it would have been to attend to the requirements of the ports of Lüderitzbucht and Walvis. As it happened, it was not until April, or more than three months after the occupation, that the Engineer and Assistant Engineer of Table Bay, with some fifty skilled artisans, arrived at Walvis and carried out some much-needed improvements, which enabled the transports to be discharged more expeditiously than had been previously possible.

It may be of interest to explain that the animals were brought to shore on rafts or floats, constructed of empty casks or oil drums—after a German pattern found at Lüderitzbucht—each capable of carrying thirty-five to forty horses or mules. The rafts were towed to buoys, moored about 50 yards from low-water mark, and were then hauled in on warps to the beach by shore gangs. As soon as the float touched bottom a ramp or gangway was run out to it, over which there was little difficulty in getting the animals to walk, although, in the case of donkeys, a good deal of gentle persuasion was often required.

The utility of the floats was so apparent, not only for the conveyance of animals, rolling stock, rails and sleepers, but also for maize, lucerne, etc., that later on there was a fleet of twenty-four, which played an important part in the discharging operations at Walvis. The average number of animals landed per diem was 1,000, though, in the strenuous days consequent on the arrival of the Burghers' Commandos, over 1,500 horses and mules were landed in a day.

The occupation of Swakopmund by the Union troops on January 15, before the completion of the Walvis-Swakopmund Railway, was an additional strain on the resources of the Naval Transport Department, as infantry, guns, ammunition, stores, etc., had to be transported thither by sea. Two tugs and two or three lighters were sent from Walvis to Swakopmund daily until the end of March, and as the pier at Swakopmund is constructed in an open roadstead, and thus exposed to a heavy south-west swell, the discharge of the lighters was fraught with considerable danger. In addition, a portion of the pier and all the cranes had been put out of action by shell fire from our ships, or had been blown up by the Germans themselves. A detachment of R.N.V.R., under Sub-Lieut. Warington Smythe and C.P.O. Lamerton, proceeded to Swakopmund daily with the lighters, and rendered good service in running up a derrick and "whip" on the pier, and also in landing troops.

The weather conditions at Walvis affected the discharge of transports to a far greater extent than is generally supposed. The feature of the harbour is its freedom from the south-west swell which is prevalent on the coast, and which renders work at Swakopmund so hazardous. The great width of the opening of the bay, however, allows considerable sea to run in with northerly winds. Fortunately, these winds are comparatively rare, but, owing to their sudden rising, much work had to be done in securing rafts and boats, or in recovering those which were driven from their moorings. The chief climatic interruptions to work were caused by the very dense morning fogs, and the strong south-west winds which spring up in the afternoons. The fogs prevented the observation of flag-signals, by which the greater part of the work of disembarkation was controlled, while the short, steep sea which gets up in the south-west breezes caused the rafts to make very heavy weather when coming in, or lying laden alongside ships; also, at times, seas washing right over the rafts entirely prevented loading.

The distance from the shore at which the transports had to anchor, practically two miles, was another factor to be considered in reviewing the work of the Naval Transport Department—a work which proceeded day and night, Sundays included, from December 25 to August 14.

It is noteworthy that the landing and subsequent re-embarkation of the troops, both at Walvis and Swakopmund, was accomplished without the slightest mishap, whilst the percentage of animals lost through accident was a negligible item.

During the campaign the following ships transported troops or stores to Walvis:—

Name of Ship.	Number of Voyages.	Nature of Cargo, etc.
Galway Castle	14	Troops, guns, wagons, supplies, etc.
Gaika	6	Troops, guns, wagons, supplies, etc.
Glenorchy	8	Animals
Den of Glamis	3	Railway material and coal.
Rufidji	8	Railway material, troops, and animals.
Monarch	7	Animals, supplies, and engineers' stores.
Ingerid	7	Supplies.
Ebani	14	Sick and wounded and medical stores.
Clan MacFadyen	3	Railway material and coal.
Clan MacPhee	10	Animals, railway material, and troops.
City of Athens	9	Troops, animals, and supplies.
British Prince	10	Animals
Hyacinthus	4	Animals.
Clan McLaren	3	Animals and supplies.
Professor Woermann	8	Troops and supplies.
Shonga	4	Animals and supplies.
Erna Woermann	7	Animals, troops, and supplies.
Clan Macbeth	1	Supplies and coal.
Clan Ogilvy	1	Railway material.
Colonial	3	Railway and coal.
Umtata	1	Aviation stores and personnel.
Borda	1	Armoured motor cars and lorries.
Karatara	2	Coal and stores.
Clan MacMillan	3	Animals, coal, etc.
Umvoti	1	Aeroplanes and stores.
Havre	1	Petrol.
Jane Kilgour	1	Sleepers.
Total number of voyages	140	

The tugs employed at Walvis Bay during the period of hostilities were: "Annie," "Sir John," "Stork," "Frontier," "Magnet," "Garth," "Eland," "Colonist," "Alert," "Kingfisher," and "Eveline."

The first three of these were perhaps the best known, as they were largely used in disembarking and embarking troops, though the masters of all alike rendered yeoman service in the performance of their arduous duties amid cheerless surroundings, and with small recognition except the consciousness of work well done.

AVIATION.

While the enemy aeronauts were reconnoitring our positions to within a few miles of the coast, we were impotently chafing at the lateness of the arrival of our own long-expected flying machines from England; often, it must now shamefacedly be admitted, forgetful of the greater and graver needs existing on the Continent. Still, the rumour had got about soon after the occupation of Swakopmund in January that aeroplanes were coming, and it was not until after the advance upon Windhuk that the aerodrome was established at Walvis to accommodate the South African Aviation Corps and several up-to-date machines. At such an enlightened epoch in Universal National Defence blame for the lack of an aeroplane section in the Union Defence Scheme cannot fairly be bestowed upon the Home authorities, and it does occur to the casual observer as strange, in view of the fact that the enemy on our border possessed an aviation section some time before the commencement of hostilities, that the Union should have seen fit to do without such a valuable adjunct to the military system of the country. Yet, in spite of its belated appearance, the Aviation Corps contrived to execute some extremely useful and hazardous work. Once our machines took to the air and were observed by the enemy, never again did the German aeroplane manifest its appearance, and from that time, until the surrender, our troops enjoyed an immunity from the bomb-dropping attention of the German aviators.

Those of us, ignorant of aviation, who had imagined that the flights of an aeroplane could be conducted with the ease attaching to the journey of a Putney 'bus, were considerably surprised at the elaborate nature of the preparations necessitated, more particularly in such wild country. At Walvis the flat, dry bed of the Kuiseb River formed an excellent exercise ground, but owing to the frequency of mists much delay was experienced in testing the machines before they could, with security, be despatched across the desert belt. At Karibib, on the opposite fringe of the desert, was the vacated German aerodrome, and this was the spot to which it was desired to convey the 'planes without a halt en route. So successful was this operation that records in aviation were established during the process. Lieut. Creed and Sub-Flight-Lieut. Hinshlewood, each flying in separate machines, covered the distance of 140 miles from Walvis Bay in one hour and a half. Only when the northward advance was made did the real difficulties commence, the country becoming so dense with bush that gangs of natives had to be sent ahead in the Aviation Corps motor-cars to clear spaces for landing. As it was, in planing down to alight at Omaruru, the first aeroplane grazed a bush on the outskirts of the clearing and was brought to earth with a suddenness that put the machine out of action straightaway.

No sooner, however, was an aerodrome created at Omaruru than the force resumed its march, and a fresh landing place was called for farther forward. At Kalkveld another open space in the bush was arranged with as much expedition as possible, the Headquarters at this juncture requiring the almost constant services of the aeroplanes on reconnaissance work, and it was nothing for our aviators to fly eighty miles north and back (often under fire from the enemy's shrapnel) before the breakfast hour, an institution honoured at that time more in the breach than in the observance.

Before a clearing could be properly effected away went the aviators upon their hazardous missions, and it was while feverish attempts were being made to enlarge the opening that Captain van der Spuy, in endeavouring to alight in the cramped space, caught one of the wings against a thorn tree and narrowly escaped a serious accident, the machine spinning round at the obstruction and bringing the pilot heavily to the ground. Fortunately, Captain van der Spuy, who was one of the senior pilots, and, with Captain Turner and Lieut. Creed, had only recently been flying at the European front, survived the ordeal with a severe shaking and a few cuts, the machine being incapacitated for further immediate flight.

In that country of illimitable bush, making casual landing impossible, it was by nothing less than a miracle that Sub-Flight-Lieut. Hinshlewood, whose engines failed him when miles from anywhere, was enabled to vol-plane down to a ploughed patch of land immediately beneath him on the enemy's side of the country, where he alighted and corrected the trouble. He had just room to allow for the preliminary run required to gather momentum for the rise. A reward offered for the discovery of another such open space in the bush would have met with poor response.

As the advance continued, from point to point, Major Wallace, O.C., S.A. Aviation Corps, closed down the latest aerodrome, packed up the intricate paraphernalia, and, with his staff, sped forward in powerful motor-cars to inaugurate new depôts nearer the retreating enemy. The value of the Aviation section was demonstrated early on the final advance, when reports were current that the enemy intended to put up opposition at Kalkveld. The Germans had actually disposed their forces with this intention, as our aviators were able to verify, but the futility of putting up a defence while under the observation of our aeroplanes, taken in conjunction with the menacing movements of our flanking columns, must have occurred to the enemy, who evacuated the position some time before our troops could get within striking distance. It was the aviators who first reported this retirement, and thereby helped to accelerate our forward movements by enabling the force to dispense with any elaborate demonstration in the form of "feelers." Later, as we pressed hard on the heels of the foe, the aeronauts took up with them bombs of, I think, 120 lbs. in weight, with which they made some bold attempts to break up the railway behind the enemy. But from an aeroplane a single railway line (and a narrow gauge at that) affords a very poor target, though some excellent practice was nevertheless made. The surrender of the enemy's forces cut short a very promising career for the S.A. Aviation Corps, which, when Peace was signed, made rapid tracks for Cape Town, en route to Europe.

"CAPTAINS ALL."

It is not in any spirit of carping criticism that I refer to the casual manner in which commissions were, in so many cases, indiscriminately bestowed, but mention it rather as an interesting psychological feature of our South African army system. Until the Sandfontein disaster brought home to the authorities the unwisdom of toying with the German Southwest campaign with a handful of men, the general attitude of some of the representatives of the Defence Force towards those who early volunteered their services was little short of offensive. Commissions earned during previous active service. it was "sniffily" explained, were not considered as any particular recommendation, while there were others who could prove the performance of "Saturday night" parades. I have nothing but admiration for the man who voluntarily sacrifices such a large proportion of his spare time in peace to qualify for a soldier in times of war, but I fail to recognise his superiority over the veteran who has experienced the real thing.

An equality may be admitted, but a preference for the soldier-in-the-making I cannot allow. Rather should previous good active service, with nights spent in doing outpost duty, than Saturday nights spent on the parade ground, ensure a man an early job at the front. Such an opinion is doubtless opposed to the teachings of the little "red (or is it purple?) book"; but, unfortunately, our South African campaigns usually decline to conform to orthodox methods, and, in consequence, the student soldier is liable to find his long years of book-lore of little or no account in an emergency.

I know of the case of an ex-Irregular officer, who had served in two previous campaigns, and who, failing to secure a regimental appointment, because he did not belong to a volunteer corps, applied in Cape Town at the beginning of hostilities for a commission in one of the departmental corps. He was regretfully told by two of the principal officials that he was ineligible for an appointment, as commissions were being given by rotation solely to those who had been working with these departments in peace times. Having just left an officer newly appointed to one of these departments who lacked previous military knowledge of any kind, our ex-Irregular friend was able to place the statement without hesitancy in its proper category. Later, he had the opportunity of noting that both these sticklers for rectitude appointed their own sons, who had been in the adolescent stage at the time of the Boer War, to commissions in the Commissariat. At times it becomes a humiliating experience to attempt to serve one's country.

But what a change when it was decided to pursue the campaign with an army of a size more appropriate to the task! Then a welcome was accorded to all and sundry. Then, curiously enough, the veteran who was put aside in the first instance for his ignorance of the "goose-step" was, after only a few parades, considered good enough to be sent forward as an efficient fighting machine—and, of course, he justified the confidence so reluctantly reposed in him.

I have been generalising so far, and now to revert to the preliminary remarks on this subject. Apart from the commissions properly granted to regiments, as the wants of the army increased in a variety of directions, commissions were thrust upon unoffending individuals who were more highly concerned with matters of a civil character, or jobs whose claims to be termed military rested upon most insecure foundations. The complaint is not mine alone against this hysterical creation of a position which might be summed up as one of "Captains All," but was reflected by the combatant section in the jocular appellation of "The Ragtime Army" to the Northern force.

Promotion, too, was of a swift and breathless order, as the following incident will serve to illustrate:—It occurred at Swakopmund, one evening, that a Post Office official was telephoning to a certain unit in the town informing it that there was correspondence awaiting the favour of Private Atkins.

"Private Atkins? Private Atkins?" queried the individual at the other end of the 'phone; "I don't know him." "Oh!" responded the overwrought official, whose strenuous duty it was to endeavour to keep pace with the lightning promotions. "he was *Private* Atkins early this morning; perhaps he's a Major by now."

Small wonder that the Sam-Brown belt was so often more abused than used in the South-west African campaign. It would be worn on an afternoon tea visit to the hospital; adorn a spectator at a tennis or football match, not even being discarded, so it was alleged, while enjoying the delights of the bath. It was recorded of one fledgling that he had to be restrained from donning the "regalia" over his pyjamas.

Then there were "O.C.'s" galore. "O.C. Loot," "O.C. Goats," "O.C. Dogs" (there were no cats), "O.C. Water." and, had it not been for the fact that the supply of liquor to the troops was controlled by an officer already possessing a lengthy alphabetical title, there would assuredly have been an "O.C. Whisky."

Still, these and other little idiosyncrasies were treated by the troops in a spirit of cheery tolerance, and afforded a constant source of amused speculation to the force generally as to what new Gilbertian command the morrow would bring forth.

IN GERMAN HANDS.

A number of our men, captured during the campaign, escaped from the Germans and met our forces at Omarassa, filtering into camp in batches, mostly in rags and tatters. According to their statements, their treatment had been nothing short of barbarous. No shelter had been provided since their capture, in some cases since the Sandfontein fight in September, and their dietary had verged on starvation. Only by volunteering for labour fatigues, for which they received credit for an equivalent of eighteenpence per day, could they attempt to satisfy their craving for food. A credit note for one day's labour obtained for them, only when available, three cups of mealies, which they themselves ground by hand into some semblance of meal. At Franzfontein Camp they were handed sacks, out of which they contrived to make clothes. Their daily rations consisted of three dessertspoonsful of flour, two of mealie-meal and one and a-half of rice, with eight ounces of meat and some raw coffee-beans. No sugar had been issued since Christmas.

A few days prior to their escape, so the prisoners say, Lieut.-Colonel Francke, the German commander, visited the camp, and in a belated apology endeavoured to mollify them by stating that there had been an evident misinterpretation of his orders.

The prisoners were furnished with lying and ridiculous reports regarding the situation in Europe, principal among which were statements to the effect that German troops had landed in England, and London was ablaze; that General French had been captured with two hundred thousand men, and that General Botha had retired on Swakopmund to put the place in a state of defence against the attack of German warships, already on their way from the North Sea. The prisoners-of-war laughed so heartily at these recitals that the practice of reading out the " latest news " was eventually discontinued. Our prisoners say they were prompted to escape when they saw our aeroplanes, and judged from that that the Union forces were close at hand.

Some of the men testified to having witnessed atrocious treatment meted out to native offenders by German soldiers. On one occasion it was alleged that a degraded party of these soldiery debated whether a native should be hanged with barbed wire or rope. Eventually the boy was strung up on a tree with cord, and a box kicked away from beneath him. This operation failed to cause instantaneous death, and, after the victim had been suspended alive for twenty minutes, a bayonet thrust in the region of the heart put a period to his misery.

After the occupation of Otaviefontein, where the majority of the prisoners-of-war had been located until a few days before our entry, we were able to confirm the statements as to their treatment in respect to their accommodation. The camp site, surrounded by a hedge of cut thorn-bush, lay in an exposed position without shelter of any kind. The dust from the limestone foundation was ankle-deep, and the whole place was in an indescribably filthy state, totally unfitted for habitation even by a Berg Damara.

Colonel Curtis, S.A.M.R., stated that some of his men who were prisoners-of-war were subjected to the inexcusable indignity of performing sanitary services for German non-commissioned officers.

The men, who had been entirely without smoking material for months, were gratified beyond measure at the attentions of their comrades, who willingly handed over contributions from their own fast diminishing stocks.

Striking testimony of the treatment of Dutch prisoners in German hands was further afforded by Lieut. Joubert Reitz, son of Senator Reitz, ex-President of the Free State. " What we felt more than starvation," he stated, " was the insulting way in which we were treated. It may surprise a good many of my countrymen to know that the Germans, who were so extremely kind as to guarantee our independence, and who·

promised to help us in such a variety of ways, despise and hate the Boers. They have, with ulterior motives, promised many things, and have spoken enthusiastically of the future of the Boer nation. But what do they do? When our men who were prisoners were shifted from Franzfontein to Otavi, Colonel Francke gave orders to separate the Dutch from the English, and to let the English ride in the carriages and the Dutch in the trucks. Are the men who do such things to become the friends and protectors of the Boers?

"Justice seems to have no place in their military system, as witness the cases of Captain Geary, of the 1st S.A.M.R. and Captain Borrow. The former was, immediately after the capture at Sandfontein, flung into a cell at Windhuk, where he was kept in solitary confinement for six months without any reason being given, and the latter was unexpectedly separated from us one afternoon and taken to Windhuk, where he had four and a-half months' solitary confinement, and they refused to tell him why."

After referring to the Germans as barbarians, Lieut. Reitz said: "They never missed a chance to submit Afrikanders to every indignity," and added that they are adepts at the game of hitting a man when he is down. Lieut. Reitz concluded thus: "What I have seen and heard has forced me to the conclusion (and I do not think there can be any doubt that my conclusion is a right one) that Germany hoped, with the assistance of the rebels, to convert the Union into a German Colony. My experience has also convinced me that no Afrikander, be he Boer or Briton, will ever be able to live contentedly under a German régime. I came across many Boers who had settled in German South-west Africa (they were, of course, conscripted), and I did not speak to a single one who was satisfied. They hate the Germans, and the Germans hate them, and the Boers of the Union as well. The representation that Germany wished to see an independent South Africa is misleading in the extreme. They do not wish for it, but only as one would wish to have a stepping-stone in a stream which would otherwise be impassable. Our independence would just now merely be a stepping-stone to annexation by Germany in a few years' time, when a pretext would easily and conveniently be found."

SOUTH AFRICAN HORSES.

It is anticipated by horse-breeders that Europe will set up a demand for horses for some years after the termination of the war, and, in view of this fact, the wonderful stamina and all-round suitability of the South African horse should not fail to earn for it a share of recognition in European markets. Long before the Boer War British officers used to pay periodical visits to the Cape to purchase mounts for the Indian Army, and freely admitted that the South African-bred pony was unsurpassed for the work required of it in the varied climates of India. Throughout the Boer War the Colonial horse outmatched the imported animal in every respect, and acquired a reputation which has since been greatly enhanced, while its more recent exploits in the South-West African campaign, often without food and water for very long intervals during exhausting marches, was a further revelation of its astonishing powers.

HOSPITAL AND MEDICAL.

In introducing the subjoined statistics relative to the number of patients treated by the Hospital and Medical staffs with the Northern Expedition, it is a pleasure to add a word of appreciation of the work of the Nursing Sisters, who, defying the innumerable discomforts of the wilderness, carried out their strenuous duties assiduously and with a commendable spirit of cheerfulness. Lieut.-Colonel R. Mackenzie acted as Principal Medical Officer at Swakopmund, and, on his return to the Union after the occupation of Windhuk, was succeeded by Lieut.-Colonel De Kock.

NORTHERN ARMY.
JANUARY 15TH TO JULY 31ST, 1915.

Officers.			Men.			Total all Ranks.			
Admitted to Hospital.	Days treated.	Deaths.	Admitted to Hospital.	Days treated.	Deaths.	Admitted to Hospital.	Days treated.	Deaths.	Remarks.
234	1,898	1	5,556	50,266	26	5,790	52,164	27	Walvis Bay and Swakopmund Hospitals.
12	118	Nil	180	1,948	Nil	192	2,066	Nil	Windhuk Hospital.

```
Died from disease in hospital ..................  22
Died from gunshot wounds in hospital ......   5
Killed in action ..............................  50
                                                 —
                        Total ..................  77
```

CENSORSHIP.

It would be unfair to the public were I to omit a reference to the manner in which the censorship, on most occasions, was conducted, for the public had every reason to be dissatisfied with its operations. My first experience of a Censor corresponded with what, at the time, was tolerantly spoken of as "Maritz's Defection," and here I found myself confronted by one who inferred that he was the chosen "F. E. Smith" (the then Chief Censor in London) of South Africa. Unfortunately, in consequence of this inflated impression, much "copy" of considerable public interest was never permitted to see daylight; although ordinary travellers were allowed to journey to and fro between Upington and the rest of the Union, free to disseminate news during the initial, and, therefore, from the journalistic point of view, the most important period of this degrading chapter in South Africa's history. Representations to Pretoria, prompted by the ridiculous treatment meted out to correspondents' despatches, led to an order that telegraphed matter would no longer be liable to a surgical operation by the local Censors, but that the authorities in Pretoria would exercise supervision. Those responsible for the appointments did not at the start appreciate the fact that postmasters, from which class of Civil Servant the Censors were chiefly drawn, are not all necessarily imbued with those qualities of tact and discretion which should be associated with the important office of Censor, and that aspirants for such appointments should be subjected to as rigid a course of training as are members of any other branch of the South African military service.

During the chase after Maritz, while the correspondents' despatches were, besides being subjected to the local Censor, also "scrutinised" by the Chief Staff Officer, it was strongly affirmed by several who had been in the firing line at the Keimoes fight that Maritz was observed suddenly to stagger, when about to mount his horse, his subsequent and immediate behaviour serving to confirm the opinion that he had been shot in the leg. This gratifying piece of information the correspondent was debarred from communicating to the public, though the *official* despatch sent off the same day contained the news, as will be seen from the extract here quoted:—

"We have been authorised to publish the following official statement: ' . . . Maritz was wounded and fled in the direction of Kakamas. . . . '"

During the attempted interception of the rebel Kemp and his following by Col. Ben Bouwer, when a spy was shot at

Kameelpoort, outside Upington (referred to in Chapter I.), I sent both a telegraphed and written message, giving an account of the trial and subsequent execution. Both these messages were carefully suppressed by the Censors, but a full account of the affair was published a few days later in a Rand newspaper, which gave as its source of information a returned member of the forces who witnessed the incident. There was always the obvious loophole for news to filter through, despite Censors, and the most absurdly stringent regulations. For a hundred and one reasons units are travelling to and fro the whole time, and so the most confidential items of news are carried out of the firing line and conveyed to friends and acquaintances, and, as the one instance recorded shows, to newspaper editorial offices.

After General Botha's initial advance from Swakopmund, an over-conscientious Staff Officer debated the point whether or no the fact that General Botha was conducting the operations in person should be telegraphed to the Press. Permission was at last grudgingly given, when it was pointed out to this youthful and over-zealous officer that the suppression of General Botha's name following upon unfounded rumours of the G.O.C.'s ill-health, circulating in the Union at the time, might only lead to the presumption of his demise. Of course, the idea influencing this particular official mind was that the enemy might learn of the General's arrival in the country, and possibly employ the information in some way to their own advantage. And, while touching on this subject of information leaking out regarding the strength of the Union forces operating in South-west Africa, I could never understand why so much concealment concerning a force of over 50,000 men, accompanied by much heavier calibre artillery than the enemy could muster, was always considered to be so necessary, when arrayed as they were against a force officially stated at the outset to be not greater than 6,500. We had nothing to conceal with respect to our numbers, at least, and should our might have become known to the enemy, he was surely entitled, under the circumstances, to enjoy whatever doubtful advantage he could conceivably gain from such discouraging intelligence.

As already mentioned, it was eventually resolved that all censoring of the correspondents' copy should be done in Pretoria, and, at the time the expedition started for Walvis Bay, such was the understanding. From a courteously permitted perusal, or "scrutiny," of messages before despatch, there grew up a tenacious idea among the various officers appointed for the purpose (first by Col. Skinner and subsequently by the Headquarters of the General Officer Commanding) of reserving to themselves the right to censor. A little acrimonious correspondence arose between General Botha's Chief Staff Officer

(Col. Collyer) and the authorities wielding the "blue pencil" in Pretoria, both insisting that theirs was the sole right to censor the news for submission to the public. Both had their own way to the end of hostilities.

The correspondent (*qua* correspondent) appeared to be tolerated as a necessary evil, and a stricter censorship was not exercised in Europe than was practised in German South-west Africa. Had Lord Kitchener not given expression to his disapproval of the principle of war correspondents, our task might have proved less onerous. But, verily, imitation is the sincerest form of flattery, and we paid dearly for the spirit of emulation which animated the breasts of many an aspiring Field-Marshal.

No information was ever voluntarily imparted to me, with the unimportant exception of a conversation, aided by a plan, regarding the fight at Riet, several days after the event. Every scrap of information had, therefore, to be ferreted out and submitted to Censor No. 1 in a form ready for transmission to Censor No. 2 in the Union capital, via the telegraph office at Swakopmund, where was installed a further official called a "Scrutineer," who was empowered to delete superfluous words for the sake of economy. Although despatches were sometimes reduced in proportions, the Chief Staff Officer cannot be accused of ever having been over-communicative and so assisting to increase their bulk. As there was only one correspondent with the Northern force, and there were many practically independent columns operating miles and miles apart, the system or principle had, as may be gathered, its disadvantages. It led to the conclusion that the proverbial reticence of the police was only exceeded by that of a budding South African Staff Officer.

Instances were all too frequent during the campaign when it really appeared as if the Chief Staff Officer himself was in competition with the public's accredited Press representative.

On the occasion of the surrender at Otaviefontein, and before the official figures had been obtained of the total number of prisoners, I endeavoured to acquaint the Union with some idea of the number of captures, and presented a telegram for despatch which gave them as "approximately 3,500" (this twenty-four hours after the actual surrender). The Chief Staff Officer, however, was horrified at the mere suggestion, and pointed out that only the exact official total could possibly be communicated to the public, and the tally at the German camp was still incomplete. "You will be acquainted with the figures as soon as they come to hand," was the promise vouchsafed me.

The following morning the numbers were publicly made known, and I hastened to send my wire. I was greeted by the C.S.O. with a triumphant smile and the remark that " he was afraid he had done me a shot in the eye," having himself already telegraphed the number of surrenders to the Union.

It is to the Upington Censor that I must give credit for the deletion of a reference, in my first despatch from there, to an occasional dead transport donkey seen along the road. Presumably the shock would have been too much for the Union taxpayer to bear!

The following was the censored paragraph: " The journey was productive of at least one discovery possibly of use to science which upsets a theory hitherto most tenaciously adhered to for many generations. This was none other than the sight of a dead donkey, and I am afraid that in the track of the necessarily hurried transport we counted more than one."

The reference, as will be seen, was not even personal.

For weeks and weeks, running into months, after the occupation by our forces of Walvis and Swakopmund, no one was permitted to mention either place as his address, though all the while the sick, sorry, and those on leave were returning to the Union and regaling their friends with full and glowing accounts of the situation as they had so recently left it. The mere reference to Walvis or Swakopmund was almost sufficient to cause an official fit.

If the system of censoring must be adopted for private correspondence, then I consider the individual is entitled to demand that his letters are only perused by responsible officers. At Swakopmund, and elsewhere, the outgoing letters of the troops were scanned by non-commissioned postal officials, in addition to the Postmaster and accredited Censor, and, however much the arrangement was to be recommended for economical reasons, and the officials for their fitness for the work, the system is one to which the troops had good cause to object.

So much money is dissipated during a campaign that a little extra expenditure upon the appointment of qualified Censors would not only be well warranted, but would create a sense of better security among troops who are drawn from all classes. As the censoring fell under the ægis of the Army Post Office, my criticism of the gentle art of suppression must not in any way be taken as a reflection upon that hard-worked and efficiently conducted department. Under Major Venning, A.D.A.P. at Walvis, and a competent and indefatigable staff throughout the country, postal arrangements were from start to finish conducted in a highly satisfactory manner, and, but for an unfortunate conflagration at Omaruru, when a consignment of mails stored in an hotel was destroyed, nothing but appreciation was heard on all sides of the Army Posts, with which were incorporated the sorely tried Telegraph Department, and, for the time being, the two Eastern Telegraph and Cable Company's officials, through whose hands passed the whole of the telegraphic matter of the Northern force until the overland lines were restored through Windhuk to the Union.

The old system of blindly forwarding letters in one lot to a regiment, possibly scattered among different points throughout the country, was no longer pursued, a constant register being maintained of the movements of every unit in the field, and, on the arrival of mails at Walvis Bay, it was possible to determine immediately where every individual man was to be found. The system worked smoothly and expeditiously, and few, if any, with the Northern force had reason to complain of the Department of Army Posts, which contrived to serve out mails right up at the advance base at Riet directly after the termination of the battle.

NATIVE AFFAIRS.

With the acquisition by the Union forces of the bulk of the territory so recently known as German South-west Africa we came into possession of a considerable legacy of natives hitherto under German rule—a rule at the least drastic, if not frequently inhuman. Adjacent to the town of Windhuk alone there was a stad, or village, of over 10,000 natives, and it was with some foresight that the Union Government early despatched Major S. M. Pritchard (Director of Native Labour in the Union) to inaugurate a system of administration more in accordance with the British notions of right and justice. Staffs of competent officials, loaned from the Native Affairs Department of the Union, were promptly installed at all the more important and newly occupied centres, and a systematic method of control was soon in smooth running order.

But, before proceeding up-country, reference must be made to the management of native affairs at the coastal base, where native labourers imported from the Union were required for railway construction and other services. A compound was established at Walvis, where the majority of the natives were employed, and every reasonable consideration was bestowed upon their welfare, with the result that a smiling and contented community might any day have been observed "chanting" at their work on the jetties and in the supply-yards, ever with time at the end of the day's labour for an indulgence in friendly banter as they lined up for their rations and a mug of steaming coffee. And our coloured helpers were not all of Bantu origin, for the Indian community contributed a large number of men for sanitary and other equally important services in the towns.

Officials with extensive native experience were appointed at the very commencement, both at Walvis Bay and at Swakopmund, as Controllers of Native Affairs, a wise precaution which was amply justified by the successful results. The interests of the natives were, in consequence, scrupulously guarded, to the obvious satisfaction of both employee and employer. Similarly willing work was being done by natives employed nearer the front on transport work, their inimitable manipulation of draught animals, especially mules, being only too well known and appreciated by South Africans.

To serve to demonstrate the extent of the particular native labour organisation brought into being solely for the campaign, it is only necessary to state that during the period of hostilities no less than 25,000 natives were recruited for service with the Union forces.

With regard to the natives of the new territory, the German census on January 1, 1913, gives the totals, with their principal habitats, as follows:—

Hereros, 21,611 (Windhuk, Okahandja, Karibib, and Amaruru).

Hottentots, 14,366 (area, Warmbad to Gibeon).

Bastards, 3,301 (Rehoboth).

Bushmen, 3,335 (Etosha Pan and neighbourhood).

The figures for the Ovambos only show those employed in towns, viz., 5,705, which, however, is no guide to the numbers of this tribe, and concerning which there are no reliable figures in existence.

Of the totals mentioned above, one-third is estimated as representing the male populations.

In Windhuk, at least, the natives paid no hut-taxes, but a monthly income-tax of 1s. was substituted, which it was the duty of the employer to deduct from his servant's wages, the revenue so accruing being devoted by the Windhuk Municipality to improvements for the benefit of local natives.

Until the discovery of the Lüderitzbucht diamond fields the policy of the German authorities towards the natives in Southwest Africa was more one of extermination than of utilisation. With the opening up of the diamond industry, the want of labour was suddenly brought home to the Germans, who were compelled to employ Cape boys from the Union, the bulk of whose wages naturally went out of the country. The attitude of the Germans to their native population may, therefore, be said to have undergone a change for the better from that period, and their new-born humanity, as I have shown, was not actuated by any solicitous regard for the natives' welfare, but merely to educate them up to a proper recognition of the dignity of labouring on the Lüderitzbucht diamond fields.

Strenuous attempts were made by the German military authorities to cause certain sections of the natives to rise in their support against the forces of the Union.

Rehoboth, as is shown by the census return, is the home of the Bastards, who, under a Captain named Cornelius van Wijk, enjoyed self-government under a properly constituted Council, and were altogether immune from German interference, although living under their aegis.

The importunities of the Germans led Van Wijk to make a trip across country on a visit to General Botha, and on April 1, accompanied by a few headmen, the Captain of the Bastards arrived at Swakopmund. Van Wijk explained that they were perfectly satisfied to come under British rule, as they were well aware of the freedom and privileges enjoyed by the Cape boys and other natives throughout the Union. They were, however, being harassed by the Germans, and desired to know what their attitude should be. They were strictly enjoined to remain neutral. But, on the return of Cornelius to Rehoboth, he learned that the Germans, in revenge, had attacked a native convoy and burned both vehicles and the female occupants. After this the Bastards could no longer be restrained, and broke out against these goads of the enemy. It is authoritatively stated that Van Wijk's small son and grown-up daughter were killed by the Germans, the daughter being shot on the doorstep, while the son was dragged to the bush and there done to death. Although it was never made known officially, the Bastards exacted a terrible retribution from the Germans, whose casualties at the hands of the infuriated coloured people have been stated by some to have exceeded those incurred by the Germans during the whole of the South-west campaign. It is, of course, impossible yet awhile to verify this statement. Colour is, however, lent to the story by the fact that the Germans were compelled to withdraw from the contest.

In sharp contrast to the treatment by the Germans of the Bastard womenfolk mentioned above, it is noteworthy that German women and children who, in the course of the encounters, found themselves prisoners in the hands of Cornelius van Wijk, were profuse in their gratitude to the Bastard Captain when they were handed safely over to the Union Army. It is recorded that the women shook hands with Van Wijk to emphasise their appreciation of the coloured people's kindly behaviour.

The South African Hospital Ship "Ebani" anchored off Luderitzbucht.

General and Mrs. Botha leaving the "Ebani" at Cape Town.

Lady Buxton on board the Hospital Ship "Ebani," at the Official Opening Ceremony.

German Civilian Prisoners being taken to Cape Town.

After South West—Homeward Bound to the Cape.

Returning Home from South West.

After the Great Work was Done.

[Photo: Nissen.

General Botha's Reception at the Union Buildings, Pretoria, 1915.

In the meantime, in the north, a German officer and a missionary were busying themselves in a vain attempt to stir up the Ovambos (a dangerous pastime, considering that this warlike tribe remains unbeaten by the Germans themselves). Gifts of a wagon-load of mealie-meal and another of rum were despatched to the Chief, but these tempting baits were returned with a message to the effect that, recollecting that the German attack upon the Hereros some years back was shortly preceded by the bestowal of a similar present, the offering must be declined with thanks. The German agents repudiated such a base suggestion, and begged leave to press their gifts, which, on the second occasion, were received—presumably with a wink. These emissaries were still busy with the Ovambos at the time of the surrender at Otavi, and there were others who were endeavouring, though unsuccessfully, to suborn Portuguese officials on the border, about whom they had so recently written in splenetic vein in the Windhuk Press: " . . . Angola has always been a Convict Settlement. Most of the Portuguese settlers in the country are descendants of criminals—hybrids between Portuguese and for-centuries-bastardised-people, and the natives of the country. . . . So long as up there in the beautiful land, favoured by Nature, the flag of the Portuguese Republic, already dipped in blood during the Revolution, flies over the worthless mob which has for centuries committed crime upon crime in the name of European culture—so long as one of the treacherous, infamous murderers breathes, so long shall we have failed to avenge the murders of Ischinga Naulila." Naulila, it may be explained, was the spot in Portuguese territory where the Germans and Portuguese came into conflict during October, 1914.

The irrational anger which characterised the utterances of the Windhuk journal whenever Britain, Boer, or our ancient allies the Portuguese came under discussion, was pitiful in its childish impotence, and succeeded in creating an effect opposite to that evidently intended, these frequent diatribes only causing humorous interludes in the more serious business in hand.

POSSIBILITIES OF SOUTH-WEST AFRICA.

On the possibilities of Walvis Bay it is perhaps a little too early to speculate, and its future must depend entirely upon the extent to which it is ultimately resolved to develop the undoubted potentialities of the interior.

The mineral wealth of the country is reflected in the returns of the mines in operation before the outbreak of war, of which records are available.

There was the cheery optimist who, five minutes after setting foot on shore at Walvis, hysterically opined that a railway constructed across the Kalahari to the Rand would bring the Gold City several days nearer to Europe. An aeroplane might also conceivably effect a still greater diminution of time, and at less expense, between Johannesburg and the northern hemisphere and would be well able to cope with the few passengers. For it is only travellers who would gain an advantage. Even as the crow flies the distance from Walvis to Johannesburg is little less than that from Cape Town. Freights would therefore suffer higher charges over the new line, without enjoying a corresponding reduction due to being carried 800 miles less by sea. Once cargo is placed in the ships' holds it appears to make very little difference whether it is borne oversea for sixteen days or fourteen. It was once pointed out to me that the freight charges on a piano from London to Cape Town were slightly higher than on one from London to Melbourne (roughly, double the distance)! Consequently, as goods would not appear to reach the Rand any cheaper than over the existing routes, it seems a little too early in the world's history to expect the expenditure of millions on the construction of a line which could only benefit a handful of tourists.

A well-known dry-land agronomist, who has had ample opportunity of realising the enormous tracts of cultivable land still untouched in the Orange Free State and Transvaal, must needs choose to recommend Walvis, where the shifting sand-dunes baffle the ingenuity of man to harness them to one foundation, as a suitable area in which to grow mealies. Such idle talk is apt to be misleading. As lief say that if sufficient soil be placed upon the Johannesburg house-tops a mealie crop could be grown. In both cases the mealies would doubtless materialise, but the cost of production would stagger the ordinary level-headed farmer of the Union.

The expert alluded to is on much sounder premises when he touches upon the probabilities of Walvis Bay as a port and as a health resort. As a harbour Walvis Bay has no equa

A Great Marble Quarry near Karibib.

A Famous British Aeroplane in South West.

Penguins on Halifax Island, off the coast of German South West.

General Botha in South West attends to his horses at 5 a.m.

The End of the African Lion Hunt.

Reproduced by courtesy of the Editor of JOHN BULL.

around the shores of the African continent, while as a resort for the delicate, owing to its temperate climate throughout the year, it might well rival the attractions of more popular and therefore more boisterous haunts of the idle.

It is a peculiar kink in human nature, this craving to exploit the more inaccessible portions of the universe, and to neglect the obvious opportunities awaiting development at our thresholds.

As I have already stated, the growth of Walvis, as a commercial port only, will be regulated by the extent to which the interior may be developed, and in the northern and copper region there already exists in the South-west Africa Co., Limited, with its subsidiary, the Otavi Mines and Railway Co., a solid example of British enterprise in Damaraland. Land concessions, mining rights and railways represent the principal interests of the company, the extraction of copper and lead ores at Tsumeb and subsidiary mines being carried on on an extensive scale.

It is interesting to recall that this British company was primarily responsible for the construction of the Swakopmund-Otavi railway. Formed in 1900 as a Germany company by the South-west African Co., for the purpose of exploiting the Tsumeb and other mineral deposits, the Otavi Company built a line from Swakopmund to Tsumeb, 354 miles long, at a cost of about £850,000, the construction being completed in 1906. About the same time the South-west Africa Co. built a branch line from Otavifontein to its headquarters at Grootfontein, a distance of $59\frac{1}{2}$ miles. Subsequently both lines were acquired by the German Government, but continued to be operated by the Otavi Company under lease. General Botha's occupation automatically displaces the German Government and creates a further asset for the conquerors.

Away from the arid coast-belt the territory from Windhuk northward becomes not only an ideal cattle country, but, judging from the flourishing farms encountered wherever water is obtainable (and boring seems to meet with very satisfactory results), it augurs well for the greater development of its agricultural resources in the future. If confirmation of this were needed, the confidence expressed by the South-west Africa Co. in its possession, under grant or concession, of some $3\frac{1}{4}$ million acres of freehold land surveyed into farms in the best parts of the territory (of which 750,000 acres have been sold to individual settlers and farming undertakings), should serve to convince the sceptical of the value of farming prospects in South-west Africa. The Germans evidently realised the farming potentialities of the Protectorate, for every farm, wherever situated, is founded on thorough and permanent lines. There is not a tin " shack " (such as one all too frequently meets with throughout the pastoral districts of the Union) in the whole of the territory, and the homesteads along the line of march were, without exception, substantially built. One such model farm was "Goabeb," a few miles north of Usakos, where much land had been put under irrigation by means of steam pumping plant, which elevated the water from wells in proximity to a river bed and dispersed it over the land by means of an elaborate and costly system of cement furrows. A feature that appealed to the Boer farmers was that few if any of the cattle farms are fenced, and yet herdsmen are almost unnecessary. The reason of this is due to the very drawback of the country—the absence of open water; for each evening the cattle may be seen trekking back to the near vicinity of the homestead, where the water awaits them, pumped into troughs from the well.

Extensive cattle ranches, established by the Germans, are to be met with in the neighbourhood of Windhuk, where the pasture is of an excellent quality and dairy farming receives much attention. At one of these farms a certain D.A.Q.-M.G. with our forces purchased hundreds of pounds of cheese for his brigade, and butter and milk too were freely obtainable at the farms along the Karibib-Windhuk line.

Figures relative to the South-west African Protectorate compiled before the war read as follows :—Area, 322,446 square miles (about six times the size of England); white population, some 14,000; railways. 1,400 miles; value of exports in 1913, £3,500,000; value of imports in 1913, £2,170,000.

APPENDICES.

I.
OFFICIAL CORRESPONDENCE BETWEEN THE IMPERIAL AND UNION GOVERNMENTS RESPECTING OPERATIONS IN GERMAN SOUTH-WEST AFRICA.

1.
Ministers to Acting Governor-General, Union of South Africa, Prime Minister's Office, Pretoria, 4th August, 1914.

Minute No. 686.

Ministers have the honour to inform His Excellency the Officer Administering the Government that immediately after the return of the Prime Minister a meeting of the Cabinet was summoned, when it was decided to request His Excellency to transmit the following message to the Right Honourable the Secretary of State for the Colonies:—

"The Government, fully recognising the obligations of the Union, in the event of hostilities, wishes to assure you of its preparedness to take all such measures as may be necessary for the defence of the Union. Should His Majesty's Government require the Imperial troops now stationed in South Africa, and who are not connected with the garrison artillery, in any other part of the world, Ministers would gladly employ the Defence Force of the Union for the performance of the duties entrusted to the Imperial troops in South Africa."

Ministers would further express the hope that they will be kept fully informed of further developments.

(Signed) LOUIS BOTHA.

2.
Acting Governor-General to Ministers. Governor-General's Office, Pretoria. 6th August, 1914.

Minute No. 9-18.

The Acting Governor-General transmits herewith for the information of Ministers with reference to their Minute 686 of the 4th August, a copy of the undermentioned document on the subject of the offer of the Union Government to undertake responsibility for the duties now performed by Imperial troops in South Africa.

(Signed) DE VILLIERS, Acting Governor-General.

[*Telegram.*]
From Secretary of State to Acting Governor-General, Pretoria. 5th August, 1914.

Your telegram of 4th of August. Please inform your Ministers that His Majesty's Government most cordially appreciate their offer to undertake responsibility for duties now performed by Imperial troops in South Africa in order to leave those troops free for other purposes if required. I will communicate with you further as soon as I am able to give definite reply.

HARCOURT.

3.
Acting Governor-General to Ministers. Governor-General's Office, Pretoria. 7th August, 1914.

Minute No. 9-18.

The Acting Governor-General informs Ministers with reference to their Minute No. 686 of the 4th August that he has received the following telegram from the Secretary of State for the Colonies:

His Majesty's Government gratefully accept your offer to release Imperial troops from South Africa and yourselves to take charge over defence and internal order. We shall accordingly recall all the troops which are not actually required in duties which cannot be otherwise performed.

(Signed) DE VILLIERS, Acting Governor-General.

4.
Acting Governor-General to Ministers. Governor-General's Office, Pretoria. 7th August, 1914.

Minute No. 9-18.

The Acting Governor-General informs Ministers that, in continuation of the message communicated in his Minute No. 9-18 of this date, the Secretary of State for the Colonies telegraphed as follows:—

If your Ministers at the same time desire and feel themselves able to seize such part of German South-west Africa as will give them the command of Swakopmund, Lüderitzbucht, and the wireless stations there or in the interior, we should feel this was a great and urgent Imperial service. You will, however, realise that any territory now occupied must be at the disposal of the Imperial Government

for the purposes of an ultimate settlement at the conclusion of the War. Other Dominions are acting in similar way on the same understanding.
(Signed) DE VILLIERS,
Acting Governor-General.

5.

Acting Governor-General to Ministers.
Governor-General's Office, Pretoria.
10th August, 1914.
Minute No. 9-18.
The Governor-General transmits herewith for the consideration of Ministers, with reference to his Minute No. 9-18 of the 7th instant, a copy of the undermentioned document on the subject of the proposed naval and military expedition against German South-west Africa.
(Signed) DE VILLIERS,
Acting Governor-General.

Telegram.
From Secretary of State.
To Acting Governor-General.
9th August, 1914.
My telegram of 6th August. His Majesty's Government regard as urgent necessity seizure of coast wireless stations at Swakopmund and Lüderitzbucht. This can only be effected in reasonable time by a joint naval and military expedition up the coast. Capture of long-distance station at Windhuk, which is of great importance, might follow another expedition against coast stations or be carried out independently from interior, but this must rest with your Government.

6.

Minister to Acting Governor-General.
Prime Minister's Office, Pretoria.
Minute No. 718. 10th August, 1914.
Ministers have the honour to inform His Excellency the Officer Administering the Government that they have given careful consideration to the important matter raised in the communications from the Secretary of State for the Colonies of the 6th and 9th instant, and that they cordially agree to cooperate with the Imperial Government and to assist in sending an expedition for the purpose indicated, the naval part to be undertaken by the Imperial authorities and the military operations to be undertaken by the Union Government. (Signed) LOUIS BOTHA.

II.

THE CAMPAIGN SUPPORTED BY PARLIAMENT.

The Parliament of the Union of South Africa met in Extraordinary Session on the 9th September, 1914. The action of the Government respecting hostilities in German South-west Africa was confirmed by both the Senate and the House of Assembly. The following are the speeches of leaders, with the voting data:—
The Governor-General (His Excellency Viscount Buxton):
The King has directed me to inform the people of the Union of his constant interest in the welfare of your country. He has received with pride and gladness the many proofs which have reached him of the loyalty to the Crown and Empire, by which South Africa, in common with all his other Dominions, is animated, and of her determination to play her part in the great conflict which has been forced upon us. As he has already informed you, your support is an invaluable source of strength to him in discharging the responsibilities which rest upon him, and he relies with confidence upon the people of South Africa to maintain and add fresh lustre to the splendid traditions of courage, determination, and endurance which they have inherited. He has noted with great satisfaction the remarkable progress that has been made in the few years since Union was established, and he is confident that when the anxieties which cloud the more immediate future are dissolved South Africa may again look forward to a time of continued progress and prosperity.

The following Address was agreed to in reply:—
To His Most Gracious Majesty George V., By the Grace of God, of the United Kingdom of Great Britain and Ireland, and of the British Dominions Beyond the Seas, King, Defender of the Faith, Emperor of India:
May it please Your Majesty.
We, Your Majesty's most dutiful and loyal subjects, the President and Members of the Senate, and the Speaker and Members of the House of Assembly of the Union of South Africa in Parliament assembled, humbly beg to tender to Your Majesty our heartfelt thanks for Your Majesty's Most Gracious Message to the people of the Union of South Africa, which was conveyed by His Excellency Viscount Buxton on the occasion of the opening of the Special Session of Parliament on the 9th September, 1914.
While deeply deploring the outbreak of the war, we are convinced that participation therein was forced upon the Empire, and we respectfully desire to be allowed to express our approval of the action taken by Your Majesty in defence of the principles of liberty and justice and of the integrity and sanctity of international obligations. In expressing our deepest sorrow on account of the inevitable hardships and suffering entailed upon Your

Majesty's subjects, we fervently trust and believe that not only will Your Majesty's Empire emerge from the gigantic struggle confirmed in the position which it has so long occupied among the nations of the world, but that the period of conflict will be succeeded by an era of beneficent and lasting peace

And we humbly assure Your Majesty of our continued loyalty and devotion to Your Majesty's Throne and Person.

In the Senate,
Senator General de la Rey said that no one could dispute that dark clouds hung over the world at the present day, and also over South Africa, and that it would be very difficult to find a way to remove them as far as South Africa was concerned. They should not act as his hon. friend Senator Wolmarans had done by using certain words, which did more harm than good. Senator Wolmarans had spoken of robbery ("roverij") and capturing booty ("buitmakerij"), but such expressions were wrong, and only tended to create ill blood. Let them remain calm. He was wholly against war, and it had always been his standpoint, since he had the honour of representing his people, that war should be avoided where they could avoid it. Before the last struggle in the Transvaal and the O.F.S. he had been against declaring war, but if his land was attacked he would defend it with all his might. Now, owing to events in Europe, they were in difficult times again in far-off South Africa. As to neutrality, as the Prime Minister had said, there could be no possible doubt about their not being neutral. When the speaker signed the treaty at Vereeniging he never thought that if Britain were involved in war he was binding his country to make war. Since the signing of the treaty at Vereeniging the people of South Africa had never taken any action that was disloyal to the British flag. He wanted to see the German power broken, because, if so, his country was free of the danger, but if the British power were broken, what would happen to this country? As far as the final result was concerned, what they did in South Africa would be as a drop in the ocean; and why then should they put their country in danger? If South Africa was attacked he would do all he could to defend it, and personally he preferred to live under the British flag rather than under the German flag. He very much regretted what had been said in another place about their not being armed in certain parts of South Africa, because such statements did them harm, and published broadcast their supposed defenceless condition. His opinion was that if they were attacked by Germany it would take much longer than three years to conquer them—it had taken Great Britain three years—but now they had the four Provinces united. He could not vote for the motion, not because he had anything against the Government, but because he had conscientious scruples—and if his support was necessary it was ever ready at the disposal of the Government for the defence of the country.

The Senate agreed to the Address by 24 votes to 5.

Minority:—Senators A. D. W. Wolmarans, H. Potgieter, C. G. Marais, I. W. B. de Villiers, and W. J. C. Brebner.

Majority:—Senators J. A. C. Graaf, C. Searle, H. G. Stuart, S. Marks, Sir Meiring Beck, Kt., Dr. A. G. Viljoen, P. J. Weeber, E. Powell, M. J. Beukes, F. O. F. Churchill, Marshall Campbell, Colonel J. J. Byron, C.M.G., E. R. Grobler, J. J. H. Claassens, T. J. Nel, J. D. Schofield, C. Southey, C.M.G., Colonel W. E. M. Stanford, C.B., C.M.G., the Right Hon. Sir Frederick Moor, P.C., K.C.M.G., H. D. Winter, W. K. Tucker, C.M.G., W. F. Lance, F. A. R. Johnstone, and J. C. Krogh.

In the Assembly.

The Prime Minister moved:

That this House, fully recognising the obligations of the Union as a portion of the British Empire, respectfully requests His Excellency the Governor-General to convey a humble address to His Majesty the King assuring him of its loyal support in bringing to a successful issue the momentous conflict which has been forced upon him in defence of the principles of liberty and of international honour, and of its wholehearted determination to take all measures necessary for defending the interests of the Union and for cooperating with His Majesty's Imperial Government to maintain the security and integrity of the Empire, and further humbly requesting His Majesty to convey to His Majesty the King of the Belgians its admiration for and its sincere sympathy with the Belgian people in their heroic stand for the protection of their country against the unprincipled invasion of its rights.

He said that never before had the Parliament of South Africa been called together at a more critical time. The Empire of which they formed a component part was involved in one of the greatest and most cruel wars which humanity had ever had the misfortune to behold. They in South Africa were, so to speak, at the extreme edge of this terrific storm. Of course, we suffered certain consequences from the storm, and privation and misery were felt in South Africa as a result thereof. But, practically speaking, that storm was still far away from us, and its full effects were not felt here. There were consequently many people in this country who did not recognise the tremendous seriousness and great possibilities of this war, and there were even some people who thought that the storm did not threaten us. This was a short-sighted conception. It was a wrong conception, which he hoped would be removed, unless they wished to create for themselves a miserable future. They to-day formed part of the British Empire. They were an ally in the British Empire, and that Empire being involved in war, South Africa was *ipso facto* also involved in war — (hear, hear) — with a common enemy. That proposition seemed so clear to him that it could not be contradicted, so he would not say much about it. For a territory which belonged to the British Empire there were only two ways open in such a case as that. The one possibility was that of faith, duty, and honour. (Cheers.) The other was of dishonour and disloyalty. He knew the South African people. There was no quality in the South African people more characteristic than its sense of honour. The history of their people was clean and unstained. (Hear, hear.) It would be the desire of their people to maintain that reputation unstained and unblemished. It would be a scandalous dishonour on their part if they chose the present moment, this time of trouble and misery, to abandon their loyalty. (Hear, hear.) Such disloyalty would make every just and fair-minded man ashamed, and it would plunge South Africa in the deepest troubles and misfortunes. It would be an action which would blacken us for ever in the eyes of every other nation. The South African people had perhaps made the greatest sacrifices any people could possibly make. He did not think any people in the world could have made greater sacrifices than the people of South Africa had made. (Hear, hear.) But if they had made sacrifices they had retained their honour, their name, and their reputation. Theirs was a people who had always looked forward to a future of greatness, but their people had always based their ideals on Christianity. That was the road of a Christian nation. Never had they endeavoured even in the darkest days of their existence to create anything by treason, and the road of treason was an unknown road amongst the Dutch-speaking people of this country. Therefore he said emphatically that the people of South Africa would not stoop to anything in the nature of disloyalty or dishonour. Their duty and conscience told them to be faithful and true to the Imperial Government in every respect in this hour of darkness and trouble. That was the attitude which he and his colleagues had determined to adopt, and they did not hesitate to think that the people of the country were in thorough accord with it. He was pleased to see that in every part of South Africa resolutions had been passed expressing loyalty and confidence. Animated by that spirit, the Government had not hesitated, as soon as it became clear that the position was serious, to cable to the Imperial Government that if the Imperial troops stationed in South Africa could be of service to the Imperial Government elsewhere, they in South Africa would be prepared to take the defence of South Africa on their own shoulders. (Hear, hear.) The Imperial Government accepted that assurance with thanks. This brought with it the necessity for calling up a part of the Defence Force. The Minister of Defence, as soon as war was declared and after consultation with the Cabinet, had at once notified the Defence Force to be ready. It could not be otherwise. People knew that the Defence Force had been called up These men had not been called up for the purpose of being sent to a particular part of the country, but were notified that the country, being in a state of war, could be placed in a proper condition of defence.

The British troops in South Africa had either gone or would speedily be leaving, and to a certain extent the country would have to be prepared to look after its own defence, and to take over the work of the troops. After that the Imperial Government had notified South Africa that certain military operations in German South-west Africa were considered to be of great strategic importance, and that if the Union could take that work on its own shoulders it would be regarded as a great service. That was a request from the Imperial Government to the Union Government. Having very carefully considered the matter, this Government had resolved to comply with the suggestion, and they did so both in the interests of South Africa and in those of the Empire. (Hear, hear.) Well, that was the request to South Africa, and in the speaker's view there was only one possible answer, unless they wished to create a very unsound position. On those grounds, therefore, the Government considered they had acted in the true interests of the South African people. The manner in which those military operations were to be carried out was obviously a question which could not be discussed in public, but he was able to give the assurance that those who would be responsible for them would go to work with the greatest possible prudence and tact.

After that request, and after that decision by the Government, he had at once arranged for an extraordinary sitting of Parliament. There would have to be a further mobilisation of the Defence Force, and it was only fair that the representatives of South Africa should be called together and informed of what had happened, so that they would be able to understand the position. That was a question on which men of understanding would meet together in order to take action in the true interests of the public. He accordingly left the whole question in the hands of the House.

Next he wished to refer to certain incidents which had taken place. Not long after the outbreak of the War the Government were informed that troops in fairly large numbers in German Southwest Africa had visited the border of the Union at several different points. They came to the border and then went back again, and they did that repeatedly. Finally they came in the direction of Nakob, and stationed themselves there near the beacons on the border. That was a position which they had never previously occupied. They had entrenched themselves there. Moreover, they had seized kopjes in the territory of the Union in a southerly direction, and had entrenched themselves there. So far as the Government knew, the troops were there still. German troops had taken up that position without warning.

Another incident arose out of the fact that a number of the subjects of the Union, a fairly large number too, were living in German territory. It seemed probable that those people had been ordered to move, with their cattle, further into the interior, or else give up their cattle. A small group refused to do that, and fled in the direction of Groot River, going to one of the islands in the territory of the Union. The islands, in fact, belonged to the Union. Then a German patrol appeared for the purpose of taking the cattle, and some fighting ensued, with the result that two Germans were shot to death there. He (the speaker) only mentioned those matters in order to show the hostile attitude which had been already taken up against the Union, and he trusted that the House and the country would thoroughly understand it.

Well, after very careful consideration the Government had arrived at the conclusion that there could be only one answer to the request of the Imperial Government.

The war had been forced on the British Government. If Great Britain had ever entered on a war with clean hands, it was this war. (Hear, hear.) It was not necessary for him to explain the history and the whole position which led to the present war. It had been done elsewhere by those on whom the responsibility rested, and he did not doubt that every one in the House had read the correspondence referred to that afternoon by Sir Percy Fitzpatrick, and that every one had perused the official correspondence which had been published in London. If that had not been done he hoped it would still be done. It was abundantly clear from the correspondence that the British Government did not want war. The British Government did its utmost to maintain peace.

They were forced into this war by Germany. (Hear, hear.) The war had been forced on them by Berlin. Had the proposals made by the British Government been accepted by Berlin the war would not have taken place. That was not simply an argument—it was a fact clearly proved by the correspondence to which he had referred. Only when the war broke out between the other Powers, and when it became impossible without loss of prestige and honour to remain out of the war, did the Imperial Government take the extreme step. (Hear, hear.) By that decision the whole of the British Empire was involved in war. The war was undertaken not with any desire of aggrandisement, nor with any desire to acquire more land. The desire which had been charged to the discredit of the British Government was absolutely unfounded. The war was undertaken out of a sense of duty, and not out of any desire to get more land. Nor was it their purpose in South Africa to capture more land, but merely to do their duty. War was declared because the British Government were bound to carry out solemn treaties concluded with other people. They had undertaken the protection of other nations who were trampled on and whose ground had been occupied by a large armed force without the smallest attention being paid to the public there, and without a declaration of war. The war was undertaken by the British Government in order to maintain the right, and it was with that in view that the British Government accepted these great responsibilities. He wanted the House to feel that whatever step the Government took there was no desire whatever to acquire fresh possessions. It was unnecessary to tell the House every step that the Government might possibly take. Everything would be done, of course, with the greatest prudence and tact. Meantime no one would deny that their future was being decided on the battlefields of Europe.

There was no one who could think

that the victory of either side would not reflect itself in the future of this country in one way or another. Proceeding, General Botha said he wished to say a few words in appreciation of the excellent spirit of co-operation which during the past few weeks had been manifesting itself in South Africa. If one looked back twelve or thirteen years to the day when the two great white races of this country were opposed to each other in a great struggle, one could not help but feel thankful for the great change that had come about and the great co-operation which to-day prevailed. (Cheers.)

The Prime Minister went on to appeal to every one to be as tolerant as possible in days like the present. They should not blame the Afrikander of Dutch origin who did not feel exactly the same as the English Afrikander did. People should not say, because the Dutch Afrikanders did not feel the same way as the English Afrikanders, that the Dutch Afrikanders were disloyal. A difficulty in assenting to what was proposed to be done should not be regarded as disloyalty. It was not that. There was no question of disloyalty. He knew the people of South Africa, and he believed in them; although there may be many who in the past had been hostile to the British flag, he could vouch for them that they would ten times rather be under the English flag to-day than under the German flag. He wished to appeal to them all for greater tolerance than ever before—(cheers)—because in times like the present rumours sprang up from everywhere like the wind—rumours in which there was no truth at all, and which would only have the effect of doing the greatest possible harm. He asked everybody to disbelieve such rumours. (Cheers.) There was another point he wished to refer to. They had in this country a large number of German people who were British subjects, and who had always co-operated for the welfare and prosperity of this country, and who, in fact, had been true and faithful assistants to South Africa. (Cheers.) Therefore he was grateful that the Minister of Defence had told certain Germans in Natal that their services would not be required in the present trouble for the Defence Force, because surely it would not be right, perhaps, to make brother fight against brother or father against son. (Cheers.) He wished to impress upon the House that they should not wage war on persons. To-day they were to fight the German Crown which was responsible for this vindictive war. (Loud cheers.) Some of them felt more strongly on this subject than others did, but it by no means followed that the latter were disloyal. They must all be as tolerant as they possibly could. Great confidence had been placed in the people of South Africa. They had received the Constitution, under which they could create a great future in the country. Let them stand by that Constitution, and he felt that the people of South Africa would prove themselves worthy of the confidence placed in them. The British Government after giving them their Constitution had regarded them, and had treated them, as a free people, as a sister State. They were free in South Africa, and on South Africa itself depended its own future.

In regard to the attitude of the British Government, he wished to refer to one incident to show how that Government had always treated them. In July last this country had tried to take up a loan of four millions, but had succeeded only in getting two millions. It would be fatal, of course, under present circumstances, to go into the market for money, and they all knew the financial difficulties with which the Union was faced. However, the British Government had come to their assistance, and had lent them seven millions. (Loud cheers.) That was a spirit of co-operation and brotherhood which had always animated the Imperial authorities. (Loud cheers.) Its own difficulty notwithstanding, the British Government had come to help South Africa out of its embarrassment. It would be indeed disastrous if a feeling of racialism were again to be revived in this country. Let them all stand together for the welfare of the whole. It was the duty of the House to see that they emerged from the present war not as a divided people, but as one united nation. (Hear, hear.)

Continuing, General Botha said there was just one other point he wished to mention. In a war like this, of course, heavy suffering and great privations must be inflicted. He felt it was the duty of South Africa to do something to relieve that suffering, and therefore he would propose that they do something and make some contribution of some kind towards the relief of the suffering. Their contribution might be in the way of mealies, tobacco for the soldiers, and brandy for medicinal purposes, though he could not say in what quantities. Possibly also it might take the form of meat, for there were many farmers in South Africa who had come to the Government and offered gifts, provided the Government would organise the matter and see to the transport. Farmers had come forward offering their products if the Government would undertake the dispatch. (Cheers.)

Concluding, General Botha said he wished hon. members to remember that in the past the Belgian and French people had come forward with many gifts to relieve the suffering in this country, and he trusted that the attitude South Africa was going to take up would be as honourable a one in the eyes of the whole world. (Cheers.)

Sir T. W. Smartt, Unionist Party, seconded amid general cheers.

Mr. F. H. P. Creswell, Labour Party, moved as an amendment to add at the end of the reply:

And, further, humbly requests his Majesty to take every possible measure to ensure that at the termination of the present war there shall be a general reduction of armaments, and that in future international differences shall be settled by arbitration and an end be put to the system by which civilised peoples are hurled into a state of war without their consent being first obtained. This House, further, considers that to promote the internal efficiency and minimise the distress and unemployment accentuated by the war, it is the duty of the Government to provide for the carrying on of all wealth-producing activities, so that there may be no unnecessary curtailment of public and other works; to this end it is of opinion that the Government should be given power to take over for the public use during the continuation of the war any natural resources of which the fullest use is not being made.

Mr. T. Boydell seconded the amendment.

Later in the debate Mr. Creswell announced that he had much pleasure in withdrawing the amendment—(cheers)—so that there might be no sort of excuse, and no side could pretend that there had been any division in the House, or imply that there had been a want of unanimity in that House to render what help they could.

General J. B. M. Hertzog, Nationalist Party, said that Parliament, as the highest authority in the country, were suddenly called on that evening to decide whether they would declare war against Germany—yes or no. (Cries of "No, no.") In reality that was the question that was put before the House, namely, whether they as the governing authority in South Africa were going to attack their neighbours in German South-west Africa. It had been represented to hon. members that an obligation to do that rested on them. It was quite true that South Africa was in a state of war in consequence of the war which existed between England and Germany, but that war was not yet the war of South Africa. It was for South Africa to say whether it would seize that part of the country. It was for South Africa to say whether as a separate Union it would pass over or take part in a war which already existed.

It was, moreover, a question the weight of which the people of South Africa knew only too well, because of the few years that had passed since it took a hand in doing what it was now again called on to do, and as a result of which the country had suffered in such a measure that it had not even yet recovered from the effects. They knew what it meant when South Africa was asked again to enter on such a struggle. Personally, he had shuddered at it, as he felt sure the House had shuddered at it. There were many in the country who reflected more deeply than those who allowed themselves to be dragged away by the excitement of the moment. It was felt far more deeply and more earnestly by the people in the country districts. It was not a question of Imperialism. It was a question of South Africa for the people of South Africa. When they were dealing with a question which might lead to the country being plunged into the deepest misery, and, as was only too possible, to the whole country being ruined, then they ought to feel that they were considering a question which required a little more consideration than it was apparently the intention of the Government to allow the House to give it.

He (the speaker) said that he was sorry that neither he nor other members of the House who were not in the secrets of the Government had been given an opportunity to consider such a serious matter and to ascertain what suggestions they would be able to make. He felt it, and the people would know it, that he had not been afforded a timely opportunity in which to consider this weighty matter.

In considering the question, he was not going to be led. Nothing else would lead him than the interests of the people and of the country. The House was asked to declare war against Germany. (Cries of "No, no.") Well, he would put it in a better way. It had been suggested to the House that they should agree to authorise the Government to make a raid on German South-west Africa. The House was asked to empower the Government to call up the burghers and to give them full powers to make a raid on that country. When South Africa undertook to do anything of that sort it ought to be done, in the first place, with the object of contributing something to the struggle which was now taking place in Europe.

In the course of his speech the Prime Minister had several times told them that it had nothing to do with any extension of territory. The speaker accepted that, but then he asked: What, then, is the reason for raiding German South-west Africa? Could they by so doing contribute so much to the obtaining of a favourable result of the struggle in Europe? Would Germany, as a consequence of the raid by the Union in German South-west Africa, send a single man there? If not, what would South Africa contribute to the struggle? Why was South Africa to sacrifice its men and spend its gold? Why expose themselves to things that might happen—though God forbid it!—but which had already happened elsewhere? Then, God help South Africa!

South Africa was to make a raid on German South-west Africa, and yet the Union did not seek for an expansion of territory. Then what were they going to do in German South-west Africa? How in doing that would they be helping England? Would it not be better if South Africa, either directly or in some other way, took a real part in the struggle in the area where it ought to be fought? There were other reasons why they should not create a position of danger, and why they should not take a step of that character. He would venture to ask this war-like Government: What was the condition of affairs with regard to the arming of the people? He felt almost obliged to say things which he would rather suppress. He did not wish to have South Africa directly dragged into the war. Let them state the facts frankly, and look the possible results in the eyes. What was the condition of the arms of the people? In the whole of the Free State there was not a single district where more than six policemen remained. The whole of the police force had been taken away from the Free State. They knew the position, and it was very possible that something might happen there, and what would the unarmed people of the Free State be able to do, being as they were totally unarmed? And yet they wanted to enter on a war with the greatest and mightiest military Power in the world whilst the population of South Africa was unarmed. The Minister of Defence knew it. The people were being called on to make war when no duty rested on them to go and look for a quarrel.

Had the Government considered the condition of the people in the country places in the Free State, for example? The condition of misery there remained almost as bad as it was a year after the war. They were without cattle, and the country had suffered badly from the drought. In a material sense the people were worse off now than they were immediately after the war, and yet the House was being asked to drag those people in that miserable state to go to war. The speaker's duty was to go to this country and to these people, and no Empire had the right to come between them. What, then, was in the interest of that people and of that country? He would not now discuss the condition of the war in Europe, but he asked himself what that condition was. They were being fed with messages from Europe, and what they were told as true one day was described the next day as lies. They did not know the true condition of affairs. Those who were perhaps acquainted with the facts—and those would include the Government—could they say that France or Belgium or the British Empire had obtained a glorious victory?

Suppose they received news that the Allies were totally defeated and ruined, would South Africa be justified in that case in beginning a war with Germany and incurring the danger of German troops being brought to South Africa? None of the members would be in favour of it. The position of affairs was not so serious as that, but, on the other hand, it was not of a nature which left the British Empire without anxiety, and even all the Allies. Why should South Africa undertake a thing which would lead to nothing else than to bringing the country into the same condition as Belgium? If South Africa went out of its way to make a raid, it would not have the right to say anything after if it were attacked.

Well, he would not go into the question as to who was to be blamed for the war. Had there ever been a war in which the one party failed to blame the other? He was not at present in a position to judge who was right, or who was wrong, and history only would be able to settle that point. But to assume at once that one was right and the other wrong—why, he had been warned against that from the very first days when he began to study the law. He put himself into the position of an intelligent Government, which took care under the circumstances that, if misery was to come, it should come as late as possible. He did not suppose that anybody would accuse him of lack of a deep feeling of compassion for Belgium. Everybody ought to have a deep feeling of sympathy with the Belgian people, especially because they were for the greater part a Dutch-speaking people of the same race as they in South Africa. But when the Government asked the House to express itself against the unprincipled assault on Belgian neutrality, he asked himself what right the House had to deliver judgment, seeing that it did not know all the facts. Was the House to decide solely on the news which was contained in the newspapers? And if they gave judgment, they should still remember that there was another side of the story, and that that ought to be laid before them. Let them show to the Belgians that the South African, who knew what war meant, had the deepest sympathy for them, but if the speaker were asked to go out of his way to express opinions on matters with which he was not fully acquainted, then he was bound to say he could not do it. He could not agree to the terms of the motion which referred to the unjust action of Germany, as it might be shown afterwards that it was no such thing.

It was not for him to suggest to the Government what ought to be done, but if the Government thought that something had to be done, then let it be done in a manner which would be effective and in a manner which would not produce more miseries in South Africa. He had never yet made a great fuss of his regard for the Empire, and he had never tried to convince others of his loyalty. No one had the right to demand that he should do any such thing. He had never done it yet, and would never do it. Not only had the people of South Africa shown that they fully esteemed all the favours which they had received, but, if it were necessary to show it still more, that, too, would be done. But they had no right to ask South Africa to do what no single part of the Empire had done, namely, that it should take direct action, cross over its borders, and act directly as a principal in the struggle which was now proceeding. Let them assume for a moment that the struggle was between America and the British Empire. Would it not in such a case be the very extremity of absurdity to demand that Canada should attack the United States? Such a thing would be the last word in folly. No one in the world had the right to demand that a country like South Africa should make a complete sacrifice of itself. No one had such a right. It would be said that he had not been asked to sacrifice himself. But the British Empire had asked for that to be done, and the British Empire had no right to ask it. It was more than South Africa ought to be asked to do.

If South Africa were a great and mighty country which could use violence and really do something, the speaker would be unable to say anything in favour of it, but what could the country do with less than 60,000 armed men, every one of whom would be necessary to perform the task which they had undertaken? The Prime Minister had undertaken to see that the honour of South Africa was preserved, and that the dangers which surrounded the countries were restrained. And no one had the right to ask South Africa to do anything more than that.

The Prime Minister had rightly stated that the Afrikander would prefer to live under the British Government rather than the German. The speaker thought that the Prime Minister had not expressed himself on that point with sufficient emphasis, believing as he did that, if it came to a question of whether South Africa should be under the British Government or under the German, they would find opinions so strong that every one in South Africa would fight to the last before he would submit to having the German flag waving over the Union. South Africa should not therefore do anything that it was not its duty to do. Could anyone say how long the war would last? It was said that it would probably last three years, and it was assumed that Germany would be defeated. Well, in that case the war would certainly last a long time, because the German people knew what the war meant and had prepared themselves for it. Everyone who had written on the subject of the war had been able to come to no other conclusion than that the war would last two or three years. And yet South Africa, in the very beginning of the war, was to place a burden on its back of at least a million pounds sterling per annum, or perhaps more, and to lose its best men in German Southwest Africa. If Germany were not defeated, where, then, would South Africa be? Where, then, would be the men whose duty it was to watch the borders of the Union? The best of them would probably have been buried in the sand in German South-west Africa, and would disappear at the same time as the Government and the people. If Germany lost, then German South-west Africa would fall like a ripe fruit into the lap of Great Britain. And then, if Germany won, would South Africa be in a position to retain German Southwest Africa? Was it not the very essence of stupidity to ask that South Africa, in the beginning of the war, should go and take German South-west Africa? In such a case the Union would have the satisfaction of having spent money and men and kept the country in a good state in order afterwards to hand it back to Germany. He could not see why they should go for a "sand egg" of that sort. He was sorry he could not be as enthusiastic as some other hon. members were in speaking of this matter. He knew what war was, and he knew the sights that it provided. He knew also what it meant to be responsible for it. For these reasons therefore, and before entering on the war, the Government must consult the people. The Prime Minister could say what he liked, but it did not reflect the opinion of the people, at any rate, not 5 per cent. of the opinion of the Free State. During his journey to Cape Town the speaker had spoken to many prominent persons in that Province, and he was able to give the assurance to the Minister of Defence that a large proportion of the inhabitants of the Cape Province were opposed to war in German South-west Africa. As a representative of a Cape constituency, was the Minister of Agriculture able to deny that? The Government would very speedily find out that they had to deal with a population which felt something was being done which ought not to be done. They felt it was not their duty to go and fight as the Government had suggested. He feared that the plan would be the ruin of South Africa, and the little reputation which South Africa won fourteen years ago would be lost. When the war of 1899 broke out he knew what the opinion of the burghers were. Everyone of them had his weapon in his hand, and felt himself strong. The measure of the confidence which the burghers had in their arms in 1899 was the measure of their distrust to-day in their old and worn-out rifles. The Government would not have the people with them when they called on the latter to do something which was opposed to their views.

In conclusion, he said he felt he had done his duty to the House and to the country, and would now allow the Government to go and take the responsibility on its own shoulders. He could not agree that the motion should be adopted, and he accordingly moved the following amendment:

This House, being fully prepared to support all measures of defence which may be necessary to resist any attack on Union territory, is of opinion that any act in the nature of an attack or which may lead to an attack on German territory in South Africa would be in conflict with the interests of the Union and of the Empire.

Mr. P. G. W. Grobler seconded the amendment.

Mr. Fremantle proposed the following amendment to General Hertzog's amendment:

This House, deeply appreciating the liberty secured to the people of South Africa under the British Crown, and fully recognising the obligation of the Union as a portion of the British Empire, respectfully requests his Excellency the Governor-General to convey a humble address to his Majesty the King assuring him of its hearty and unreserved sympathy in the calamity which the war has brought upon the Empire, and of the determination of the people of South Africa to discharge to the full their obligations; and, further, humbly requesting his Majesty to convey to his Majesty the King of the Belgians its admiration for and its sincere sympathy with the Belgian people in their heroic stand for the freedom of their country, and, further, that this House——

Mr. J. H. B. Wessels seconded the amendment.

The House divided, with the following result:

For the motion, 91:—J. J. Alberts, M. Alexander, W. H. Andrews, W. Duncan Baxter, H. C. Bekker, S. Bekker, Sir W. Bisset Berry, Kt., W. W. J. J. Bezuidenhout, G. Blaine, General the Rt. Hon. Louis Botha, P.C., T. Boydell, D. M. Brown, the Hon. H. Burton, K.C., the Hon. W. F. Clayton, F. H. P. Creswell, Colonel the · Hon. Sir Charles Crewe, F. R. Cronje, Sir Thomas Cullinan, Kt., M. J. de Beer, Dr. A. L. de Jager, H. de Waal, the Hon. N. J. de Wet, K.C., G. J. W. du Toit, A. Fawcus, Sir Percy FitzPatrick, K.C.M.G., L. Geldenhuys, W. H. Griffin, C. H. Haggar, Colonel Sir David Harris, K.C.M.G., C. B. Heatlie, J. Henderson, C. Henwood, J. W. Jagger, C. J. J. Joubert, M. Kentridge, J. G. King, C. J. Krige, General L. A. S. Lemmer, Colonel the Hon. Sir George Leuchars, D.S.O., G. A. Louw, Dr. Donald Macaulay, Dr. J. C. MacNeillie, T. Maginess, the Hon. F. S. Malan, P. G. Marais, the Rt. Hon. John X. Merriman, P.C., I. J. Meyer, H. M. Meyler, M. W. Myburgh, E. Nathan, Dr. A. M. Neethling, J. A. Neser, R. G. Nicholson, H. A. Oliver, O. A. Oosthuizen, T. Orr, C.M.G., J. W. Quinn, J. M. Rademeyer, W. Rockey, W. Runciman, H. W. Sampson, J. H. Schoeman, T. L. Schreiner, Major P. A. Silburn, D.S.O., the Hon. Sir Thomas Smartt, K.C.M.G., General the Hon. J. C. Smuts, K.C., General T. Smuts, J. P. G. Steyl, G. L. Steytler, C. F. W. Struben, the Hon. H. S. Theron, P. J. G. Theron, J. A. P. v. d. Merwe, F. J. W. v. d. Riet, K.C., J. v. d. Walt, J. W. van Eeden, the Hon. H. C. van Heerden, J. A. Venter, H. C. W. Vermaas, A. I. Vintcent, J. A. Vosloo, the Hon. Sir Edgar Walton, K.C.M.G., E. B. Watermeyer, A. H. Watkins, the Hon. Sir Thomas Watt. K.C.M.G., Dr. H. W. Wessels, H. Wiltshire, Colonel Sir Aubrey Woolls-Sampson, K.C.B., the Hon. Hugh Wyndham; and Dr. J. Hewat and H. Mentz, tellers.

Against the motion, 12:—C. G. Fichardt, H. E. S. Fremantle, E. N. Grobler, P. G. W. Grobler, General the Hon. J. B. M. Hertzog, J. H. Marais, H. P. Serfontein, N. W. Serfontein, C. A. van Niekerk, C. T. M. Wilcocks; and J. H. Brand Wessels and J. G. Keyter, tellers.

III.
GENERAL BEYERS' RESIGNATION.

Letter to the Minister of Defence, and the Minster's Reply.

Pretoria,
15th September, 1914.

To the
Right Hon. General J. C. Smuts, Minister of Defence, Pretoria.

Hon. Sir,—You are aware that during the month of August last I told you and General Botha by word of mouth that I disapproved of the sending of commandoes to German South-west Africa for the purpose of conquering that territory. I was on the point then of resigning, but, hearing that Parliament was to be called together, I decided to wait, hoping that a way out of the difficulty would be found. To my utmost surprise, however, Parliament confirmed the resolution adopted by Government, namely, to conquer German South-west Africa, without any provocation towards the Union by Germans. Government must be aware that by far the great majority of the Dutch-speaking people of the Union decidedly object to crossing the frontier, and the two conferences of Commandants recently held in Pretoria bore eloquent testimony to this. I challenge Government by an appeal to the people without making use of compulsion, to obtain any other result. It is said that Great Britain has taken part in this war for the sake of right and justice, in order to protect the independence of small nations, and to comply with treaties. The fact that three Ministers of the British Cabinet resigned shows that even in England there is a strong minority which could not be convinced of the righteousness of a war with Germany.

History teaches us, after all, that whenever it serves her interests Great Britain is always ready to protect smaller nations, but, unhappily, history also relates instances in which sacred rights and the independence of smaller nations has been violated, and treaties disregarded, by the same country. In proof of this I have only to indicate how the independence of the South African Republic and Orange Free State was violated, and of what weight the Sand River Convention was. It is said that war is being waged against the barbarity of the Germans. We have forgiven but not forgotten all the barbarities perpetrated in this, our own country during the South African war.

With very few exceptions all farms, not to mention many towns, were Louvains, of which we now hear so much. At this critical moment it is made known in Parliament that our Government was granted a loan of seven millions sterling by the British Government. This is very significant! Any one can have his own thoughts about that. In the absence of legitimate grounds for the annexation policy of the Government you endeavour to intimidate the public by declaring that Government possesses information showing that Germany has decided—should opportunity arise—to annex South Africa.

My humble opinion is that this will be hastened if, from our side, we invade German territory without having been provoked thereto by the Germans. And as to the alleged German annexation scheme this is nothing more than the result of the usual national suspicion attending such matters. The allegations made in Parliament, namely, that Germans have already violated our frontier, are unfounded (see the official report of the Information Bureau, corroborated by Lieut.-Colonel Maritz and his officers, who are on or near the frontier). Apparently Government longed for some transgressions by the Germans of German South-west Africa, but have been disappointed in this, for so far not a single German soldier has crossed our frontier.

As you know very well the report is perfectly correct regarding an involuntary transgression of the frontier some time ago and the tendering of an apology for so doing. Whatever may happen in South Africa, the war will be decided in Europe in any case, so if Germany triumphs and should decide to attack us, then, even if Great Britain should be unable to help us, we should at least have a sacred and clean cause in defending our country to the utmost, provided we stay inside our borders in the meanwhile.

In case we are attacked our people will arise as one man in defence of its rights. Besides, I am convinced that a commando of 8,000 Germans, as at present stationed in German territory, will not be so foolish as to attempt an attack on our country. I have always said and repeated at Booysens recently, that if the Union is attacked Boer and Briton will defend this country side by side, and in such a case I will deem it a great honour and privilege to take up my place at the head of our forces in defence of my fatherland. I accepted the position of Commandant-General under our Defence Act, the first section of which provides that our forces can only be employed in the defence of the Union. My humble opinion is that this section cannot thus be changed by informal resolution of Parliament, such being contrary to Parliamentary procedure. So the Defence Act does not allow us to go and fight the enemy over the frontier and to light the fire in that way, but should the enemy penetrate into our country it will be our duty to drive him back and pursue him in his own territory.

In his speech General Botha speaks about the help we had from the Belgians and the French after the South African war. This is still appreciated by me and by all our people, but we must not forget that the Germans also were not behindhand, and have always been well disposed towards us. So why should we deliberately make enemies of them? As circumstances are I see no way of taking the offensive, and as I sincerely love my country and my people I must strongly protest against the sending of the Union Citizen Forces over the frontier. Who can foretell where the fire the Government has decided to light shall end? For the reasons enumerated above I feel constrained to resign my post as Commandant-General as also my commissioned rank. For me this is the only way of faith, duty, and honour towards my people, of which mention was made by General Botha. I have always tried to do my duty according to my best convictions, and it sorely grieves me that it must end in this way.

I have the honour to be,
Honourable Sir,
Your obedient Servant,
(Signed)
CHRISTIAN FREDERICK BEYERS.
Department of Defence, Pretoria.
19th September, 1914.

Sir,—It was with regret that I received your letter of the 15th inst., tendering your resignation as Commandant-General of the Union Defence Forces and as an officer of the Union. The circumstances under which that resignation took place and the terms in which you endeavour to justify your action tend to leave a very painful impression. It is true that it was known to me that you entertained objections against the war operations in German South-west Africa, but I never received the impression that you would resign. On the contrary, all the information in possession of the Government was communicated to you, all the plans were discussed with you, and your advice was followed to a large extent, the principal officers were appointed on your recommendation and with your concurrence, and the plan of operations which is now being followed is largely the one recommended by yourself at a conference of officers.

My last instruction to you before I left for Cape Town to attend the special session of Parliament was that in my absence you should visit certain regiments on the German South-west border, and it was well understood between us that immediately the war operations were somewhat further advanced and co-operation with the various divisions would be practicable, you should yourself undertake the chief command in German South-west Africa. The attitude of the Government after this remained unchanged and was approved by Parliament after full discussion. One would have expected that this approval would make the matter easier for you; but now I find that you anticipated that Parliament would disapprove of the policy of the Government and that your disappointment in this became the reason for your unexpected action. In order to make your motive clear, the reasons for your resignation were explained in a long political argument, which was immediately communicated to the Press and came into the hands of the Government long after publication.

I need not tell you that all these circumstances in connection with your resignation have made a most unpleasant impression on my colleagues and myself. But this unpleasant impression has even been aggravated by the allegation contained in your letter. Your bitter attack on Great Britain is not only entirely baseless, but is the more unjustifiable, coming as it does in the midst of a great war, from the Commandant-General of one of the British Dominions. Your references to barbarous acts during the South African war cannot justify the criminal devastation of Belgium, and can only be calculated to sow hatred and division among the people of South Africa.

You forget to mention that since the South African war the British people gave South Africa her entire freedom under a Constitution which makes it possible for us to realise our national ideals along our own lines, and which, for instance, allows you to write with impunity a letter for which you would, without doubt, be liable in the German Empire to the extreme penalty.

As regards your other statements, they have been answered and disposed of in Parliament. From these discussions it will be apparent that neither the British Empire nor South Africa was the aggressor in this struggle. War was in the first instance, declared by Austria-Hungary and thereafter by Germany under circumstances in which the British Government employed its utmost powers to maintain the peace of Europe and to safeguard the neutrality of Belgium. So far as we ourselves are concerned our coast is threatened, our mail boats arrested, and our borders threatened by the enemy.

This latter incident did not occur, as you say, in an involuntary manner and with an apology, which latter at any rate, was never tendered to the Government.

Under these circumstances it is absurd to speak of aggressive action on the part of the Union, seeing that, together with the British Empire, we have been drawn against our wish and will, and entirely in self-defence, into this war.

As regards your insinuation concerning the loan of £7,000,000, which the British Government was kind enough to grant us, and for which the public of the Union, as evidenced recently in Parliament, are most grateful, it is of such a despicable nature that there is no necessity to make any comment thereon. It shows to what extent your mind has been obscured by political bias. You speak of duty and honour. My conviction is that the people of South Africa, in these dark days, when the Government, as well as the people of South Africa, are put to the supreme test, have a clearer conception of duty and honour than is to be deduced from your letter and action.

For the Dutch-speaking section in particular I cannot conceive anything more fatal and humiliating than a policy of loyalty in fair weather and a policy of neutrality and pro-German sentiment in days of storm and stress. It may be that our peculiar internal circumstances and our backward condition after the great war will place a limit on what we can do, but, nevertheless, I am convinced that the people will support the Government in carrying out the mandate of Parliament, and in this manner, which is the only way, legitimately fulfil their duty to South Africa and to the Empire and maintain their dearly-won honour unblemished for the future.

Your resignation is hereby accepted.
I have the honour to be, Sir,
Your obedient servant,
(Signed)   J. C. SMUTS,
Minister of Defence.
To the Hon. General C. F. Beyers,
Pretoria.

IV.
THE TREACHERY OF MARITZ.

Maritz told the forces under him in the following words of his decision to join the Germans. The speech was made in a camp near Keimoes, on the North-west of the Cape Province, on the 10th October, 1914.

Now, men, I am here to address you on a critical subject. It is a matter which never previously occurred in the history of South Africa. As you all know, I was a Commandant in the late Boer War and have always cared for my country and always will do so no matter what the consequences may be. The Minister of Defence has instructed me to cross the border with you, but we have just decided we are not going to fight against the Germans. There are several reasons for the decision. One of them is that we do not want unnecessary bloodshed. We don't want to be ruled by the Jews and financiers of England.

General Beyers, General de Wet, and myself have decided to form an independent South African Republic, and have entered into an agreement with the Governor of German South-west Africa, who has been authorised by his King to do so, the agreement being that in return for helping them to annex Walfish Bay and the islands near it, they will form a German volunteer corps in German South-west Africa to help us fight against the British. They will provide us with arms and ammunition, guns, etc., and also help us to take Delagoa Bay, the natural port of the Union, from the Portuguese King. In the event of anything going wrong, and any of us escape to German territory, they will give us protection and recognise us as German subjects.

Now, my young friends, this step has not been decided in a moment of haste, it is a course for which we have worked for some time. The Botha Government has caused this step, first by excluding General Hertzog from the Cabinet; secondly, by invading German South-west Africa against the people's wishes. You must remember that the Government has got you here by false pretences. They called you for training, and while you were undergoing training in the camp, I was ordered to raise my force and cross the border, which I have refused to do. The force is not properly equipped. I asked the Government for assistance, and they sent a little lieutenant and a few men with a couple of maxims.

On this step depends the freedom of the masses of the country. I love my wife and children, but I love my country better. Lieut. Freer has asked me to allow him to retain his maxim and ammunition and he will fight us. I have refused this because in my opinion it would cause unnecessary bloodshed.

V.
THE MARITZ PROCLAMATION.

"With reference to the establishment of the South African Republic." This document, printed in Dutch, was extensively circulated in certain parts of South Africa in the early days of the Rebellion:—

To the People of South Africa.

The day of liberation has dawned. The burgher population of South Africa has already risen and has begun the fight for freedom against the undesirable and forcibly imposed British overlordship. The troops of the newly-formed South African Republic have now commenced war against the troops of the British Government. The Government of the South African Republic is provisionally represented by the hon. gentlemen,
GENERAL MARITZ,
COMMANDANT DE VILLIERS,
JAN DE WAAL-CALVINIA.

The Government will give back to the people of South Africa the long-deprived freedom, from which they have been robbed for the last 12 years. Burghers, countrymen, and all who desire to see South Africa free, willingly and freely do your duty towards the beloved and beautiful "Vierkleur Flag." Unite to the last man to regain your freedom and rights.

The German Government, whose victory is already assured, has, being the mightiest Power, sanctioned the right of establishment of the S.A. Republic, and thereby it is proved that it had no intention of conquering South Africa, as was declared by Messrs. Botha and Smuts in the Parliament of the Union.

Kakamas, Z.A.R.,
October, A.D. 1914.
The Government of the South African Republic.
(Signed)
MARITZ.
DE VILLIERS.
JAN DE WAAL.

VI.
GERMAN PROCLAMATION.

"To the Dutch Inhabitants of South Africa," which was freely circulated at Kakamas by the German contingent with Maritz:—

Whereas English troops have taken Raman's Drift, invaded the German borders and thereby transferred the war from Europe to South Africa, therefore I declare emphatically that the Germans are not making war against the Dutch inhabitants of South Africa, that, on the contrary, they are using all measures to ward off the attacks of British troops at all points, and that they will carry on the war against the English, and against the English only, to the utmost.

(Signed) SEITZ,
Imperial Governor of German South-west Africa.
Windhuk, 16th September, 1914.

VII.
TREATY (SO-CALLED).

"Made and entered into by and between the Imperial Government of German South-west Africa, as the representative of His Majesty the Emperor of Germany, and General S. C. Maritz, who is acting in the name and on behalf of a number of officers and men who are prepared to declare the Independence of South Africa, that is to say:—

I. The said General S. C. Maritz has declared the independence of South Africa and commenced war against England.

II. The Government of German South-west Africa acknowledges all African forces which operate against England in (blank) forces, and they will, after further discussion, support the war against England.

III. In the event of British South Africa being declared independent, either partially or as a whole, the Imperial Government of German South-west Africa will take all possible measures to get that State or States acknowledged as such by the German Empire as soon as possible, and bring them under the terms of the general conclusion of peace.

IV. In consideration of such assistance, the newly-formed State or States will have no objection to the German Government taking possession of Walfish Bay and the Islands opposite German South-west Africa.

V. The centre of the Orange River will in future form the boundaries between German South-west Africa and the Cape Province.

VI. The German Empire will have no objection to the above-named States taking possession of Delagoa Bay.

VII. If the rebellion fails, the rebels who enter German territory will be recognised as German subjects and be treated as such."

VIII.
GENERAL CHRISTIAN DE WET'S SPEECH.

Delivered at Vrede, October 21, 1914. General de Wet compelled the Magistrate of Vrede to attend to listen to this speech, which gave rise to the term "The Five Bob Rebellion."

Ladies, gentlemen, and burghers,—

I have asked you to come here to hear me explain my position. Magistrate, I want you to take down every word that I am going to say, because whatever I may do in the future I can never commit a greater act of rebellion than I have already committed. I am going through to Maritz, where we will receive arms and ammunition, and from there we are going to Pretoria to pull down the British flag and proclaim a free South African Republic. All those who side with me must follow me, and those who side with the Government must go to them.

I signed the Vereeniging Treaty and swore to be faithful to the British flag, but we have been so downtrodden by the miserable, pestilential English that we can endure it no longer. His Majesty King Edward VII. promised to protect us, but he has failed to do so, and has allowed a Magistrate to be placed over us (he is one of the pestilential English) who is an absolute tyrant, and has made it impossible for us to tolerate it any longer. I was charged before him for beating a native boy. I only did it with a small shepherd's whip, and for that I was fined 5s.

Yes, I did plead guilty. (The Magistrate had here interrupted the speaker, who also retorted that if he did not hold his tongue he would make him.)

After the Magistrate had delivered judgment, instead of reprimanding the boy and ordering him in future to be obedient and do his duty, he looked at the native as if he would have liked to give him a kiss. The Magistrate is a brother-in-law of a man for whom I have the greatest respect, and who is very dear to me—President Steyn—and for that reason I will give him another chance. Otherwise I would have taken him prisoner and handed him over to the Germans. The Magistrate's father was one of the staunchest pillars of the Church, and if he were alive to-day he would be heart and soul with me in this movement, and would condemn this dastardly act of robbery which the Government is going to commit.

The ungodly policy of Botha has gone on long enough, and the South African Dutch are going to stand as one man to crush this unholy scandal. Some of my friends have advised me to wait a little longer until England has received another knock, but it is beneath me and my people to kick a dead dog. England has got her hands full enough. I hate the lies which are continually being spread to the effect that thousands of Australians, Canadians, and Indians can be sent to fight us. Where will England get them from? She has enough to fight her own battles.

I am going through the town to take the following six articles:— Horses, saddles, bridles, halters, arms and ammunition, and if anybody should refuse to hand to my men these articles, if they should be found in their possession, I will give him a thrashing with a sjambok. I order the shopkeepers to come and open their shops, and I will select men to go round and take whatever I require apart from the above articles, and they will give receipts for what they take, and if they don't open their shops willingly I will open them in another way. My advice to you English is to remain quiet in your houses and not interfere with my men, and if you don't, beware when I come back. I have got my eight sons and sons-in-law here with me, and the only people left on my farm are my wife and daughter. Anybody can go and see if they like, and I request the Magistrate to give them any help they may require if he will do so.

IX.

DECLARATION BY PIETER DE WET RESPECTING MARITZ'S NEGOTIATIONS WITH THE GERMANS.

Translated.

I have resided at Windhuk since 1912. In January, 1905, I left Carnarvon, and entered German South-west Africa, and in April, 1914, I became a German subject. I am married to a Boer girl. At the end of May, or the beginning of June, 1913, I was in the Cape Province to purchase mules for the German Government. I went overland as far as Upington, and from there to Prieska by motor-car.

There I visited Maritz for a few days. At that time Maritz was stationed there as a major of the Defence Force. He had an office there and a few clerks. There was then no camp, and Maritz did not wear a uniform. I know Maritz well from the time of our war days. I was intimate with him. Maritz one night said to me: "Look here, Piet; we have a plan, should there be war one day in Europe, to free our country from the English Government, and they have now placed me here to try and find out whether we can get into touch with the Germans, so that they can provide us with arms in case we undertake anything in this way. Now, have the Germans many guns and rifles in German South-west?" I said that I did not know, as the guns were very strictly guarded in the artillery depôt, but that he should try to get into touch with influential persons in German South-west.

We finally decided that I should see the Governor after my return, and ask him whether he could send Gustav Voigts, a person of importance and highly thought of by the Government, on a visit to the Union for the purpose of getting into touch with Maritz. Maritz further said that a certain number of Boers had been trained as staff officers, and that these persons, as well as General Beyers, General de Wet, and other persons, were in favour of the idea. We discussed many matters, but these were the most important. We then separated. I returned by sea, and did not therefore see Maritz again.

After my arrival here in June, 1913, I went to Gustav Voigts. He said to me: "Pieter, I shall go and see the Governor at once and communicate to him your message from Maritz." Some time afterwards Voigts told me that he had written a letter to Maritz, saying, "Your wish will be realised."

I did not see Maritz again until August, 1914, as will appear here.

Shortly after the outbreak of war I was in Windhuk, and a certain Max Tienert—a large and influential farmer in the Okahandja district, and a great friend of Maritz—came to see me. He told me that he had instructions from the Governor to get into personal touch with Maritz, and that he wished that I should accompany him. We then left for the south. When we reached Warmbad I told Tienert that it was not advisable for him to cross the border, but that I should go alone. It was arranged that I should cross the border with a document signed by Hauptmann Beyer, to the effect that I, as a British subject, had been forbidden on the outbreak of war in Europe to remain in German South-west territory. In this manner I would then cross the border and see Maritz, and this was accordingly done. By means of this document I was allowed by an English corporal to cross the border at Schuit Drift.

I then first went to Kakamas. There I was informed by Piet Joubert that Maritz would within a few days come to Kakamas. I waited there. Two or three days later Maritz came. Maritz, on seeing me, said: "What are you Germans doing here?" I laughed, and said that I had fled. He laughed, and entered the house of Stadler. I also entered with Joubert.

Maritz then said to Joubert and me: "I wish to tell you a secret. You know the Government now wish to attack German South-west, and I have just been at a meeting at Pretoria, at which there were present members of Parliament and Boer ex-officers. Generals Botha and Smuts proposed to take German South-west, and fifty-eight of the sixty members present voted against it. De la Rey became so angry that he left the meeting. A large proportion of the people is also against it, but it appears that the intention of Generals Botha and Smuts to carry out the plan will be put into execution, and, as I told you last year, if I fight I do not fight against the Germans. What is now the position in regard to the rifles and ammunition we last spoke about? If we rebel we must be armed. What did the Governor say about my message?"

I said: "Gustav Voigts told me that he wrote you about it."

He replied: "Voigts wrote me a short, rubbishy note, in which he says, 'Your wish will be realised,' but from that I did not conclude much. They should have sent somebody to see me personally." He then asked: "But what is the position? Have the Germans got rifles and ammunition there, and will they help us if we want these things?"

I replied: "The Germans are very secret in such things, but Tienert is here on the German side of Schuit Drift, where you can see him." I then told him how Tienert had come, and how Tienert had been left behind on the other side of the border. Maritz then wished me to return at once to ascertain about guns and rifles. I said: "Yes, but how am I to evade the police and cross the river again?" He replied: "You ride along with me to Schuit Drift, and the police can go to blazes."

We then left Maritz, and I said I wished that Maritz should see Tienert personally. When we arrived at Schuit Drift the police were away to investigate the Liebenberg incident lower down. Maritz then took the boat himself, and we crossed the river. I then introduced Maritz to the German sergeant Samel, who was in charge of the German post there. Tienert was not there. He had returned to Ukamas. Maritz then asked Samel whether he (Maritz) could be placed in telephonic communication with Tienert. This was done. I was present at the conversation.

Maritz then told Tienert what he had told Joubert and me. Tienert said that the German Government had a large supply of artillery, and that the Germans could give him (Maritz) a sufficient number Maritz wished to be assured by Tienert as to whether the German Government could also supply Maritz with artillerists. It was then arranged and decided that Tienert and I should immediately return to see the Governor, and inform Maritz precisely of everything. Maritz further said that he would like the Governor and General Beyers to meet each other. Tienert proposed that Beyers should come to the border. At this point the conversation over the telephone came to an end. Maritz then further said to me: "We do not, however, wish to fight on a loose footing. I should like, if we fight, that Beyers and Seitz should meet each other, so that they can frame a proper treaty. I will endeavour to get Beyers to visit the camp which I am establishing; then you or Tiernert have to be at Nakob, so that when I let you know of Beyers' arrival you can immediately notify Seitz, so that these two can meet each other. I hope to have Beyers here between the 7th and 15th of September." Thereupon I left.

The following day Tienert and I arrived at Windhuk. We then immediately went to the Government buildings, where we met the Governor and von Heydebreck. We told them everything. Seitz was mysterious, as all Germans always are. He looked at von Heydebreck, who said, "Yes, guns we have enough, but we are short of personnel." Finally Seitz said, without, however, mentioning any number:

"Yes, we will assist the Boers as far as possible with artillery and small arms." Seitz also said that he was willing to meet Beyers at any time to treat with him. We then separated.

Tienert, as arranged with Maritz, returned to Nakob the following day, and I remained here at Windhuk. Tienert had to await a message there as to when Beyers would arrive. As nothing was, however, heard from Maritz as to Beyers' arrival, Seitz left four or five days before the 15th September for the south, in order to be as near as possible to the border on Beyers' arrival. I was informed of this by the officers here, in whose entire confidence I was.

I now wish to refer to the raising of the volunteer corps. After I returned from Maritz in August, 1914, I wrote to my brother, Andries de Wet, who at that time was, and still is, resident in the district of Grootfontein. Thereupon my brother came to Windhuk. He said that he was going to propose to the Governor to allow him to raise a corps to help our people in the Union. This he did. The Governor said that he would assist us with artillery, as also with money, where necessary. Thereupon the well-known "Oproepbrief" (manifesto) was drafted. This letter was written by the Rev. Mr. Leonard at the dictation of my brother, and printed by the *Zuidwest Bode*. When this corps was at its strongest it numbered about 120 men. When we crossed the border with this corps it numbered ninety-eight men. A battery of four guns and two pom-poms had been attached to the corps. The guns and pom-poms were under the command of Uber-Leutnant Hausdenk and eighty men. Hausdenk was under the command of my brother. The officers of that corps were Andries de Wet (Commandant), Pieter de Wet (Chief Field Cornet), and Hausdenk (Assistant Field Cornet). Other well-known farmers in the corps were Christoffel Esterhuizen (supplies), Jan Delport (subsequently Field Cornet), Hans Grootbeer (of Ermelo, since killed), four brothers Kotzee (of Gibeon), and Jacobus Coetzee (subsequently Field Cornet).

This corps crossed the river at Nakob on October 9, and joined Maritz at Van Rooy's Vlei on October 10. After the surrender of arms at Upington in the beginning of February the corps was disbanded, partly at Ukamas and partly at Kalkfontein. My brother had already resigned in the beginning of November, and then returned to his farm. The position of my brother as Commandant was filled by Stoffel Schoeman, a German subject. I myself surrendered my arms at Ukamas after the disbandment of the corps.

A day after Seitz had left to meet Beyers my brother also went south. When he arrived at Keetmanshoop he received a telegram from Dr. Seitz to the effect that he had at once to proceed to Ukamas to confer with Seitz. On arrival there Seitz was dissatisfied, as no message had yet been received from Maritz regarding Beyers's arrival. He (Seitz) told my brother that von Heydebreck had become greatly dissatisfied at the delay of Maritz, and that he (von Heydebreck) had lost good chances for fighting, but that he could do nothing until Beyers put in an appearance.

My brother replied that he could not himself understand why Maritz was delaying so much, and suggested that it might be owing to the fact that the drifts had in the meantime been so strongly guarded that it was impossible for Maritz to send a message across. (This was before we had heard of the death of General de la Rey. A rumour to that effect reached us a day or two after his death.) My brother then proposed to the Governor that the English police stations should be attacked and captured in order to restore communication with Maritz. My brother undertook, at the request of the Governor, to take Nakob (also called Groendoorn) that night, and that the Germans would also that night take Stolzenfels and Rietfontein. Early the next morning my brother surrounded and took Nakob. Stolzenfels and Rietfontein were, however, only taken some days later. We, however, did not hear anything from Maritz, and the Governor then returned to Windhuk. When he left we were already in possession of the news of De la Rey's death.

The Governor left Von Zastrow behind to discuss all matters with Beyers or Maritz, and to enter into a treaty. Von Zastrow had written authority from the Governor to act as his representative. As Beyers, however, did not come, the well-known treaty was subsequently entered into between Maritz and von Zastrow.

I have to explain that I was not present at the meeting between the Governor and my brother. To me, as leader, however, everything was told by my brother, and von Zastrow himself told me that he remained behind as the Governor's representative. I myself met the Governor at Gibeon on his return, and he (the Governor) congratulated me on my brother's success at Nakob.

(Signed) PIETER DE WET.

The above statement was made by Pieter de Wet in my presence, and recorded by me in writing. De Wet told me everything voluntarily, and has perused the statement and signed it as correct.

(Signed) D. DE WAAL, Major,
Provost Marshal.

Windhuk, May 27, 1915.

X.
THE POISONED WELLS.
Communiqué issued from Pretoria, 8th May, 1915.

On the occupation of Swakopmund by the Union troops on the 14th January, 1915, it was discovered that six wells from which water was to be drawn for human consumption had been poisoned by means of arsenical cattle dip. In some instances bags full of this poison were found in the wells.

On February 13th General Botha addressed a letter to Lieut.-Colonel Franke, the Commander of the German Forces, drawing his attention to the fact that such an act was contrary to Article XXIII. (a) of the Hague Convention, and informing him that if the practice was persisted in he would hold the officers concerned responsible, and he would be compelled, though with reluctance, to employ such measures of reprisals as might seem advisable.

To this letter Lieut.-Col. Franke replied under date February 21st, that the troops under his command had been given orders "if they can possibly prevent it not to allow any water supplies to fall into the hands of the enemy in a form which allows such supplies to be used either by man or beast. . . . Accordingly the officer who was in charge when Swakopmund was evacuated had several sacks of cooking salt thrown into the wells . . . But we found that the salting of the water could be rendered ineffective in a short time. Thereafter we tried kopper dip, and we found by using this material any enemy occupying the town would for some time have to rely on water brought from elsewhere."

Lieut.-Col. Franke also claimed that in order to prevent inflicting "injury to the health of the enemy" instructions had been given that the wells so treated should be marked by warning notices; and stated that he had sent one of the oldest of his staff officers to Swakopmund to examine what had been done.

To this General Botha replied on February 28th expressing regret that this use of poison apparently received the support of the German military authorities. He again drew attention to the breach of Article XXIII (a) of the Hague Convention, and pointed out that the offence against the customs of civilised warfare was in no degree lessened by the exhibition of warning notices, even if displayed. He added that, as a matter of fact, no such notices had been found when Swakopmund was occupied.

Finally, General Botha repeated his intention to hold the officer commanding responsible, and reiterated the hope that the German military authorities would refrain from similar practices in the future. On March 22nd, however, a message, dated March 10th, sent by Capt. Kruger, of the German Protectorate troops, to an outpost at Pforte, was intercepted. It reads as follows:—

The patrol Gabib has been instructed thoroughly to infect with disease the Ida Mine. Approach Swakop and Ida Mine with extreme caution, and do not water there any more.

Since their evacuation of Aus, Warmbad, and other places, the German troops have consistently poisoned all wells along the railway line, in their retirement.

XI.
SPEECH BY THE EX-GERMAN GOVERNOR, DR. SEITZ.

The Landesrath or Parliament of German South-west Africa (which is purely advisory) met at Windhuk in March, after the campaign had been six months in progress. The following is a translation of Dr. Seitz's speech:—

Gentlemen,—I welcome you heartily to the sixth session of the Diet. Since, under the present circumstances, many members are prevented from being present here, I have invited a few gentlemen from various districts and various spheres of interest to attend our meeting as guests, with the right of giving advice. I expect these gentlemen to attend to the business of the House with the same conscientiousness as the members.

During the last decennia, gentlemen, much has been said and written about the fatal hour towards which the German people was advancing. This fatal hour has struck, gentlemen; we are in the midst of it, and we can rightly say: This great time has not found Germany a small generation! We see how our people are fighting against a superior force, as has hardly ever been done by any people on earth!

We, too, in this Protectorate, share in the strife, and I may say that here, too, everything has been done that could possibly be done in this war, and I believe it is our duty and firm resolve also in the future to emulate our brethren at home in loyalty to Emperor and Empire, and to be prepared, as they are, to sacrifice joyfully everything for the honour of the Fatherland!

Although we are in the midst of war and the enemy is actually within our borders, I have nevertheless convened the Diet to discuss the general condition of the country, and to submit to you a kind of "urgency" Estimate. We are unfortunately not in a position to fix decisive Estimates, and on account of the unsatisfactory connection with the Mother Country, it was also impossible to get war Estimates granted us from home. As long ago as May last we indeed discussed the Estimates for 1915, but we do not know what has become of them, nor in what form they have been presented to the legislative bodies. We must, therefore, decide upon domestic Estimates for the first six months of 1915. Further, a synopsis of the condition of our finance will be furnished to the Diet. I also consider it expedient to put before you a general survey of the development of affairs here, since the beginning of the war.

The first official intimation of the threatened war we received on 29th of July, in a telegram from the Colonial Office, which stated "that the Powers were endeavouring to localise the war between Austria-Hungary and Servia, and that there was no danger for the Protectorates." In spite of these latter words, we began at once the necessary preparations, particularly by ordering the removal from the coastal towns of the official balance of foodstuffs. On August 1st we received a further telegram containing only the following: August 2nd first day of mobilisation! Against whom we mobilised was not mentioned; we learned, however, from other telegrams, which arrived some time after, sometimes in cypher, that war with Russia had broken out, and that war with France was imminent.

On August 6th another telegram arrived reading: "War with England, France, Russia!" As this made war also probable for us, Martial Law was declared in German South-west Africa. Volunteers were called for, and, in order to make possible the payment of numerous claims for cash now reaching the Government in large numbers, five millions' worth of Treasury notes were issued. These measures were taken in consultation with representatives of the banks and the merchants. A large number of these notes have been redeemed by us in the meanwhile.

Though in the beginning there was reason to doubt whether the Union of South Africa would join England against us, this doubt was soon dispelled by the speeches of the Union Ministers Botha and Smuts in Parliament, and on other occasions. So we had to reckon not only with an attack by the English, but also with one by the Union. The revolt in South Africa which collapsed completely in January of this year, might retard this development, but could not frustrate it. So the position now is that the English are in the occupation of the Orange Line, Lüderitzbucht, the railway as far as Garub, and the Swakop Valley.

Our relation to Angola is still the reverse of clear, as it has been from the beginning. In spite of several inquiries, we have not been able to find out whether Angola—or rather Portugal—is at war with us or not. Officially Portugal seems still to be neutral; but in any case, that is not a loyal neutrality, since Portuguese politics seem to have been taken completely "in tow" by the English. Our condition is characterised by the murder—the cowardly and dastardly murder—committed on District Magistrate Schultze-Zena, Chief Lieut. Rosch, and farmer Roder, in Naulila. I believe that now, however, both Angola and Lisbon have become aware, after the brilliant armed success of our Protectorate Troop Commander and his brave men, at Naulila, that even in difficult times the Germans do not let the murder of their countrymen go unavenged! (Hear, hear.)

In any case, gentlemen, we need not fear an attack from the North for some time to come, on account of the fact that in the North of Angola a revolt has broken out which will fully occupy the Portuguese; further, the geographical position and the climatic conditions of the border districts are against such an attack.

And so we have succeeded for eight months to hold South-west against a superior force. Great sacrifices have we made! Apart from the many who, in battle, on account of wounds or the loss of horses, have fallen into the hands of the enemy; apart from the women and children who, in flagrant violation of all principles of international law, have been deported by the English to South Africa, the number of victims is still very great. Besides Col. von Heydebreck, the meritorious former Commander of Protectorate troops, we have lost up to now six officers, 14 non-commissioned officers, and 37 mounted men. Regarding the losses in the fight on the Swakop we have not yet received particulars....

In any case the colonies have proved that they know their duty, and the theory so long and so emphatically preached at home, namely, that the fate of the colonies was going to be decided at home—in the North Sea—has been proved to be false.

And so I come to the condition of affairs in Europe. The war at sea has taken a quite unexpected course in Europe. Though we have to deplore heavy losses at sea, especially so the loss of our Eastern Squadron, it is nevertheless certain that England has lost more ships and larger ships than we. But, above all, the often threatened attack by the English fleet on the German fleet has never come off, and, further, England, powerful at sea, must experience an effective blockade over her entire coast. That it is effective is not only made clear by the suspension of sailings by 22 English steamship lines, but it can also be verified from the shipping at Cape Town. In former years about 1,100 entered Table Bay every year. All ships of any size, now-a-days, carry wireless installation, and all these ships announce their arrival to the respective ports.

By this means we could make sure that only 17 ships have arrived at Cape Town, among which were two Portuguese, one Swede, and quite a number of ships bound for Australia, and one ship that came from Australia and indicated as its port of distination—remarkable to relate—Trinidad. From this we can gather that the sea traffic of the English merchant fleet has been reduced to about one-third of the normal. . . .

Victory will be gained by whichever can best stand the economic and financial strain. And in this respect Germany is altogether in a better position than her adversaries. . . . We may conclude with great probability that England is to-day already living on her capital. . . .

We see from all this: Germany stands at present just as powerful and strong as was ever the case in the best times of the Middle Ages, and we may cherish the hope that it will end this war victoriously. This hope, however, must encourage us to defend our land here with all our strength against the enemy, must show us there can be but one motto for us: "Fight to the end." . . .

The Governor gave expression to his conviction that the Empire would give full compensation for all damage and loss sustained through the military operations in South-west, and concluded:

I believe that after this war the Empire will feel obliged to make particularly high grants to the colonies as war indemnification. For a certain inward arrear in moral reproaches will certainly remain with many at home, and also many of those gentlemen who opposed me on the question of the diminution of troops will now appreciate their mistake.

XII.

TERMS OF THE GERMAN SURRENDER.

As agreed to by the Government of the Union of South Africa, and accepted by His Excellency, Dr. Seitz, the Imperial Governor of the Protectorate of German South-west Africa and Commander of the military forces of the Protectorate; and signed at Kilo 500, on the railway line between Otavi and Khorab, on the 9th day of July, 1915.

(1) The military forces of the Protectorate of German South-west Africa, hereinafter referred to as the Protectorate, remaining in the field under arms and disposal at the command of the Commander of the said Protectorate forces, are hereby surrendered to General the Right Hon. Louis Botha, Commanding-in-Chief the Forces of the Union of South Africa in the field. Brigadier-General H. T. Lukin, C.M.G., D.S.O., acting on behalf of General Botha, shall be the Officer in Charge with arranging the details of the surrender and giving effect to it.

(2) The active troops of the said forces of the said Protectorate surrendered in terms of paragraph one shall, in the case of officers, retain their arms, and may give their parole, being allowed to live each under that parole at such places as he may select. If for any reason the Government of the Union of South Africa is unable to meet the wish of any officer as regards his choice of abode, the officer concerned will choose some place in respect of which no difficulty exists.

(3) In the case of other ranks of the active troops of the said forces of the said Protectorate, such other ranks shall be interned under proper guard in such place in the Protectorate as the Union Government may decide upon, each non-commissioned officer and man of the other rank last referred to shall be allowed to retain his rifle but no ammunition, one officer shall be permitted to be interned with the other ranks of the artillery, one with the other ranks of the remainder of the active troops, and one with the other ranks of the police.

(4) All Reservists, Landwehr, and Landsturm, of all ranks, of the said forces of the Protectorate now remaining under arms in the field shall, except to the extent as is provided for in paragraph six below, give up their arms upon being surrendered in such formation as may be found most convenient and after signing the annexed form of parole shall be allowed to retire to their homes and resume their civil occupation.

(5) All Reservists, Landwehr, and Landsturm, of all ranks, of the said forces of the Protectorate who are now held by the Union Government prisoners of war taken from the said forces of the Protectorate upon signing the form of parole above mentioned in paragraph four shall be allowed to resume their civil occupation in the Protectorate.

(6) The officers of the Reserve Landwehr and Landsturm of the said forces of the Protectorate who surrender in terms of paragraph one above shall be allowed to retain their arms provided they sign parole above mentioned in paragraph four.

(7) All officers of the said forces of the Protectorate who sign the form of parole above mentioned in paragraph four shall be allowed to retain the horses which are nominally allotted to them in their military establishments.

(8) The police of the Protectorate shall be treated as far as they have been mobilised as the active troops. Those members of the police who are on duty on distant stations shall remain at their posts until they are relieved by Union troops, in order that the lives and property of non-combatants may be protected.

(9) Civil officials in the employment of the German Imperial Government, or of the Government of the Protectorate, shall be allowed to remain in their homes, provided they sign the parole above mentioned in paragraph four. Nothing, however, in this statement shall be constructed as entitling any such officer to exercise the functions of the appointment which he holds in the service of either of the Governments aforesaid or to claim from the Union Government the emoluments of such appointments.

(10) With the exception of the arms retained by the officers of the Protectorate forces and by the ranks of the active troops, as provided for in paragraph two above, all war material, including all field and mountain guns, small arms ammunition, and the whole of the property of the Government of the Protectorate shall be placed at the disposal of the Union Government.

(11) His Excellency the Imperial Governor shall appoint a civil official of the Protectorate service, who shall hand over and keep a record of all Government property of the civil departments, including records which are handed over to the Union Government, in terms of paragraph ten above, and the Commander of the said forces of the Protectorate shall appoint a military officer, who shall hand over and keep a similar record of all Government property of the military departments of the Protectorate.

Given under our hands on this ninth day of July, 1915.
LOUIS BOTHA, General Commanding-in-Chief the Union Forces in the Field.
SEITZ, Imperial Governor of German South-west Africa.
FRANKE, Lieutenant-Colonel Commander of the Protectorate Forces of German South-west Africa.

Form of the parole:
I the undersigned hereby pledge myself on honour not to re-engage in hostilities in the present war between Great Britain and Germany.

XIII.
GENERAL ORDER TO THE VICTORIOUS FORCES.
By Major-General the Hon. J. C. Smuts, K.C. Issued from Pretoria, 12th July, 1915

The Minister of Defence desires to express to the General Officer Commanding the Union Expeditionary Forces in the Field, to his Staff, and to all ranks of the Forces who are now, or have been, under his command his warmest congratulations on the successful issue of the campaign.

Not only is this success a notable military achievement and a remarkable triumph over very great physical, climatic, and geographical difficulties; it is more than these, in that it marks in a manner which history will record for all time the first achievement of a united South African nation, in which both races have combined all their best and most virile characteristics, and bent themselves resolutely, often at the cost of much personal sacrifice, to overcome extraordinary difficulties and dangers in order to attain an important national object.

If differences of opinion, minor disappointments, and petty grievances and jealousies have arisen in the course of this great task, now successfully completed, these can speedily be forgotten and buried in oblivion, when the broad result, creditable in equal measure to all those who have striven to attain it, is considered.

The Minister desires further to convey to the Staff of the Defence Headquarters and to all Defence Officers and Establishments in the Union controlled by him, his thanks for and appreciation of the great services they had rendered in their respective spheres in bringing about the results which have been attained. Almost without exception the work they have been called upon to perform has been extremely arduous and very often trying and difficult. Considering the very rudimentary stage of development which the Union Defence organisation had reached when it was called upon to undertake the tasks it has actually accomplished, the results can broadly be stated to be most satisfactory and highly creditable to those who have striven incessantly to bring about their attainment.

There have, of course, been mistakes and shortcomings, but the Minister trusts that investigation will prove that these have not really been serious. The task now remains so to profit by the invaluable experience gained during the last eleven months to bring the military organisation of the Union to such a high standard of efficiency, combined with economy, that it may continue to be a legitimate source of pride to the people of South Africa.

XIV.—OFFICIAL CASUALTY TOTALS.

KILLED OR DIED OF WOUNDS :—
G.S.W.A. Campaign—
  English descent.... 76
  Dutch descent .... 46— 122
Rebellion—
  Dutch descent 81
  English descent.... 51— 132— 254

WOUNDED :—
G.S.W.A. Campaign—
  English descent....205
  Dutch descent ....113— 318
Rebellion—
  Dutch descent 183
  English descent.... 94— 277— 595

PRISONERS 612
DIED OF DISEASE AND MISADVENTURE 153
                        1,614

UNION TROOPS UNDER ARMS
(Estimated).
For the G.S.W.A. Campaign—
  English descent 27,500
  Dutch descent ....22,500—50,000

For the Rebellion—
  Dutch descent 20,100
  English descent...... 9,900—30,000

ENEMY TROOPS: THE CAPTURES AND SURRENDERS.

Captured during hostilities—
  Officers............ 39
  Rank and file...... 859— 898
Surrendered—
Officers:
  Active troops and Police 110
  Reserve .... 177— 287
Rank and file:
  Active troops and Police 1,548
  Reserve .... 2,575 –4,123–4,410
                        5,308
Guns Surrendered—
  Field............. 37
  Machine .... 22— 95

THE CASUALTY LIST.
(Excluding the Rebellion).

NOTE.—The Rebellion was officially declared over on December 10, 1914.

KILLED OR DIED OF WOUNDS OR DISEASE.

Name and Rank.	Corps.	Place and Date.
Aldridge, Corpl. J. A.	5th S.A.M.R.	Sandfontein, 26.9.14
Anderson, Pte. W. E.	Kimberley Regt.	Trekkopjes, 26.4.15
Burnett, Pte. G.	5th Mounted Rifles	Swakopmund, 21.1.15
Bulakoff, Sgt. P.	18th M.R.	Upington, 26.1.15
Badenhorst, Tpr. J. P.	Kalahari Horse	Wounded Schaapkolk, 19.3.15. 25.3.15
Beukes, Lt. R.	11th Mounted Rifles	Plattbeen, 27.3.15
Braithwaite, Q.M.S. C.	11th Mounted Rifles	Kabus, 19.4.15
Breytenbach, Cpl. H. J.	Middelburg B. Com.	Swakop River, 30.4.15
Brokensha, Lt. H. V.	Natal Light Horse	Gibeon, 27.4.15
Coulter, Cpl.	5th S.A.M.R.	Nakob, 16.9.14

THE CASUALTY LIST—continued.
KILLED OR DIED OF WOUNDS OR DISEASE—continued.

Name and Rank.	Corps.	Place and Date.
Clayton, Pte. C. F.	1st Rhodesian Regt.	Swakopmund, 7.2.15
Coetzee, Pte. C. F.	Rand Light Infantry	Garub, 24.2.15
Campher, Bgr. F. H.	Wolmaransted Com.	Jackalswater, 20.3.15
Cameron, Lt. W. M.	2nd Transvaal Scottish	Trekkopjes, 26.4.15
Cameron, Lance-cpl. T. A.	Kimberley Regt.	Trekkopjes, 26.4.15
Cooper, Cpl. H. E.	S.A. Field Teleg. and Postal Corps	Kalkfeld, 24.6.15
Croon, Tpr. F.	1st I.L.H.	Grasplatz, 26.9.14
Dyke, Pte. E. P. C. (Died of wounds)	5th Mounted Rifles	Swakopmund, 21.1.15
de Meillon, Capt. C. K.	Intelligence Dept.	Garub, 22.2.15
du Preez, Lieut.	18th Mounted Rifles	Upington, 26.1.15
de Meyer, Burgher, W. A.	Ermelo Commando	Jackalswater, 20.3.15
de Jager, Tpr. J. J. (Died of wounds)	Natal Light Horse	Gibeon, 27.4.15
du Preez, Sergt. F. J. I.	Pietersb'g Commando	Otjimbingue, 30.4.15
du Plessis, Cpl. P. M. J. (Died of wounds)	Lemmer's Scouts	Osambimbani, 12.5.15
Erasmus, Tpr. J.	Du Plessis' Cradock Commando	Upington, 26.1.15
Etzebeth, Sergt. J.	Kalahari Horse	Wounded Kirüss West, 13.4.15
Engelbrecht, Bgr. A. J.	Middelburg B Com.	Swakop River, 30.4.15
Fuller, Rfn. C. L.	1st S.A.M.R.	Sandfontein, 26.9.14
Filer, Lance-cpl. D. A.	Kimberley Regt.	Trekkopjes, 26.4.15
Ferguson, Bgr. J. H.	Botha's Scouts	Otajakatjongo, 17.6.15
Fletcher, Sergt. H. M.	Natal Light Horse	Gibeon, 27.4.15
Franks, Cpl. M.	Natal Light Horse	Gibeon, 27.4.15
Groneau, Tpr. C. H.	1st I.L.H.	Grasplatz, 26.9.14
Grobler, Pte. A.	1st Eastern Rifles	Lüderitzbucht, 17.10.14
Good, Pte. A. H.	2nd Kimberley Regt.	Trekkopjes, 26.4.15
Greyling, Tpr. A. J.	Natal Light Horse	Gibeon, 27.4.15
Hadley, Rfm. E. A.	4th S.A.M.R.	Raman's Drift, 17.9.14
Harris, Battery S. M. A. E.	Trans. Horse Artillery	Sandfontein, 26.9.14
Handfield, Cpl. C. R. (Died of wounds)	Natal Light Horse	Gibeon, 27.4.15
Harmse, Bgr. N. C.	Pietersb'rg Commando	Otjihangwe, 17.6.15
Hattingh, Bgr. J. J. N. (Died of wounds)	Pietersb'rg Commando	Otjihangwe, 17.6.15
Holtzhuizen, Tpr. L. C. (Died of wounds)	Botha's Scouts	Otavi, 1.7.15
Hollingsworth, Lt. F.	1st Rhodesian Regt.	Trekkopjes, 26.4.15
Harrison, Capt. F. (Died of wounds)	2nd Kimberley Regt.	Trekkopjes, 26.4.15
Hardie, Sgt. J. S.	Natal Light Horse	Gibeon, 27.4.15
Hill, Tpr. W. A.	Natal Light Horse	Gibeon, 27.4.15
Harris, Tpr. R. S.	2nd I.L.H.	Gibeon, 27.4.15
Jacobus, Christian	Intelligence Corps	Sandfontein, 26.9.14
Joubert, Pte. L. F. (died of disease)	Western Province Rifles	— 9.10.14
Joyner, Tpr. D. K.	1st I.L.H.	Garub 16.12.14

THE CASUALTY LIST—*continued.*
KILLED OR DIED OF WOUNDS OR DISEASE—*continued.*

Name and Rank.	Corps.	Place and Date.
Jacobs, Bgr. P. J.	Scouts	Jackalswater, 20.3.15
Jooste, Bgr. F.P. J. J.	Krugersdorp Com.	Jackalswater, 20.3.15
Joubert, Bgr. J. J.	Middelburg Com.	Ghaub, 3.7.15
Jackson, Tpr. G. A.	Natal L.H.	Gibeon, 27.4.15
Jeffreys, Cpl. A. G.	1st Natal Carbineers...	Gibeon, 27.4.15
Kobus, Rfm. W. C. P.	1st S.A.M.R.	Sandfontein, 26.9.14
Keeping, Cpl. H. T.	12th Citizen Battery...	Tschaukaib, 17.12.14
Kritzinger, Pte. W.	8th M.R.	Lutzputs, 17.1.15
Kenthorn, Tpr. C. J.	Natal L.H.	Gibeon, 27.4.15
Lindsay, Rfm. G.	1st S.A.M.R.	Sandfontein, 26.9.14
Louw, Cpl. J. C. A.	Naude's Scouts	— 3.1.15
Lourens, Act. S.M. H. J.	Marico Commando	Jackalswater, 20.3.15
Levine, Bgr. C.	Scouts	Jackalswater, 20.3.15
Linde, Bgr. G. J. H. (died of wounds)	Lemmer's Scouts	Osambimbani, 12.5.15
Lambie, Pte. A.	2nd Kimberley Regt...	Trekkopjes, 26.4.15
Lester, Cpl. H.	N.L.H.	Gibeon, 27.4.15
Macdonald, R.Q.M.S.	1st S.A.M.R.	Sandfontein, 26.9.14
Mutlow, Rfm. E. D. (Wounded 15.9.14)	5th S.A.M.R.	Schuit Drift, 8.10.14
Minnaar, Lt. W. H.	Van Zyl's Commando	Nous, 22.12.14
Mulder, Trp. B. H.	7th Mounted Rifles...	Lutzputs, 17.1.15
Mitchell, Trp. D. J.	Scott's Kimberley Central Commando	Near Upington, 24.1.15
Mey, Bgr. J. A.	Ermelo Commando	Jackalswater, 20.3.15
Meyer, Bgr. F. W.	Potchefstroom Com...	Jackalswater, 20.3.15
McLean, Cpl. R. (Died of wounds).	Natal Light Horse...	Gibeon, 27.4.15
Madsen, Sgt. A. (Died of wounds).	1st Natal Carbineers..	Gibeon, 27.4.15
Mynhardt, Bgr. Z. A.	Pietersburg Com.	Otjibangwe, 17.6.15
Mitchell, S. M. F.*	Brand's 5th O.F.S. Schutters.	Otavi, 1.7.15
Matheson, Lt. R. T.	Natal Light Horse.	Gibeon, 57.4.15
Northway, Lieut.	1st S. A. M. R.	Sandfontein, 26.9.14
Nesbit, Rfm. R. R. (Wounded 15.9.14).	5th S. A. M. R.	Schuit Drift, 26.10.14
Neethling, Lt. J. (Died of wounds).	Remounts Dept.	Kakamas, 3.2.15
Nel, S. M. J. F.	Scouts.	Jackalswater, 20.3.15
Norman, Bgr. C. G. (Died of wounds).	Ermelo Commando.	Jackalswater, 20.3.15
Nicholls, Tp. C. N.	Natal Light Horse.	Gibeon, 27.4.15
Olivier, Lieut. H. J.	Van Zyl's Commando	Nous, 23.12.14
Oldewage, Tpr. S. P.	18th Mounted Rifles...	Upington, 26.1.15
Oosthuizen, Bgr. D. J.	Ermelo Commando....	Jackalswater, 20.3.15
Olsen, Tpr. K. L.	2nd I.L.H.	ibeon, 27.4.15
Pickering, Corpl. N. J.	Trans. Horse Artillery	Sandfontein, 26.9.14
Poldon, Pte. J. J.	Pretoria Regt.	Tschaukaib, 18.1.15
Potgieter, Tpr. J. H.	Malan'sHanover M.R.	Upington, 26.1.15

THE CASUALTY LIST—*continued.*
KILLED OR DIED OF WOUNDS OR DISEASE—*continued.*

Name and Rank.	Corps.	Place and Date.
Payne, Sgt. W. S. (died of wounds)	Natal Light Horse	Gibeon, 27.4.15
Pascoe, Tpr. F. D.	Natal Light Horse	Gibeon, 27.4.15
Pearce, Tpr. C. H.	Natal Light Horse	Gibeon, 27.4.15
Pescod, Sgt. W. T.	2nd Imperial L.H.	Gibeon, 27.4.15
Pexton, Tpr. H.	1st Natal Carbineers	Gibeon, 27.4.15
Pyke, Tpr. E. P. C.	5th Mounted Rifles	Swakopmund, 21.1.15
Quinn, Rfm. J. P.	1st S.A.M.R.	Sandfontein, 26.9.14
Rossouw, Tpr. P. A. W.	Studer's Springbok Commando	Lutzputs, 23.1.15
Rabinson, Pte. B.	1st Rhodesian Regt.	Swakopmund, 7.2.15
Reid, Pte. G. S.	2nd Trans. Scottish	Trekkopjes, 26.4.15
Strachan, Sgt.-Major (accident)	1st Eastern Rifles	Grasplatz, 23.12.14
Short, Rfm. J. G.	1st S.A.M.R.	Sandfontein, 26.9.14
Stumke, Lieut. (wounded 27.9.15)	Intelligence Corps	Hasuur, 9.10.14
Smit, Sgt. J. J.	Van Zyl's Commando	Sandfontein, 3.2.15
Swart, Capt. L. J.	Scouts	Jackalswater, 20.3.15
Syffert, Bgr. W. J.	Potchefstroom Com.	Jackalswater, 20.3.15
Sacks, Tpr. B.	Bloemhof Commando.	With Northern Force, 16.4.15
Smit, Bgr.. C. J. (Died of wounds)	Pietersburg Com.	Otjimbingwe, 30.4.15
Strydom, Tpr. G.	Brand's 5th O.F.S. Schutters	Otavi, 1.7.15
Spargo, Cpl. J. E.	S.A. Field Telegraph Corps	Gibeon, 27.4.15
Thompson, Pte. M. (Died of disease)	Rand Light Infantry	Lüderitzbucht, 23.11.1
Troski, Cpl. J. M. (Died of wounds)	Lemmer's Scouts	Osambimbani, 12.5.15
Tapp, Tpr. A. H.	Natal Light Horse	Gibeon, 27.4.15
Ulys, Lt. J. N.	Wolmaranstad Com.	Jackalswater, 20.3.15
van Baalen, Rfm. J. P.	5th S.A.M.R.	Raman's Drift, 17.9.14
v. Lille, Conductor D.	Transport	n Namaqualand,23.9.14
Visser, Tpr. E. P. J.	Studer's Springbok Commando	Lutzputs, 23.1.15
Vosloo, Sgt. J. A.	Du Plessis' Cradock Commando	Upington, 26.1.15
v. Hoven, S.S.M. F. H.	Middelburg Com.	Jackalswater, 20.3.15
v. Tonder, Bgr. W. M.	Carolina Commando	Jackalswater, 20.3.15
Venter, Bgr. A. J.	Middelburg B. Com.	Swakop River, 30.4.15
v.d. Heever, Bgr. J. O.	Pietersburg Com.	Otjimbingwe, 30 4.15
v.d. Berg, Bgr. J. D.	Pietersburg Com.	Otjimbingwe 30.4.15
v. Rensburg, Bgr. H. V. (Died of wounds)	Pietersburg Com.	Otjimbingwe, 30.4.15
v. Rensburg, Tpr. D. C. (Died of wounds)	Brand's 2nd O.F.S. Schutters	Otavi, 1.7.15
Winslow, Tpr. W. L.	1st I.L.H.	Grasplatz, 26.9.14

THE CASUALTY LIST—continued.
KILLED OR DIED OF WOUNDS OR DISEASE—continued.

Name and Rank.	Corps.	Place and Date.
Winslow, Tpr. R. L.	1st I.L.H.	Grasplatz, 26.9.14
Water, Rmf. G. G.	1st S.A.M.R.	Sandfontein, 26.9.14
Wilkins, Capt. C.	Sutherland Commando	— 20.1.15
White, Tpr. E. B.	Bloemhof Cammando	With Northern Force, 16.4.15
Webb, Pte. R. W.	1st Trans. Scottish	Aus Nek, 28 4.15
Wells, L.Cpl. J. R.	Kimberley Regt.	Trekkopjes, 26.4.15
Watt, Major J. H.	N.L.H.	Gibeon, 27.4.15
Woolley, Cpl. R.	Umvoti M.R.	Gibeon, 27.4.15
Williams, Tpr. S. (died of wounds)	N.L.H.	Gibeon, 27.4.15
Wattmore, Pte. W. J. L.	Kaffrarian Rifles	Aus Nek, 15.4.15

WOUNDED.

Name and Rank.	Corps.	Place and Date.
Andrews, Bgr. H. C. F.	Standerton Com.	Jackalswater, 20.3.15
Allwright, Gunner A. F.	Trans. Horse Artillery	Sandfontein, 26.9.14
Anderson, Sergt. J. K.	8th Mounted Rifles	Nous, 22.12.14
Anderson, Bgr. C.	Pretoria Commando	East of Winduk, 19.5.15
Adie, Tpr. S.	1st Natal Carbineers	Gibeon, 27.4.15
Bethel, R. S. M. R.	Scott's KimberleyCentral Commando	Upington, 26.1.15
Bowker, Capt. D. M. P.	7th Mounted Rifles	Lutzputs, 17.1.15
Botha, Bgr. P.	Ermelo Commando	Jackalswater, 20 3.15
Browne, Lieut. S. B.	2nd Trans. Scottish	rekkopjes, 26.4.15
Boxall, Colour-Sergt. C.	2nd Kimberley Regt.	Trekkopjes, 26.4.15
Burnett, Pte. H.	2nd Trans. Scottish	Trekkopjes, 26.4.15
Booysen, Bgr. J.	KlerksdorpCommando	Northern Force, 2.5.15
Booysen, Bgr. D. M. P.	KlerksdorpCommando	N rthern Force, 2.5.15
Baumann, Gunner C.	Trans. Horse Artillery	Sandfontein, 26.9.14
Brighton, Tpr. W. P.	1st Natal Carbineers	Garub, 16.12.16
Benade, Bur. P. J.	Van Zyl's Commando	Nous, 22.12.14
Bowker, Cpl. D. M.	8th Mounted Rifles	Ncus, 22 12.14
Bloem, Lance-corpl.	8th Mounted Rifles	Nous, 22 12.14
Bolus, Pte. M.	8th Mounted Rifles	Nous, 22.12.14
Brown, Pte. J. M.	8th Mounted Rifles	Nous, 22.12.14
Bezuidenhout, Bgr. M. J. F.	Potchefstroom Com.	Jackalswater, 20.3.15
Blackett, Lieut. M. C.	Natal Light Horse	Gibeon, 27.4.15
Bennett, Tpr. F. R.	Natal Light Horse	Gibeon, 27.4 15
Brunton, Lieut. W. G.	2nd I.L.H.	Gibeon, 27.4.15
Bands, Tpr. E. W.	Natal Light Horse	Gibeon, 27.4.15
Boult, Tpr. J. S.	Natal Light Horse	Gibeon, 27.4.15
Coltman, Gunner W. V.	Transvaal Horse Art.	Sandfontein, 26.9.14
Coltman, Gunner A. O.	Transvaal Horse Art.	Sandfontein, 26.9.14
Coulson, Gunner R.	12th Citizen Battery	Tschaukaib, 17.12.14

THE CASUALTY LIST—continued.
WOUNDED—continued.

Name and Rank.	Corps.	Place and Date.
Coetzee, Pte. J. P.	8th Mounted Rifles	Nous, 22.12.14
Celliers, Staff-Sergt. C. D.	20th M.R.	Kabus, 19.4.15
Comley, Sergt. A. N.	20th M.R.	Kabus, 19.4.15
Compian, Tpr. C. D.	20th M.R.	Kabus, 19.4.15
Cane, Tpr. R. P. G.	Natal Light Horse	Gibeon, 27.4.15
Colman, Cpl. S. M.	Natal Light Horse	Gibeon, 27.4.15
Comey, Tpr. L.	Natal Light Horse —	Gibeon, 27.4.15
Cox, Cpl. H. H.	2nd I.L.H.	Gibeon, 27.4.15
Chandley, Tpr. P. E.	1st Natal Carbineers	Gibeon, 27.4.15
Coetzee, Tpr. L. O.	20th Mounted Rifles	Upington, 26.1.15
Conradie, Tpr. D. S.	20th Mounted Rifles	Upington, 26.1.15
Campbell, Tpr. T. H.	Scott's Kimberley Central Commando	Upington, 26.1.15 Jackalswater, 20.3.15
Coetzee, Bgr. P. A.	Ermelo Commando	
Coetzee, Bgr. A. D.	Middelburg Com.	Jackalswater, 29.3.15
Church, Pte. J.	2nd Kimberley Regt.	Trekkopjes, 26.4.15
Collinson, Pte. J.	2nd Kimberley Regt.	Trekkopjes, 26.4.15
Calvin, Pte. J. W.	2nd Kimberley Regt.	Trekkopjes, 26.4.15
Cooper, Pte. A. F.	2nd Kimberley Regt.	Trekkopjes, 26.4.15
Cosgrove, Pte. G. H.	2nd Kimberley Regt.	Trekkopjes, 26.4.15
Cadermole, Pte. G. F. M.	2nd Transvaal Scottish	Trekkopjes, 26.4.15
Cross, Pte. R. G.	1st Rhodesian Regt.	Trekkopjes, 26.4.15
Chrystal, L.Cpl. A. T.	1st Rhodesian Regt.	Trekkopjes, 26.4.15
Campbell, Pte. A.	1st Rhodesian Regt.	Trekkopjes, 26.4.15
Chapman, Tpr. J. D.	5th M.B. Machine-gun section	Otavi, 1.7.15
Coetzee, Bgr. A.	Botha's Scouts	Otjakatjongo, 17.6.15
Crane, Bgr. D.	Botha's Scouts	Otjakatjongo, 17.6.15
Cadman, Rfm. P.	1st S.A.M.R.	Sandfontein, 26.9.14
du Preez, Tpr. P. A.	Conroy's Commando	Upington, 26.1.15
Dingwey, Bgr. D. M.	Ermelo Commando	Jackalswater, 20.3.15
de Meillon, Capt. K.	Intelligence Depart.	Grasplatz, 26.9.14
Douglas, Gunner G.	Transvaal H.A.	Sandfontein, 26.9.14
Dykeman, Pte. J.	1st Transvaal Scottish	Lüderitzbucht 17.10.14
Day, L.Cpl. J.	Rand L.I.	Garub, 24.2.15
Dixon, L.Cpl. H. H.	Rand L.I.	Garub, 24.2.15
Davidson, Pte. G.	11th M.R.	Plattbeen, 27.3.15
Dique, Lt. A. F.	Pietersburg Com.	Otjimbingwe, 30.4.15
de la Salle, Capt. C. A. B.	Natal Light Horse	Gibeon, 27.4.15
Dippenaar, Bgr. M.	Krudersdorp Com.	Osmogonto, 26.4.15
Davies, D.S.O., Lt.-Col. W. T. F.	2nd I.L.H.	Gibeon, 27.4.15
Dawler, Tpr. W. C.	Natal Light Horse	Gibeon, 27.4.15
Downing, Sgt. N. O.	8th Mounted Rifles	Lutzputs, 17.1.15
Elliott, Sgt. E.	1st I.L.H.	Grasplatz, 26.9.14
Edden, Pte. A. H.	2nd Kimberley Regt.	Trekkopjes, 26.4.15
Edmunds, Pte. W. S.	2nd Kimberley Regt.	Trekkopjes, 26.4.15
Egerton, Pte. W. C. H.	2nd Kimberley Regt.	Trekkopjes, 26.4.15
Ellis, Lieut. J. A.	Brand's 4th U.F.S. Schutters	Otavi, 1.7.15
Eybers, Sgt. J. N.	Pietersburg Com.	Otjihangue, 17.6.15
Edwards, Cpl. L.	Transvaal Horse Artillery	Sandfontein, 26.9.14

THE CASUALTY LIST—continued.
WOUNDED—continued.

Name and Rank.	Corps.	Place and Date.
Egerton, Bomb. T. J.	Transvaal Horse Artillery	Sandfontein, 26.9.14
Ewbank, Pte. J. J.	Rand Light Infantry	Rothkuppe, 8.12.14
Esterhuizen, Pte. P. H. J.	11th Mounted Rifles...	Plattbeen, 27.3.15
Eaton, Lieut. H. L.	Natal Light Horse ..	Gibeon, 27.4.15
English, Sgt. W.	Natal Light Horse ...	Gibeon, 27.4.15
Featherstone, Lieut. N. E.	20th Mounted Rifles...	Upington, 26.1.15
Fitzhenry, Tpr. W. H.	Pohl's Graaff Reinett Commando	Jackalswater, 25.3.15
Fourie, Q.M.Sergt. P. J.	Ermelo Commando ...	Jackalswater, 20.3.15
Featherstone, Lt. N. E.	20th Mounted Rifles	Upington, 26.1.15
Fitzhenry, Tpr. W. H.	Pohl's Graaff-Reinet Commando	Upington, 26-1.15
Fourie, Q.M.S. P. J.	Ermelo Commando ...	Jackalswater, 20.3.15
Fyvie, Pte. A.	2nd Transvaal Scottish	Trekkopjes, 26.4.15
Forbes, Bgr. H. H.	Botha's Scouts	Otjakatjongo, 17.6.15
Forbes, Bomb.	Transvaal Horse Artil.	Sandfontein, 26.9.14
Fulke, Cpl. J. W.	1st S.A.M.R.	Sandfontein, 26.9.14
Farge, Rfm. F.	1st S.A.M.R.	Sandfontein, 26.9.14
Fogerty, Lt. J. F.	12th Citizen Battery	Tschaukaib, 17.12.14
Froud, Tps. S.	N.L.H.I.	Gibeon, 27.4.15
Frazer, Tpr. D. A.	2nd Light Horse	Gibeon, 27.4.15
Fly, Tpr. E. W.	1st Natal Carbineers	Gibeon, 27.4.15
Grobelaar, Tpr. H. P.	Malan's Hanover Mounted Rifles	Upington, 26.1.15
Groenwaldt, Rflm. F. P.	S.A.M.R.	In Namaqual'nd, 23.9.14
Grant, Lt.-Col. R. C.	1st S.A.M.R.	Sandfontein, 26.9.14
Geary, Capt. W. J.	1st S.A.M.R.	Sandfonteln, 26.9.14
Griffin, Rfm. A. N.	1st S.A.M.R.	Sandontein, 26.9.14
Gibbon, Bomb. P.	12th Citizen Battery	Tschaukaib, 17.12.14
Gibb, Pte. W. W.	S.A. Engineer Corps...	Nous, 23,12.14
Gouws, Pte. L. G.	Vermaas' Scouts	——, 3.1.15
Germishuizen, Tpr. J. N.	Naude's Scouts	Nabas, 6.3.15
Gray, Lt.-Col. W. Park	Natal Light Horse ...	Gibeon, 27.4.15
Griffiths, Tpr. R. P.	Natal Light Horse ...	Gibeon, 27.4.15
Gullett, Sgt. A. E.	2nd I.L.H.	Gibeon, 28.4.15
Heroldt, Tpr. S. G.	Malan's H.M.R.	Upington, 26.1.15
Hockley, Bgr. A. E.	Ermelo Commando ...	Jackalswater, 20.3.15
Herschell, Capt. A.	2nd Transvaal Scottish	Trekkopjes, 26.4.15
Hermiston, L.Cpl. W. A.	2nd Kimberley Regt.	Trekkopjes, 26.4.15
Harris, Pte. A. G.	2nd Kimberley Regt.	Trekkopjes, 26.4.15
Hood, Cpl. H.	2nd Transvaal Scottish	Trekkopjes, 26.4.15
Henderson, L.Cpl. J. A.	1st Rhodesian Regt....	Trekkopjes, 26.4.15
Holliday, Tpr. J. J.	Brand's 5th O.F.S. Schutters	Otavi, 1.7.15
Human, Rlfm.	5th S.A.M.R.	Nakob, 16.9.14
Holcroft, Capt. L. A.	S.A.M.R.	Sandfontein, 26.9.14
Hattingh, Scout W.	Intelligence Corps.	Sandfontein, 26.9.14
Hutchings, Gunner R.	12th Citizen Batt. ...	Tschaukaib, 17.12.14
Hoole, Tpr. D. C.	8th M.R.	Nous, 22.12.14
Homan, Lt. J. L.	Potchefstroom Com....	Jackalswater, 20.3.15

THE CASUALTY LIST—continued.
WOUNDED—continued.

Name and Rank.	Corps.	Place and Date.
Heydenrich, Tpr. L.	20th M.R.	Kabus, 19.4.15
Heugh, Sgt. H. W.	20th M.R.	Kabus, 19.4.15
Haines, Cpl. A. L.	N.L.H.	Gibeon, 27.4.15
Hargreaves, Sgt. W.	N.L.H.	Gibeon, 27.4.15
Harmer, Cpl. C.	N.L.H.	Gibeon, 27.4.15
Hall, Tpr. R.	2nd I.L.H.	Gibeon, 27.4.15
Jacobs, Lt. J. H.	Ermelo Commando	Jackalswater, 20.3.15
Joubert, Lt. J. H.	Ermelo Commando	Jackalswater, 20.3.15
Jones, Capt. C. la Turner.	1st S.A.M.R.	Sandfontein, 26.9.14
Johnston, Gunner R. E.	Trans. Horse Artillery	Sandfontein. 26.9.14
Jones, Lt.	Rand Light Infantry	Lüderitzbucht, 22.10.14
James, Tpr. A. W.	Natal Light Horse	Gibeon, 27.4.15
Koen, Bgr. J. J.	HeidelbergCommando	Jackalswater, 20.3.15
King, Pte. R. R.	2ndTransvaal Scottish	Trekkopjes, 26.4.15
Kirsten, Bgr. A. D.	KlerksdorpCommando	With Northern Force, 2.5.15
Koen, Bgr. G. H.	KlerksdorpCommando	With Northern Force, 2.5.15
Koen, Bgr. S. P.	KlerksdorpCommando	With Northern Force, 2.5.15
Koen, Bgr. G. A.	KlerksdorpCommando	With Northern Force, 2.5.15
Kirk, Rfm. K.	1st S.A.M.R.	Sandfontein, 26.9.14
Kimack, Sgt. R. N.	Transvaal Horse Artil.	Sandfontein, 26.9.14
Koen, Rfm. E. L.	5th S.A.M.R.	Sandfontein, 26.9.14
Krankamp, Tpr. P. C.	20th Mounted Rifles.	Kabus, 19.4.15
Kirby, Tpr. W. H.	Natal Light Horse	Gibeon, 27.4.15
Liebenburg, Tpr. P. J.	Conroy's Commando.	Upington, 26.1.15
Labuschagne, Bgr. F. G.	Ermelo Commando	Jackalswater, 20.3.15
Lombard, Bgr. D. B.	Carolina Commando.	Jackalswater, 20.3.15
Lotz, Bgr. J. N.	Heidelburg Com.	Jackalswater, 20.3.15
Lennon. Colour-Sergt. J.	2nd Kimberley Regt.	Trekkopjes, 26.4.15
Lowe, Pte. G.	2nd Trans. Scottish.	Trekkopjes, 26.4.15
Loder, Rfm. E. R.	1st S.A.M.R.	Sandfontein. 26.9.14
La Croix, Lance-Sergt. D. E.	1st S.A.M.R.	Sandfontein, 26.9.14
Louw, Q.M -Sergt. D. J.	Lichtenburg Com.	Jackalswater, 20.3.15
Le Grange, Sergt. L.	Kalahari Horse.	Kiriis-West. 13.4.15
Langridge, Pte. C. A. W.	Rand Light Infantry.	Ausnek, 28.4.15
Livingstone, Cpl. E. M.	1st Natal Carbineers.	Gibeon, 27.4.15
Meintjes, Capt. C.	20th Mounted Rifles.	Upington, 26.1.15
McCabe, Tpr. G.	Pohl's Graaff-Reinet Commando	Upington, 25.1.15
Meyer, Lieut. C. H.	Ermelo Commando	Jackalswater, 20.3.15
Mey, Bgr. J. F.	Ermelo Commando	Jackalswater, 20 3.15
Manning, Pte. F. S.	2nd Kimberley Regt.	Trekkopjes, 26.4.15
Milne, Lance-cpl. W. G.	2nd Trans. Scottish.	Trekkopjes, 26.4.15
Marshall, Petty Officer W.	Naval Motor Division	Trekkopjes, 26.4.15
Mare, Major Troskie	5th Mounted Brigade Staff	Otavi, 1.7.15
McDougal, Rifleman	1st S.A.M.R.	Sandfontein, 26.9.14
McCalgan, Tpr.	1st I.L.H.	Lüderitzbucht, 6.10.14

THE CASUALTY LIST—continued.
WOUNDED—continued.

Name and Rank.	Corps.	Place and Date.
Marais, Pte. J. K.	8th Mounted Rifles	Nous, 22.12.14
Michau, Cpl. M.	8th Mounted Rifles	Nous, 22.12.14
McLeod, Pte. S. G.	Rand Light Infantry	Garub, 24.2.15
Mackintosh, Tpr. M.	20th Mounted Rifles	Kabus, 19 4.15
Millar, Tpr. J. C. A.	20th Mounted Rifles	Kabus, 19.4.15
Morcom, Tpr. G. L.	Natal Light Horse	Gibeon, 27.4.15
Messer, Capt. J. F.	Natal Light Horse	Gibeon, 27.4.15
MacDougall, Lieut. J.	Natal Light Horse	Gibeon, 27.4.15
Masson, Cpl. D.	Natal Light Horse	Gibeon, 27.4 15
Matthews, Tpr. M.	Natal Light Horse	Gibeon, 27.4 15
McQueen, Tpr. M.	2nd I.L.P.	Gibeon, 27.4.15
Mathers, Tpr. G.	2nd I.L.P.	Gibeon, 27.4.15
Moore, Tpr. T. C.	2nd I.L.P.	Gibeon, 27.4.15
Middlemass, Tpr. J. G.	Umvoti Mo'nted Rifles	Gibeon, 27.4.15
Nell, Tpr. W. R.	20th Mounted Rifles	Kabus, 19.4.15
Neethling, Bgr. P. J.	Middelburg Com.	Ghaub, 3.7 15
Nicholson, Tpr. R. N.	2nd Natal Carbineers	Gibeon, 27.4.15
Nell, Lieut. D. H.	Ermelo Commando	Jackalswater, 20.3.15
Nelson, Sgt. J. H.	S.A. Field Telegraph Corps	Kabus, 19.4.15
Nesbit, Rfm. R. B.	5th S.A.M.R.	Raman's Drift, 17.9.14
Nel, L-Cpl. T. G.	1st S.A.M.R.	Sandfontein, 26.9.14
Nel, Tpr. P. S.	8th Mounted Rifles	Nous, 22.12 14
Nicol, Tpr. J. A.	18th Mounted Rifles	Upington, 22.2.15
Nel, Tpr. P.	Calvinia Commando	Kakamas, 3.2.15
Nel, Bgr. A. P.	Heidelberg Commando	Jackalswater, 20.3.15
Neser, S.-M. S. J.	Potchefstroom Com.	Jackalswater, 20.3.15
Nieuwholt, Bgr. G. W.	Scouts	Jackalswater, 20.3.15
Oberholzer, Tpr. G. J.	Brand's 5th O.F.S. Schutters	Otavi, 1.7.15
Owen, Lt. W.	1st S.A.M.R.	Sandfontein, 26.9.14
Ogilvie, Bomb. J. P.	Transvaal Horse Art.	Sandfontein, 26.9.14
Ovens, Cpl. J.	5th S.A.M.R.	Sandfontein, 26.9.14
O'Kelly, Pte. P. D.	18th Mounted Rifles	Nous, 22.12.14
Potgieter, Tpr. S. P. J.	Du Plessis' Cradock Commando	Upington, 26.1.15
Potgieter, Tpr. F. J.	Du Plessis Cradock Commando	Upington, 26.1.15
Pollock, Tpr. K. A.	1st S.A.M.R.	Sandfontein, 26.9.14
Partington, Gunner S. A.	12th Citizen Battery	Tschaukaib, 17.12.14
Prins, Tpr. J.	Calvinia Commando	Kakamas, 3.2.15
Parkin, Tpr. D. I.	Natal Light Horse	Gibeon, 27.4.15
Pretorius, Bgr. S. P.	Middelburg Com.	Ghaub, 3.7.15
Pearce, Lt. J. W.	N.L.H.	Gibeon, 27.4.15
Porter, Tpr. J.	N.L.H.	Gibeon, 27.4.15
Pitt, Tpr. L. von. A.	2nd I.L.H.	Gibeon, 27.4.15
Pollard, Tpr. B. E.	2nd I.L.H.	Gibeon, 27.4.15
Pavy, Sgt. W.	1st Natal Carbineers	Gibeon, 27.4.15
Power, Cpl. H. N.	1st Natal Carbineers	Gibeon, 27.4.15
Potgieter, Bgr. P. J.	Malan's H.M.R.	Lutzputs, 17.1.15
Pescod, Sgt. W. T.	2nd I.L.H.	Gibeon, 27.4.15
Pexton, Tpr. H.	1st Natal Carbineers	Gibeon, 27.4.15
Pyke, Tpr. E. P. C.	5th Mounted Rifles	Swakopmund, 21.1.15

THE CASUALTY LIST—continued.
WOUNDED—continued.

Name and Rank.	Corps.	Place and Date.
Quinn, Rfm. E. J.	1st S.A.M.R.	Sandfontein, 26.9 14
Quinn, Rfm. J. P.	1st S.A.M.R.	Sandfontein, 26.9.14
Roos, Tpr. P. J.	Malan's H.M.R.	Upington, 26.1.15
Ramsay, Bgr. A. J.	Ermelo Commando	Jackalswater, 20.3.15
Richardson, R.S. M. J.	2nd Kimberley Rgt.	Trekkopjes, 26.4.15
Reid, Cpl. W. C. S.	2nd Transvaal Scottish	Trekkopjes, 26.4.15
Rose, Rfm. T. A.	1st S.A.M.R.	Sandfontein, 26.9.14
Rose, Tpr. F.	1st Natal Carbineers	Garub, 16.12.14
Reid, Cpl. W.	1st I.L.H.	Swakopmund, 21.1.15
Richards, Capt. W.	Rand Light Infantry	Garub, 24.2.15
Rossouw, Segt. P. A.	Scouts	Jackalswater, 20.3.15
Reeder, Tpr. H.	Natal Light Horse	Gibeon, 27.4.15
Renski, Bgr. R. A.	Botha's Scouts	Otjakatjongo, 17.6.15
Ringham, Tpr. G. A.	2nd I.L.H.	Near Bethany, 18.4.15
Rush, Tpr. E. F.	Natal Light Horse	Gibeon, 27.4.15
Reid, Tpr. M.	2nd I.L.H.	Gibeon, 27.4 15
Richards, Tpr. P.	1st Natal Carbineers	Gibeon, 27.4.15
Rossouw, Tpr. P. A. W.	Studer's Springbok Commando	Lutzputs, 23.1.15
Rabinson, Pte. B.	1st Rhodesian Regt.	Swakopmund, 7.2.15
Reid, Pte. G. S.	2ndTransvaal Scottish	Trekkopjes, 26.4.15
Stevenson, Sgt. J. W.	8th Mounted Rifles	Lutzputs, 17.1.15
Smit, Bgr. H. J.	Carolina Commando	Ghaub, 3.7.15
Sloan, Tpr. H. T.	1st I.T.H.	Grasplatz, 26.9.14
Strydon, Tpr. H.	Malan's . Hanover Mounted Rifles	Upington, 26.1.15
Steenkamp, Cpl. S.G.M.	Ermelo Commando	Jackalswater, 20.3.15
Sloop, Bgr. A. A.	Ermelo Commando	Jackalswater, 20 3.15
Spies, Bgr. P.	Standerton Com.	Jackalswater, 20.3.15
Sarak's, Pte. P. G.	2ndTransvaal Scottish	Trekkopjes, 26.4.15
Scott, Pte. J. L.	2ndTransvaal Scottish	Trekkopjes, 26.4.15
Sterling, Sapper H.	S.A. Engineer Corp-	Trekkopjes, 26.4.15
Scott, Acting-S.-M. J. F.	Klerksdorp Commando	With Northern Force, 2 5.15
Sterling, Bgr. N. W.	Botha's Scouts	Otjakatjongo, 17.6.15
Spohr, Rfm. C. J.	1st S.A.M.R.	Sandfontein, 26.9.14
Snyman, Rfm. J.	1st S.A.M.R.	Sandfontein, 26.9.14
Scholk, Rfm. A. P.	1st S.A.M.R.	Sandfontein, 26.9.14
Swanson, Sgt. T.	5th S.A.M.R.	Sandfontein, 26.9.14
Stewart, Lt.	Rand Light Infantry	Rothkuppe, 8.12.14
Sutherland, Gunner, V.C.	12th Citizen Battery	Tschaukaih, 17.12.14
Sellar, Pte. R.	Rand Light Infantry	Garub, 24.2.15
Stols, Bzr. L. J.	Lichtenburg Com.	Jackalswater, 20.3.15
Slabbert, Tpr. J. F.	Kalahari Horse.	Schaapkolk, 19.3.15
Steyn, Tpr. T. J.	Kalahari Horse.	Kees, 11.4.15
Stevens, Tpr. E. J. H.	Bloemhof Commando	With Northern Force, 16.4.15
Stewart, Sgt. A. B.	Natal Light Horse.	Gibeon, 27.4.15
Strachan, Sgt.-Major (Accident)	1st Eastern Rifles	Grasplatz, 23.12.14
Short, Rfm. J. G.	1st S.A.M.R.	Sandfontein, 26.9.14
Stumke, Lt. (Died of wounds, 27.11.15)	Intelligence Corps	Hasuur, 9.10.14
Smit, Sgt. J. J.	Van Zyl's Commando	Sandfontein, 3.2.15

THE CASUALTY LIST—*continued*.
WOUNDED—*continued*.

Name and Rank.	Corps.	Place and Date.
Swart, Capt. L. J.	Scouts	Jackalswater, 20.3.15
Syffert, Bgr. W. J.	Potchefstroom Com...	Jackalswater, 20.3.15
Sachs, Tpr. B.	Bloemhof Commando	With Northern Force, 16 4.15
Smit, Bgr. C. J. (Died of wounds)	Pietersb'rg Commando	Otjimbingwe, 30.4.15
Strydom, Tpr. G.	Brand's 5th O.F.S. Schutters	Otavi, 1.7.15
Spargo, Crp. J. E.	S. A. Field Telegraph Corps.	Gibeon, 27.4.15
Theron, Lt. J. M.	20th Mounted Rifles	Upington, 26.1.15
Taute, Bgr. F.	Ermelo Commando	Jackalswater, 20.3.15
Traher, L.-Cpl. T. W.	2nd Transvl. Scottish	Trekko jes, 26.4.15
Till, Sgt. H. G.	Tvl. Horse Artillery	Sandfontein, 26.9.14
Tainton, Cpl. A. G.	Tvl. Horse Artillery	Sandfontein, 26.9.14
Turton, Cpl. H. G.	Natal Carbineers	Garub, 11.3.15
Thomsen, Tpr. W. O.	2nd I.L.H.	Gibeon, 27.4.15
Trollip, Bgr. N.	8th Mounted Rifles	Lutzputs, 17.1.15
Thompson, Pte. M. (Died of disease).	Rand Light Infantry	Lüderitzbucht, 23.11.14
Troski, Cpl. J. M. (Died of wounds).	Lemmers Scouts	Osambinbani, 12.5.15
Tapp, Tpr. A. H.	Natal Light Horse	Gibeon, 27.4.15
Ueckerman, Cpl. H. J.	Rand Light Infantry	Rothkuppe, 8.12.14
Uys, Lieut. J. M.	Wolmaranstad Com...	Jackalswater, 20.3.15
Van der Lingen, Tpr. J. C.	18th Mounted Rifles	Upington, 26.1.15
Venter, Tpr. C.	Du Plessis' Cradock Commando	Upington, 26.1.15
Van der Walt, Sgt. M. J. H.	Malan's Hanover Mounted Rifles	Upington, 26.1.15
Victor, Tpr. F. G.	Malan's Hanover Mounted Rifles	Upington, 26.1.15
Van der Merwe, Q.M. Sgt. J. P.	Ermelo Commando ..	Jackalswater, 20.3.15
Voss, Bgr. F.	Middelburg Com.	Jackalswater, 20.3.15
Van Wren, Bgr. J. B.	Heidelberg Commando	Jackalswater, 20.3.15
Visser, Lt. L. I.	Klerksdorp Commando	With Northern Force, 2.5.15
Venter, Bgr. M.	Pietersburg Com.	Otjihangwe, 17.6.15
Venter, Tpr. J. A.	Brand's 5th O.F.S. Schutters	Otavi, 1.7.15
Van Tonder, Bgr. J.	Botha's Scouts	Otjaka'jongo, 17.6.15
Villey, Rfm. L. A.	1st S.A.M.R.	Sandfontein, 26.9.14
Vice, Cpl. G. L.	8th Mounted Rifles	Nous, 22.12.14
Van der Walt, Pte. J. H.	8th Mounted Rifles	Nous, 22 12.14
Venter, Pte. J. H.	8th Mounted Rifles	Nous, 22.12.14
Van Wyk, Pte. J. W. C.	Vermaas' Scouts	—. 3.1.15
Van Biljoen, Sergt. P. J.	Lichtenburg Com.	Jackalswater, 20.3.15
Van Heerden, Q.M.-Sergt. H. S.	8th Mounted Rifles	Lutzputs. 17.1.15
Viljoen, Tpr. J. P.	Kalahari Horse	Schaapkolk, 19.3.15
Van Baalen, Rfm. J. P.	5th S.A.M.R.	Raman's Drift, 17.9.14
v. Lille, Conductor D.	Transport	In Namaqualand, 23.9.14
Visser, Tpr. E. J. P.	Studer's Springbok Commando	Lutzputs, 23.1.15

THE CASUALTY LIST—continued.
WOUNDED—continued.

Name and Rank.	Corps.	Place and Date.
Voslov, Sgt. J. A.	Du Plessis Cradock Commando	Upington, 26.1.15
v. Hoven, S.S.M. F. H.	Middelburg Com.	Jackalswater, 20.3.15
v. Tonder, Bgr. W. M.	Carolina Commando.	Jackalswater, 20.3.15
Venter, Bgr. A. J.	Middelburg Com.	Swakop River, 30.4.15
v.d. Heever, Bgr. J. O.	Pietersburg Com.	Otjimbingwe, 30.4.15
v.. Berg, Bgr. J. D.	Pietersburg Com.	Otjimbingwe, 30.4.15
v. Rensburg, Bgr. H. V. (Died of wounds).	Pietersburg Com.	Otjimbingwe, 30.4.15
Will, Lt. F. G.	Malan's Hanover Mounted Rifles	Lutzputs, 17.1.15
Will, Sgt. A. M.	Malan's Hanover Mounted Rifles	Lutzputs, 17.1.15
Wright, Tpr. J. C.	18th Mounted Rifles.	Upi. gton, 26.1.15
West, Tpr. M. S.	Du Plessis Cradock Commando.	Upington, 25.1.15
Wood, Cpl. L. F.	1st Rhodesian Regt.	Trekkopjes, 26.4.15
Willis, Sgt. J.	Brand's 5th O.F.S. Schutters	Otavi, 1.7.15
Wakefield, Lt. H. S.	1st S.A.M.R.	Sandfontein, 26.9.14
White, Rfm. H.	1st S.A.M.R.	Sandfontein, 26.9.14
Watson, Gunner W. A.	12th Citizen Battery.	Tschaukaib, 17.12.14
Watson, Pte. H. R.	Rand Light Infantry.	Tschaukaib, 17.12.14
Wakeford, Pte. W. J.	8th Mounted Rifles	Nous, 22.12.14
White, Pte. H. T.	8th Mounted Rifles	Nous, 22.12.14
Wild, Tpr. G.	Bloemhof Commando.	With Northern Force, 16.4,15
Wallis, L.-Cpl. J.	Rand Light Infantry	Aus nek, 28.4.15
Waters, Rfm. A.	—	Kubis (East of Keelmanshoop), 19.4.15
Warby, Major E. W.	Natal Light Horse	Gibeon, 27.4.15
Waugh, Sgt. E. M.	Natal Light Horse	Gibeon, 27.4.15
Wilson, Tpr. D. R.	Natal Light Horse	Gibeon, 27.4.15
Wilson, Tpr. E. G.	Natal Light Horse	Gibeon, 27.4.15
Williamson, Cpl. P. W.	Natal Light Horse	Gibeon, 27.4.15
Warren, Tpr. F. D.	2nd I.L.H.	Gibeon. 27.4.15
Willis, Tpr. P. W.	2nd I.L.H.	Gibeon, 27.4.15
Wilson, Tpr. R.	2nd I.L.H.	Gibeon, 27.4.15
Zeeman, Lt.	Vermaas' Scouts	— 3.1.15

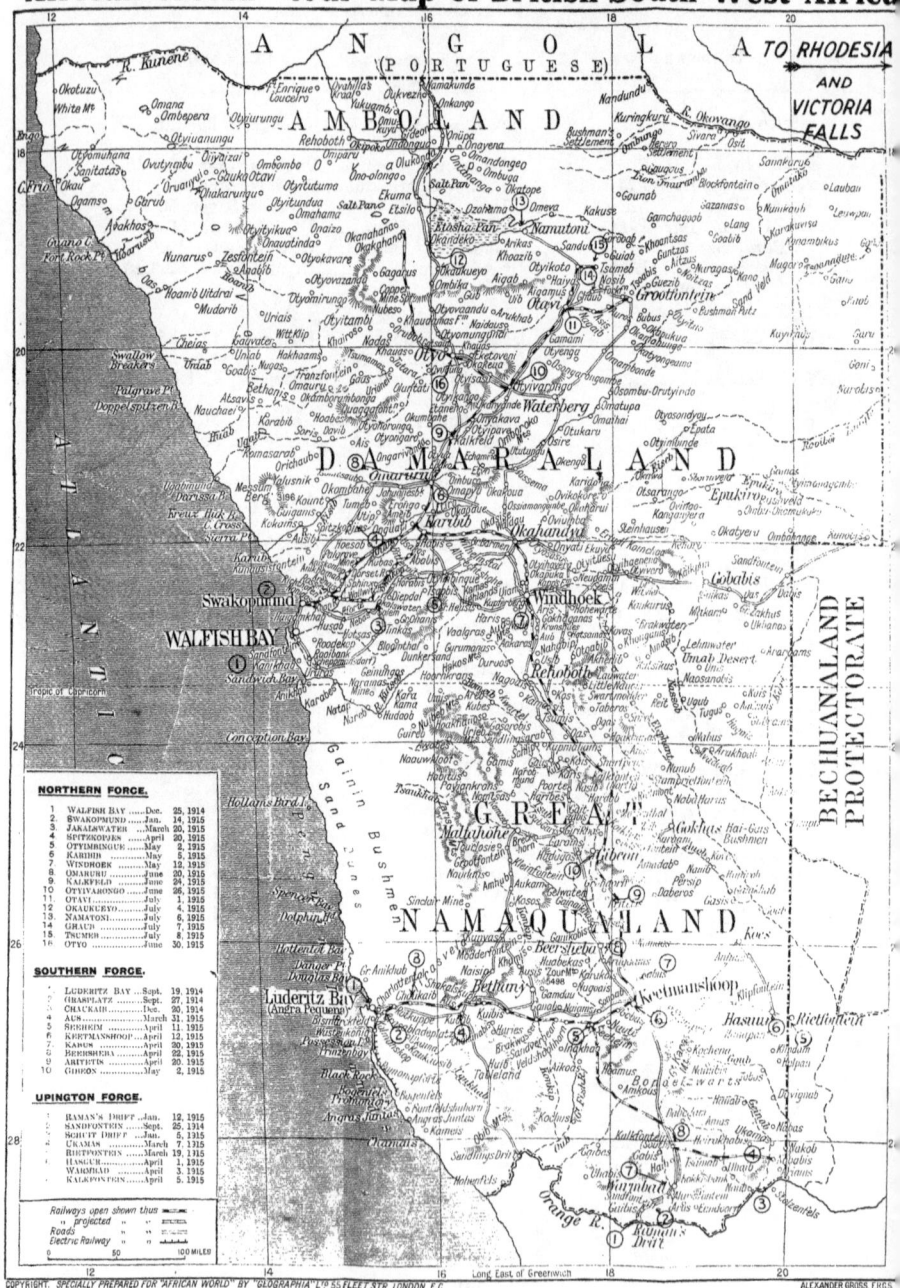

www.ingramcontent.com/pod-product-compliance
Lightning Source LLC
Chambersburg PA
CBHW031132160426
43193CB00008B/113